A History of Ancient Philosophy
I. From the Origins To Socrates

Giovanni Reale

A History of Ancient Philosophy

I. From the Origins to Socrates

EDITED AND TRANSLATED FROM THE FOURTH ITALIAN EDITION

John R. Catan

State University of New York Press

Published by
State University of New York Press, Albany

©1987 State University of New York

For information, address State University of New York
Press, State University Plaza, Albany, N.Y., 12246

Library of Congress Cataloging-in-Publication Data

Reale, Giovanni.
 A history of ancient philosophy.

 (SUNY series in philosophy)
 Bibliography: v. 1, p.
 Includes indexes.
 Contents: 1. From the origins to Socrates.
 1. Philosophy, Ancient.   I. Catan, John R.
II. Title.   III. Series.
B171.R4213   1986   180   86–14559
ISBN 0-88706-292-X (v. 1)
ISBN 0-88706-290-3 (pbk. : v. 1)

10 9 8 7 6 5 4 3 2 1

The American edition and translation is dedicated
to the memory of Claire Avena Stack

TABLE OF CONTENTS

Introduction
THE ORIGIN, NATURE, AND DEVELOPMENT OF PHILOSOPHY AND THE PHILOSOPHICAL PROBLEMS OF ANTIQUITY

First Part
THE PHILOSOPHERS OF NATURE: THE IONIANS AND THE ITALIANS. THE PROBLEMS OF NATURE, OF BEING, AND OF THE COSMOS

First Section
PRELUDE TO THE COSMOLOGICAL PROBLEM

Second Section

THE MILESIANS AND HERACLITUS

Third Section

PYTHAGOREANISM

Second Part
THE SOPHISTS: THE TRANSITION FROM
THE PHILOSOPHY OF NATURE TO MORAL PHILOSOPHY

First Section
THE ORIGIN AND NATURE OF THE MORAL PROBLEM

Second Section
THE SOPHISTS

Second Appendix
DETERMINATIONS OF THE FUNDAMENTAL CHARACTERISTICS OF THE GREEK CONCEPT OF PHILOSOPHY

FOREWORD

This *History of Ancient Philosophy* is the result of twenty-five years of scientific research in conjunction with almost as many years of teaching.

The content has been anticipated – but only in a limited and partial way – in my *Problems of Ancient Thought* 2 vols. (Milan: Celuc, 1971-73) as a kind of "first run" and then radically revised and completed in five volumes between 1974 and the beginning of 1979. While we were proceeding in the drafting of the work as a whole, the individual volumes were published and were sold out and then totally re-edited. At the time of the completion of the fifth volume (January, 1979) the first two had already gone through three editions, and the third and fourth volumes had also gone through two editions. Let us now turn to the general plan of the work.

The first volume contains the treatment of the Naturalists, the Sophists, Socrates, and the minor Socratics.

The second volume is wholly concerned with Plato and Aristotle.

The third volume studies the Hellenistic Age. First it outlines the progressive decline of the Academy and the Peripatos as well as the exhaustion of the Socratic schools. Next it examines the philosophic systems created by the spirit of the new age (Epicureanism, Stoicism, Scepticism, and Eclecticism) and follows their development to the end of the Pagan era.

The fourth volume reconstructs pagan philosophy during the first centuries of the Christian era. It examines the final phase of the traditional schools and their exhaustion, pausing especially on those currents of thought that, by going back to teachings derived from the Classical or Hellenistic Age, bring about changes in them, fueled by the demands and anxieties of the new age, or even resort to infusing unforeseen elements in them. We carefully analyzed especially neo-Aristotelianism, neo-Scepticism, neo-Stoicism, the encounter of Hellenism and the biblical theology of Philo of Alexandria, Middle Platonism, Neo-Pythagoreanism, and Neo-Platonism.

The fifth volume, finally, contains: *a*) a lexicon or an explanatory index of the principal concepts of ancient thought (practically a philosophical dictionary); *b*) a listing of the exponents of the various schools and of the available philosophical writings of the ancient thinkers with appropriate philosophical references (principal critical editions, translations, commentaries, lexica, and critical literature); *c*) a general index of the names of ancient authors who are treated and mentioned in the course of the entire work.

We will mention the characteristics of the interpretations we propose to offer, of the periods and the authors treated throughout, in the prefaces of each individual volume. Here we will simply limit ourselves to the distinctive features of the first volume.

After a preface of a theoretical nature, we consider, in a short introduction, the origins of philosophy which is already very well known to be the creation of the Hellenic genius (probably their most well known creation).

The ancient philosophy that emerged from the claims of the Ionians is: *a)* an attempt to explain the totality of things or the whole of reality and being, *b)* on the basis of *logos* alone or chiefly on that basis, *c)* for purely theoretical purposes and not for its utility, that is, out of a disinterested love for the truth. Only the cultural, social, political, and economic conditions of ancient Greece offered the conditions under which philosophy could arise, because it presupposed an essential liberty, from which no one of the nations that had reached civilization before the Greeks had been able to benefit (and it is for this reason that philosophy arose in the colonies to the East and West of Greece, precisely because these colonies acquired those freedoms before their motherland did).

We have offered an interpretation of the philosophy of nature *(physis)* in an ontological mode. The "science" of the Ionic and Italic philosophers is, in fact, the first attempt to explain *all beings,* and their cosmology is an attempt to explain *the totality* of the things that exist in function of one or more "principles." We gave special attention to the Eleatics, because they pose some basic problems for ancient philosophy that will not only condition the systems of the Physical Pluralists, but will decisively impact on the formation of Platonic and Aristotelian philosophy. We not only spend time with Parmenides, who is the founder of Eleaticism, but also with his followers Zeno and Melissus. The latter, in fact, as we have already shown in another work (cf. Reale, G. *Melisso, Testimonianze e frammenti* [Florence: La Nuova Italia, 1970]), is the true systematizer of Eleatic thought, while Zeno is, instead, the inventor of dialectic that has such importance in the subsequent history of Greek philosophy. The arguments against movement and multiplicity, far from being vacuous sophisms, bristle with the strength of the *logos* that contests experience itself in proclaiming the omnipotence of its own laws (in our view, it reaches the same heights speculatively that from the poetical viewpoint were achieved by the *Odes* of Pindar and the lyric poetry of Sappho).

We propose an interpretation of the Sophists that benefits from the profound re-evaluation of their thought made in this century. They represent that crisis of development that is verified by the discovery and founding of *moral philosophy.* As many have already recognized, Socrates would be unthinkable without the Sophists; he is truly one of their number, and has been able to hold on to the best of Sophism.

We propose an unusual thesis about Socrates that takes up, but with radical changes, the very familiar thesis of J. Burnet and A. E. Taylor according to which Socrates is one of the first to have given to the term *psyche* the western meaning of *soul,* the meaning that we today give to the word. It is in function of this discovery of the soul as the seat of intelligence and morality of human beings (and hence as the essence of what it is to be human) that we read over again the various Socratic doctrines, that is, the entire ethics and its methodology, about which we furnish abundant documentation. In addition, it would seem that on the basis of the testimonies handed down to us we may speak of a theology and of a teleology of Socrates, constructed on an intuitive and ethical basis, which will have important consequences. We give major prominence to Socrates because we are convinced that his words and his spirit are of an unquestionably exemplary character, not only in comparison to those of Plato and Aristotle but in their own right as well. Not only is Plato inconceivable without Socrates, but all of Hellenistic philosophy is profoundly impregnated with the Socratic spirit and it is only in the Imperial Age that ancient philosophy forgets Socrates.

The teachings of the minor Socratics are interpreted as different and onesided reductions of the multiple ramifications of Socratic thought and as anticipations of some requirements that will come to the forefront in the Hellenistic Age.

Commencing with the third edition, two appendices complete this first volume. The first concerns Orphism and the originality of its teachings, and contains a series of documents that are indispensible to the comprehension of some necessary aspects of Presocratic and Platonic thought. The second appendix concerns a series of determinations of the Greek conception of philosophy, which is most important for understanding the whole work. It makes more precise and clarifies the reasons for what we presented in the *Foreword* and in our *Introduction* as well, and it explains and argues for what, in our judgment, is the correct key in order to read and understand the message of the Greeks, the message of "theorein."

Giovanni Reale

PREFACE

In the field of modern studies it cannot be said with any accuracy that histories of philosophy are numerous, especially those about ancient philosophy; in point of fact there are very few.

Strangely, in the last few years, a kind of mistrust of philosophy and especially of philosophy as it has been classically understood seems to have caught many scholars. To such a degree is this true, from more than one quarter, that one is led to wonder whether philosophy as it is classically understood has not suffered the fate of the columns of Heracles that were destroyed and are now forever lost.

We live at a time in which within the crisis of philosophy is included as a kind of philosophy, the philosophy of the crisis of philosophy. We mean a philosophy that theorizes about the demise of philosophy. Joined to the crisis of philosophy is a parallel crisis in theology which is also, in some cases, so convinced of the crisis of philosophical values that it maintains that everything Christian thought has accomplished is valueless, in its structuring by philosophy and in particular by ancient philosophy. As thus understood, these currents proclaim in a loud voice the necessity of de-hellenizing Christianity. It is almost as though Christianity, because it had taken up speculative categories of classical philosophy, had become imprisoned in them to the point of becoming impotent because of them, that is, by becoming in some way Hellenic itself.

Moreover, in all these tendencies there lurks, in reality, an authentic loss of the meaning and character of the speculative dimension, that is, of the dimension that is most properly philosophic. Some theorize about the end of philosophy because they have lost the meaning of philosophy. The technical scientific mentality has habituated us to believe that something is valid only when it can be verified, certified, or controlled by experience and calculation and when it is productive of tangible results. In addition, the new political mentality has conditioned us to believe that only what can accomplish changes has relevance in things; not theory but praxis—it preaches—is what counts. It is of no use to contemplate reality, one has to actively intervene in it. Thus, on the one hand, this mentality wishes to impose on philosophy a method taken from the sciences that would make philosophy into scientism, and, on the other hand, it wishes to impose on philosophy the conditions that would reduce it to activism and thus be debased to the level of an activist ideology. In either case it absurdly pretends to be "doing" philosophy in the very process of destroying it.

We will discuss this point further in the course of the work, since it is not of minor importance, in our judgment. As we will see more fully in the course of our treatment, philosophical problems arise and develop as an attempt to understand and explain the whole, that is, the totality of things, or at least as the *problematic of the totality*. Philosophy remains such if and only if it attempts to determine the whole and searches for the perspective of the meaning of the whole. On the contrary, the sciences have arisen as rational considerations restricted to the parts or sectors of reality. They have an elaborate methodology and technique of inquiry that changes in function of the structure of these parts, and their value resides in these parts, and hence they are not of value for the whole of reality.

The accuracy of the scientific method necessarily supposes structural simplifications and restrictions with respect to its limits. Consequently, the application or the pretense of applying the methods of the sciences to philosophy (to the whole of reality, as philosophy is always and only, as we said, a consideration of the whole) produces that *monstrum* that we call scientism.

Thus when philosophy renounces contemplation for action it abandons once again its own nature. In fact, the practical commitment inexorably carries it to interest-ladened elaborations of its ideas reduced to their pragmatic aim, instead of to a disinterested vision and contemplation of the truth, and consequently it is transformed from philosophy into ideology.

The new currents of the theological avant-garde have committed in a certain sense even more spectacular mistakes. They risk, by indiscriminately rejecting the Greek *logos*, rejecting the *logos* as such. It is true as a matter of historical fact that Christian thought has in part taken notions strictly bound to Hellenic culture that hence are historically conditioned. But it is likewise true that in addition to these notions it has absorbed others that, although Hellenic in origin, are rational notions of universal validity, products of reason insofar as it is reason and not insofar as it is "Greek" reason. So a new irrationalism lurks under this de-Hellenization of theology when it does not directly hide a specific philosophy that is antithetical to Greek philosophy, although that philosophy is not recognized in its true nature, only because of its surreptitious acceptance.

Against these tendencies, this *History of Ancient Philosophy* hopes to contribute to a recovery, on the one hand, of the meaning of the speculative dimension and, on the other, it hopes to demonstrate that some of the categories elaborated by ancient Greek philosophy remain structurally indispensible for the start of any theological problematic, even if, as we will see, the Greek vision of the world and life remains essentially different from the Christian vision. In fact, it is certainly not the case that the categories proper to science and ideology can, in some way, shed light on the problem of the whole or even on the theological problem.

Today many philosophers, or self-styled lovers of philosophy, essentially remain such by using a fashionable idiom, while some have personalities which are inauthentic and thus incapable of assuming their own basic responsibilities; they are personalities, that is, who do not wish to renounce either philosophical ambition or those more valued empirical and concrete advantages of science and politics. These remarks ought not be construed as an attack on science or politics, because both science and politics are obviously more necessary than philosophy, but it is equally true that they are other than philosophy since they have a different aim, a different nature, and different categories. The sciences are simply a moment of the whole, whereas philosophy is structurally bound to the whole.

But what purpose is there to philosophizing today, in a world in which science, technology, and politics seem on the whole to divide the power, in a world in which the scientist, the technocrat, the politician become the new magicians moving all the levers?

The purpose, in our judgment, remains always the same for philosophy as it has from its beginning, the aim of *demythologizing*. The ancient myths were those of poetry, of fantasy, of imagination; the new myths are those of science, of technology, and of ideology, that is to say, the myths of power.

Certainly the task of demythologizing is more difficult today than it was with the ancients, because in the beginning it was sufficient that philosophy opposed the *logos* to fantasy in order to destroy the myth of poetry. Instead, the new myths of today are constructed by reason itself, at least in great part, since science and technology would seem to lead directly to the triumph of reason. But – and this is the essential point – it is a reason that, once it has lost the meaning of the totality, the sense of the whole, risks losing even its own identity.

So the task of philosophy today will be that of challenging the very sciences it has created. As is well known, it is from the matrix of western philosophy that the various western sciences have arisen; but then, quite often these sciences have pretended like children to dress-up in their mother's clothes. They do not have the prudence to be solely and uniquely themselves, limiting themselves and limited to a determined part of reality, but they have often attempted to extend themselves beyond their aim and their categories of limited and determined value to the totality of things, to the ultimate meaning of life. Worse yet, it was the attitude of politics, which too often has presented the truth as *freely* manipulable, for the purpose of making the reality of things more plastic in order to serve the aims that they propose.

To state this is not only to recover the meaning that philosophy can have today in rediscovering the meaning of the whole, and thus to locate the just place of things in the whole, but it is likewise to communicate the urgency of this recovery.

As we have said above, only a recovery of the meaning of pure contemplation can dissolve the plethora of ambiguities from which we suffer and can make us capable of understanding that there are or can be more things on earth and in heaven (to paraphrase a celebrated Shakespearean phrase) than science, technology, and certain political ideologies might imagine.

The Greeks can guide us to this recovery better than any other human beings, because they were the first to teach the world what it is to philosophize. Hence we have given to this *History of Ancient Philosophy* an outline depending chiefly on its problems, seen in their birth, in their development, and in their dissolution. We have tried as much as possible to say not only *what* the philosopher said but *why* he asserted it. Often various histories of philosophy are limited to telling us *what* such and such a philosopher thought about this and that but they do not tell us *why* he thought what he did, what links his thought had to those preceding him, and the impact he had on those who followed him. By not doing this, notions become disconnected from the problems that generated them and these disconnected notions almost inevitably turn into a conceptualism against which today there is just criticism from many quarters.

We have therefore avoided as much as possible displays of erudition and in general the insistence on those parts and those details that would lead to the loss of the vision of the principal lines. Instead, documentation is always furnished, or the references to the documentation. In fact, it has been our constant concern to trace a synthesis, and of not falling into the generic or loose citation. A true synthesis presupposes the completion of an accurate analysis, and its precision depends always on the precision with which that analysis has been conducted.

In order to conclude this preface let us return to the theoretical problem we raised above. In the service of honesty to the reader, our personal theoretic position is neo-classical not simply to the extent that we are acquainted with the doctrines of this or that classical thinker, but insofar as it seems to us that the metaphysical dimension of the philosophy proclaimed by the classical philosophers, as we said above, is the one that gives the aforementioned meaning to philosophy. Some, in response to our previous works, have believed erroneously that our position is that of an Aristotelian-Thomist; on the contrary, our sympathies lie with Plato, Plotinus, and Augustine, or better, to the way in which these philosophers posit and resolve the problems rather than with their particular solutions.

Hence, this *History of Ancient Philosophy* will not be an aseptic reconstruction that treats the ancients as museum pieces who have arisen from the dust of centuries with nothing further to say. To those who hold this view, and today their number is not small, ancient philosophy is nothing other than a museum and ancient philosophers are exhibits in this museum. We wish to remind them of the splendid epigraph of Paul Valéry that was placed above the entrance to the "Museum of Man" in Paris and in a few short phrases touches the basic problem and solves it:

> It depends on those who pass
> Whether I am grave or treasure
> Whether I speak or am mute
> On you only this depends
> Friend enter not without desire.

PREFACE TO THE AMERICAN EDITION

I began to write this work at the same time as the outbreak and rapid dispersion of the revolution of '68, that is, at a moment of time in which there had begun a rejection, in a categorical and massive manner, both the usefulness, and in general, the validity of philosophical argumentation, especially one which would attempt to repropose ancient thought (which has a basic and strong metaphysical inspiration), for the consideration of modern man, which has problems just as diverse.

In '68 I had just published my detailed and complete commentary to the *Metaphysics* of Aristotle (2 vols. Naples: Loffredo 1968) which quickly generated an interest and response from readers, much to everyone's surprise. But even more surprising has been the great success of this *History of Ancient Philosophy* in a few short years of its publication, (1975-1980) to the point that, just while I am writing the *Preface to the American Edition,* the publisher *Editrice Vita e Pensiero* has requested that I prepare the fifth Italian edition (1986).

What has happened? What are the reasons which have suddenly turned around the tendency which from '68 and during the '70s affected public opinion in what seemed to be an irreversible direction?

The basic reasons are threefold.

In the first place, some people quickly understood that man in his revolutions can destroy many things, but he cannot destroy his history. And in a special way he cannot destroy the history of his own thought. In particular, some have understood that the "project" itself of a future that '68 presented as a unique aim, was a pure ideological illusion. In fact, a "project" for the future remains a pure fantasy and a chimerical aspiration if it does not go forward in a constructive way with respect to that which has already been achieved but instead only wishes to destroy the past in an iconoclastic manner. In short: the "future" as it came to be conceived by the revolution of '68 was chiefly of a mythical character, arising from irrational passions.

In the second place, some people have understood, going a little more deeply into it, that if the past is eliminated, so also with the very same stroke is the future. In fact the past is like the roots of a large tree. If the roots are cut and pulled out because they are underground and do not bring forth any flower or fruit (which are of value to the present) and hence the tree is seen as useless, the loss of the roots rapidly destroys the flowers and fruits and hence the very life and production of the tree in the future.

This notion has been expressed recently in a very effective manner for example by Konrad Lorenz, a Nobel laureate in medicine and psychology. This scientist in his book *Der Abbau des Menschlichen* (Munich, 1983) has shown that cultural progress and change has profound analogies with the progress and changes of living species. The rate of change of a species is beneficial only if it is measured and contained, otherwise it endangers the species itself. Every excessive change produces abnormal and negative phenomena. Hence, it is necessary to evaluate and correctly preserve the values of the past, for adequate adaptation and emergent novelty to take place. In other words, it is necessary "to communicate traditional information accumulated within the course of cultural evolution, and at the same time open the door to the acquisition of new information." In particular, Lorenz states quite well: "... it is a mistake to maintain that if we throw away an old culture a new and better culture will automatically arise in its place."

Therefore, an ethologist who on the basis of accurate experience about the evolution of species grasps a sound principle which is of value also for culture and spirit as a form of life.

But there is also a third reason which explains a revival of interest in the thought of the ancients.

By now contemporary epistemology has shown that the "sciences," which began at the time of the great scientific revolution with which the modern era opened, were believed to be an expression of the ultimate truth and generally to be irrefutable in all respects. Science not only did not have an organic and cumulative development, and did not achieve an ultimate and incontrovertible truth, but, on the contrary, the very sources of its growth were contained in its "falsifications" and "anomolies." The book of Th. Kuhn, *The Structure of Scientific Revolutions* (Chicago: The University of Chicago Press, 1963) is in my judgment a masterpiece of the very first magnitude. I myself agree with all of Kuhn's positions excepting those contained in his final chapter.

In any case, even if most people have not yet been impacted by Kuhn's theses and those of contemporary epistemology, some have begun to think in various ways that science does not have the ultimate response to the problems of man.

Clearly, I do not mean a response to the problems of man as *homo faber* (that is, to the practical and technical problems of man), but to the problems of man *as man,* that is, of man who is not only the most refined of the animals, but who is something more, because he poses himself as a problem, namely, his meaning within the totality of things, the consideration of the "whole."

In short: I believe that for some, at least in part, the great affirmation of Aristotle (who in addition to being a great philosopher was also a great scientist), according to whom *all the other sciences are more necessary and more useful than philosophy, but none is superior to philosophy* is beginning to be considered as true, or at least, as able to be proposed through a changed cultural climate and development.

Clearly, philosophy is superior with respect to the problems which it has confronted and about which it has been concerned. Actually, these are the problems about which none of the *special sciences* can offer solutions, but about which we nonetheless ask questions: Why do I exist? What sense does my life have? What meaning is their to the whole of reality? Why is there being and not nothing?

But it is precisely concerning these issues that the Greeks have been at their greatest. And some problems that they asked and certain of their responses have not only given meaning to the whole of particular "paradigms," to use the terminology of Kuhn but they have relevance and value meta-paradigmatically.

In short: the way of proposing certain problems on the part of the ancients and some of their answers, or at least their way of confronting and proposing these answers remains valid even today. If to pose and solve *particular problems* man needs methods which are valid today, some of the solutions offered by the ancients to *general and global problems* are still valuable as they are concerned with the nature of man which remains always the same.

The reader will by now have understood quite well what I have attempted to accomplish in this *History of Ancient Philosophy.* I did not want to be simply a pure and abstract philosophical technician and treat the message of the ancients as removed from us, as if the men of past had absolutely nothing to do with the men of today. I believe, in other words, that human thought, in general, really is in search of the truth, and that sometimes in some way and with different expressions, although in a purely limited way, it finds the truth, or it can find it. And in this perspective I have tried to re-read the great history of the thought of the past.

A reviewer (F. O'Farrell) has this judgment about my work: "...this is not just another good history of Greek philosophy. It is something far better and far rarer. It is a work capable of guiding safely and securely those engaged in the study of Greek philosophy from the enthusiastic beginner to the over-cautious expert." The reader may place in parentheses this evaluation and reserve his own judgment. But this statement accurately reflects my own aims, that is, I have tried to address everyone, *not only the expert but also the intelligent layman.*

I hope that in America this work of mine will have a success analogous to that which the series enjoyed in Europe. I wish to thank wholeheartedly John Catan for the great labor that he has taken on in this translation, evidently he also is convinced about certain enduring truths contained in this discussion of the ancients. I also wish to thank State University of New York Press for the beautiful typography and design with which they have presented the American edition.

Giovanni Reale
Milan, 1986

TRANSLATOR'S PREFACE

After the present volume, the next volume of the series to be published would have been the second, on Plato and Aristotle, but Professor Reale requested that the fourth volume on the Imperial Age be published before it. His reasons are sound and acceptable, namely that he is preparing a full revision of the Plato section of volume two, the content of which heavily depends on two other volumes. The first, his own monograph on Plato in Italian published in the Spring of 1986, as well as the already published work of Hans Krämer entitled *Platone e i fondamenti della metafisica* (Milan: Vita e Pensiero, 1982), which Reale translated into Italian. It is anticipated that both volumes will be published by State University of New York Press in 1987-88.

I have tried to be consistent in the format of this volume, the first in the original ordering, with the previously published third volume of the series. I wish to thank Professor Reale and his wife for their invaluable assistance and many kindnesses on my behalf. The work of translation, although at times laborious, nevertheless provides many joys, not least among which is the knowledge that such translations will make a substantial contribution to the knowledge of the philosophy of the ancient period to which so many scholars have dedicated much time and energy. I am delighted to be able to make my own small but necessary contribution for the Anglophone.

I would also like to thank my colleague and Department Chairperson Dr. George Stack and dedicate this volume to the memory of his wife, Claire Avena Stack, who is sorely missed. To my friends who have accepted my absences from the circle of fellowship and still persevere in our friendship, I extend my gratitude. A full cup of thanks to Professor Tony Piccione of SUC Brockport for saving me from many infelicities of grammar and expression, although I am fully responsible for any such errors. Finally a word of thanks to my friend and associate, Melody Brinkman, for all that she has done to bring this volume to press both in encouragement and the discussion of many issues that arise in the course of completing a work of this magnitude. I should also like to thank the State University of New York Press and Mr. William Eastman for their commitment to scholarship.

I would also like to thank Harvard University Press for permission to use extracts from the Loeb Classical Library Series, as well as Random House for permission to quote from their edition of Aristotle. Finally, for permission to quote from Kathleen Freeman's *Ancilla to the Presocratics,* I am grateful again to Harvard University Press as well as Cambridge University Press for permission to use some references to Kirk & Raven's *The Presocratic Philosophers.*

J.R. Catan
Adams Basin, New York

From the Origins to Socrates

«ὁ δὲ ἀνεξέταστος βίος οὐ βιωτὸς ἀνθρώπῳ.»

"A life without inquiry is not worth living."

Plato *Apology* 38A

Introduction

The Origin, Nature, and Development of Philosophy and the Philosophical Problems of Antiquity

«ἀναγκαιότεραι μὲν οὖν πᾶσαι ταύτης, ἀμείνων δ᾽ οὐδεμία.»

"All the other sciences are more necessary than this one, but none is superior to it."

Aristotle *Metaphysics* A 2.983a10

I. The Birth of Philosophy in Greece

1. Philosophy as a creation of the Greek genius

"Philosophy," both in its semantic sense (that is, as a lexical term) as well as in its conceptual content, is a creation peculiar to the Greeks. In fact, in every other respect practically all the other components of Greek civilization are to be found in other peoples of the East, who achieved a certain level of progress prior to the Greeks. Whereas with respect to philosophy, there is no corresponding achievement or even something resembling it to be found. From the Greeks, the whole of the West called and still calls this unique creation philosophy.

A variety of beliefs and religious cults, artistic manifestations, knowledges and technical abilities, political institutions, and military organizations existed both in nearby Eastern peoples, who make an appearance in civilization prior to the Greeks, and also in the Greeks. It is, consequently, possible to make a comparison (if only or at least within certain limits) and to establish whether and in what measure the Greeks in these areas can be or actually have been debtors with respect to the peoples of the East. It can also be ascertained in what measure the Greeks surpassed in their various enterprises the peoples of the East. Oppositely, in the matter of philosophy, we find that it is a new phenomenon that has neither any identical counterpart in the Eastern peoples, nor anything which could be compared with the philosophy of the Greeks or which prefigures philosophy in an unequivocal way.

To emphasize this means to recognize neither more nor less that in this area the Greeks were creators, that is, that they gave to civilization something that it did not possess, and that, as we will see, will be revealed to be of such a revolutionary character as to change the course of civilization itself. Therefore, if the superiority of the Greeks with respect to the Eastern peoples in other areas is acknowledged as being of a mere *quantitative* nature, then in what concerns philosophy their superiority is instead naturally *qualitative*. He who does not consider this will end in not understanding why the civilization of the entire West has taken, under the impetus of the Greeks, a direction completely different from that of the East, further he will not understand why science originated only in the West and not in the East. In addition, he will not understand why an Easterner, when he wishes to benefit from Western science and its results, must also appropriate in a goodly measure the categories, or at the least some categories necessary to Western logic. In fact, it is precisely philosophy that created these categories and this logic, a wholly new mode of thinking; and it is philosophy that generated, in function of these categories, science itself and, indirectly, some of the principal consequences of science. To recognize this means to recognize that philosophy had the merit of making a truly exceptional contribution to the history of civilization. Therefore we must justify in a critical manner what we have said and must adduce some very detailed proofs.

2. The inconsistency of the thesis of a presumed derivation of philosophy from the East

Actually, there has been no lack of attempts on the part of some of the ancients or on the part of modern historians of philosophy, especially of the romantic age, as well as by well known orientalists to maintain the thesis of a derivation of Greek philosophy from the Orient on the bases of observations of various kinds and of different characters. But none of them has succeeded in their intention. The most rigorous critics, even beginning from the second half of the nineteenth century, have assembled a series of counter-arguments that at this time can be considered as incontrovertible objections to this thesis.[1]

Let us examine, especially, how the idea of a presumed Eastern origin of Greek philosophy arose in ancient times. The first supporters of the Eastern origin of Greek philosophy were precisely certain Easterners, undoubtedly under the influence of a nationalistic motivation. They wanted to deny to the Greeks, and to vindicate, for their own people, that most unique title to glory resulting from the discovery of the highest form of knowledge. On the one hand, there were Egyptian priests, who during the time of the Ptolemies became acquainted with Greek thought and tried to maintain that it was derived from the preceding wisdom of the Egyptians. On the other hand, there were Jews of Alexandria who had absorbed Hellenistic culture and tried to maintain the origin of Greek philosophy from the teachings of Moses and the Prophets contained in the Bible. Next there were Greeks themselves, who gave credence to this thesis. The Neopythagorean Numenius will write that Plato is nothing other than a "Greekified Moses."[2] Many others would maintain an analogous thesis, especially the last of the Neoplatonists, that the teachings of the Greek philosophers were merely elaborations of doctrines of Eastern origin and originally received by Eastern priests through divine inspiration from the Gods.

But these affirmations have no historical basis for the following reasons.

a) In the ancient-classical period of the Greeks, neither historians nor philosophers give even the slightest hint of a so-called origin of philosophy from the East. Herodotus (with the exception of his derivation of Orphism from the Egyptians, which is contrary to all the evidence) says absolutely nothing. Plato, who admired the Egyptians, emphasized their practical and anti-speculative spirit, which was so contrary to the theoretical spirit of the Greeks,[3] whereas Aristotle attributed to the Egyptians only the discovery of mathematics.[4]

b) The thesis of the Eastern origin of philosophy is given credence in Greece only at the time when philosophy had lost its speculative strength and self-confidence and no longer trusted in reason, but rather in a higher revelation for its own foundation and justification.

c) Greek philosophy, on the other hand, became in its final stage a mystical and ascetic doctrine that could easily find analogies with certain prior Eastern doctrines and hence be believed to have a dependence on them.

d) In their turn the Egyptians and the Jews were able to discover coincidences between their "wisdom" and Greek philosophy only by quite arbitrary allegorical interpretations, some from Egyptian myths and some from the biblical narrative.

But why do modern scholars continue to defend the thesis of the Eastern origin of philosophy? In a certain sense it is because they accept as valid the statements of the ancients, whom we mentioned above, without taking into account their lack of credibility, that is, they do not consider what we have argued above. But, in general, it is because they give credence to the uncovering of some analogies of content and possible contacts between the Eastern peoples and particular doctrines of the Greek philosophers. Following this path scholars arbitrarily and whimsically infer imaginary conclusions that reached outlandish proportions with Gladisch.[5] This German scholar (whom we mention because of the torturous lengths to which he forces the thesis that we are arguing against, and because he represents to a large extent the absence of a critical view that would arise from following such criteria) claims even to conclude, from the consideration of internal concordances, that the five principal Presocratic systems were derived, with few exceptions, from the five principal Eastern peoples, precisely: 1) the Pythagorean from Chinese wisdom; 2) the Eleatic from Indian wisdom; 3) the Heraclitean from Persian wisdom; 4) the Empedoclean from Egyptian wisdom; and 5) the philosophy of Anaxagoras from Judaic wisdom.

We agree that, carried to such extremes, these theses become nothing other than works of fiction; but the fact always remains that even if they become attenuated, particularized, and toned down, thus losing their fictional character, they still remain simply conjectures and, what is more, without historical foundation. In fact, they would still have to contend with the following detailed data that factually frustrates their claims to credibility.

a) It has been historically demonstrated that the Eastern peoples with whom the Greek have come in contact possessed, it is true, religious convictions, as well as theological and cosmological myths, but they did *not* possess a *scientific philosophy* in the true sense of the word. They did not possess what the Greeks themselves were the first to create, namely, philosophy. The archeological evidence that has come to light at present does not authorize us in any way to go further than this conclusion.

b) In the second place, granted also (but not conceded) that the Eastern peoples with whom the Greeks came in contact had philosophical doctrines, the possibility of communicating them to Greece would be anything but easy to explain. Zeller has written quite accurately: "When strictly philosophical concepts are considered, especially in the infancy of philosophy, in comparison to their connections to linguistic expression; when we remember how rarely the knowledge of foreign tongues is encountered among the Greeks, and how little on the other hand the interpreters, as a rule well versed only in commercial transactions and for the explanations of curiosities, would consequently be capable of being guides to the understanding of philosophical teachings; and when we add to all of that the fact of the utilization of Eastern writings on the part of Greek philosophers and the translation of such writings, nothing further is said that in the least merits belief; when we ask in addition through what means the doctrines of the Indians and the other peoples of the Far East could have come to Greece before Alexander, then these difficulties will be found sufficiently weighty."[6]

Note that it would be beside the point to object that the Greeks, notwithstanding this, were able to draw from the Eastern peoples certain beliefs and religious cults as well as certain arts, at least on the experiential level. In fact, such things are easier to communicate in contrast to philosophy, as Burnet has stressed, because they neither require abstract language nor the vehicle of knowledgeable men, but simply imitation: "We," writes Burnet "do not know, in the period with which we are concerned, any Greek who knows the Eastern language well enough to read an Egyptian book or even to understand the words of Egyptian priests, and only at a much later date do we hear mention of Eastern teachers who write and speak Greek."[7]

c) In the third place (and this has until now not been sufficiently attended to), many scholars who claim to uncover similarities between Eastern wisdom and Greek philosophy are victims without being fully aware of optical illusions insofar as, on the one hand, they understand the Eastern doctrines in function of Western categories and, on the other, they color the Greek doctrines in Eastern tints so that these correspondences have, in the final analysis, little or no credibility.

d) Finally, even if it could be demonstrated that certain ideas of the Greek philosophers actually had antecedents in Eastern wisdom and it could be historically proven that they attained them, such similarities would nevertheless not change the core of the problem. Philosophy, from the moment of its birth in Greece, represented *a new form of spiritual expression such that, in the moment itself in which it acquired content as a fruit of other forms of the spiritual life, it structurally transformed it.* This final remark puts us in a position, as a consequence, to also understand another very interesting fact, that is, how and why those same arts, and in particular the knowledge of mathematics and astronomy, which the Greeks received (the fact seems to be historically undeniable), from the Egyptians and from the Babylonians, respectively, were essentially transformed by them.

3. The unique theoretical transformation of the Egyptian and Chaldaic knowledges produced by the Greek spirit

It is quite beyond doubt that the Greeks derived their first knowledge of mathematics and geometry from the Egyptians. But, as has been correctly emphasized by Burnet,[8] they were radically transformed by the Greeks.

As we can note from a papyrus of the Rhind collection, Egyptian mathematics chiefly consisted of the determination of arithmetic calculations for essentially practical purposes, e.g., the weighing of cereals and fruits, the calculation of the ways of dividing given quantities of things between a number of persons, etc. Whatever has been said to the contrary, it corresponds quite well to what Plato notes in the *Laws* about the arithmetical operations taught to children in the Egyptian schools.

Analogously, geometry had an essentially practical character (as can be inferred from the aforementioned papyrus of the Rhind collection and from Herodotus[9]), both in determining the dimensions of fields after the flooding of the Nile, and in the construction of the Pyramids or similar projects. But mathematics as the general theory of numbers and the theoretic science of geometry were created and developed by the Pythagoreans. Some scholars object to Burnet's arbitrarily positing a distinction between the theoretical and practical and, hence, between the practical interest (of the Egyptians) and the theoretical interest (of the Greeks). Thus Burnet develops a separation of the two interests that is in itself incorrect, because in the measure in which the Egyptians were able to determine their practical rules they were precisely involved in a theoretical activity. Moreover, insofar as the above is undeniable, it is still true that the prominence given to the properly theoretical aspect and the speculative clarification of mathematico-geometrical questions was the work of the Greeks. This rational procedure itself, on which philosophy was grounded, permits it to purify mathematics and geometry and to elevate them to the speculative level.

An analogous argument is true as well for the astronomy of the Babylonians, which has at times been noted. It was concerned with celestial phenomena, with the astrological purpose of foreseeing events and making predictions. Hence it had a purely utilitarian aim that was not properly scientific and speculative. Even if it has been emphasized that the conceptions of the Chaldaic astrologers implicitly contained rather important speculative concepts, as for example the notion that number is the instrument for the knowledge of all things, the notion that all things are linked by an intimate connection, and hence the idea of the unity of all things, and perhaps even the notion of the cyclical character of the cosmos and others like it, nevertheless the points made above are still true: namely, that it is the Greeks who are to be credited with having explained these concepts, and that they accomplished it in terms of their speculative spirit, that is, in virtue of the spirit that created philosophy.

4. Conclusions

At this stage of current research, it is impossible to speak of a derivation of philosophy or speculative science from the East. Certainly the Greeks took from the peoples of the East with whom they came into contact notions of various kinds and on this point the current research may bring to light new facts and new perspectives. One point is nevertheless secure, namely, that the Greeks *qualitatively* transformed whatever they received. Therefore we want to conclude with R. Mondolfo (who, it should be noted, was very insistent on the importance and positive character of Eastern influence on the Greeks and on the spiritual fecundity of that influence) as follows: "... these assimilations of elements and cultural stimuli [coming from the East] cannot at all weaken the boast of the originality of Greek thought. It has negotiated the decisive passage from technical utility and from myth to pure and disinterested science; it has first affirmed systematically the logical requirements and the speculative needs of reason. It is the true creator of science as a logical system and of philosophy as the rational awareness and solution of questions of the whole of reality and life."[10]

But what we have established brings to light further problems. What reasons will explain in whole or in part how and why only the Greeks, and not other civilized peoples before them, created philosophy and science? We shall now reply to this question.

II. The Forms of the Intellectual Life of the Greeks that Prepared for the Advent of Philosophy

1. The Homeric poems

The uncontested educators of the Greeks, prior to the birth of philosophy, were the poets, especially Homer, whose poems, as has been accurately said, were the Bible of the Greeks in the sense that the first Greeks looked for their necessary and chiefly spiritual sustenance in the Homeric poems, from which they drew models of life, materials for reflection, stimuli for the imagination, and hence, all the necessary elements typical of spiritual formation and education.

Now the Homeric poems, as is presently well-known, contain some aspects that clearly differentiate them from all the poems that we find at the beginnings of various peoples, and already contained in themselves some of the qualities of the Greek spirit that produced philosophy.

In the first place, it has been emphasized that the two poems were produced by a rich and varied imagination producing marvelous or fantastic situations and events that do not fall, except rarely at times, into descriptions of the *monstrous* and the *deformed* as, in general, instead occurs in the first artistic representations of primitive peoples. The Homeric imagination is structured according to a sense of harmony, rhythm, proportion, limit, and measure; they will reveal themselves as constants of Greek philosophy that will result in the elevation of measure and limit especially to the height of a metaphysically determined principle.

In addition, it has also been stressed that, in the poetry of Homer, *the art of motivation* is a constant, in the sense that the poet does not only narrate a chain of facts, but analyzes them, although purely on a poetic-imaginative level, for *reasons.* Homer, Jaeger correctly writes, "does not passively accept tradition: he does not relate a simple succession of events, *he presents a plot that develops by its own compulsion from stage to stage, governed by an unbreakable connection of cause and effect.* . . . And the plot does not develop in a loose chronological sequence. It is ruled throughout by the principle of sufficient reason. Every action has its roots in character."[1] This poetic mode of seeing things is the antecedent to the philosophical inquiry into the "cause," the "principle," the "why" of things.

A third characteristic of the Homeric epic prefigures the philosophy of the Greeks. They both "*present the structure of reality in its entirety,* although philosophy presents it in its rational form, whereas the epic shows it in mythical form. In Homer, the theme of 'the position of man in the universe,' that is, the classical theme of Greek philosophy, is already present at every moment, and Homer never loses sight of it."[2]

Finally, the Homeric poems were decisive in fixing a specific conception of the Gods and the Divine as well as fixing some fundamental types of life and ethical characters of men that will become authentic models. But we must leave aside the importance of this factor, because on this point the argument would carry us beyond Homer and encompass all that is Greek.

2. The Gods of state religion and their relation to philosophy

Scholars have emphasized many times that between religion and philosophy there is a structural bond (Hegel will even say that religion expresses through the way of representations the same truth that philosophy expresses by way of concepts). It is true both when philosophy takes up from religion a determined content as well as, again, when philosophy tries to challenge religion (in this latter case the challenging function is again nourished and hence conditioned by the challenged goals). Moreover, if this was true in general it was done in a paradigmatic way among the Greeks.

But when we speak of Greek religion it is necessary to make a clear distinction between the *state religion* that has its most noble manifestation in Homer and the *religion of the mysteries,* since between the former and the latter is a very clear distinction. In many respects, the spirit that animates the religion of the mysteries is rejected by the spirit animating, on the contrary, the state religion. Now a historian of philosophy who concentrates only on the first aspect of the religion of the Greeks is prevented from understanding completely an entire and very important current of speculation that moves from the Presocratics to Plato and to the Neoplatonists, and hence inevitably distorts the general perspective. This happened even to Zeller and to numerous groups of his followers (and hence to many of the manualists who for a long time slavishly followed the interpretation of Zeller).

The German scholar was well aware of the nexus between the Greek state religion and Greek philosophy (and on this point we will reproduce his keen remarks that are still valuable today); but then he fell into a wholly one-sided vision, misconceiving the consequences of the mysteries, and especially that of Orphism, with the absurd consequences about which we will speak.

But, first, let us see the nature and importance of the state religion of the Greeks. In what sense and in what respect did the state religion have an influence on philosophy? For Homeric man and for the Greek man, inheritor of the Homeric tradition, it may correctly be said that *everything is divine,* in the sense that everything that happens is a work of the Gods. All natural phenomena are initiated by the Gods, the thunder and the lightning are hurled by Zeus from the height of Olympus, the waves of the sea are aroused by the trident of Poseidon, the sun is carried by the golden chariot of Apollo, and so on. But even the phenomena of the interior life of the individual Greek man, as well as his communal life, the destiny of his city, and its wars, are conceived as essentially linked to the Gods and conditioned by them.

But who are these Gods? They are, as we recognize today, natural forces in idealized human shape. They are aspects of humankind sublimated and hypostatized. They are powers of man presented in a very attractive form. In conclusion, the Gods of natural Greek religion are nothing other than *human beings amplified and idealized*; they are, hence, *quantitatively* superior to us, but not *qualitatively* different. Therefore the Greek state religion is certainly a form of *naturalistic* religion. It is, in fact, naturalistic to such an extent that, as Walter Otto has correctly remarked, "sanctity cannot find a place in it,"[3] since by their very essence the Gods do not desire, nor in any manner could they elevate man above themselves. As a matter of fact, if the nature of the Gods and men, as we said, is identical and they are different *only in degree*, man can see himself in the Gods. In order to raise himself up to them he must not at all enter into conflict with himself. He must not compromise his own nature or aspects of his own nature. He must not in any way die to himself. Rather he must simply be himself.

Hence, as Zeller has said so well, what is required by the Gods from man is "not at all a profound change in his manner of thinking, it is not even a struggle with his natural tendencies and impulses; since quite the reverse everything that for man is natural is valued also basically by divinity as legitimate; the most divine man is the one who unfolds in the most vigorous way his human power; and the accomplishment of his religious duty consists essentially in this, that man do for the honor of the divinities that which conforms to his own nature."[4]

And as naturalistic as the religion of the Greeks was, so also "...their most ancient philosophy was naturalistic; and even when ethics acquired pre-eminence...its motto was conformity with nature."[5]

This is undoubtedly true and well said; but it only illuminates one face of the truth.

When Thales says that "everything is full of Gods," he will move without doubt in an analogous naturalistic sphere. The Gods of Thales will be derived from a natural principle of all things (water). But when Pythagoras speaks of the transmigration of the soul, Heraclitus of an ultraterrestrial destiny for souls, and Empedocles explains the way of purification, then naturalism is broken profoundly and *such a break is not comprehensible except by going back to the religion of the mysteries and especially to Orphism.*

But before speaking about this, we must explain another essential characteristic of Greek religion which had a particular influence on the possibility of the origination of philosophical reflection.

The Greeks did not have sacred books or divine revelations. They did not have, hence, fixed and unchanging theological dogmas. (The Homeric poems and the *Theogony* of Hesiod were the principle sources in the matter.) And consequently, in Greece there was to be no priestly caste as custodians of dogma. (The priests in Greece were a very weak force and scarcely relevant, since they did not have the task of guarding and communicating a dogma, nor did they have the exclusive office of being sacrificers.)

Moreover, the absence of dogma and their custodians left plenty of room for philosophical speculation. It did not find any obstacles of a religious character analogous to those that were to be found with Eastern peoples, and that would be overcome only with difficulty. Therefore, scholars correctly underline this fortunate historical circumstance in which the Greeks found themselves. In antiquity it was unique and of truly inestimable value.

3. The mystery religions: the influence of Orphism on the establishment of the problematic of ancient philosophy

That a religion of the mysteries flourished in Greece is a clear symptom that *for many the official religion was not sufficient*, that is, that many did not find adequate satisfaction for their authentic religious desires.

In this respect we are not interested in tracing, not even in outline, a history of the mystery religions, since only Orphism had an impact on the philosophical problematic in a way that can be determined. The Orphics maintained that the founder of their movement was the mythical Thracian poet Orpheus (who, contrary to the type of life incarnated in the Homeric heroes, spoke of a more interior and spiritual type of life) and from him they derived their name. We do not know whence the movement had its origin and how it was spread throughout Greece. Herodotus gives Egypt as its source,[6] but this is impossible because the Egyptian documents do not contain any traces of Orphic doctrines and, in addition, the care of bodies and their practice of embalming clearly contrasts with the spirit of Orphism that rejects the body as the prison and the bond of the soul. The movement is later than the Homeric poems (which do not contain any traces of it) and Hesiod. Certainly it flourished or reflourished in the sixth century before the Common Era. The fundamental nucleus of the beliefs taught by Orphism, stripped of their various encrustations and amplifications that several times were added to them, consists in the following statements.

a) A divine principle dwells in man, a *daimon* fallen into a body because of an original fault.

b) This *daimon* that pre-existed the body is immortal and hence does not die with the body, but is destined to be re-incarnated several times in successive bodies through a series of rebirths in order to expiate its faults.

c) The Orphic life, with its practice of purifications, is the only one that can put an end to the cycle of re-incarnations.

d) Consequently, he who lives the Orphic life (the initiated) enjoys, after death, the promised reward in the beyond (liberation); whereas for the non-initiated there is punishment.

Now many scholars have acknowledged that the doctrine of transmigration of souls has come to the philosophers from Orphism. However, everyone has not seen the most important consequences that this acknowledgment involved.

The first is that the *dualistic conception* of the soul (= *daimon*) and body (= the place of expiation of the soul) arose with Orphism. For the first time, that is, man sees in himself two opposed principles, locked in combat, precisely because the body is seen as a prison and a place for the punishment of the *daimon*. The naturalistic vision of which we spoke in the previous section is broken, and thus man begins to understand that not all tendencies that are contained in himself are good, that some, on the contrary, must be repressed and contained, and that a *purification* of his divine element is necessary and hence a mortification of the body.

So now we come to the premises of the revolution of the entire vision of life connected to the state religion. The virtue of the Homeric hero, the traditional *arete*, ceases to be *authentic* virtue; life is seen according to a wholly new dimension.

Now, *without Orphism we cannot explain Pythagoras, nor Heraclitus, nor Empedocles, and naturally not Plato and whatever was derived from him.* Zeller objected that Orphic beliefs in these philosophies merely parallel scientific theories and in these theories "no lacuna could be found if that [Orphic belief] were missing."[7] But the objection is simply historically inaccurate. In fact, the philosophical schools in Sicily and in Magna Graecia, where Orphism was particularly strong, *take on different characteristics in comparison to the schools established in Asia Minor.* They are concerned with a somewhat different problematic, and they even create a different theoretical atmosphere. If it is true that the Italic philosophers did not produce a complete synthesis between their scientific doctrines and their Orphic beliefs, it is likewise true that if we separate those Orphic doctrines from them we will first of all lose even the *content* that, at first, is juxtaposed to the naturalistic doctrines and, in the second place, will bring about their being superseded. But Zeller writes again later: "Only in Plato is faith in the immortality of the soul grounded philosophically, but it is difficult to imagine that a similar belief would have been impossible for him without the myths that he will adopt for their expression."[8] So in this case, Zeller once again goes against historical truth because, in point of fact, that Plato began to speak about immortality when he began to speak about the Orphic myths can be confirmed. It will be the promptings of the Orphic vision that will move Plato to undertake his "second voyage," that is, to undertake the way that will lead to the discovery of the supersensible world.

4. The political, social, and economic conditions that favored the birth of philosophy among the Greeks

The unique role of *freedom* that characterized the Greeks in comparison to the Eastern peoples is given great emphasis by historians. The Eastern peoples were held by blind obedience to religious and thus to political power sources. We have already considered the degree of freedom the Greeks enjoyed from religion. The argument is more complex in regard to political conditions; however, it is possible to say that the Greeks enjoyed, even in this area, a privileged situation. The Greeks did not feel any antithesis between the individual and the State with the creation of the *polis*, nor any limitation on their freedom, but instead were moved to self-acceptance *not accidentally but essentially* as citizen of a specific State, of a particular *polis*. The State became and remained up to the Hellenistic Age the arena of activity for the Greek man and, hence, the individual citizen considered the goal of the State to be his own goal, the good of the State his own good, the glory of the State his own glory, the freedom of the State his own freedom.

But there were two concrete political facts "that stand out above all the others,"[9] in the development of Greek civilization prior to the rise of philosophy, as has been noted by Zeller: *a*) the birth of the republican system, and *b*) the expansion of the Greeks toward both East and West with the founding of colonies in both directions.

Both of these facts were decisive for the birth of philosophy.

With respect to the first point, again Zeller correctly notes: "In the stresses and struggles of this political turmoil [that carried the Greeks from the old aristocratic to the republican and democratic forms of government] all forces must be mobilized and exercised; public life opened the way to science, and the sense of their youthful freedom must give to the spirit of the Greek people an impetus that had an impact on scientific activity. Hence, if contemporaneously with the transformation of political conditions, there was posited the foundation of the artistic and scientific flowering of Greece in a vigorous way, the connection of the two phenomena can be clearly recognized; moreover, the culture is, for the Greeks, entirely and in a stronger way what it will always be in any healthy life of the people: at the same time an effect and a condition of freedom."[10]

But there is a fact to be noted that confirms this in a stronger way (and that we mentioned above as the second phenomenon of Greek history). Philosophy *arose first in the colonies before it arose in the mother country*; it was born first in the colonies to the East in Asia Minor, thence in the colonies to the West in the lower half of Italy, and only then did it move to the mother country.

Why did this occur? It is because, as scholars have noted, the colonies with their productiveness and their commercial activity achieved well-being and hence culture. And it is also because of a certain openness that the distance from the mother country permitted and that allowed them to freely grant constitutions to themselves before the homeland could.

Thus it was the more favorable socio-economic conditions of the colonies that permitted the birth and the flourishing of philosophy, which then was passed on to the mother country, where it achieved its highest perfection, not in Sparta or in other city-states, but only at Athens, that is, in that city-state in which there was the most freedom, as Plato himself recognized, that the Greeks had ever enjoyed.

III. The Nature and Problems of Ancient Philosophy

1. The defining characteristics of ancient philosophy

Until now we have spoken of philosophy without determining in a specific way its definition; it is only in the light of the preceding considerations that we can do so at this point.

We must first point out that the tradition claims that Pythagoras was the inventor of the term. As a matter of fact, the issue cannot be settled by historical evidence, but it is, however, a plausible claim. The term was certainly coined within a religious milieu. The milieu presupposed that "wisdom" as a secure possession was possible in its highest form only for the Gods, whereas it considered that human beings could only tend toward wisdom, and so continually draw near to it with love. It was a love that is never wholly satisfied, whence the appropriateness of the term "philosofia," which means "love of wisdom."

But what did the Greeks understand by this wisdom which they sought and loved? It is possible to establish what *in principle* ought to be called philosophy, prescinding from various fluctuations and uncertainties that as a matter of fact are met in the use of the term. These uncertainties are yet quite great because from time to time various authors and various currents of thought included in philosophy either too much or too little, according to the circumstances. It is, nevertheless, possible to decide what has a right to be called philosophy, and what from Thales onward *as a matter of fact* was thought to be so by those who are correctly called philosophers. The uncertainties arose only because some philosophers, in dealing with what we will see can be said to be truly philosophy, were also concerned with many other kinds of knowledge that made claim with equal validity to be called philosophy, following the opinion that, since it is the one person who searches, the sciences that he possesses must also be one.

Moreover, from the moment in which it arose, scientific philosophy presented in a very clear way the following characteristics with regard to, respectively, *a)* content, *b)* method, and *c)* aim.

a) With respect to content, philosophy wanted to explain the *totality of things*, that is, *the whole of reality* without the exclusion of any part or aspect of it, thus distinguishing itself structurally from the special sciences that instead are limited to explaining particular sections of reality, groups of particular things, or particular phenomena. This aspect of philosophy is already present in all its import in the first philosopher's (Thales) question— what is the principle of *all things*?

b) With respect to method, philosophy wanted to explain the totality which is its object in a *strictly rational manner. What is of value in philosophy is its rational argument, its rational purpose, or simply, its logos.* It is not enough for philosophy to confirm and ascertain the data derived from experience on a factual level; philosophy must go beyond the fact and the experience in order to discover the reasons, the causes, and the principles.

It is this last attribute that confers the scientific character on philosophy. Such a quality is also common to the other sciences, in fact, insofar as they are sciences they never simply verify and ascertain the data empirically, but are always seeking the causes and the reasons; but the difference lies in the fact that, while the special sciences look for the causes of individual realities or of parts of individual realities, philosophy instead seeks the causes and principles of the whole of reality (as moreover the first above-mentioned characteristic necessarily states).

c) Finally, we must clarify the aim or purpose of philosophy. On this point Aristotle has offered the best explanation; he states that philosophy has a purely theoretical character, that is, it is a contemplation. It simply seeks the truth for its own sake, prescinding from its practical use. Philosophy is not sought because of any advantage that is extrinsic to it, but it is sought just for itself. Therefore philosophy is "free" insofar as it does not serve any practical purpose, and it is completed and realized in the pure contemplation of the truth. It is also from this viewpoint that the name philosophy is really appropriately given to it; a love of wisdom for its own sake, a disinterested love of the truth.

Here are some statements of Aristotle that are particularly enlightening:

> That it is not a science of production is clear even from the history of the earliest philosophers. For it is owing to their wonder that men both now begin and at first began to philosophize; they wondered originally at the obvious difficulties, then advanced little by little and stated difficulties about the greater matters, e.g., about the phenomena of the moon and those of the sun and of the stars, and about the genesis of the universe. And a man who is puzzled and wonders thinks himself ignorant (whence even the lover of myth is in a sense a lover of wisdom, for the myth is composed of wonders); *therefore since they philosophized in order to escape from ignorance, evidently they were pursuing science in order to know, and not for any utilitarian end.* And this is confirmed by the facts; for it was when almost all the necessities of life and the things that make for comfort and recreation had been secured that such knowledge began to be sought. *Evidently then we do not seek it for the sake of any other advantage; but as the man is free, we say, who exists for his own sake and not for another's, so we pursue this as the only free science, for it alone exists for its own sake.*[1]

The argument that we have constructed to this point concerning the originality of the scientific philosophy of the Greeks should be clear.

Eastern wisdom is profoundly tied to imaginative fictions, and in them the imaginative and mythical element predominates and for this reason they lack scientific character. The Eastern sciences and arts (Egyptian mathematics and geometry, Chaldaic astronomy) although they call for the use of reason, they lack the element of the theoretical, that is, of speculative freedom and naturally, as particular knowledges, also the first of the elements of the definition pointed out above. The absolute originality of this wonderful creative synthesis of the Greek genius that was called philosophy should by now be clear. Even its stature, not eulogistically called sublime, is so because it elevates man to the very summit of his potentialities.

Aristotle will call it "divine" because in addition to bringing man to a knowledge of God it shares the same characteristics that the knowledge of God itself possesses, that is, a disinterested, free, and complete contemplation of the truth. Therefore, Aristotle again was correct in saying, "all the other sciences will be more necessary than this, but none will be superior."[2]

We wish to conclude with this remark since today the category of interest or utility, not the category of disinterest, is placed at the summit of the scale of values. When based on the scale of values of marxist thought or a thought of marxist extraction, it is asserted that the task of philosophy is not to contemplate but to change reality; and hence that ancient philosophy which chooses only contemplation must be set aside by a form of philosophy which descends to reality in order to change or to make changes. Further, when this is said, what is being asked for is not simply the substitution of one philosophical vision for another, but what amounts to the death of philosophy. To change reality can only be a consequent aspect, dependent on discovering and finding the truth, whereas to change reality is at best a corollary to philosophizing. Change can only be an ethical, political, educative task. It can never be from the philosophic point of view in a primary position because it structurally presupposes that we know and have confirmed in a preliminary fashion the nature and extent of the change. Hence it always presupposes a theoretical moment (a philosophical one) as its necessary condition. It does no good to object, with those who too quickly assert against the objection of activists that it is true that to change reality is not to philosophize but that nevertheless, the modern man must philosophize *in order to* change something. Even this position is deceptive. In fact, he who philosophizes with this attitude *has lost his freedom* because the anxiety produced by aiming at change inevitably conditions and disturbs the contemplative dimension of his thought. It disturbs it to the point that it overturns the goals and agitates the vehicle of action. Pure contemplation then becomes ideology and ceases to be philosophy.

In this also the Greeks have been and are our teachers. It is philosophy if and only if it is totally free, that is, if and only if it is absolutely free, a contemplation and search for the truth as such, without any further purpose determining it. Whatever follows as a practical effect of the truth that is found and contemplated is again necessarily external to the properly philosophical moment.

2. The problems of ancient philosophy

We have said that philosophy claims to know the totality of reality with a rational method and a purely theoretical purpose. Now it is clear that the totality of reality is not a monolithic block, but rather a collection of distinct things, even if organically and strictly connected. Hence the philosophical problem in general must necessarily be subdivided, that is to say, separated into problems that are more particular and determined so that their connections are in accord with the manner and measure in which the realities that they have as their objects are joined. It is clear again *a priori* that these particular questions, in the sphere of the general problem, will not come to light simultaneously but slowly over time.

Thus, at first, the totality of reality, *physis*, is seen as *cosmos* and hence the pre-eminent philosophical problem was contained in the cosmological questions, "how did the cosmos come into being?," "what is its principle?," "what are the stages and the phases of its generation?," etc. This is more or less consistently the essential problematic that arose in the first phase of Greek philosophy.

But with the Sophists the situation changed, the problematic of the cosmos, for reasons that we will discuss, is put aside and the reality that attracts their attention is that of man. Therefore the philosophies of the Sophists and Socrates will concentrate their energies on the nature of man and virtue, or *arete*; thus the moral problem arose.

The philosophical problematic is further differentiated and enriched by Plato and Aristotle. They distinguish areas and parts of problems that then become points of reference for the whole subsequent course of the history of philosophy.

First, Plato discovers and demonstrates that reality or being is not a single genera. In addition to the sensible cosmos, there exists an intelligible, supersensible, and transcendent reality from which there will be derived the Aristotelian distinctions of physics, or the doctrine of sensible reality, and metaphysics, or the doctrine of supersensible reality. Further, moral problems are specified by distinguishing two aspects of the life of man: one as an individual and the other in his communal life. Thus the distinction arose between authentic ethical problems and those that are properly political (problems which for the Greeks are still more intimately connected than they are for us moderns).

Again with Plato and especially with Aristotle, the epistemological and logical questions are determined (again, largely as they emerge from the preceding philosophers). It will not be difficult to see that these questions are explained and have a particular character according to their unique philosophical quality, that is, *the method of rational inquiry*. What is the way that man must travel to achieve the truth? What is the verifying nature of the senses, and what is it with respect to reason? What is the nature of truth and falsity? And again, in general, what are the logical forms through which men think, judge, and reason? What are the rules of correct thinking? Finally, what are the conditions that allow an argument to qualify as scientific?

In connection with the logico-epistemological problems, there also arose the problem of the determination of the nature of the arts and beauty, of artistic expression and language; and hence there arose what are called today aesthetic problems. And again, in connection with these there arose the problem of determining the nature of rhetoric and rhetorical discourse, that is, the discourse which has as its purpose conviction and persuasion.

Post-Aristotelian speculation will treat all these problems as present and they will choose to re-arrange them into 1) physics, 2) logic, and 3) morality. One of the characteristics of philosophy, at first sight, that post-Aristotelian speculation will seem to change is its *purely theoretical character,* that is, the *disinterested practice of philosophy.* In fact, the Hellenistic-Roman schools will essentially aim to construct the ideal life of the sage, that is, the life that guarantees tranquility of soul, happiness, and they will resolve physical and logical problems only in function of their contribution to those of morality. But it is easily seen that the purely contemplative spirit of philosophy is not exactly rejected, but only determined in a different way. Destroy the polis and tear down the traditional hierarchy of values that the polis supported and the philosopher will ask philosophy to furnish him with new ones. What the philosopher in this period will not generally ask of philosophy is that it change others and things, but rather that it change him. He will seek from philosophy the truths that will enable him to live according to the truth.

In conclusion, ancient philosophy in the final period, especially Neoplatonism, will be enriched through a mystico-religious problematic; facing a nascent and triumphant Christianity, Greek thought will try to add to man a vision of the All and a type of life in the All that contrasts and overcomes those preached by Christianity. But it will achieve in this attempt the opening of further areas of metaphysical interest, not conquering them except for a short period in the confrontation, because Christianity is presented as a messenger of a Word that will dissolve the Greek vision of the world and will lead thought to another landfall.

IV. The Periods of Ancient Philosophy

Greek philosophy has a history of over a millenium, beginning from the sixth century before the Common Era and going on to the year 529 of the Common Era, the year in which by the Edict of the Emperor Justinian the philosophical schools were closed, their libraries destroyed, and their followers dispersed.

In this course of time we can distinguish the following phases, stages, or periods.

1) The so-called *naturalistic* period characterized, as we said previously, by the problem of *physis*, that is, by the cosmo-ontological problem (Ionians, Pythagoreans, Eleatics, and the Pluralists).

2) The so-called *humanistic* period, which is identified in part with the previous stage and with the dissolution of naturalistic speculation, and which has as its protagonists the Sophists, who posited the speculative problem concerning man. Socrates, who was among their number, was the first to attempt philosophically to determine the nature of man.

3) The period of the great syntheses of Plato and Aristotle characterized especially by the discovery of the supersensible and the explanation and unified formulation of various philosophical problems.

4) The period characterized by the Hellenistic Schools with the birth and development of the three great systems, Stoicism, Epicureanism, and Scepticism and with the successive diffusion of eclecticism.

5) The religious period that coincided almost in its entirety with the Christian epoch. It involved, for the first time, the meeting between Biblical revelation and the Hellenic culture of Alexandria. A revival of Stoicism at Rome (that will take up this doctrine with religious overtones, indeed, strongly spiritualistic ones). A reinterpreted Pythagoreanism, and especially an imposing rebirth of Platonism, at first with so-called Middle Platonism and next especially by the magnificent movement of Neoplatonism.

In a *History of Ancient Philosophy* understood as Greco-Roman philosophy, the nascent problematic of Christian thought is not included, but only the thematic of those thinkers who did not accept the new Christian problematic, since this, far from crowning Greek thought, placed it in crisis and prepared for a new way of thinking and a new age, that is, the middle ages. Therefore this problematic is to be examined and adequately understood not as the conclusion of ancient speculation, but as the premise and foundation of mediaeval thought and philosophy.

First Part

The Philosophers of Nature: the Ionians and the Italians. The Problems of Nature, of Being, and of the Cosmos

«... οὔτε γίγνεσθαι οὐθὲν οἴονται οὔτε ἀπόλλυσθαι.»

"...they believe that nothing is generated and nothing is destroyed."

Aristotle *Metaphysics* A3.983b12

PRELUDE TO THE COSMOLOGICAL PROBLEM

«καὶ ὁ φιλόμυθος φιλόσοφός πώς ἐστιν.»

"He also who loves myths is in some way a philosopher."

Aristotle *Metaphysics* A2.982b18

I. The Theogonic and Cosmogonic Myths

It has been remarked many times that the antecedent of philosophical cosmology is the mythico-poetic cosmogonies and theogonies, in which Greek literature abounds. The paradigmatic prototype is the *Theogony* of Hesiod, which is the result and inheritance of the preceding mythological tradition, and which traces an imposing synthesis on all the material, unifying, re-elaborating, and systematizing it. The *Theogony* of Hesiod narrates the birth of all the Gods and why some Gods are identified with parts of the universe and with phenomena of the cosmos. In addition, theogony also becomes cosmogony, that is, it provides imaginative explanations of the genesis of the universe and cosmic phenomena.

Hesiod imagines himself, in his introduction, at the foot of Mount Helicon, in Boetia, having had a vision of the Muses and having received from them a revelation of the truth of which he immediately becomes the herald. At first, he says, *Chaos* was generated, then *Gaia* (Earth), in whose ample bosom all things reside, and in the depths of the Earth the dark Tartarus was generated, and finally, Eros (Love) who then was the origin of all other things. From Chaos was born Herebus and Night, from which was generated the Aither (the high Heaven) and Hemera (the Day). Uranus was generated (the starry Skies) from the Earth alone, as well as the mountains and the seas; then, united to the Heaven, Earth generated Ocean and the waves.

Proceeding in a similar way, Hesiod tells of the origin of the various Gods and divine messengers. Zeus belongs to the final generation. In fact, he was generated by Cronos and Rhea (who in their turn were generated by Earth and Uranus), and thus with Zeus they take part in the final generation of all the other Gods of the Homeric Olympus, that is, those Gods that the Greeks then venerated.

Now, as we said, there is no doubt that the *Theogony* of Hesiod and in general its theogonic-cosmological presentations are the antecedent of philosophical cosmology. However, it is likewise indubitable that between these attempts and philosophical cosmology (even the most primitive, that of Thales) there is a very clear gap. In order to grasp the difference of the one from the other, we must consider three characteristics that we mentioned above and that are distinctive of philosophy: *a*) The description of the totality of reality, *b*) the method of rational explanation, *c*) the purely theoretical interest. Now, it is clear that theogonies possess the first and the third of these characteristics, but *they lack the second one, that is, the specifying and determinative one.* They proceed in terms of myth, with imaginative descriptions, poetic license, and intuitive analogies suggested by sensible experience. Therefore they are not on the rational level, that is, the level of rational explanation.

When Aristotle says that the lover of myths is in some way a philosopher,[1] what he says refers precisely to the fact that, just as philosophy, so myth arose in order to satisfy the desire for the marvelous, or the simple desire to know, and not for any pragmatic purpose.[2] But myth is always myth, related to philosophy but not philosophy.

Because this point has recently been taken up again, and some have wanted to deny the existence of this gap, it is well that we go on and point out some concepts which we maintain as essential. Jaeger has written: "Hesiod's *Theogony*, again, is a rational system, deliberately built up by logical inquiry into the origin and nature of the world. Yet within that system the old force of mythological thinking is still active, it lives on in what we think of as 'scientific' philosophy, in the work of the Ionian 'physicists'; and without it we could not explain the astonishing ability of the early scientific age to create great new philosophical systems. Love and Hate, the two natural forces of binding and separation in the philosophy of Empedocles, have the same intellectual ancestry as Hesiod's cosmogonic Eros. Thus we *cannot* say that scientific thinking began either when rational thinking began or when mythical thinking ended. Even in the philosophy of Plato and Aristotle we can find genuine mythologizing, for instance, the Platonic myth of the soul, or Aristotle's description of the love that all things have for the unmoved Mover of the Universe."[3] But Jaeger is the victim of an optical illusion. No one denies that before the advent of philosophy reason existed and no one affirms that in the *Theogony* of Hesiod (as well as in the Homeric epics) there is only myth and imagination without reason; so also no one denies, conversely, that in philosophy there remained for a long time mythical and imaginative elements. But the essential point is in the *specifying role* that each of these factors played. We will immediately see that in Hesiod and in the authors of theogonies the specifying role is precisely that of the imaginative and mythico-poetic element, whereas in Thales it will be given to the logos and reason. It is thus precisely for this reason that the tradition has denominated Thales as the first philosopher, recognizing quite accurately that in his type of discourse something was radically changed from that of the poets, and that this something signaled precisely the change from myth to logos.

Moreover, in the *Theogony* of Hesiod, the characteristic that would qualify it as philosophical cosmology is missing, that is, *the attempt to specify the first unconditioned principle, the absolute source of everything.* Jaeger himself, contradicting his own thesis that we quoted above, remarks as follows: "The geneological thought of Hesiod considered even chaos as generated. He does not say in principle it was chaos but *first there was generated chaos*, then the earth, etc. To this point the question is proposed whether there is also to be a beginning to becoming by what has not come into being. To this question Hesiod has no answer, as a matter of fact no one posed it. It presupposed a logical thought far distant from his."[4]

But keep in mind that Hesiod did not pose the question and he could not pose it precisely because the imagination that was fed by the sensible and analogies taken from the sensible invoked chaos to answer the question, that is, it cannot imagine any further form, it was at an end of its resources. The imagination can recognize as generated chaos itself, that is, the primary reality, precisely because it sees everything as generated (both Gods and things). In order to represent it as ungenerated, it would have to put aside imagination, and hence to deny itself. This is indeed what philosophy is right from its inception, it will go contrary to fantasy and imagination as well as the senses. It will confer on its speculative productions the power of the logos, challenging myth and sensible appearances and thus creating something completely new.

When it is said that the *Theogony* is very important for the advent of philosophy, it is correct. But the advent of philosophy presupposes the acquisition of a new level of the logos, that is, it involved a revolution, as we will immediately see.

Second Section

THE MILESIANS AND HERACLITUS

«ἐκ πάντων ἓν καὶ ἐξ ἑνὸς πάντα.»

". . .from all things the one and from the one all things."

Heraclitus *Fragment* 10

I. Thales

1. The philosophical propositions attributed to Thales

Aristotle is the source of our knowledge of the following views concerning Thales,[1] from whom we have nothing written.

a) Thales was the founder of the philosophy of *physis*, insofar as he was the first to affirm the existence of a unique principle and cause of all things that exist and he said that this principle was water.[2]

b) He stated that the world is full of Gods.[3]

c) He said that the magnet possesses a soul, because it is capable of moving things (and hence the soul is the principle of movement).[4]

Naturally, the first is the most important of all these statements. For, as has been correctly stated, this proposition is "the most fundamental, and is...it could be said, the first philosophical proposition of what we today call western civilization..."[5]

But what did Thales mean by what Aristotle calls the notion of a principle [*arche*]? How and why did he identify it with water? What is the precise connection between the water-principle and individual things?

2. The meaning of "principle"

The term "principle" [*arche*] is certainly not to be attributed to Thales (it was first coined, it would seem, by his follower Anaximander), but it is nonetheless clear that this term better than any other points to the notion that water is *the origin of all things*. Moreover, the water-principle has absolutely nothing in common with the Hesiodian chaos, nor with any other mythological notion of principle. It is, as Aristotle says, "that from which all things *have their origin* and that into which all things *are dissolved*." It is "a reality that remains identically the same throughout the changes in its characteristics," that is, a reality "that continues to exist unchanged"[6] throughout the process of the generation of everything. Hence it is *a*) the source or origin of all things, *b*) the focus and final goal of all things, *c*) the permanent sustainer (substrate, we can say with a term of later usage) of all things. In short, the "principle" is that from which all things come, that through which they exist, that into which they are resolved. Such a principle was denominated by these first philosophers (if not previously by Thales himself) as *physis*, a word that means, not "nature" in the modern sense of the term, but rather *the primary, original, and fundamental reality*. It means, as has been well stated, "that which is primary, fundamental, and persistent, in opposition to that which is secondary, derivative, and transitory."[7]

3. Water as the principle

Why did Thales think that water was the principle? It is Aristotle again who informs us in detail:

> Thales, the founder of this type of philosophy, says the principle is *water* (for that reason he declared that the earth rests on water), getting the notion perhaps from seeing that the nutriment of all things is moist, and that heat itself is generated from the moist and kept alive by it (and that from which a thing is generated is always its first principle). He derived his assumption, then, from this, and from the fact that the seeds of all thing have a moist nature, and that water is the origin of the nature of moist things.[8]

As can be seen, it is through a series of reasons that have been handed down through the oral tradition that recognized the incontrovertible presence of the logos, that is, of properly rational reasons. The principle is water because it is wholly from water that life itself comes and into which it dissolves. Hence, nothing here is derived from the imagination, nothing of a poetic or fantasy-ladened nature; we have decisively turned from myth to logos. This is the way philosophy arose.

Actually, some ancients thought they could find thoughts similar to Thales in those statements (for example, in Homer) which propose Ocean and Tethys respectively as father and mother of all things. They had likewise recalled the ancient belief according to which the Gods swore oaths on Styx (which is a river and hence water). They also noted that that by which one swears is in fact what is primary and supreme. Modern thinkers have echoed this position by pointing out numerous analogies in Eastern conceptions. But Aristotle already opposed these conjectures in his written statement:

> It may perhaps be uncertain whether this opinion about nature is primitive and ancient, but Thales at any rate is said to have declared himself thus about the first cause.[9]

And Simplicius writes:

> It is a tradition that Thales was the first to turn the Greeks to the study of nature, as has been maintained by Theophrastus as well as many other researchers. But Thales so surpassed those who preceeded him that everyone has forgotten them.[10]

In conclusion, the ancients had already begun to realize that the thought of Thales was something wholly new. In point of fact, Ocean, Tethys, and Styx are imaginative symbols, poetic fictions, products of the imagination, while the propositions of Thales are based on logos. In the former it is solely myth, while in the latter it is philosophy.

It does not seem that Thales took up the third problem which we mentioned, or at least nothing is stated by him about it with any clarity.

4. Other propositions of Thales

The second statement is spoken about in these terms:

> Certain thinkers say that soul is intermingled in the whole universe, and it is perhaps for that reason that Thales came to the opinion that *all things are full of Gods.*[11]

On this statement that all things are full of Gods (Plato had recorded it before Aristotle and then the doxographers repeated it)[12] light is cast by a passage from Diogenes Laertius according to which Thales had said that "God is most ancient because ungenerated."[13] If Thales had said this, there is no doubt that he was referring to his water-principle, the source, sustainer, and font of all things.

Hence there should be no doubt about the meaning of the proposition that we have been concerned with, namely, all things are full of Gods *because all things are derived from water as principle.*

The theological dimension (the theological dimension of a naturalistic character) is, hence, quite clear in Thales.

Lastly, the meaning of the third proposition is also clear.

Aristotle says:

> Thales, too, to judge from what is recorded about him, seems to have held soul to be a motive force, since he said that the magnet has a soul in it because it moves iron.[14]

So, if water as a principle is not only the source of all things, but that *from which* and *into which* they go, it is clear that all things must participate in the being and the life of this principle and therefore all must be alive and animated; and the example of the magnet must be a proof that Thales adduced in favor of this general thesis.

In conclusion, what has come down to us from later sources,[15] that Thales thought that soul was immortal, if actually stated by our philosopher (in our judgment he did so state it), can only be understood in connection with his general orientation. Thales can only be considering soul as that principle or an aspect of that principle which is present in all things (water), and through which all things exist. Individual things change, but their principle remains immortal. It is an immortality, hence, that has nothing to do with *personal immortality,* a notion which the successive philosophers of nature derived from the Orphics, but which, as we will see, is opposed to the foundation of their doctrine (namely, the philosophy of nature).

II. Anaximander

1. The infinite as the principle and its characteristics

It is Anaximander[1] (as seems to be philologically certain, or at least highly probable) who introduced the term *arche* in order to designate the *primum*, the primary and ultimate reality of things, that is, the *physis* about which we spoke in discussing Thales. (Let us remember that the title of the work of Anaximander is Περὶ φύσεως *On Nature*.)

But, contrary to Thales, he maintained that the principle was not water but the *apeiron*, that is to say, the *infinite* or *unlimited*. Our ancient sources write:

> Anaximander of Miletus...said that the first principle of existing things is *the unlimited* (*apeiron*), introducing for the first time the term "principle"; and he said that it is neither water nor any other of those things that are called elements, but another of an unlimited nature (*physis*) from which arose all the heavens and the universes contained in them.[2]

All ancient doxographers, on this point, have no doubts.

But what is this *apeiron*?

First we must point out that the term *apeiron* is only imperfectly translated with the terms "un-limited," or "in-finite" because it involves something more than the two words can render. "*A-peiron*" means that which is lacking a *peras*, that is, not only *external* but *internal* limits or determinations as well. In the first meaning, *apeiron* indicates unlimited space, unlimited quantity, that is, a *quantitative unlimited*. In a second meaning, instead, the unlimited is according to quality, that is, the *qualitative unlimited*. The unlimited of Anaximander must have, at least implicitly, these two connotations. In fact, insofar as it generates and embraces infinite universes, it must therefore be *spatially unlimited*, and insofar as it is not determined as water, air, etc. are, it is *qualitatively unlimited*.

In this form of thinking, there is undoubtedly an originality and profundity that in the Greek mentality, as we will see, is somewhat exceptional. The source, the basic reality of things, can only be unlimited precisely because, as such, it has neither principle nor goal. It is ungenerated and imperishable and *for this very reason* it is capable of being the principle of all things. Aristotle writes, referring to Anaximander:

> Everything is either a principle or derived from a principle. But there cannot be a source of the infinite or the unlimited, for that would be a limit of it. Further, as it is a beginning, it is both ungenerated and imperishable. For there must be a point at which what has come to be reaches completion, and also a termination of all passing away. That is why, as we say, there is no principle of this, but it is this that is held

to be the principle of other things, and to encompass all and to steer all, as those assert who do not recognize anything else, alongside the unlimited. . . . Further they identify it with the divine, for it is deathless and indestructible as Anaximander says, with the majority of the physicists.[3]

The passage that we have just read, in addition to giving reasons why Anaximander must have posited the unlimited as principle, gives further and important descriptions. The unlimited *encompasses* and *circumscribes* and *rules* and *governs all things*. Now, there can be no doubt about the meaning of these terms (which are almost certainly genuine). *To encompass* (περιέχειν), *to rule* (κυβερνᾶν) indicate and specify precisely the function of the principle, that is, to embrace and to rule all things because all things are generated from the principle and they co-exist and have existence in and through the principle.

Finally, the Aristotelian passage also stresses the precise *theological* meaning of the principle. Anaximander considered his principle as divine, because it is immortal and incorruptible (the exact words of Anaximander were "eternal and ever-youthful").

This (as we have seen above) must already have been stated by Thales, and as Aristotle says, "also by the greater part of the physicists." It is clear that water for Thales and the unlimited for Anaximander must be considered as God, or more exactly, as "the divine" (τὸ θεῖον, neuter). In fact, they take up in themselves, as principle, as *arche* or *physis* of all things, the characteristics that Homer and the tradition considered the necessary prerogatives precisely of the Gods: they are immortal, insofar as rulers, and governors of all things. Jaeger correctly states that Anaximander (but implicitly even Thales) goes beyond this, saying that the immortality of the principle must be such as to forbid not only an *end*, but also, a *beginning*. If this is so, then the very basis of the theogonies and genealogies of the various Gods is undermined; as the divine cannot die, so also it cannot be born, thus it is infinite and eternal. "It would be an error," Jaeger then concludes, "to deny the religious importance of this sublime conception of the divine beginning from preconceived theories and opinions about the nature of true religion, affirming for example, that it is impossible to pray to the God of Anaximander or that physical speculation is not a religion. No one would argue that for us there cannot be any higher form of religion without the idea of the infinite and the eternal that Anaximander joined to his new concept of the divine."[4]

These statements are accurate, but only in the measure in which they correct the old conception of the Presocratics as materialists and atheists or irreligious in the modern sense. It still needs correction on an important point. The idea that distinguishes the conception of the Divine in Anaximander and in the Presocratics is and always remained *naturalistic* in the sense that, rather than seeing in the Divine *something other* than the world, they see in it the essence of the world, the *physis* of all things. They do not attribute to it any of those characteristics given in later categories of thought, which will be called spiritual. They do not even attribute to it the highest faculty that can be found in man, that is to say, *thought*. The best proof that confirms what we have been saying is that Anaximander, as has been expressly handed down, "says that the unlimited heavens were Gods,"[5] and therefore he does not hesitate to call by the name of "Gods" the unlimited worlds that, as we will immediately see, *arise* from the unlimited principle and that are, it is true, of a very long duration, but then are subject to death. This may also certainly be said of the Gods insofar as they are unlimited manifestations of the unlimited principle. Therefore, even for Anaximander, as for Thales and in the same meaning as Thales, it is possible to say that *all things are full of Gods, all is divine.*

2. The origin of all things from the infinite

How do things arise from the unlimited, through what process, and by what causes?

Our sources agree that it would be by separation or a disjunction of the opposites (hot-cold, moist-dry, etc.) from the one principle due to eternal movement.[6]

This "separation" or this "disjunction" would be somewhat obscure, considered in isolation, if it were not for the presence of an authentic fragment of our philosopher that states:

> But into those from which the existing things have their coming to be,
> do they also pass away, according to necessity; for they give justice
> and make amends to one another for their injustice, according to the
> ordering of time.[7]

The fragment (that has been interpreted and distorted by scholars in various ways) identifies, beyond any possibility of refutation, the *birth* and *dissolution* with a *fault* or an *injustice* and with the necessity for an *expiation of this fault.*

Probably Anaximander referred in this passage to the contraries that tend precisely to overwhelm *each other.* The injustice is the injustice proper to this overwhelming, and time is seen as the judge, insofar as it assigns limits to each of the contraries, putting an end to the predominance of one over the other and vice versa. But it is clear that not only the alternating condition of the contraries is an "injustice," but also the rising of the contraries themselves, for each contrary that arises immediately sets itself up against the other. That is why the world arises with the separation of the contraries in what is seen as the primary injustice that will be expiated with the death of the world itself according to a determined period of time. Therefore, as some have correctly noted, there is a double injustice, and hence a double necessity for expiation: the first is on the part of being born in the world during the separation which is opposed to the unity of the principle; the second necessity is based on "the attempt after the separation is completed by every one of the opposites in hatred of the others to usurp the condition of the unique surviving and dominating contrary, which would be at the same time the usurping of the position and the rights *of the divine that is immortal and indestructible.*"[8]

It would seem undeniable that in this thought (and this has been noted in different ways by various scholars) there is a profound infiltration of religious conceptions, probably Orphic. So it would seem to be undeniable that there is a certain basic pessimism that sees joined to birth an "overwhelming defect" and a "fault," so that as in death, it sees an "expiation," although one tempered by the overarching thought of a "balancing justice."

3. The infinite worlds and the origin of our world

As the principle is infinite, so also are the worlds that arise from the principle. Worlds are unlimited not only in temporal succession, in the sense that a world dies and then is reborn an unlimited number of times, but likewise in its spatial co-existence, that is, in the sense that there exists together an unlimited number of worlds, every one of which has an origin and an end going on into infinity.

How our world specifically is derived from the unlimited is difficult to reconstruct with accuracy. The testimonies that are extant speak of an *eternal movement* that produces the separation of the contraries, and they speak of the hot and the cold as the primary pair of opposites, but they are not specific as to how, step by step, they become and then constitute all things.

The hot formed a sort of sphere of circumambient fire that then broke up into three spheres; in this way the sun, moon, and stars originate. The cold, instead, must originally have been in a liquid state; because of fire this is transformed into air that, perhaps through its expansion provoked by being heated, broke up, as we said, the sphere of fire into three spheres, it encircles them and almost encloses them, and then it drags them with it in a circular motion. In the air many openings of a tubular shape are formed from which fire is emitted; the heavenly bodies that we see are precisely the light that is emitted through these small holes (so likewise the eclipses result from the momentary halt at these small openings).[9]

In their turn, earth and sea are formed from the liquid element.

Here is how Alexander writes about the doctrine of Anaximander:

> Some physicists maintain...that the sea is a residue of the originative moisture. The area about the earth in fact would be moist, and afterwards a part of this moistness would be evaporated by the sun and the winds would arise and the rotation of the sun and the moon....Whatever of this moistness that would remain in the area scooped out of the

earth would be the sea that is precisely diminishing because it is
continually evaporated by the sun, until it becomes totally dry...[10]

The earth is at the center and it is of a cylindrical shape and it is
supported by a kind of equilibrium of forces:

it remains suspended without any support, but remains fixed because
it is at an equal distance from all of its parts.[11]

And as the liquid element was originative, so also from the liquid element
by the action of the sun the first living things are born. Here is a testimony:

According to Anaximander, the first living things were born in a liquid
element, with a spiny covering; growing to a certain age they leave the
water and come on to dry land, and after the breaking of the covering
being torn that covers them, after a while they change their way of
living.[12]

Thus from simple living things were born more complex living things
which slowly come to be transformed and adapt themselves to their
environment.

Some superficial readers will perhaps smile condescendingly at these
conceptions that seem to be puerile. On the contrary, in our judgment, they
are strongly anticipatory and almost prophetic with respect to some very
modern scientific truths. It is for this reason that we wanted to present
them. It is enough here to recall two of these scientific truths: first, the
boldness of the representation of the earth that has no need of any material
support (even for Thales the earth floated on water), and that it is supported
by an *equilibrium of forces*;[13] and second, the modernity of the notion that
the origin of life began with acquatic animals and the consequent virtual
presence of the notion of the evolution of species through adaptation to the
environment.[14] And this is already in itself sufficient to demonstrate how
far the logos of Anaximander is beyond myth.

III. Anaximenes

1. Air as the principle

Anaximenes,[1] a follower of Anaximander, corrected the doctrine of his teacher in this sense: the primary principle is, it is true, unlimited in magnitude and quantity, but it is not indeterminate: it is air, unlimited air. All things are derived, therefore, from air and from its differentiations. Theophrastus writes:

> [The air] is distinguished into various substances according to the differences in rarefaction and condensation: and thus by dilation it gives origin to fire, while by condensing it gives origin to the wind and then to the clouds; and because of greater amounts of density it forms water, then the earth and hence the rocks; the other things are then derived from these.[2]

Why did Anaximenes change the principle of his teacher?

We saw that Anaximander, in a certain sense, had made a jump from his unlimited to the generation of things: in fact, it is not possible to fully understand in what way the contraries, by separating, generated various things; for this reason Anaximenes undoubtedly believed that he had to search for another solution. He may have been guided to this other solution by the following considerations.

An ancient testimony states that Anaximenes posited the air as *arche*, because *the air better than anything else lends itself to variations* and, consequently, better than anything else lends itself to being thought as a principle capable of generating everything.[3]

In fragment two we read:

> Just as our soul, which is air, sustains and governs us, so breath and air embrace the entire cosmos.[4]

It could be argued from these words that Anaximenes inferred his principle based on the consideration of living things, which live precisely as long as they breathe, that is, they inhale and exhale air, and die when they exhale their last breath. Just as the air is necessary to the life of human beings and living things, so it must likewise be necessary for all other things and the entire cosmos (which Anaximenes conceived as a living organism).

Finally, some scholars have noted that even the observation of the fact that from the heaven (that is, from the air) rain (water) falls and lightning strikes (that is, fire) and steam and fumes rise to the heavens could have forced Anaximenes to choose the air as a principle: how much more appealing as an explanation would air be, since its confines are lost to sight, and hence it lends itself to being thought of as unlimited.[5]

This is the specific characteristic of air:

> When it is absolutely uniform, it is *invisible*; it becomes visible when cold, when hot, when moist and in movement.[6]

And there is complete agreement with this in a fragment which has wrongly been labeled inauthentic:

> The air is close to the *incorporeal*: and because we come to be by its flow, it is necessary that it be unlimited and rich, by being never less.[7]

In this fragment that "closeness to the incorporeal" expresses exactly "being invisible," that is, imperceptible, so it also expresses being without limit, that is, the unlimited being of the air, unlike all the remainder of things which are derived from it, which are instead visible, definite, and limited.

It is quite creditable that Anaximenes called the air "God," as was stated by the ancients,[8] and it is creditable as well that the things which were derived from the air were called Gods.[9] We are by now quite familiar with the precise meaning of such language which is common to the three Milesians.

2. The derivation of all things from air

Air is conceived by Anaximenes as naturally endowed with movement and, through its very mobile nature, it lends itself (even better than the unlimited of Anaximander) to be conceived in perpetual motion.

But Anaximenes, as we have previously stressed, also specified the nature of *the process by which things are derived from air*. For him, it is a matter of *condensation* and *rarefaction*, as all of our sources state. The rarefaction of air gives rise to fire, its condensation to water, and then to the earth.

Plutarch writes:

> Anaximenes says that the cold is the matter which contracts and condenses, while the hot is the matter which expands and *loosens* (this is the expression which he used). Hence, it is not without reason, according to Anaximenes, that a man lets go from the mouth cold and hot: the breath, in fact, is cooled if it becomes compressed by closed lips, but instead if it leaves from the open mouth it becomes hot by dilation.[10]

This clearly must be one of the arguments taken from experience which Anaximenes used to prove his thesis.

3. The relationship of Anaximenes to his predecessors

Anaximenes is for the most part judged by the historians of philosophy as inferior to Anaximander, but this view is wrong. It is true instead that

Anaximenes, as some scholars have become aware, signals a progress over his predecessors by trying to explain rationally the *qualitative* difference of the things which are derived from a *quantitative* difference of the originating principle (condensation and rarefaction are precisely quantitatively differentiated). Burnet then noted that Anaximenes's influence on the ancients was greater than that of his predecessors. In fact, when the ancients speak of Ionian philosophy they refer to Anaximenes as a model, seeing in him the more finished and accurate expression of the thought of the School.[11] Actually, it is impossible not to acknowledge that Anaximenes, precisely by his introduction of the process of condensation and rarefaction, supplied that dynamic cause which allows for the derivation of all things from their principle, an issue about which Thales had nothing to say and that Anaximander could only specify by a conception inspired by the Orphics. Hence, he gave a cause which is *in complete harmony with the principle*, making Ionic naturalism in that way fully coherent with its premises. When Ionian philosophy is recovered, or will attempt to be recovered, with Diogenes of Apollonia,[12] it will appropriately begin from Anaximenes.

IV. Heraclitus of Ephesus

1. The perpetual flux of all things

Heraclitus[1] carried the philosophical discourse of the three Milesians to what was to a great extent a new and decidedly advanced position.

The Milesians had chiefly concerned themselves with the problem of the principle of things and on the coming into being of the cosmos from the principle. In doing this, they had pointed out *the universal dynamism* of reality, the dynamism of things which come to be and perish, the dynamism of the whole cosmos or of the cosmos which comes to be and perishes, the dynamism of the principle itself which gives being to various things because it is endowed with perpetual movement. However, they did not explain this dynamism, nor did they take their discussion of it to the thematic level of the whole of reality; neither, consequently, were they able to reflect on the many implications of this universal dynamism itself.

It is exactly this issue which instead Heraclitus did address.

First, he emphasized the perpetual motion of all things which exist. Nothing is immobile and nothing is permanently fixed or stable in one state or condition, but everything moves, all is changing, all is transformed without exception.

Heraclitus himself, in order to express this insight, made use of the image of a running stream in fragments which are extremely well known:

> Upon those who step into the same rivers different and again different waters flow.[2]

> It is impossible to descend twice into the same river and it is impossible to touch a mortal substance twice in the same condition, but because of the impetuosity and speed of the changes, it is scattered and gathered together, it comes and it goes.[3]

> We descend and do not descend into the same river, we are and are not ourselves.[4]

The meaning is clear. The river is *apparently* always itself, while in reality it consists of water which is always changing, which comes and goes. It is impossible to descend into the same river twice, precisely because at the second descent that water is already gone and a different water flows. Further, we ourselves change at the moment in which we complete our immersion into the river, thus we are different when we emerge; so the waters are constantly changing as is he who bathes in them. So Heraclitus can correctly say, from his point of view, that we enter and do not enter into the river. He can also say that we exist and we do not exist because in order to be what we are at a given moment, we can *no longer* be that which we were at a preceding moment, so that, in order to continue to be, we shall soon have not to be any longer what we are in this moment. That is precisely the case, according to Heraclitus, in every situation, without exception.

Therefore, nothing is permanent and everything is changing, or if you wish, the becoming of things is the only permanent feature of reality, in the sense that, for Heraclitus, things do not have any reality except insofar as they ceaselessly change.

It is this aspect of the doctrine of Heraclitus which undoubtedly became the most well known. It was immediately encapsuled in the phrase "all things are flowing" (πάντα ῥεῖ). It is that aspect which his followers emphasized, carrying it to extreme consequences. (Cratylus, for example, drew as a consequence that if all is flowing so rapidly, it is impossible for any knowledge of things to exist, and "he ends in the belief," says Aristotle, "that no one can speak. As to him, he confined himself to mere pointing, and criticized Heraclitus for having said that it is impossible to step *twice* into the same river, Cratylus, in fact, thought that it was impossible for anyone to step once.")[5]

Nevertheless, the philosophy of Heraclitus is far from being reduced to the mere proclamation of the universal flux of things. In fact this is, for him, almost the starting point of an arduous and quite profound inference, which we must now try to specify and state with precision.

2. The opposites in which becoming unfolds and their hidden harmony (the synthesis of opposites)

The becoming of which we spoke is characterized by a continual change of things from one contrary to the other: "cold things warmed themselves, warm cools, moist dries, parched is made wet"[6]; the young age, the living die, and similars.

Becoming is hence a continual conflict of the contraries which follow one another. It is a perpetual war of one against the other, it is a perpetual warfare. But because things have reality, as we saw, only in their perpetual becoming, then it necessarily follows that war is the foundation of the reality of things:

War is the father of all things and the king over all.[7]

But keep in mind that this war is at the same time peace, this contrast is instead harmony; so that the perpetual flowing of things and the universal changing is revealed as a *harmony* or *synthesis of contraries*, that is, as a perpetual pacification of the belligerent, and the conciliation of the contentious. Fragment eight states:

Whatever is opposed is reconciled and from different things are born the most beautiful harmony, and all things are generated by a contrasting way.

In Fragment fifty-one:

> They do not apprehend how being at variance it agrees with itself: there is a connection working in both directions, as in the bow and the lyre (trans. Kirk).

It is through this higher harmony that the contraries not only are able to contend with each other, but they give to each other their proper meaning:

> Disease makes health pleasant and good, hunger satisfaction, weariness rest;[8]
>
> No one can know the name of justice except he commit an offense.[9]

And it is through this harmony and in this harmony that the opposites coincide at the highest level:

> The way up and down is one and the same.[10]
>
> Beginning and end are common in the circle.[11]
>
> The same thing is the living and dead and the waking and sleeping and the young and old. For these original things having changed are their opposites, and the things which have changed are in their turn again their opposites.[12]

It is clear, finally, that the multiplicity of things is gathered into a dynamic higher unity:

> Out of all things can be made a unity, and out of unity, all things.[13]
>
> Having listened not to me, but to the *logos*, it is wise to agree that all things are one[14] (trans. J. Owens).

In conclusion, if things have a reality only insofar as they change, and if changing is from opposites which are related to each other and their opposition is reconciled in a higher harmony, then it is clear that *in the synthesis of opposites lies the principle which explains the whole of reality*, and it is evident, consequently, *that in this synthesis of opposites precisely consists God and the Divine*. In fact, Heraclitus expressly says in Fragment sixty-seven:

> God is day-night, winter summer, war peace, satiety hunger (trans. Kirk).

This means, precisely, that God is *the harmony of contraries, the unity of opposites*.

3. Fire as the principle of all things

The reader will certainly have noticed the powerful originality of Heraclitean thought and will probably realize that it, in a certain sense, anticipates in an impressive way the basic notion of Hegelian dialectic. It was Hegel himself who recognized it, writing expressly: "there is no proposition of Heraclitus that I do not agree with in my logic."[15]

Nevertheless, if this is true, it is likewise true that Heraclitus is not doing logic and even less is he doing dialectic in the modern sense; in fact, the philosophy of the Ephesian did not leave the area of inquiry defined by *physis* and, whatever some critics claim to the contrary, the remarks of Burnet are irreproachable: "The identity in diversity which he proclaimed *was purely about physis;* logic did not exist yet. ... The identity which he presents as consisting in diversity is simply that of the primary substance manifesting itself in all things."[16]

Almost all of the ancient doxographers,[17] in referring to the thought of Heraclitus, indicate that the essential notion of our philosopher is that *fire is the fundamental element* and that all things do not exist except that they are transformed by fire. The fragments also fully confirm it:

> All things are an equal exchange for fire and fire for all things, as goods are for gold and gold for goods[18] (trans. Kirk);

> This (world-) order (*the same for all*) did none of gods or men make, but it always was and is and shall be: an everliving fire, kindling in measures and going out in measures[19] (trans. Kirk);

> Fire's changes: first sea, and of sea the half is earth, the half lightning-flash[20] (trans. Kirk).

Why Heraclitus singled out fire as the "nature" of all things becomes clear as soon as we pay attention to the fact that *fire expresses in a paradigmatic way the characteristics of perpetual change, struggle, and harmony,* as well as adverting to the fact that fire is always moving. It is a life which lives from the consuming of the combustible. It is incessantly changed into smoke and ashes, it is just as Heraclitus says about his God "satiety and hunger,"[21] that is, it is a unity of contraries, the hunger of things, which makes things exist; and it is the satiety of things which hence destroys and makes things die.

With this in mind, is also clear that God or the Divine for Heraclitus (which we have already said is night-day, hunger-satiety, war-peace, that is, a unity of contraries) coincides with this fire. Let us read Fragment sixty-four:

> Thunderbolt (i.e., *Fire*) steers all things (trans. Kirk).

The thunderbolt is precisely the divine fire; and Heraclitus attributes to his fire-God the eschatological function of supreme judge:

> Fire having come suddenly upon all things will bring them to trial and secure their convictions (trans. Kirk).[22]

And in Fragment thirty-two we read:

One thing, the only truly wise, does not and does consent to be called by the name of Zeus (trans. Kirk).

What Heraclitus wanted to say in this fragment is evident: "He wished to be called by it [with the name of Zeus], because it is in truth what under that name is venerated; but he does not even wish to be called by it, because this name evokes anthropomorphic images which do not belong to his primordial being, that is, because this name is an inadequate designation."[23]

But, while the Milesians did not attribute intelligence to the primary divine principle, it is instead clear enough that Heraclitus attributed it to it. Fragment seventy-eight states:

Human nature has no knowledge, divine nature, has (it).

The very famous Fragment forty-one, given different translations and interpretations, can be rendered as follows:

There is only one wisdom: to recognize the intelligence who steers all things through all things.

It seems almost certain that Heraclitus called his principle *logos*, which, as many maintain, does not really mean *reason* and *intelligence*, but rather *a rule according to which all things are accomplished and a law which is found in all things and steers all things* and generally includes rationality and intelligence.[24]

Finally it is clear that, for Heraclitus, the truth cannot exist except through the grasp, understanding, and expression in general of this logos in all things. It is understandable, consequently, that he warns against trusting the *senses*, because they grasp only the appearances of things. Just as he rejects the common *opinions* of men, because they are blind, or like men who walk around as if in sleep. Finally, it is clear that he rejects the wisdom of other philosophies because he considers it vain erudition which simply piles up a multiplicity of particular notions without yielding any universal law. Consequently, the haughty and proud tone which he uses throughout his work in relation to all other views is understandable; since he has grasped the *logos*, he realizes he is its herald, its only spokesman. Lastly, the type of language and expression adopted by him in his work is understandable. It is the language of the prophets, the oracles, and the Sibyls, that is, a language which speaks and does not speak, which both hides and reveals; a language, in conclusion, marked by the impress of the *logos* which he wished to reveal.

4. The soul

Heraclitus also expresses some thoughts about the soul which go beyond those of his predecessors. On the one hand, he, like the Milesians, identified the nature of the soul with the nature of the principle, and he said that it is fire and even stated that the wiser the soul the drier and, consequently, he made madness coincide with the soul's wet condition.[25]

But, in addition to this way of thinking, he expresses a second way with a different tenor that leads him to discover in the soul something having properties completely different from the body. Let us read the beautiful Fragment forty-five:

> You would not by your going discover the limits of soul though you traveled over every path, so deep has it a *logos*.

Snell has noted that this conception of the "depth of the soul" involves its clear differentiation from any organ or physical function. It makes no sense to speak of a deep hand or a deep ear.

This scholar also writes: "the image of depth is used in order to point out the characteristic of the soul, *which is that of having a particular quality which does not involve space or extension*. ...With it Heraclitus wished to signify that the soul is extended to infinity, contrary to what is physical."[26]

This second way of thinking is in line with the religious aspect of Orphic thought, of which there is an echo in Fragment sixty-two:

> Immortals mortal, mortals immortal, living their death, dying their life.

It expresses with the language of Heraclitus the Orphic belief according to which the life of the body is the mortification of the soul and the death of the body is the life of the soul. With the Orphics, Heraclitus must admit rewards and punishment after death and hence a personal immortality, as he expressly states in Fragment twenty-seven:

> There await men after they are dead things which they do not expect or imagine (trans. K. Freeman).

But it is a way of thinking that poorly fits in with his general vision, in which there is no room for a *personal* soul nor for a beyond. Nevertheless, it is a way of thinking that we will find often in the Presocratics, unreconciled and unreconcilable with their doctrine of *physis*, but which, because of this, will reveal itself as quite fruitful, in that sense which we will adequately explain in regard to Plato.

But before leaving Heraclitus we want to discuss some of his moral thinking, which must have been inspired more by his Orphic vision of the soul than by his doctrine of reality. Happiness, says Fragment four, cannot consist in pleasures of the body. If it were so, cows would be happy when they have their fodder. The most beautiful Fragment, eighty-five, further specifies this notion:

> The struggle against desire is difficult, because it must be purchased

at the *price of the soul.*

This is a thought in which there is encapsulated the nucleus of the ascetic morality of the *Phaedo*. To satisfy the body means to lose the soul.

Third Section

PYTHAGOREANISM

«... φασὶ δ᾽ οἱ σοφοί... καὶ οὐρανὸν
καὶ γῆν καὶ θεοὺς καὶ ἀνθρώπους τὴν
κοινωνίαν συνέχειν καὶ φιλίαν καὶ
κοσμιότητα καὶ σωφροσύνην καὶ
δικαιότητα, καὶ τὸ ὅλον τοῦτο διὰ
ταῦτα κόσμον καλοῦσιν...»

"...The wise say...that heaven, earth,
Gods and men are held together by order,
by wisdom, and by rectitude: and it is
proper for such a reason that they call
them this totality a 'cosmos'..."

Plato *Gorgias* 507E-508A

I. The Reason that We Speak about the Pythagoreans in General and Not about Individual Pythagoreans. The Characteristics of the Pythagorean School.

We move with the consideration of the Pythagoreans from Ionia to the southern part of the Italian peninsula. Here, philosophy created a new climate; it perfected, it improved, and began to reach the extreme limits of that concept of *physis* which had been opened up by the Ionians. This work of refining, we will see, will be conducted by both the Pythagoreans and the Eleatics. But the Pythagoreans certainly have a right to claim the creation of this new atmosphere from which the Eleatics were to benefit (the ancient sources inform us that Parmenides, the founder of Eleaticism, was introduced to philosophy, as a matter of fact, by a Pythagorean).[1]

But we must explain first why we speak about Pythagoreans in general, and not rather about individual Pythagoreans.

a) First, it is impossible to distinguish Pythagoras from the Pythagoreans, that is, the teacher from the disciples, because Pythagoras did not write anything and very little has been attributed to him with any accuracy, and much of the late *Life of Pythagoras* is thought to be a fiction. Even a little after his death (and perhaps in the final years of his life) Pythagoras had lost, in the eyes of his disciples, human characteristics and was regarded and venerated as a divinity.[2]

b) The school that Pythagoras founded on his arrival in Italy did not have as its principal aim scientific research, but rather the *realization of a particular kind of life-style* with respect to which scientific inquiry was not the *goal*, but mostly the *means*, as we will see better further on. The Pythagorean school arose as a confraternity, or better, as a sect or religious order, organized according to precise rules for the living together of the members. (The order was, then, involved in politics and was implicated in quite turbulent happenings.) Since science was a means to the accomplishment of its goals, it was as a *common property*, a commonwealth from which all the initiates drew and to which all tried to add by inquiry and study. It was because of this *commonwealth* of science that the anonymity of individual contributions belonged as a necessary consequence.

c) The doctrine of the School, in addition, was considered a *secret* which could only be shared with the initiates, and this impeded the spread and knowledge of the doctrines, unlike the doctrines of the other Schools.

d) The first Pythagorean to publish a work was Philolaus,[3] who lived at the time of Socrates. By this time the doctrine had surely evolved, but it is very difficult to establish how much was due to the first Pythagoreans and how much to later ones. All the criteria proposed to the present have been shown to be arbitrary or at least purely conjectural.[4] Therefore, for these reasons, the Pythagorean school is to be viewed as a seamless whole.

e) If it is true that from the end of the sixth century to the beginning of the fourth it could enrich its own spiritual inheritance, it is also otherwise true that the presuppositions and foundations on which it produced them *were substantially homogeneous* and hence, it is not only correct, but necessary, to give a global consideration of the doctrine. (The foundation on which the Pythagoreans worked, instead, will be different when they revive it on the threshold of the Christian Era, but this new stage also required a change of name. It is clearly and rightly called "Neopythagoreanism." And this further development will be treated in its proper place.)

f) Aristotle did not know anything of Pythagoras and almost nothing of *individual* Pythagoreans and treated them as a group, calling them with the famous phrase "the so-called Pythagoreans,"[5] a phrase which unfortunately has been the object of disparate interpretations, although clear in its meaning, as has been very well explained by Timpanaro Cardini.[6] Aristotle placed particular emphasis on the adjective *so-called* "... because it is based on a strange fact; the first philosophers he mentions each spoke for himself; each clearly had fellow-scholars and followers but without any special ties to a School. The Pythagoreans instead were a new phenomenon. They studied and worked, to use a modern term, as a *team*; their name is a program, a symbol. Finally, it is a technical term, indicating a given mental orientation, a certain vision of reality on which men and women of diverse countries and conditions agreed. Aristotle grasped this characterization, and felt that in introducing the Pythagoreans into the flow of the argument he would in a certain sense prevent a sort of surprise on the part of those who heard or read him. So! Up to this point, have not well differentiated philosophers been presented; and now a group is named, whose name is well known, but whose members are anonymous? Thus were they called, Aristotle assures us, such is their official denomination which they have as a School, and in the course of time their group name represents the unity and the continuity of their doctrine."[7]

In conclusion, Pythagoreanism and the doctrines which it elaborated between the end of the sixth century and the beginning of the fourth century before the Common Era must be seen together. Anyone who ruptures this unity also breaks that spirit which has made Pythagoreanism a School different from all the rest, and hence they compromise the possibility of understanding this spiritual movement in its innermost reality.

II. A New Conception of the Principle

1. Number as the principle of all things

We have emphasized the fact that for the Pythagoreans science was less a goal than a means to the realization of a new life style. Therefore, although it is owing to methodological reasons that are required by the exposition of the problems which we take up in this work which led us to speak first of the science and then of the faith of the Pythagoreans, nonetheless the reader must not be lead into the error of thinking that this primacy of place that we thus give to science mirrors its hierarchical priority in relation to faith, since in point of fact the hierarchical precedence belongs, on the contrary, to faith.

Moreover, from the point of view of science, Aristotle had already clearly established that that *principle* which the Ionians had pointed out in water, in the *apeiron*, in air, and in fire, with a clear change of perspective, *was instead identified by the Pythagoreans with number and with the constitutive elements of number.* Here is the famous Aristotelian passage:

> The so-called Pythagoreans, who were the first to take up mathematics, not only advanced this study, but also having been brought up in it they thought that its principles were the principles of all things. And since of these principles *numbers* are by nature the first, and in numbers they seemed to see many resemblances to the things that exist and come into being—more than in fire and earth and water...since again, they saw that the modifications and the ratios of the musical scales were expressible in numbers—since, then, all other things seemed in their whole nature modeled on numbers, and numbers seemed to be the first things in the whole of nature, *they supposed the elements of numbers to be the element of all things, and the whole heaven to be a musical scale and a number.*[1]

The Aristotelian passage states very clearly the reasons that forced the Pythagoreans to see the principle in number, thus radically changing the Ionian view of things. The Pythagoreans were the first systematic cultivators of mathematics, and as such they were the first to note that a whole series of realities and natural phenomena are translatable into numeric representations. In the first place, the Pythagoreans must have seen that music (which they practiced as a means of purification) was translatable into number and specific ratios. The diversity of sounds which the hammers produce when beating on the anvil depends on the differences in their *weight*. The differences in the sounds of stringed instruments depends on the differences in the *length* of the strings. In general, they discovered the harmonic ratio of the octave, of fifths, of fourths, and the mathematical laws which govern them. Since they also studied the various phenomena of the cosmos, in this area as well they must have recognized the determined occurrence of number. There are precise numerical laws which determine the year, the seasons, the days, etc. There are precise numerical laws which rule the period of incubation of the fetus, the cycles of development, and the various phenomena of life. It is, hence, understandable on the bases of these individual correspondences between phenomena of various kinds and numbers that the Pythagoreans would then be moved to construct even non-existent correspondences and, in this way, they would fall into the arbitrary and sterile position of identifying the various aspects of reality with number, which goes beyond reason into the fantastic.[2] In any case, the process through which they arrived at conceiving number as *the principle of all things* is quite clear.

But the modern reader will with difficulty grasp the sense of this affirmation of the Pythagoreans, unless he adopts the proper mental attitude and tries to recover *the original sense and the archaic attitude toward number.* For us number is the result of the operations of our mind. It is the result of abstraction and hence it is a mental entity. Vice versa, for the ancient way of thinking (and such way of thinking will be corrected only by Aristotle) *number is a real thing, in fact the most real of things,* and as such can be the constitutive principle of other things. To wonder whether the Pythagorean notion of number is both the *material* principle or the *formal* principle of things as was done first by Aristotle[3] and then many moderns following him would involve the introduction of later categories (matter and form) and inevitably would falsify the more ancient viewpoint of the Pythagoreans. The truth is that number is the principle of things just as water was for Thales or air for Anaximenes, that is, it was an integral principle (using later categories we would say that it is a material principle *and* a formal principle *and* an efficient principle). Therefore, Zeller correctly notes: "It is this way of thinking which gives us an impression of strangeness; but if we reflect on what an impression must have been made by the first discovery of the profound and invariable mathematical regularities in the phenomena upon a sensitive mind by these things, then we can grasp how number came to be venerated as a cause of all order and every determination as a foundation of all knowledge, as a divine power dominating the world, and how hence it was hypostatized for being the essence of all things by a thought which in general was habituated to move not on the terrain of abstract concepts but rather on that of sensible intuitions as well."[4]

2. The elements of number: their fundamental opposition and harmony

The Aristotelian passage which we have read above not only says that numbers in general are the principle of things, but it specifies that "the *elements* of numbers are the elements of all things." This means that numbers as such are not the absolute *primum*, but they are themselves derived from further elements or principles.

What are these elements or principles?

First, numbers are wholly divisible into two kinds, the *odd* and the *even*. (*One* is an exception insofar as it is capable of generating both the odd and even. By adding one to an even number, the odd number is generated while by adding one to an odd number, the even number is generated. This shows that the one has in itself the generative capacity of both the odd and the even and therefore participates in both their natures.) Therefore, as we know, everything is reducible to number, everything is an expression of an odd or an even number. Philolaus says:

> Numbers are two special kinds, the odd and the even: a third results from a mixture of these two, it is the odd-even. There are many forms of odd and even numbers and each thing displays them intrinsically.[5]

But odd and even are still not the ultimate elements. Philolaus (expressing or perfecting a conception which must have already been present among the first Pythagoreans if not with Pythagoras himself) speaks expressly of the *unlimited* (or *unterminated* or *infinite*) and of the *limit* or *limiting* (or *terminating*) as the supreme principles of all things:

> All things are necessarily either limited or unlimited or both limited and unlimited. Only unlimited things or limited things are able to exist. Since it is clear that the things which exist cannot be constituted either solely of limited elements or solely of unlimited elements, it is evident that the universe and the things which exist in it are constituted of the harmony of the limited and unlimited elements.[6]

Now this harmony of unlimited and limiting elements is precisely number, so that the ultimate elements from which numbers result are the *unlimited* and the *limiting*. Because in its turn number constitutes each of the things which exist, it itself functions as a determining and hence limiting principle.

But number is generated from indeterminate and determining elements insofar, as it is generated by a "bridling" of the unlimited or indeterminate within the confines of the limited and the determined. It is clear that although it functions as a limiting element "it is not in this sense a stranger," Timpanaro Cardini says correctly, "to the ἄπειρον (that is, to the unlimited). Indeed, it (the number) feeds on the ἄπειρον, and determines it more and more within the schemes of its own arithmo-geometrico relations."[7]

Therefore it is no surprise that the Pythagoreans, on the basis of the observations which we will clarify below, saw in *even* numbers almost a jutting out of the indeterminate element and in the *odd* numbers almost a jutting out of the determined and determining element and they consider the *odd* and *even* within number precisely as the equivalent of the indeterminate and determinate.

This identification (even = unlimited and odd = limited) is explained well by referring to the primitive way of presenting number as geometrically arranged points used by the Pythagoreans. Now if we represent in this way any even number, we will see that the process of division symbolized by the arrow does not meet any limit, to infinity:

On the contrary, in every odd number divisibility encounters a halt in the unity, which indeed makes the number odd, as the figure shows.

An ancient testimony states:

> When the odd number is divided into two parts it remains a unity in the middle; but when the even is divided into two parts it remains an empty field without determination and without number, showing that it is defective and incomplete.[8]

In conclusion, the unlimited and the limited are primary principles; numbers have their origin from them, they are a synthesis of each element, but a synthesis such that it sees in its depth, precisely in the even series, a prevalence of the unlimited element, and in the odd series a prevalence of the limiting element. As a synthesis, however, number always represents a bridling of the unlimited by the limited, and hence as such it can be in its turn a delimiting and determining element of things.

3. The transition from number to things

It is necessary to say that for the Pythagoreans there is no difficulty concerning the problem of the derivation of things from numbers. It constitutes instead an insurmountable difficulty for those interpreters who are ignorant of the properly Pythagorean conception of number, which is, as we have already said, a strongly archaic notion unifying arithmetic and geometry, an arithmo-geometry, as has been correctly stated by a well-known historian of ancient science.[9] Numbers were represented both as pebbles and as points, hence they were *seen* just like a figure is seen. Thus the points were conceived as occupying space, as having magnitude; number was seen also as a solid figure. Therefore the transition of number to figure, to things, for that primitive way of thinking about numbers was wholly natural.

Moreover, that the Pythagoreans, right from the beginning, would have thought that numbers are spatially extended is clear if we keep in mind the following. The antithesis of unlimited and limited constituted the fundamental notion of Pythagoreanism and goes back, although in a rather inchoate form, certainly to the first Pythagoreans, if not to Pythagoras himself. The ancient Pythagoreans conceived the unlimited as a void surrounding everything, and recognized the universe as springing from a kind of "inspiration" of this void aside from the One (how it forms itself, we do not know). This unlimited void, inspired into the One, was conceived as the cause of the distinction of things and of numbers themselves.[10] (This conception clearly echoes the thought of Anaximander and Anaximenes.) Numbers and things are hence thought of as spatially determined, that is, they are both placed on the same level. The succeeding Pythagoreans improved the system, but remained within these parameters.

When the Pythagoreans say that the one is a point, two is a line, three a surface, four a solid, it is clear that they can only be understood on the basis of the premises that we have clarified. Analogously, again on these bases the attempt (which seems to be of Philolaus) of assimilating the four elements to the geometrical solids can also be nicely clarified. The earth is assimilated to the cube, fire to the pyramid, air to the octahedron, water to the icosahedron (the solidity of the cube analogically reflects that of the earth, the pyramidal form the tongues of fire, etc., and the analogy can authorize the deduction within the area of that viewpoint).[11]

Thus the mode in which the transition from the primal elements to number is clear (arithmo-geometrically understood), and from number to all individual things.

4. The foundation of the concept of the "cosmos": the universe is an "order"

If the remarks we made are taken into consideration it will not be difficult to understand how the universe of the Pythagoreans must have acquired a new meaning as compared to that of the Milesians. It is a universe in which the contrasting elements are pacified into a harmony; it is a universe constituted by number, with number, through number. It is a universe wholly dominated by number, not only in its totality, but also in its individual parts and in each individual thing contained in it. *Thus it is clear why this universe must be considered by the Pythagoreans as a "cosmos," which means an "ordered whole."*

> The wise say...that heaven, earth, Gods, and men are held together by order, by wisdom, and by rectitude: and it is proper for such a reason that they call them this totality a "cosmos" [that is, an ordered whole].[12]

"Cosmos," therefore, is a term that was used for the first time by the Pythagoreans in this sense, and in this sense it will remain a definitive acquisition of western thought.

The logos has now reached one of its definitive stages. The world has ceased to be dominated by obscure forces, it is no longer a place of mysterious and indecipherable power; on the contrary, it has become an "ordered whole," and as such it has become transparent to the mind. Order indicates number and number bespeaks rationality, conceivability, and openness to thought. Philolaus states:

> All the things which can be known have a number; without this nothing could possibly be thought or known.[13]

> The nature of number and harmony admits of no falsehood; for this is unrelated to them. Falsehood and envy belong to the nature of the unlimited and unintelligent and the irrational. Falsehood can in no way breathe on number; for falsehood is inimical and hostile to its nature, whereas truth is related to and in close natural union with the race of number.[14]

Hence, *the rule of number means the rule of rationality and truth.*

If all this is taken into consideration, namely, that the whole universe is a harmony and number and that music itself is harmony and number, it would not seem so surprising that the Pythagoreans thought that the heavens, rotating according to number and harmony, would produce a quite beautiful harmony, the celestial music of the spheres. It is a music which we do not hear, either (as some Pythagoreans thought) because we are accustomed to it from birth and thus cannot distinguish it, or (as some other Pythagoreans said) because it is beyond the range of our ears' capacity to hear.

We have moved from the Chaos of Hesiod to a Cosmos. Thanks to the Pythagoreans, man has achieved a new vision of his world.

III. The Pythagorean Faith:
Man, His Soul, and His Destiny

We have pointed out in the preceding pages that Pythagorean science was not cultivated as an *end*, but as a *means* for a further goal, and it is this goal that we must now explain.

Pythagoras is certainly the first philosopher who taught the doctrine of metempsychosis, that is, the doctrine according to which the soul is constrained to be reincarnated many times in successive bodies, not only in the form of man, but likewise in the different forms of animals, in order to expiate the guilt of an original fault. On this point our sources agree from the most ancient, which is that of Xenophanes[1] (who is almost a contemporary of Pythagoras), facetiously needling this belief, up to the more recent ones.[2]

Now, that Pythagoras himself was the inventor of such a doctrine, as Wilamowitz[3] believed, is wholly unlikely. All scholars, at present, agree in maintaining that Pythagoras received it from Orphism, which surely existed prior to his time. If the Orphics honored Dionysus and the Pythagoreans Apollo, then that, as we will see, is possible to explain. Since Pythagoreanism will reform Orphism on some essential points, and in fact precisely on these points which made possible its conjunction with philosophy, the change of the tutelary divinity is plausible. Instead of Dionysus, in whose name frenzied and sacred orgies were celebrated, Apollo was substituted, to whom reason and science were sacred.

Hence, the soul is immortal, it pre-exists the body and continues in existence after the body. Its union with the body is not only not in conformity with its nature, but is even contrary to it. The nature of the soul is divine and eternal, whereas the nature of every body is mortal and corruptible. The union of body and soul, as was said, is a punishment for a hidden original fault committed by the soul, and is the expiation of that fault. Consequently, the life of man is built on the basis of a wholly new vision which is different from that of Homer, which the Greeks had previously taken as certain.

Man must live not for the body, which is a "prison" and a "jail" for the soul, a place in which the soul must expiate its original fault, but for his soul. But to live for the soul means to live a life which is capable of "purifying it," that is, of cleaning up those connections to the body which it has contracted because of its original fault.

But if Orphism and Pythagoreanism agree in the need for an ultraterrestrial eschatological goal and in the meaning of life indicated by the "purifications" which enable the soul to be liberated from the cycle of reincarnations and which carry it to union with the divinity where it belongs, then they are clearly different in the choice of the means and in the manner in which they believe that this purification of the soul can be achieved. The Orphics maintained that the means of purification are the celebrations and the religious practices of the sacred mysteries (which elevated the soul from level to level until it experienced the God in itself and was brought to ecstatic union with him); therefore they remained mired in a magical mentality committed almost entirely to the power of thaumaturgic rites. The Pythagoreans, on the contrary, *pointed out the way of purification chiefly in science.* In the Pythagorean prescriptions, understood as a rule of daily life, there were present (which is quite natural) numerous empirical rules dictated by superstition or, generally, things wholly extraneous to science. But the Pythagorean life is clearly different from the Orphic life precisely in its cultivation of science, which became the highest of the "mysteries" and hence the most effective means of purification.[4]

Therefore, the Pythagoreans realized a type of life wholly new for the Greeks, answering the needs which the traditional forms of religion did not know how to address, and which the religion of the mysteries only imperfectly addressed. So it is not difficult to appreciate the enthusiasm which the Pythagoreans aroused both in the acceptances and the successes which they achieved.

The medical rules of purgation and the ascetic rules of abstinence were aimed at purifying the body in order to render it docile to the promptings of the soul. The practices of purification of the soul were at first concentrated on music which, as we know, must have been a vehicle leading to the theory of numbers, and to the arithmo-geometrical system of the Pythagoreans. With this, the meaning of all the complex prescriptions through which knowledge was communicated to the new initiates is likewise clear. The novices, in the first period in which they were admitted to the brotherhood, must only be *silent* and *listen* (which were considered the most difficult things to learn). Having grasped this, they could go on and ask questions about music, arithmetic, and geometry (writing down whatever they had learned). Finally, they went on to the study of the whole of nature and the cosmos. The teacher, in addition, spoke hidden behind a curtain, as though to separate the knowledge from the person who physically communicated it and thus to give that knowledge an hieratic quality similar to the response of an oracle. The formula through which the teacher communicated his knowledge was «αὐτὸς ἔφα», *ipse dixit,* that is, "he himself said it," the divine Pythagoras, the greatest authority. This formula became proverbial. A silence, then, must be maintained by the initiate about the doctrines and anyone who broke it was punished.[5] In conclusion, the sacred mysteries were indeed celebrated by the Pythagoreans, but they were the sacred mysteries of science.

The Pythagoreans were, in some way, the initiators of that kind of life which was later called (or which perhaps was already so-called by the Pythagoreans themselves) «ὁ βίος θεωρετικός»,[6] that is, the contemplative life, and which also came to be called simply "the Pythagorean life," a life which sought purification in the contemplation of truth, hence through knowledge and wisdom. Plato gave to this type of life its most perfect exemplification in the *Gorgias*, and especially in the *Phaedo*.

IV. The Structural Aporias of Pythagoreanism

1. The aporias concerning God and the Divine

Zeller, in his treatment of the Pythagoreans, has not only tried to separate Pythagorean *science* from Pythagorean *faith*, but has opposed the one to the other, and has even maintained that it is a mistake to evaluate Pythagorean philosophy wholly in terms of what is independent of the doctrine of numbers. But whatever the amount of agreement this thesis received in the past, today it has been abandoned. Many scholars, in fact, agree with the idea that Pythagorean science is rooted in an essential manner in Pythagorean faith, because "the Pythagorean life" can only be realized through science, according to what we have detailed above. Man cannot achieve purification except through knowledge, and hence Pythagorean faith is structurally bound to that knowledge. Pythagorean mysticism thus differs radically from forms of Eastern mysticism, since instead of making an appeal to a-logical and a-rational forces, to the abolishment of consciousness, it appeals to the *logos*, to reason, to science, and to awareness. The first exemplars, then, of this mystical and rational union are the Pythagoreans, and afterwards such a union is repeated many times in the Western world.

Nevertheless, there is some truth in the assertion of Zeller apropos the doctrine concerning the Gods of the Pythagoreans. He writes that the "Pythagoreans in all likelihood did not place their theology in any scientific connection with their philosophical principles." And then he adds: "That their idea of God had nevertheless, insofar as it is a religious idea, the greatest importance, cannot be placed in doubt, but, there is very little which is characteristically theirs in what has been handed down to us in relation to their theology..."[1] But, that the Pythagoreans did not place their theology in relation to their scientific doctrines is not correct; it is true, on the contrary, that they attempted to do so, although they failed for structural reasons which we will now clarify. It is a consequence of this fact that they had nothing unusual to say about the Gods.

Moreover, on the basis of what we have said about the conception of the divine among the Milesians and in Heraclitus, it is tempting to speculate that the Pythagoreans even identified God and the Divine with the primary principles. Instead, it did not happen this way. That it did not happen this way is not due to chance, but rather for authentic and sound reasons. The Pythagoreans admitted, as we have seen, the unlimited and the indeterminate or infinite as one of the two primary principles. Now, the unlimited or infinite was synonymous with the *un-intelligible*, the *ir-rational*, and *evil* and hence could not in any way be identified with God. God was instead identified with perfection and hence with harmony and thence with number. It is certain that the Pythagoreans had linked the power of number in general, and of certain numbers in particular, with the Divine. Therefore, Philolaus says in the eleventh fragment:

> One must study the activities and the essence of number in accordance with the power existing in the decade; for it [number] is great, complete, all-achieving, and the *origin of divine and human life and its leader*, it shares...the power also of the decade. Without this, all things are unlimited, obscure, and indiscernible.[2]

A little further on:

> And you may see the nature of number and its power at work not only in supernatural and divine existences but also in all words and human activities everywhere, both throughout all technical production and in music as well.[3]

And in fragment twenty, which is not certainly attributed to Philolaus but which is certainly an expression of Pythagorean thinking, God is identified with the number seven. In addition Philo writes:

> The Pythagoreans instead compared (the number seven) to the ruler of all things; because what does not generate or is not generated remains unmoving...and what alone does not move or is moved is the ancient teacher and ruler, of which many properly can say that the number seven is the image. My words are confirmed also by Philolaus, where he says: "for it is ruler and teacher of all things; it is God, one, ever-existing, stable, unmoving, itself alike to itself, different from the rest.[4]

There is another ancient source which tells us:

> The reason that Philolaus called the number seven "motherless": it alone, in fact, through its nature neither generates nor is generated: now, what is not a generator nor generated is unmoving....Now such is God, as the teacher from Tarantum himself affirms, when he says thus: "for it is ruler and teacher of all things; it is God, one, ever-existing, stable, unmoving, itself alike to itself."[5]

Let us note, finally, this important fact. Philolaus, as in general all the Pythagoreans, continued to speak of God and of the Gods in the traditional sense of the term, that is, without connecting them to number and the doctrine of number. More logically and coherently, the Neopythagoreans made the Divinity and the One, from which all numbers are derived, coincide; but the ancient Pythagoreans, it seems, did not certainly come to this stage of differentiation of the doctrine. Further, the Pythagoreans also speak of "*daimons*," which are souls without bodies; but they do not say what relation these have with the Gods and the Divine, nor what relation they have to number.

2. The aporias concerning the soul

The Pythagoreans, in addition, did not say what the nature of the relation of our souls was with number. As all other things, the soul must be a number. But, in the first place, we have to note that, if Divinity can be differentiated from other things by being identified with certain privileged numbers, it is not the case with souls, which are very numerous (all living things, without distinction, have their own souls, and moreover, there are also numerous souls without bodies awaiting bodies or which have finished the cycle of rebirths). In order to preserve the individuality of each of these souls, they must each be identified with different numbers (which is absurd), and if all were to have a unique number, then each would be differentiated from the others.

If Philolaus, or generally certain Pythagoreans, identified soul with the harmony of the bodily elements, then that would place it in contrast with the doctrine of the soul-daimon, or inevitably place the sensible soul side-by-side with the soul-daimon without resolving the problem but, instead, further exacerbating it.

These aporias are insuperable if we remain in the area of the Pythagorean philosophy of number or generally within the sphere of the philosophy of *physis*. In order to resolve such difficulties Pythagorean philosophy would have to go explicitly outside the realm of *physis*, but in order to do this it would have to wait for Plato, and then it would with him understand what, with a most attractive image, he himself will call "the second voyage." Pythagoreanism would need to discover the supersensible.

Fourth Section

XENOPHANES AND THE ELEATICS

«χρὴ τὸ λέγειν τε νοεῖν τ᾽ ἐὸν ἔμμεναι
ἔστι γὰρ εἶναι, μηδὲν δ᾽ οὐκ ἔστιν.»

"One should both say and think that being is; for to be is possible, and nothingness is not possible."

Parmenides D-K 28B6

I. Xenophanes

1. The position of Xenophanes with respect to the Eleatics

The cosmological theme, which has characterized Ionian thought and in part the Pythagorean, is notably transformed with Xenophanes.

Traditionally, Xenophanes has been considered the founder of the Eleatic School, but this view has been abandoned by more recent scholarship and modern scholars tend to completely detach Xenophanes from the philosophers of Elea. Xenophanes was born in the Ionian colony of Colophon, which he left early, and he remained in the western colonies in Sicily and in lower Italy.[1]

That Xenophanes cannot be the founder of the Eleatic School is demonstrated by the following reasons. In the first place, his *concerns* are completely theological, whereas those of the Eleatics are exclusively ontological. In the second place, his *dialectic* so destructive of traditional opinions does not have anything to do with Eleatic dialectic, because the former does not derive from a precise principle while the latter is hinged on the principle of the immutability of being, and hence has a totally different import. In the third place, the tradition says nothing precise about the relationship between Xenophanes and Elea. Finally, Xenophanes himself, in a fragment too often overlooked, tells us clearly that he had been traveling without a fixed abode until the ripe old age of ninety-two;[2] and if until he was ninety-two he lacked a fixed abode, it is clear that he did not found a School at Elea, nor is there any probability that he founded the School after his ninety-second year. The ambiguity which gave birth to the idea that Xenophanes founded the School at Elea is to be found in a passage of the *Sophist* in which Plato, opposing to the philosophers who admit a plurality of principles those who on the contrary reduce everything to a unity, writes:

> Our Eleatic tribe, beginning from Xenophanes and *even before*, explains
> in its myths that what we call all things are actually one.[3]

Plato was not speaking historically, but rather theoretically. He understood by the "Eleatic sect" that philosophical group which reduces all to a *unity*, and for this reason (but only for this reason) he considered Xenophanes as the chief source of this way of thinking about this matter. Further, he immediately corrects his assertion with the subsequent phrase that such a manner of thinking about things had begun "even before" Xenophanes. Therefore, the Platonic assertion lacks solid historical basis. Further, we will see that the unity of the cosmos-God of Xenophanes is totally different from the unity of the Eleatic being. This means, as the most recent scholarship has shown, that although Xenophanes and the Eleatics can be in general placed together in the group of the philosophers who reduced all to the One, still they are completely independent and, in fact, strangers to each other especially for their manner of conceiving the One.[4]

2. The criticism of the conception of the Gods and the destruction of the presupposed traditional religion

The basic theme developed in the verses of Xenophanes is chiefly a criticism of the conceptions of the Gods which were expressed in a paradigmatic way by Homer and by Hesiod and which were proper to traditional religion and Greek society in general. Our philosopher detailed to perfection the basic error from which arose all the absurdities which were connected with such conceptions. This error was *anthropomorphism*, that is, the conviction that the Gods and the Divine in general have the attitudes, forms, sentiments, and tendencies precisely like those of human beings, only more grand, more vigorous, more imposing, and hence that there exists between God and man a purely quantitative and not a qualitative difference. To this view he objected:

> But if oxen (and horses) and lions had hands or could draw with hands and create works of art like those made by men, horses would draw pictures of Gods like horses, and oxen of Gods like oxen, and they would make the bodies (of their Gods) in accordance with the form that each species itself possesses.[5]

And again:

> Ethiopians have Gods with snub noses and black hair, Thracians have Gods with grey eyes and red hair.[6]

Hence, the Gods do not have and cannot have a human semblance, but less so is it thinkable that they have human form, and especially that they commit illicit and nefarious actions as mythology portrays them.

> Both Homer and Hesiod have attributed to the Gods all things that are shameful and a reproach among mankind: theft, adultery, and mutual deception.[7]

Analogously, it is impossible that the Gods are born, because if they are born they must also die.

> But mortals believe the Gods to be created by birth, and to have their own raiment, voice, and body.[8]

And it is even impossible for God to move and to wander from place to place, as the vagabond Gods of Homer:

> And he always remains in the same place, not moving at all, nor is it fitting for him to change his position at different times.[9]

And finally, the various celestial and terrestrial phenomena, which popular belief identified with the various divinities, are explained as natural phenomena, as for example the rainbow, which was believed to be the Goddess Iris:

> And she whom they call Iris, she too is actually a cloud, purple and flame-red and yellow to behold.[10]

Here is philosophy only a brief period from its birth, already showing all its creative power, cutting through very firm beliefs that were held for centuries, but only because they were presented in the way of thinking and feeling which is typically Greek. Philosophy not only challenged their validity but it also entirely revolutionized the Greek vision of ancient man. After the criticism of Xenophanes, Western man could no longer comfortably conceive the divine according to a human form and measure.

3. God and the Divine according to Xenophanes

But if the categories used by Xenophanes were sufficient to destroy the anthropomorphic conceptions of the Gods, they were insufficient to positively determine the concept of God. After having negated with wholly adequate arguments that God can be conceived in the form of man, he tried to affirm that *God is the cosmos.* A much more profound elaboration of theoretical categories is necessary in order to achieve the conception of God not only as *other than human*, but likewise as *other than the cosmos.*

But let us see in the concrete, the affirmations of Xenophanes out of which arose not a few ambiguities. Fragment twenty-three states:

> One, God, the highest among Gods and men, not at all like mortals in body or in mind.[11]

Some interpreters do not hesitate to understand the fragment as if it said: "There exists a single and only God," and to speak, consequently, of monotheism. But that would involve a decidedly a-historical interpretation.

In the first place, it is contrary to the mental attitude of the entire Greek outlook, which, as we will see, was always indifferent to the problem as to whether God is one or many because it did not ponder the contradictory character of the affirmations that God is one and that God is many, but rather maintained as wholly natural that the divine in its very nature involved multiple manifestations and multiple affirmations. (Plato himself will conceive the divine as essentially multiple as well as Aristotle, whose tendency to monotheism is limited to the demands of an astronomical system, since he does not hesitate to link the immobile Movent, although in a purely subordinate hierarchy, with fifty-five other co-eternal movents.)

In the second place, the verse of Xenophanes, at the very moment in which he speaks of "God" in the singular, compares it to the Gods in the plural and puts it above them. In addition, he speaks of God in the singular and Gods in the plural indiscriminately in all the fragments.[12] But there is more. Fragment twenty-three, quoted from a Christian source,[13] is exclusively concerned with stressing a presumed agreement of ancient philosophers with Christian doctrine. The source cut up and thus falsified the original thought, but fortunately we are now in a position to reconstruct the original. Aristotle writes:

> Xenophanes, before these [Parmenides and Melissus] was the first who affirmed the unity of everything...in no way clearly [concerning the nature of this one, whether it is material or formal]...but, *extending his consideration to the whole world, said that the one is God.*[14]

Aristotle has here quoted from the passage from which our fragment was taken, which hence must have read like this:

> The universe...is one, God, highest among the Gods and men, similar neither in body nor in mind to human beings.[15]

Hence, the one God of which Xenophanes speaks is the cosmos-God, which does not exclude admitting other Gods or divine entities (they would be parts of the cosmos, or forces within the cosmos, or other things which from the scarce fragments it is impossible to go back and determine). If the God of Xenophanes is the cosmos-God, then it is easy to understand the other famous philosophical statements about him:

> He sees as a whole, thinks as a whole, and hears as a whole.[16]

And again:

> But without toil he sets everything in motion, by the thought of his mind.[17]

And we can understand also the negation of movement that we have already read:

> And he always remains in the same place, not moving at all, nor is it fitting for him to change his position at different times.[18]

All these statements, read according to the parameters which we have indicated, are expounded and explained in a satisfactory fashion: to see, to hear, and to think, therefore to have the power to move all things, are all activities which are attributed to God, rather than in the human dimension, in *the cosmological dimension.*

Therefore, Xenophanes is not a monotheist, because he speaks indifferently of "God" and of "Gods" in both the singular and the plural. Further, no Greek has ever felt an antithesis between monotheism and polytheism; he is not a supernaturalist because his God is the cosmos, and the category of the spiritual is entirely beyond the area of interest of his speculation (and it will remain so for all the Presocratics). He is not, consequently, a dualist (the first philosopher to oppose the spiritual to the material, as a matter of fact, will be Plato).[19]

May we conclude, then, that Xenophanes is a pantheist? There are many who do agree with this conclusion. We think that such an interpretation is less removed from the truth, but that it is well to support it with much more nuance than its upholders usually exercise.

The conception of Xenophanes is very archaic and the categories of *immanence* and *transcendence*, of *pantheism* and *theism* presuppose the possession of well determined categories. These categories are therefore always dangerous in the sense that, when they are applied to ancient thought which has not yet acquired them, they inevitably determine and bend it in a particular direction and so risk falsifying it.[20] The truth, hence, is that Xenophanes, if he identified God with the whole world, also continued to speak of Gods without determining their relationship with the world. Even less so did he specify the relations between the cosmos-God and the individual events and phenomena of the cosmos. Thus Xenophanes achieved some intuitions about the divine, but he lacked all those metaphysical categories which only those who came after him were able to construct.[21]

4. The physics of Xenophanes

One of the more plausible criticisms of what we have stated is given by the so-called Xenophanean "physics," which scholars have tirelessly attempted to connect with the doctrine about the Divine. Actually Xenophanes did not have a physics in the Ionic sense, still less a physics of that-which-appears in the Parmenidean sense.

He posited, in some fragments, the earth as principle:

> For everything is born of the earth, and everything goes back to the earth.[22]

In another fragment he speaks, on the contrary, about the earth and water at the same time:

> All the things which are born and grow are earth and water.[23]
> We are all born from the earth and from water.[24]

It would seem that Xenophanes, by using earth and water, wanted to explain *only terrestrial beings* and not the whole cosmos. Therefore, his principle is different than *the principle* of the Ionians, who wanted to explain not only terrestrial things, but the entire cosmos as well. On the other hand, if he denied that the cosmos was born, changes, and is moved, as a matter of fact, he did not deny that individual things in the cosmos are born, change, are moved and move, because his physics can in no way be the Parmenidean physics of that-which-appears.[25]

Perhaps there is truth in the thesis of Untersteiner, according to which the conception of earth-as-principle of Xenophanes is nothing other than the notion of Gaia, the Earth-Goddess (Gaia means indeed Earth), which has been transformed from myth to *logos*, yet keeping its original religious meaning.[26] In that case, the Xenophenean physics would more readily agree with his theology. And, generally, it is certain that Xenophanes was pre-occupied with providing rigorous scientific observations to support his physics and that the theses of his physics are not, in any case, derived just from the presence of the pre-Hellenic notion of Gaia.

5. Moral notions

Xenophanes also expresses a moral ideal of the highest value and, in particular, he affirms, against the then current prejudices, the clear superiority of what we will call spiritual values such as virtue, intelligence, and wisdom over purely vital values such as the purely physical powers of athletes.[27] From the former values the city-state will get a better order and a greater happiness than from the latter ones.

Here is the well-known Fragment two, in which he expresses with vivacity his notions:

> But if anyone were to win a victory with fleetness of foot, or fighting in the Pentathalon, where the precinct of Zeus lies between the springs of Pisa at Olympia, or in wrestling, or in virtue of the painful science of boxing, or in a dread kind of contest called Pancration: to the citizens he would be more glorious to look upon, and he would acquire a conspicuous seat of honor at competitions, and his maintenance would be provided out of the public stores by the city-state, as well as a gift for him to aside as treasure.
>
> So too if he won a prize with his horses, he would obtain all these rewards, though not deserving of them as I am; for my craft (wisdom) is better than the strength of men or horses. Yet opinion is altogether confused in this matter, and it is not right to prefer physical strength to noble wisdom. For it is not the presence of a good boxer in the community, nor of one good at the Pentathlon or at wrestling, nor even of one who excels in fleetness of foot—which is highest in honor of all the feats of strength seen in men's athletic contests—it is not these that will give a city-state a better constitution. Small would be the enjoyment that a city-state would reap over the athletic victory of a citizen beside the banks of Pisa! These things do not enrich the treasure-chamber of the state (trans. Freeman).

But these notions, however noble they are, are not philosophically grounded on general considerations of the nature of man. We will see this repeated consistently by all the Presocratics.

II. Parmenides

1. The three ways of inquiry

The interpretation of Xenophanes that we have given above will help us to better understand the originality of Parmenides,[1] who is not a continuator or a re-elaborator of thinking already outlined by others, but rather is a radical innovator and, within the realm of the Presocratics, a revolutionary. Cosmology receives a profound shock through him and is transformed or tends to be decisively transformed into something new and more mature, that is, into a *theory of being*.

In the poem of Parmenides—as the most recent studies bring more and more into evidence—there would seem to be three possible "paths" of inquiry. There is only one of these which is absolutely *true*. A second way, on the contrary, is considered absolutely *fallacious*. The third is seen to be (or tries to be seen) in some way or other as *similar to the way of truth*.

The Goddess expressly says[2] (she is the protagonist of the poem and is imagined as a Goddess who reveals to Parmenides the whole of truth) at the end of the prologue:

> You will inquire into everything:
> [1] both the motionless heart of well-rounded truth
> [2] and also the opinions of mortals, in which there is no true reliability;
> [3] but nevertheless you shall learn these things also—how one should go through all the things-that-appear, without exception, and test them (trans. Freeman).[3]

Therefore, there are three ways: one of unconditioned truth, one of false opinions or unconditioned falsity, and one of plausible opinion. Let us go along from one to the other together with Parmenides, or better, together with the Goddess of whom Parmenides is the prophet and messenger.

2. The way of unconditioned truth

The great Parmenidean principle, which is the very principle of truth, is this: *being is and necessarily is; not being is not and necessarily is not*. Being, hence, is and must be affirmed, not being is not and must be denied and this is the truth; to deny being or to affirm not being is instead unconditioned falsehood. Fragment two states:

> Come, I will tell you—and you must accept my word when you have heard it—the ways of inquiry which alone are to be thought; the one that *it is*, and it is not possible for *it not to be*, is the way of plausibility, for it follows truth; the other, that *it is not*, and that *it is bound not to be*: this I tell you is a path that cannot be explored; for you could

neither recognize that which is not, nor express it.[4]

And Fragment six:

> It is both necessary to say and think that being is; for to be is possible, and nothingness is not possible.[5] This I command you to consider; for from the latter way of search first of all I debar you. But next I debar you from that way along which wander mortals knowing nothing, two-headed, for perplexity in their bosoms steers their intelligence astray, and they are carried along as deaf as they are blind, amazed, uncritical hordes, by whom to be and not to be are regarded as the same and not the same, and (for whom) in everything there is a way of opposing stress.

And Fragment eight begins by proclaiming:

> ...Only one way remains open to say: that being is...[6]

Being and not being in the context of Parmenidean discourse are taken in their integral and univocal meaning: being is *purely positive* and not being is *purely negative* or, better still, being is simple and unconditioned positivity devoid of any negativity whatsoever and vice versa; not being is the absolute contradictory of this unconditioned positivity.

The affirmation of being and the negation of not being are justified by Parmenides, as has been seen already to some degree in Fragment six, by a single possible way. Being is alone conceivable and expressible. To think *is to conceive being* in the sense that being and thought coincide, that is, to the point that only what can be can be the subject of thought. Vice versa, not being is wholly inconceivable, inexpressible, and hence impossible. In Fragment three we read:

> (1) In fact it is the same thing to think and to be.

And in Fragment eight:

> (2) Thinking and that in function of which it is thought are the same because without being, in what is expressed, thought will not be found: in fact there is or will be nothing whatever outside of being...[7]

In this Parmenidean principle, interpreters have seen for the first time an important formulation of the principle of contradiction, that is, of that principle which affirms the impossibility that contradictories can at the same time be true. In our case, the contradictories are precisely the two highest contradictories: "being" and "not being." If there is being, says the Eleatic, there cannot be any not being. It is this great principle which was given its most well known formulation and defense by Aristotle, and which will constitute not only the capstone of ancient logic but also of the entire western tradition of logic. In addition, Parmenides will apply the principle almost exclusively by means of its entitative status, and only Aristotle will systematically develop its logical and epistemological status.

If we consider the meaning that we have called integral and univocal of Parmenidean being and the meaning likewise integral and univocal which the principle of contradiction is given, then it will not be difficult to grasp how all or almost all the important affirmations which we will encounter in the poem are nothing more than simple corollaries which necessarily follow upon such a premise once posited.

Being, in the first place, is *un-generated* and *in-corruptible*.

It is impossible that it be generated, insofar as, if it were to be so, it would have to be derived either from being or from not being. To be derived from not being is impossible, because not being is not; from being likewise is impossible because it would already be and thus not be generated. By this same reasoning, it is impossible for it to pass away.

Being hence does not have any *past* (because in that case it *would no longer be*), nor any *future* (because in that case it *would not yet be*), but it is in an *eternal present or now* without any beginning or end. Let us read the great Fragment eight:

> There is only one other description of the way remaining, *that it is*. To this way there are very many sign-posts: that being has no coming-into-being and no destruction, for it is whole of limb, without motion, and without end. And it never *was*, nor *will be*, because it is now, a whole all together, one, continuous; for what creation of it will you look for? How, whence sprung? Nor shall I allow you to speak or think of it as springing from not being; for it is neither expressible nor thinkable that what is not is. Also what necessity impelled it, if it did spring from nothing, to be produced later or earlier? Thus it must be absolutely, or not at all. Nor will the force of credibility ever admit that anything should come into being, besides being itself, out of not being. So far as that is concerned, justice has never released in its fetters and set it free either to come into being or to perish, but holds it fast. The decision on these matters depends on the following: *it is*, or *it is not*. It is therefore decided—as is inevitable—(that one must) ignore the one way as unthinkable and inexpressible (for it is not a true way) and take the other as the way of being and truth. How could being perish? How could it come into being? If it came into being, it is not; and so too if it is about to be at some future time. Thus coming into being is quenched, and destruction also into the unseen.[8]

Being is, in addition, *unmoved and absolutely immobile*, is shut up again, says Parmenides, in the *bonds of limit*, of inflexible Necessity. It is perfect and complete and, as such, does not lack anything and has no need of anything, and hence it remains in itself identical to itself.

> But it is motionless in the limits of mighty bonds, without beginning,

without cease, since becoming and destruction have been driven very far away, and true conviction has rejected them. And remaining the same in the same place, it rests by itself and thus remains there fixed; for powerful Necessity holds it in the bonds of limit, which constrains it round about, because it is decreed by Destiny that being shall not be unlimited. For it is not lacking; but if it were (spatially infinite), it would be lacking everything.[9]

Being, then, is indivisible into different parts, and hence is a *wholly equal* continuum, since every difference implies not being.

Nor is being divisible, since it is all alike. Nor is there anything (here or) there which could prevent it from holding together, nor any lesser thing, but all is full of being. Therefore it is altogether continuous; for being is close to being.[10]

And again:

Nor is there not being which could check it from reaching to the same point, nor is it possible for being to be more in this direction, less in that, than being, because it is an inviolate whole. For in all directions equal to itself, it reaches its limits uniformly.[11]

Parmenides, then, proclaimed many times that being is limited, that is, determined and finite, but he did not deduce this quality, which is evidently derived from the Pythagorean presupposition that only the finite is perfect.

Equality and finitude together evidently suggest the image of *the well-rounded sphere*, which the Eleatic explicitly applies to being:

But since there is a limit, it is complete on every side, like the mass of a well-rounded sphere, equally balanced from its center in every direction.[12]

It is clear that a similar image of being postulates also the attribute of *unity*. Actually, Parmenides affirms this attribute, but only in passing[13] and without insisting on it and especially without justifying it. As we will see, it will be Zeno and especially Melissus who will insist on this characteristic and bring it to the forefront.

The only truth is, therefore, that being is ungenerated, incorruptible, unmovable, unchangeable, equal, spherical, and one, the rest are only empty names:

Therefore all things that mortals have established, believing in their truth, are just a name; becoming and perishing, being and not being, and change of position, and alteration of bright color.[14]

Before going on to the remaining two ways, let us ask what is the nature of this Parmenidean notion of "being." It is clear that it is not a question of immaterial being, as some have claimed. The characteristic of the sphere and the expression "wholly full of being"[15] and similars speak against this interpretation in a persuasive enough fashion. But not for this reason ought we to insist on its material nature. This category is still a long way from being uncovered. Nevertheless it is clear that the Parmenidean notion of being is the being of the visible cosmos, immobilized, and to a great extent purified, but still clearly recognizable. It is, if a paradoxical mode of speech will be permitted, the being of the cosmos without the cosmos.

The difference between this being and the principle of the Ionians is evident. Like the principle of the Ionians, Parmenidean being is ungenerated and incorruptible, but it is not "a principle" because for Parmenides there are no "things derived from the principle." This is so because being, in addition to being ungenerated and incorruptible, is also *without alteration or movement*, whereas the principle of the Ionians generates all the things which can be altered and moved. And finally this is so because being is absolutely equal and undifferentiated and undifferentiable, whereas the principle of the Ionians generates things which are differentiated and changing. Thus the being of Parmenides is in an ambiguous state. It is not a principle, nor a cosmos, nor is it yet other than the naturalistic being of the cosmos.

But let us see the other two ways, so that they may help us to grasp this unusual position of Parmenides.

3. The way of error

The way followed above is the way of reason and the logos. It is the logos, in fact, and only the logos which affirms being and rejects not-being. On the contrary, the senses would attest to becoming, movement, living and dying, and hence both being and not-being. But it is to their senses that all men are bound and for this reason the Goddess objects and points out the dangers derived from faith in the senses contrary to the dictates of the logos and proclaims the need to follow the logos alone. In fact, to allow *being and not-being together* means essentially to admit not-being as being, therefore it is to grasp why Parmenides considered the affirmation that nothing is is to be very close to the affirmation that there is being together with not-being. In fact, both contravene the great principle by allowing (although in different ways) the possibility of contradictory negation (not-being), which is inconceivable and inexpressible and hence absurd. Let us read again Fragment six:

> It is both necessary to say and think that being is; for to be is possible, and nothingness is not possible. This I command you to consider; for from the latter way of search first of all I debar you. But next I debar you from that way along which wander mortals knowing nothing, two-headed, for perplexity in their bosoms steers their intelligence astray, and they are carried along as deaf as they are blind, amazed, uncritical hordes, by whom to be and not to be are regarded as the

same and not the same, and (for whom) in everything there is a way of opposing stress.

And Fragment seven:

For this can never predominate, that that which is not exists. You must debar your thought from this way of search, nor let ordinary experience in its variety force you along this way, allowing the eye, sightless as it is, and the ear, full of sound, and the tongue, to rule; but you must judge by means of the logos the much-contested proof which is expounded by me. There is only one other description of the way remaining, that being is.

The root of the error of the "opinions of mortals," hence, is in the admission of not-being as equal to being and in the admission of the possibility of a passage from one to the other and vice versa.

4. The third way: the explanation of the plausibility of phenomena and the Parmenidean "doxa"

Traditionally, the thought of Parmenides has been hardened into a position of absolute negativity in relation to *doxa*.[16] Recently, however it has clearly emerged that some fragments demonstrate that Parmenides, by simply denying any validity to the fallacious opinion of mortals, was not entirely adverse to conceding to "appearances," appropriately understood, their own plausibility, and hence to granting some validity to the senses. If this is true, it is necessary to conclude, as we have previously stressed, that Parmenides, recognized in addition to truth and the fallacious opinions of mortals, the possibility and the appropriateness of a certain kind of discourse that tries to give an account of the phenomena and appearances without going contrary to his great principle, that is, without admitting both being and not-being together.

We have already read the end of the prologue of the poem in which the Goddess says that after truth and the false opinions of mortals Parmenides must also grasp this:

...how one should go through all the things that appear, without exception, and test them.[17]

At the end of Fragment eight, the Goddess also says:

This world order I describe to you throughout as it appears with all its phenomena, in order that no intellect of mortal men may outstrip you.[18]

The clearest opposition between the exposition of the plausible ordering of the world to the conviction which mortals have is found in the Prologue. But then, in the course of the exposition of that which traditionally has come to be considered the false opinions of mortals, we find a form and definition which brings to mind rather closely the language of truth. It means that here Parmenides has not espoused pure error, for which he usually uses a different terminology.

Hence, Parmenides has espoused a "plausible opinion" in addition to the fallacious, and he has tried, in his own way, to explain the phenomena.[19] How?

"Mortals" are in error—we saw—in admitting being and not being to equal validity. In a more determined manner, in Fragment eight it says that mortals have posited as the two highest forms, "light" and "night," conceiving them as contraries (as being and not-being) and deducing from them the rest of things.

What precisely is the object to which Parmenides alludes in speaking of these two forms is not clear. However, it is quite clear that he intends to correct the errors of mortals:

> They have established naming two forms, the unity of which is not necessary: that is where they have gone astray.[20]

Mortals, hence, have erred *because they have not understood that the two forms are included in a higher necessary unity, meaning in the unity of being.*

And thus Fragment nine, which in the past was wholly obscure, is clarified:

> But since all things are named light and night, and names have been given to each class of things according to the power of one or the other, everything is full equally of light and invisible night, *as both are equal, because to neither of them belongs nothingness* (ἐπεὶ οὐδετέρῳ μέτα μηδέν).[21]

"Light" and "Night" are equal because neither of them is nothing, and hence *they are both being.*

That this is indeed the thought of Parmenides is confirmed on another basis in addition to that read from the fragments, namely, from information transmitted by Theophrastus according to which a corpse (which is cold, that is, obscure night) perceives:

> But that he [Parmenides] regards sensation as also due to the opposite as such [= the principle which is said by Parmenides to be "night"] he makes clear when he says that a corpse does not perceive light, heat or sound owing to its deficiency of fire [= the principle which Parmenides called "light"], *but that it does perceive their opposites [scil.,* to those of the fiery principle] cold, silence and so on.[22]

Insofar as it seems strange at first glance if not absurd to affirm that a corpse can still perceive anything, on a moment's reflection we can see that it follows from the Parmenidean premises. The obscure "night" (and the cold) in which the corpse is resolved is not pure not-being, that is, nothing. But like the "light" (and the hot) it *is*. Hence it *is being*. Therefore, in some way the corpse lives.

5. The structural aporia of Parmenidean philosophy

That the reconstruction of the world of phenomena must therefore proceed in relation to the highest principle means *rejecting not-being and affirming only being*. But this attempt (which in terms of the scarce fragments of the second part of the poem we cannot reconstruct in its details, but only in its general lines as indicated above) was destined necessarily to fail in the hands of Parmenides. Once having been recognized as "being," *light and night* must lose any clear differentiation and become identical, because being is always and only "equal," that is, identical to itself, and does not admit differences of kind, whether qualitative or quantitative. Thus as the two principles must be inevitably absorbed and lost in the equality of being, so even must all the things derived from the principles. Once recognized as being, any thing must necessarily be recognized insofar as it is being, likewise as ungenerated, incorruptible, and unmoved. Therefore, in the same moment in which Parmenides attempts to reconstruct the world of phenomena in a plausible manner, that is, without being in contradiction with his own principle of truth, he unfortunately empties the world of all its richness and variety and imprisons it in the immobility of being.[23]

If the great principle of Parmenides as it is thus formulated by him preserved being, it also lost the phenomena. Philosophy after Parmenides and the Eleatics will need to find a new way that will permit it to save the phenomena in addition to being.

III. Zeno of Elea

1. The origin of dialectical demonstration

The doctrine of Parmenides must have quickly elicited a vigorous polemic by reason of its aporetic and paradoxical nature. Its adversaries must have attacked it chiefly on the issues which more jarringly clashed with the data of experience, like the negation of becoming and movement and the negation, more implicit than explicit, but in any case effective, of multiplicity.

It was the task of a disciple of Parmenides, Zeno of Elea,[1] to defend the teachings of the master from these attacks in a work which has justly become famous and in which the argument was cast in a surprisingly new form.

Plato, in the *Parmenides*, places in the mouth of Zeno this judgment about his own work:

> "Yes, Socrates," said Zeno, "but you have not perceived all aspects of the truth about my writings. You follow the arguments with a scent as keen as a Laconian hound's but you do not observe that my treatise is not by any means so pretentious that it could have been written with the intention you ascribe to it, of disguising itself as a great performance in the eyes of men. What you mentioned is a mere acci-dent, but *in truth these writings are meant to support the argument of Parmenides against those who attempt to jeer at him* and assert that if the all is one many absurd results follow which contradict his theory. Now this treatise opposes the advocates of the many and gives them back their ridicule with interest, *for its purpose is to show that their hypothesis that existences are many, if properly followed up, leads to still more absurd results than the hypothesis that they are one.* It was in such a spirit of controversy that I wrote it when I was young, and when it was written someone stole it, so that I could not even consider whether it should be published or not.[2]

Apart from the excessive emphasis which Plato accords to the problem of the one and the many (which certainly was not *the theme* par excellence of the book of Zeno, but *one* of the themes, and which Plato, therefore, emphasized in this way because this was the theme of his dialogue), it needs to be stated that the characterization of the method of Zeno is perfect. The reinforcement of the thesis of Parmenides is presented by way of the refutation of the contradictory thesis.

Thus was born that method of demonstration which, instead of directly proving a given thesis beginning from determined principles, tries to prove this thesis by reducing to absurdity the contradictory thesis.

Zeno used this method with an ability which drew forth the admiration of the ancients. It is again Plato, who certainly shared that admiration, although accompanied by a smidgen of his accustomed irony, who says of

Zeno that:

> ...he has such an art of speaking that the same things appear to his
> hearers to be alike and unlike, one and many, stationary and in
> motion.[3]

Aristotle considered him the founder of the art of dialectic.[4]

2. The dialectical arguments against movement

The arguments of Zeno which have been handed down are concerned
with movement and multiplicity.

The most famous are those which argue against the possibility of a
coherent account of movement, which Aristotle himself found very difficult
to refute.

The first argument, called "the dichotomy," maintains that movement is
absurd and impossible because a body in order to traverse a distance must
first traverse and reach a half of that distance; but first it must reach half
of the first half and again half of that half, and so on to infinity because
there is always a further half which it must traverse.

Here is the clearest of the presentations of this argument which the
ancients have handed down to us:

> The first argument is this: if movement exists, it is necessary that the
> mobile traverse an infinite number of points in a finite time; but this
> is impossible, hence movement does not exist. Zeno demonstrated his
> position affirming that whatever is moved must traverse a certain
> distance: but any distance is divisible to infinity, what is moved must
> first traverse half of the distance and then the whole of it. But first he
> must traverse the entire half of the distance, and the half of that and
> the new half of the previous half. But if the halves are infinite in
> number since for every whole taken it is possible to take half, then it
> is impossible to traverse in a finite time an infinite number of points.
> ...Then, given that every magnitude admits of infinite divisions, it is
> impossible to traverse any magnitude in a finite time.[5]

The second argument, called the "Achilles," maintains that movement is
so absurd that, if, granted but not conceded, we put the fleet-footed Achilles
in a race with a tortoise, he would not succeed in winning it because the
same difficulty seen in the preceding argument would be present in a
different form. Achilles would first have to reach the point from which the
tortoise started, but by that time the tortoise will have moved farther on.
When he has covered the further distance, the tortoise will again have
moved on farther, and so on to infinity. Here is Aristotle's presentation of
the argument:

> The second is the so-called "Achilles," and it amounts to this, that in
> a race the quickest runner can never overtake the slowest, since the

pursuer must first reach the point whence the pursued started, so that the slower must always hold a lead. This argument is the same in principle as that which depends on bisection, though it differs from it in that the spaces with which we successively have to deal are not divided into halves. The result of the argument is that the slower is not overtaken: but it proceeds along the same lines as the dichotomy argument (for in both a division of the space in a certain way leads to the result that the goal is not reached, though the "Achilles" goes further in that it affirms that even the quickest runner in legendary tradition must fail in his pursuit of the slowest).[6]

The third argument is called the "flying arrow" and shows that a flying arrow, which the opinion of mortals would claim is in motion, in reality is at rest. In fact, in each instant into which the time of the flight is divisible, the flying arrow occupies an identical space; but what occupies an identical space is at rest; hence the flying arrow, just as it is at rest in each instant, so also is it in the totality of them. Here is how Aristotle and Simplicius present the argument:

> The third is that. . .the flying arrow is at rest, which result follows from the assumption that time is composed of moments: if this assumption is not granted, the conclusion will not follow. . . Zeno's reasoning, however, is fallacious, when he says that if everything when it occupies an equal place is at rest, and if that which is in motion is always occupying such a place at any moment, the flying arrow is therefore motionless.[7]

> The argument of Zeno, beginning from the premise that everything which occupies a space equal to itself either is in motion or is at rest, that nothing is moved in an instant and the mobile always occupies in each instant a space equal to itself, seems to adjust itself in this way: the flying arrow in every instant occupies a place equal to itself, and thus, for the whole time of its motion. But what occupies in an instant a place equal to itself does not move because nothing is moved in an instant. Hence the flying arrow, as long as it is in motion, does not move for the whole time of its flight.[8]

The fourth argument is called "the Stadium"; it shows instead the relativity of velocity, and hence of movement itself of which the velocity is an essential property and, with this demonstration of its relativity, it excludes the coherent account and hence the reality of movement.[9]

There is probably a fifth argument[10] contained in Fragment four, which we will read:

> What is moved, is not moved either in the place in which it is, nor into the place in which it is not.[11]

It is not moved in the place in which it is, because, if it is in the place in which it is, it is at rest; it does not move into the place in which it is not because it is not there; hence a coherent account of movement is impossible.

3. The dialectical arguments against multiplicity

Zeno used an analogous procedure in order to demonstrate the impossibility that being is multiple, that is, that there exists a multiplicity of beings.[12] The principal arguments tend to demonstrate that in order for there to be multiplicity there would have to be multiple *units* (on the supposition that multiplicity is indeed composed of a multiplicity of units); but reasoning shows that such unities (which common experience would attest) are inconceivable because they result in insuperable contradictions and hence are absurd and therefore cannot exist. The sense of this argument is clearly expressed in this ancient testimony:

> Zeno of Elea, arguing against those who ridiculed the doctrine of his master Parmenides, who affirmed that being is one, went to his defense, trying to show that it is impossible that multiplicity actually exists. In fact, he says, if multiplicity exists, since this is constituted from a multiplicity of units, it is necessary that these multiplicity of units exist of which the multiplicity consists. If, hence, it is demonstrated that it is impossible that a multiplicity of units exists, it is evident that the existence of a multiplicity is impossible because multiplicity is composed of units. If it is impossible that multiplicity exists, and if, on the other hand, it is necessary that either one or multiples exist, since it is impossible that multiples exist, then it is necessary to admit that only the one exists [*scil.*, the unconditioned unity of being].[13]

Zeno, in favor of this general thesis, adduced at least four particular arguments, which are worthwhile referring to in order to be able to fully grasp the meaning of his dialectic.

His first argument demonstrates that if beings were multiple, they must be both *infinitely small* as well as being *infinitely large:*

> If beings are multiple, it is necessary that they be both small and large, so large as to be infinite in size, so small as to have no size at all.[14]

Each of the many beings, in order to be one, must have neither magnitude, nor thickness, nor weight (because, otherwise, they would be divisible into parts, and hence they would no longer be one). But such a one, so infinitely small as to be devoid of magnitude, is nothing; so true is this that if you were to add such a *one* to something else, it would not increase it and if you were to subtract such a *one* from something else, it would not make it smaller. And it is only the *nothing* that is added or subtracted which gives such a result. On the other hand, it is not possible to conceive of a one with magnitude since, no matter how small, every magnitude not only, as we said already, is divisible into parts, but it is divisible *into an infinity* of parts and thus having infinite parts it must be infinite in magnitude.[15]

A second argument analogous to the first shows that by admitting that beings are multiple they must be both finite and infinite *in number* (besides being so in magnitude), which is absurd. Here are the actual words of Zeno:

> If beings are many, they must be as many as they are and neither more nor less than this. But if they are as many as they are, they must be *finite*. If beings are many, they are infinite in number. For there are always other beings between those that are, and again others between those. And thus beings are *infinite* in number.[16]

A third argument is centered on the negation of space (which is a condition of the existence of the multiple), a fragment of which has come down to us:

> If space exists, it must be found in something; now what is in something is in place; consequently space must be found in one place, and thus to infinity. Hence space does not exist.[17]

A fourth argument denies multiplicity based on the contradictory characteristics belonging to many things considered together with respect to each (or part of each) taken singly. For example many millet seeds, falling, make a sound, while one millet seed (or part of one) does not do so. But if the witness of experience were true, similar contradictions could not exist, and a single seed (or a part of one) falling would make a sound, with due proportion, as the many seeds make falling. Here is an ancient testimony concerning the argument:

> In this way he resolved also the question raised by Zeno of Elea, who asked the Sophist Protagoras the following questions:
>
> Tell me, Protagoras, does one falling grain of millet seed or one ten-thousandth part of a grain of millet seed make a sound?
>
> And Protagoras having replied that the ten-thousandth part of a grain did not make a sound, he adds:
>
> But a small piece of a grain of millet seed, does it make a sound or not, when it falls?
>
> And Protagoras having replied that it made a sound, Zeno presses the issue:
>
> But is there not perhaps a proportion between a small piece of a grain of millet seed and a single grain and between the millet and its ten-thousandth part?
>
> And Protagoras having admitted that there is, in response Zeno said:
>
> And then ought there not to be the same mutual relationship between the sounds? As there is a proportion between the things which produce the sounds, so there must be a proportion between the sounds; but

this were so, if the small piece of the grain makes a sound also the grain alone makes a sound and even its ten-thousandth part.

Zeno thus argued this way.[18]

4. The importance of Zeno

The results of the thinking processes of Zeno are important. In the realm of Eleaticism he contributed to shifting the theme of the highest pair of concepts, being and not being, on which Parmenides has concentrated his energies, to another pair, the one and the many, which in succeeding metaphysics will have great importance. Zeno helps bring forth the theme of the one-many dialectically; Melissus will salvage it systematically.

In addition, the fierce arguments that Zeno used against the phenomenal appearances of the multiple and movement showing their intrinsic contradictory character were to destroy structurally any possibility of giving to them any plausibility, even a relative one (also that relative plausibility which Parmenides had conceded to the phenomena), since *doxa* must always and only be fallacious. Even in this case Melissus will take the arguments of Zeno to their extreme consequences, denying appearances systematically (not just dialectically) and declaring that the world of phenomena is pure illusion.

Finally, in regard to Zenonian dialectic, its influence went well beyond the Eleatic School. It deeply affected the Sophists, the Socratic method itself, the Megarics, and in general it contributed in a not indifferent way to the formation of the various types of argumentation and to the birth of logic. The demonstration which is called *ad absurdum* is in essence a discovery of Zeno.

IV. Melissus of Samos

1. The systematization of Eleaticism

Melissus[1] can be described as the "systematizer" of Eleatic thought. Parmenides left poetically undetermined some of the attributes of being, and especially some which he simply affirmed and did not reason out, or only imperfectly reasoned out, and thus he even made statements which were inconsistent with the principles of the system. Zeno—we saw—was limited to an indirect defense, to supporting the doctrine by reducing to absurdity the thesis of its adversaries. Melissus tried, instead, in limpid prose, to give structure to the doctrine, to rigorously deduce all the attributes, and to correct what could not be subsumed, or be badly subsumed, within the foundation of the system.

2. The attributes of being and their deduction

Melissus understood being in the same way as Parmenides, and like him he demonstrated its ingenerability and incorruptibility. However, instead of conceiving the eternity of this being wholly wrapped in an a-temporal "now" without past and future, he preferred to spread it out to infinity and to conceive it as an "always was and always will be," as we read in Fragment one:

> That which was, was always and always will be. For if it had come into being, it necessarily follows that before it came into being, nothing existed. If however nothing existed, in no way could anything come into being out of nothing.[2]

Many scholars have maintained that the Melissean description "that which was, was always and always will be" reintroduced temporality. But this view is mistaken because Melissus intended his being as rigorously a-processive, from always and through always it was wholly actual, and with "always was" and "always will be" he only wanted to stress the infinite layers of eternity (Christian theology itself, in order to express the concept of eternity, will go back to the Melissean description).[3]

But the most obvious originality of Melissus is without doubt the affirmation that being is *infinite*. Parmenides had said that being is *finite* only in homage to the presupposition (of Pythagorean origin, then from him it became the inheritance of Greek culture) that the infinite is imperfect and only the finite is perfect. Melissus, on the contrary, reasoned in this way:

> Since therefore it did not come into being, it is and always was and always will be, and has no beginning and no end, but it is eternal. For if it had come into being, it would have a beginning (for it would have come into being at some times, and so begun), and an end (for since it

had come into being, it would have ended). But since it has neither begun nor ended, it always was and always will be and has no beginning nor end. For it is impossible for anything to be, unless it is completely.[4]

Here the final proposition is ultimate, insofar as it is *all*, being is *both* eternal *and infinite*. In modern terms we would say, insofar as it is *absolute*, being is in-finite both in the dimension of eternity and in the dimension of space. Melissus further argued that if it were limited it would be confined by the void, that is, by not being, which is inconceivable.[5]

In addition to being eternal and infinite, being is *one*. Even in the content of this attribute Melissus is original, since, as we know, Parmenides affirmed the attribute without reasoning to it, and Zeno allowed it to emerge only dialectically. Being is one *because infinite*, as we read in Fragment six (and this is also one of the arguments that Christian theology will use in order to demonstrate the unicity of the Godhead):

> If it is infinite, it must be one; for if it were two, these could not be infinite, but each would be bound by the other.[6]

Being, in addition, as Parmenides stated, is *equal*, it is *unalterable* either qualitatively or quantitatively, it is *immobile*. All these qualities are the subject of better reasoned arguments than in Parmenides, in particular the last one:

> Nor is there any void; for the void is nothing; and so that which is nothing cannot be. Nor does it move; for it cannot withdraw in any direction, but all is full. For if there were any void, it would have withdrawn into the void; but as the void does not exist, there is nowhere for it to withdraw.[7]

Finally Melissus says that being is *incorporeal*:

> If, hence, being is, it must be one. And being one, *it must not have a body.*
>
> Being one, *it must not have a body*; in fact, if had thickness, it would have parts, and hence, it would not be one.[8]

Scholars have expended a great deal of energy giving a correct historical sense to this Melissean affirmation.[9] Being has no body, not because it is spiritual but because it is *one-infinite*, and as such is not determined either by internal limits or by external limits, nor by those of the Parmenidean "well-rounded sphere." Not having a body hence coincides with not having limits, with having *infinite magnitude*. Hence Melissus is *not* a proponent of the notion of the spiritual, as some have maintained ("without a body" has a quite different meaning than "without matter"); but it is nonetheless not the case that he is a materialist, as others have stated. Like Parmenides and all the Presocratics, Melissus is still short of the distinctions of these categories, and it is historically erroneous to judge him in terms of them. So much is this true that according to how we apply these categories Melissean being (and in general Eleatic being) appears sometimes as spiritual and sometimes as material. This demonstrates that it is not, properly speaking, either; or better, that it has characteristics which locate it in both categories but the determinations of a physical nature prevail.

3. The elimination of the domain of experience and of "doxa"

The final originality of Melissus is the systematic elimination of the world of the senses and *doxa*. Here is the Melissean reasoning contained in the famous eighth Fragment. *a*) Multiple things that the senses attest to would truly exist and our sensible awareness would be veracious on only one condition, *viz.*, on the condition that each of these things remain always as they appeared for the first time, that is, on the condition that things would remain always identical with themselves, unchanging, ingenerable, incorruptible. In short, multiplicity would be creditable only on the condition that it would be as the One-Being is. *b*) On the contrary, on the basis itself of our empirical awareness, we can argue that the multiple things which are the objects of sensible perception do not ever remain identical, but they change, they are generated, and they perish continually. That is precisely the contrary of what is necessary to attain the stature of being and truth. *c*) Hence there is a contradiction between what, on the one hand, reason recognizes as an absolute condition of being and truth and, on the other hand, to what the senses and experience attest. *d*) The contradiction is eliminated by Melissus with the determined negation of the validity of the senses and of what the senses proclaim (because in essence they proclaim not being). *e*) Hence the single reality is Being-One, the hypothetical multiplicity would exist only if it were like Being-One. These are affirmations that must be grasped in order to understand the Pluralists:

If the many existed, they would have to be such as the One is.

This great fragment is worth reading in its entirety, since in it the audacity of the Eleatic *logos* achieves its most extreme position:

This argument is the greatest proof that being is one only; but there are also the following proofs. If things were many, they would have to be of the same kind as I say the one is. For if there is earth and water and air and fire and iron and gold, and that which is living and that which is dead, and black and white and all the rest of the things which men say are real: if these things exist, and we see and hear them correctly, each thing must be of a such a kind as it seemed to us to be in the first place, and it cannot change or become different, but each thing must always be what it is. But now, we say we see and hear and understand correctly and it seems to us that the hot becomes the cold and the cold hot, and the hard soft and the soft hard, and that the living thing dies and comes into being from what is not living, and that all things change, and that what was and what now is are not at all the same, but iron which is hard is worn away by contact with the finger, and gold and stone and whatever seems to be entirely strong is worn away; and that from water, earth and stone come into being. So that it comes about that we neither see nor know existing things.

So these statements are not consistent with one another. For although we say that there are many things, everlasting, having forms and strength, it seems to us that they all alter and change from what is seen on each occasion.

It is clear therefore that we have not been seeing correctly, and that those things do not correctly seem to us to be many; for they would not change if they were real, but each would be as it seemed to be. For nothing is stronger than that which is real.

And if it changed, being would have been destroyed, and not being would have come into being. Thus therefore if things are many, they must be such as the one is.[10]

Thus Eleaticism ends with the affirmation of eternal being, infinite, one, equal, unchanging, immobile, incorporeal (in the sense explained), which excludes every possibility of multiplicity because it cuts off at the root every claim of the phenomena to be recognized.

It is clear that being as the Eleatics have described it can only be the being of God, that is, *a privileged being and not the whole of being*, but the Eleatics could not distinguish the being of God and the being of the world. Hence God and the world, because of their "being," have *a single meaning*, an integral sense. The only escape from this aporia would be to distinguish between being and being, that is, to distinguish different levels and meanings of being. But this was not yet the proper time for this move.

As is known, Aristotle reproached the Eleatics in general and Melissus in particular for coming close to folly, the folly of a reason which does not aim at recognizing anything other than itself and its own laws, rejecting categorically experience and its own data.[11] But if this is true, it is likewise true that the most powerful exercise of succeeding thought, both of the Pluralists and, at a higher level, that of Plato and Aristotle, *consisted in the attempt to undo this "folly" by trying to recognize both the reasons of reason and the reasons of experience*, or to try to preserve the principles of Parmenides and at the same time to preserve the phenomena, as we will see.

Fifth Section

THE PLURALISTS AND THE ECLECTIC PHYSICISTS

«τὸ δὲ γίνεσθαι καὶ ἀπόλλυσθαι οὐκ ὀρθῶς
νομίζουσιν οἱ Ἕλληνες· οὐδὲν γὰρ χρῆμα
γίνεται οὐδὲ ἀπόλλυται, ἀλλ᾽ ἀπὸ ἐόντων
χρημάτων συμμίσγεταί τε καὶ διακρίνεται.
καὶ οὕτως ἂν ὀρθῶς καλοῖεν τό τε γίνεσθαι
συμμίσγεσθαι καὶ τὸ ἀπόλλυσθαι διακρί-
νεσθαι.»

"The Greeks have an incorrect belief on
coming to being and passing away. No
thing comes into being or passes away,
but it is mixed together or separated from
existing things. Thus they would be correct if they called coming into being 'mix-
ing,' and passing away 'separating-off.'"

Anaxagoras *Fragment* 17

I. Empedocles

1. The four "elements"

Empedocles[1] was the first thinker who tried to resolve the Eleatic aporia. On the one hand, he attempted to preserve the principle that nothing comes to be and nothing perishes and that being always perdures, and on the other, the phenomena that experience attested to.

A very clear affirmation of the Eleatic principle is found in Fragments eleven and twelve:

> Fools! for they have no long-sighted thoughts, since they imagine that *what previously did not exist comes into being, or that a thing dies and is utterly destroyed.*[2]
>
> From what in no way exists, *it is impossible for anything to come into being; and for being to perish completely is incapable of fulfillment and unthinkable; for it will always be there, wherever anyone may place it on any occasion.*

Hence, "coming-into-being" and "passing-away," understood as a coming-into-being from nothing and a passing-away into nothingness, are impossible because *being is*; however, to come-to-be and to pass-away have their plausibility and reality if understood as *a coming from things which are and a change into things which also exist.* Fragment eight states:

> And I shall tell you another thing: there is no *coming-into-being* of substance in any one of mortal existences, nor any end in execrable *death*, but only *mixing and exchange* of what has been mixed; and the name nature is applied to them by human beings.

Birth and death are, respectively, *mixture and dissolution* of determinate substances which are *not born* and are *indestructible*, that is, of substances which are eternally equal. These substances are precisely four: *fire, water, aither* or *air*, and *earth*. These are the substances which are called the "four elements," but which Empedocles poetically designated with the expression "the roots of all things." He also called them with the names of Gods in order to accent their eternality and hence their divinity.

> Hear, first, the four roots of things: bright Zeus, and life-bearing Hera, and Aidoneus, and Nestia who causes a mortal spring of moisture to flow with her tears.[3]

Empedocles accepted the water of Thales, the air of Anaximander, the fire of Heraclitus, and in a certain sense the earth of Xenophanes, but he most importantly changed the prior conception of the principle. In fact, the principle of the Ionians *is changed qualitatively* by becoming all things, while in Empedocles water, air, earth, and fire are *qualitatively unalterable and unchangeable.* There arose, in this way, the notion of "element" as something *originative and qualitatively unchangeable,* having the ability only to unite and separate spatially and mechanistically with respect to each other. It can be seen then as a notion which resulted from the Eleatic experience and the attempt to go beyond it. The so-called pluralistic conception also arose which definitively goes beyond the monistic vision of the Ionians. The root and principle of things is not single, but structurally plural. Pluralism is also a perspective that can be affirmed at a level of critical awareness only after surpassing the radical monism of the Eleatics.[4]

Why, then, Empedocles believed that there were only four elements is not difficult to explain. On the one hand, it may have been suggested by the Pythagorean tetrad, that is, by the conviction of the privileged nature of the number four. But it was certainly determined by attention to experience, which seems to attest that everything is derived from air, water, fire, and earth, as can be seen from Fragment twenty-one:

> But come, observe the following witness to my previous discourse, lest in my former statements there was any substance of which the form was missing. Observe the sun, bright to see and hot everywhere, and all the immortal things (heavenly bodies) drenched with its heat and brilliant light; and (observe) the rain, dark and chill over everything; and from the Earth issue forth things based on the soil and solid (Freeman trans.).

2. Love and Hate

We have said that birth and death for Empedocles are actually nothing other than *a mixture and separation of the four elements,* which are qualitatively unchanging. But what enables the elements to mutually unite and separate? The elements would not be mixed with the others of themselves, therefore, the necessity now arises of introducing a further cause, a cause which Aristotle will call the cause of movement. Before the speculations of the Eleatics, the need for such a cause could not arise but it did later, within the perspective of a recovery of the phenomena (specified precisely by movement) which must necessarily be thrust into the forefront. Empedocles introduced Love and Hate (Friendship and Discord) conceived as cosmic powers and (together with the elements) they are Divinities, causes of the union and separation of the elements.

Naturally we cannot speak of spiritual powers, and interpreters have, in general, well understood that we are basically faced here with natural forces (like the elements). Hate which separates and Love which joins are co-eternal like the elements. But precisely because they are co-eternal and equal powers, the effects of Love and Hate annul each other and no longer explain the process of the generation and corruption of things, and all would stay suspended in the same state if they could not in some way overcome each other. Actually, Empedocles speaks of alternating dominance first by one and then the other power, a constant cycle determined by Destiny. Thus when love predominates, the elements move into a unity. When Hate predominates, they separate. Finally, it is the interweaving of the influences of Love and Hate that produces things.

Here, then, is how Empedocles tried to satisfy both Eleatic *being* and the *reality of the phenomena* and explain *becoming:*

> All these elements are equal and of the same age in their creation; but each presides over its own office, and each has its own character, and they prevail in turn in the course of Time. And besides these, nothing else comes into being, nor does anything cease. For if they had been perishing continuously, they would be no more; and what could increase the whole? And whence could it have come? In what directions could it perish, since nothing is empty of these things? No, but these become different things at different times, and are ever continuously the same.[5]

And likewise this view is clearly expressed in Fragment twenty-six:

> In turn they [Love and Hate] get the upper hand in the revolving cycle, and perish into one another and increase in the turn appointed by Destiny. For they [the elements] alone *exist*, but running through another *they become* men and the tribes of other animals, sometimes uniting under the influence of Love into one ordered whole, at other times again each moving apart through the hostile forces of Hate, until growing together into the whole which is one, they are quelled. Thus insofar as they have the power to grow into one out of many, and again, when the one grows apart and many are formed, in this sense *they come into being* and have no stable life; but insofar as they never cease their continuous exchange, in this sense they remain always unmoved as they follow the cyclic process [of the universe].

3. The Sphere (Σφαῖρος) and the cosmos

As the reader has confidently understood, on the basis of what we have said and especially from the last of the fragments read, our cosmos is *not* constituted by the prevalence of Love but by the prevalence of Hate.

When Love prevails absolutely, no one of the elements is distinguished from the others, but all are gathered together and together are united in a way which forms a compact whole, a unity which is said by Empedocles to be *One* or a *Sphere* (Σφαῖρος), which calls to mind the sphere of Parmenides:

> But he is equal in all directions to himself and altogether eternal, a rounded sphere enjoying a circular solitude.[6]

> For there do not start two branches from his back; no feet, no swift knees, no organs of reproduction; but he was a sphere, and in all directions equal to himself.[7]

When Hate absolutely prevails, the elements are instead absolutely separate, and in this case the cosmos or individual things can in no way exist.

The cosmos and things in the cosmos arise, instead, in the two periods of the change in the cycle as it goes from the predominance of Love to that of Hate and later from the predominance of Hate to that of Love. In each of these two periods there is a progressive birth and destruction of a cosmos, which therefore necessarily presupposes the action of both forces together.

It is then clear that Love is not conceived simply as a force that produces coming-into-being and Hate simply as a power which produces destruction. In fact Love, prevailing, *dissolves the cosmos*, welcoming the elements into the undifferentiated sphere so when Hate returns to the sphere the conditions are posited for the *birth of the cosmos*; and conversely, Love *brings to birth* the cosmos by bringing together the elements after they were separated by the prevalence of Hate, and which Hate in turn *destroys* when it predominates, overturning everything.

Thus it is clear that the moment of absolute perfection is not in the cosmos but in the Sphere (Σφαῖρος).

4. Knowledge

The observations made by Empedocles about the way in which various beings are born, especially organic beings, as well as how organic beings live and grow, are interesting and for the most part ingenious. But especially interesting is the explanation that he gives of the phenomena of human knowledge. From things, and from the pores of things, the effluvia go forth which strike the bodily sensory organs, and the parts of our organs similar to them recognize their similars in the efflux coming from things. The fire knows fire, water water, and so on (in vision instead the process is reversed and the effluvia go from the eyes, but the principle according to which like knows like is always basic). Fragment 109 expressly states:

> We see earth by means of earth, water by means of water, divine air
> by means of air, and destructive fire by means of fire; love by means
> of love, hate by means of baneful hate.

Even thought is explained in the same way and with the same principle, since Empedocles does not distinguish, as did moreover all the Presocratics, the spiritual from the corporeal. He expressly says in Fragment 105:

> [The heart] nourished in the seas of blood which courses in two opposite
> directions: this is the place where is found for the most part what men
> call thought; *for the blood round the heart is thought in mankind.*

Finally, the fact that he attributed knowledge and thought to every thing without distinction is very suggestive:

> For everything, be assured, has intelligence and a portion of thought.[8]

5. The soul and the Divine

In addition to the Περὶ φύσεως [*On Nature*], Empedocles also composed the Καθαρμοί [*Purifications*], in which he defended the Orphic-Pythagorean conceptions that we have previously discussed and presented himself as their prophet and messenger.

Man, or better, the soul of man, is a *daimon* which because of its original fault has been banished from the sacred precincts of Olympus and has fallen into a body and been ensnared in the cycle of re-births:

> There is an oracle of necessity, an ancient decree of the Gods, eternal, sealed fast with broad oaths, that when one of the divine spirits whose portion is long life sinfully stains his own limbs with bloodshed, and following hate has sworn a false oath—must wander for thrice ten thousand seasons far from the company of the blessed, being born throughout the period into all kinds of mortal shapes, which exchange one hard way of life for another. For the mighty air chases them into the sea, and the sea spews them forth on to the dry land, and the earth (drives them) towards the rays of the blazing sun; and the sun hurls them into the eddies of the aither. One (element) receives them from the other, and all loathe them. Of this number am I too now a fugitive from heaven and a wanderer, because I trusted in raging hate.[9]

> For by now I have been born as boy, girl, plant, bird, and dumb sea-fish.[10]

> How great the honor, how deep the happiness from which <here among mortals I wander exiled from Olympus>.[11]

Men who have been *purified* (and for these purifications he gave rules and norms) are then reborn into a most noble life and existence, whence they escape from the cycle of rebirths and return to being Gods among the Gods:

> At the last, they become seers, and bards, and physicians, and princes among earth-dwelling men, from which state they blossom forth as Gods highest in honor.[12]

And they enjoy a blessed life:

> Sharing the hearth of the other immortals, sharing the same table, freed from the lot of human griefs, indestructible.[13]

6. The Empedoclean aporias

Scholars in the past have discoursed at length on the relations which link the two poems and quickly add in conclusion that they are in contradiction with each other, not seeing any possibility of reconciling the physics of the poem *On Nature* with the mystical *Purifications*.[14]

But todays scholars have tended to markedly dissent from this conclusion.

Empedoclean physics is not at all like modern physics and Empedoclean naturalism is not modern materialism. We have seen, in fact, that the four elements are considered divinities and are even called with names of the Gods, just as Hate and Love are divinities. Furthermore, the cycle of births and deaths of the cosmos is made to depend on the play of Hate and Love, and in an analogous manner the cycle of births of individual men originate from an act of Discord and Hate, and in their termination from an act of Love, or generally from an act of total extinction by Hate. Therefore, Empedoclean naturalism contains right from its beginnings a mystical character, and with this it is in agreement with the mystical Orphism of the *Purifications*. Nevertheless, Orphic mysticism fits better into Empedoclean physics than it would fit into the doctrine of numbers of the Pythagoreans.

In fact, the Pythagoreans have only been able to join the soul-daimon to numbers, while Empedocles expressly said that all things are derived from the four elements and from Love and Hate: fish, beasts, men and women, and even the "long-lived Gods":

> But in (the reign) of Hate they are all different in form and separate, while in the (reign of) Love they come together and long for one another. For from these (elements) come all things that were and are and will be; and trees spring up, and men and women, and beasts and birds and water-nurtured fish, *and even the long-lived Gods who are highest in honor*. For these (elements) alone *exist*, but by running through one another *they become* different; to such a degree does mixing change them.[15]

The souls are (or can be) these "long-lived Gods." Nevertheless, it is (and at a higher level) the basic aporia which we have previously verified in all the Presocratics who have encountered Orphism. It consists in the *impossibility of allowing to re-enter within the rigid area of interest of the philosophy of nature (even understood as Empedocles intends it) the conception of a soul as structurally different from the body*, of a soul which must maintain in some way its own individuality, because then it can expiate its original fault and because then it can enjoy its final reward when it is purified. But in order to solve this aporia, it was necessary to reach the dimension of the spiritual and immaterial. The "second voyage" about which Plato speaks was also necessitated through the dissolution of this aporia.

Analogous remarks can be made about the Empedoclean conception of the Divine. Divinities are for him the four roots, Love and Hate as well as the "long-lived Gods" derived from them, and the Sphere (Σφαῖρος) is itself Divine. Even for Empedocles everything is full of Gods, as it was for the first Ionians. They are Gods which are far from being other than the principles of nature. They are rather identical with them, just as they are for the Ionians. Empedocles writes in Fragment 134:

> For this he is not equipped with a human head on his body, nor from

his back do two branches start; (he has) no feet, no swift knees, no hairy genital organs; but his is mind, holy and ineffable, *and only mind, which darts through the whole universe with its swift thoughts*

He does not refer, as some have thought, to a spiritual God beyond those mentioned above, since all things possess thought; but he certainly refers, as the similarity with Fragment twenty-nine proves, if not to the Sphere (Σφαῖρος) itself, to one of the elements (for example to fire or to the sun) or to one of the other two forces (Love).

The "second voyage" is necessary in order to surpass the naturalistic conception of the Divine.

II. Anaxagoras of Clazomenae

1. The homoiomeries

Anaxagoras[1], as well as Empedocles, tried to firmly maintain the Eleatic principle of the permanence of being and together with it to give an account of the phenomena. His attempt was undoubtedly progress compared to what the philosopher from Agrigentum was to accomplish. The Eleaticism of Anaxagoras emerges with total clarity especially in Fragment seventeen:

> The Greeks have an incorrect belief on *coming to being* and *passing away*. No thing comes into being or passes away, *but it is mixed together or separated from existing things*. Thus they would be correct if they called coming into being "mixing," and passing away "separating-off."[2]

But what are these things, these "existing things" which are composed; do they not generate all things and then decompose? They are not only four, as Empedocles claimed, but they are *infinite in quantity and number*. Let us read Fragment four:

> ...one must believe that there are many things of all sorts in all composite products, and the seeds of all things, which contain all kinds of shapes and colors and pleasant tastes. And men too were fitted together, and all other creatures which have life...

These "seeds" (σπέρματα) are hence the originative qualities of every kind, they are *qualitatively originative* and conceived in the Eleatic manner as immobile.

In order to understand this affirmation of Anaxagoras, we cannot prescind from the doctrine of Melissus,[3] who said, describing a negative hypothesis (an hypothesis of impossibility, we would say in modern terms), that the "many" *would be* only if *they were permanently always what each of them is*. Thus they would always be permanently identical as the Eleatic One-Being is. Well then, the Anaxagorean seeds (as previously the Empedoclean *roots*) are precisely the positive overturning of the negative hypothesis of Melissus. The *many*, therefore, are not only the many phenomenal things which appear and disappear, since they are the "the seeds of all things which contain all kinds of shapes and colors and pleasant tastes," where the term "seeds" means precisely originating, but they are also the terms "shapes (ἰδέας), colors, and tastes" which express the different qualities of the originative plurality.

These originative qualitative pluralities are, according to Anaxagoras, unlimited or infinite, as we previously noted. Fragment one states:

> All things were together [*scil.*, things in the sense of seeds], infinite in

number and in smallness. For the small also was infinite...

And Fragment three explains:

> For in small there is no least, but only a lesser: for it is impossible that being should not be; and in great there is always a greater. And it is equal in number to the small, but each thing is to itself both great and small.

The thought of Anaxagoras is hence as follows. The seeds have no limits in their magnitude, in the sense that each and every one is qualitatively unlimited and inexhaustible. They are not limited in their smallness, in the sense that each and every one is infinitely divisible. It is possible to divide any seed whatever (any substance-quality, we would say in non-Anaxagorean terms) into continually smaller parts because we can never arrive at nothing, which *is not* (what *is* can never *not be* says Anaxagoras expressly, with a strongly Eleatic vocabulary). It is easy to understand why the seeds must be unlimited even qualitatively, besides being so quantitatively, although this goes beyond what the fragments say and is suggested by the whole context of Anaxagorean discourse.

These seeds are commonly called *homoiomeries*, which means that when they are subdivided they always yield parts or things which are *qualitatively identical* (if hair is divided, the parts of hair that result are still hair; if gold is divided gold always results, etc.; no matter how much it is divided it always retains its identity). Such a term is to be kept because it has been ratified by many centuries of usage even if we are not entirely certain that it is authentic (perhaps it was coined by Aristotle; in favor of its authenticity there is only the use of it by Lucretius, *nunc et Anaxagorae scrutemur homoeomerian*).[4]

At first these *homoiomeries* were mingled all together in the original mixture, in which each of them were indistinguishable:

> Before these things were separated off, all things were together, nor was any color distinguishable, for the mixing of all things prevented this, the mixing of moist and dry and hot and cold and bright and dark, and there was a great quantity of earth in the mixture, and seeds infinite in number, not at all like one another.[5]

From this chaotic mixture, the various things were generated because of the movement produced, as we will immediately see below, from the divine intelligence. However, all the things which were generated are always a form of mixture. The mixture is qualitatively determined by the prevalence of this or that quality. They remain, each and every one, a mixture by containing, even if in the smallest parts, the seeds of all things which exist. "Everything is in everything,"[6] says Anaxagoras with a phrase that has become quite famous; or again: "in everything there are parts of everything."[7] Especially interesting is Fragment ten with the comment of the doxographer[8] who quoted it:

> Anaxagoras, having accepted the ancient opinion that nothing comes
> from nothing, eliminated coming-into-being and introduced the division
> in the place of coming-into-being. He said in fact that all things are
> mixed one with the other and grow through dividing. Also in the seed
> itself there are hairs, nails, veins, arteries, skins and bones and they
> are invisible in the smallest of their parts, but growing little by little
> through division. "As in fact," he says, "could there be produced from
> that which is not hair hair and flesh from that which is not flesh?"
> And he says this not only of bodies, but also of colors; in fact, black is
> contained in white and white in black, and the same with regard to
> weights, he maintains that the light is mixed with the heavy and this
> with that.

Here, therefore, is why coming-into-being, development, and the growth
of things are possible; because the all is in all and consequently it is possible
that all can arise from all.

These propositions would be incomprehensible outside the context of
the Eleatic problematic in general, and in particular that of Melissus, as
Calogero has explained well: "Flesh cannot arise from not flesh, nor hair
from not hair, insofar as the prohibition of Parmenides that 'nothing is,'
prevents it. This prohibition is tied by Melissus to each single thing-named
existent, and hence a guarantee of the continual perdurance of each single
thing-named existent. Since the precise shape of each single thing is found
in the infinity of its constituents and in the constituents of these constituents, even if next to them there are to be found the constituents of other
things, as each reality present in the appearance the shape of the constituents that are prevailing in it. This world of the 'homoiomeries' is a world
essentially 'formed,' a world which is hardened, so to speak, and has sublimated every form insofar as all the infinite differences of reality are
justified in their innumerable variety. The world of the 'homoiomeries' is
even shown to be infinitely more true than we think, since it is immensely
more vast in its greatness as well as in its smallness."[9]

In this way the Eleatic principle is preserved with regard to *quality* and
analogously with regard to *quantity*. The totality of things is always equal,
it neither grows nor diminishes:

> These things being thus separated off, one must understand that all
> things are in no way less or more (for it is not possible for them to be
> more than all), but all things are forever equal.[10]

2. The divine Mind

We have said that things are born from the original mixture because of
the *movement* impressed on it by *mind* or voῦς. We ought now to determine
what is the nature and role of mind. Here is how Anaxagoras describes it

in the very fine Fragment twelve:

> Other things all contain a part of everything, but mind is infinite and self-ruling, and is mixed with no thing, but is alone by itself. If it were not by itself, but were mixed with anything else, it would have had a share of all things, if it were mixed with anything; for in everything there is a portion of everything, as I have said before. And the things mixed (with mind) would have prevented it, so that it could not rule over any thing in the same way as it can being alone by itself. For it is the finest of all things, and the purest, and has complete understanding of everything, and has the greatest power. All things which have life, both the greater and the less, are ruled by mind. Mind took command of the universal revolution, so as to make (things) revolve at the outset. And at first things began to revolve from some small point, but now the revolution extends over a greater area, and will spread even further. And the things which were mixed together, and separated off, and divided, were all understood by mind. And whatever they were going to be, and whatever things were then in existence that are not now, and all things that now exist and whatever shall exist – all were arranged by mind, as also the revolution now followed by the stars, the sun and moon, and the air and aither which were separated off. It was this revolution which caused the separation off. And dense separates from rare, and hot from cold, and bright from dark, and dry from wet. There are many portions of many things. And nothing is absolutely separated off or divided the one from the other except mind. Mind is all alike, both the greater and the less. But nothing else is like anything else, but each individual thing is and was most obviously that of which it contains the most.

The fragment undoubtedly contains one of the most powerful intuitions conceived and expressed in the whole course of Presocratic philosophy; the intuition, that is, that the principle is an infinite reality, separate from everything else, "the finest" and "the most pure," equal to itself and especially intelligent, wise, and precisely, insofar as it is such, it moves and orders all things. His contemporaries, but especially the subsequent philosophers, will heartily agree that this intuition implies something truly new.

In addition, we need to beware of believing that Anaxagoras had now achieved the concept of the immaterial and the spiritual, as many modern scholars maintain, especially under the influence of the interpretation of Zeller, who translated the Anaxagorean term *Nous* by the German "Geist," that is, the English "Spirit," and wrote: "There is no doubt that Anaxagoras truly thought [mind] was an incorporeal being. [It could be concluded] just from this conception which so stresses the superiority of spirit, its being in itself, its unmixed character, its absolute homogeneity, its power and its wisdom..."[11] But Zeller himself regretted in part some of these assertions immediately after making them, and he modified them as follows: "...and even if from the fact that the concept of the incorporeal does not appear very clearly in his exposition that should not be charged solely to the inadequacy of his language, even if perhaps he had really conceived the notion of spirit as one of the finest material which moves itself in space, penetrating all things, all this manner of speaking did not disguise his intention."[12] Consequently, Zeller feels constrained to speak of a "semi-materialism"[13] which ends by contradicting what he has said above. The embarrassment of Zeller is even more evident when responding to those scholars who correctly deny that there is in Fragment twelve any discovery of the immaterial. He has only this argument to offer, "Anaxagoras certainly did not speculate in a clear and obvious way about the immateriality of Nous, but in any case he intended to distinguish it in its essence from everything which is composed."[14] But anyone can see that this argument proves nothing. The fact that Nous is not composed does not imply at all, simply by that fact, that it is immaterial. It is simply a matter which, by its privileged nature, can be involved with other things without thereby being mixed with them or them being mixed with it.

The truth is that Anaxagoras did not possess the concept of immateriality just as he did not possess the concept of the *material as such*. As we know through having met the issue many times in preceding thinkers, the speculative area of interest of the Presocratics *did not embrace the two categories of matter and spirit* and introduction of these categories as hermeneutic canons belongs to an incorrect understanding of the thought of these philosophers. It has justly been observed that with Anaxagoras "the thought about the Divine improved, but did not succeed in getting away from its naturalistic presuppositions."[15] We add - and this we will provide with more than ample confirmation - that in order to free itself from such a presupposition ancient thought must be truly overturned, and this will only result from the epic "second voyage" of Plato.

3. The Anaxagorean aporias

The pluralism of Anaxagoras had a kind of resonance, but not many were to follow it. Many obscurities are involved in the doctrine of the *seeds* and the *mixture*. Moreover, modern scholars themselves not only did not succeed in understanding some difficulties implicated in these concepts, but they have even multiplied them incredibly. The interpretation that we have given must necessarily be simplified and skim over these specific difficulties (which would be discussed properly only in a monograph). However we can say in brief that it is a matter fundamentally of difficulties arising from the attempt to extend to qualitative multiplicity the status of Eleatic being. In order to be admitted without falling into aporias, qualitative multiplicity demands, as Plato will teach, a kind of "killing of Parmenides," since Eleatic being structurally destroys any differences.

We have previously spoken about the character of the concept of Nous. It remains to add the criticism that Plato and Aristotle will make and that we can summarize in these brief statements. Anaxagoras – says Plato[16] – promised to explain things in terms of Nous, but then in great part he did not fulfill that promise, continuing to explain things physically, as did his predecessors. Anaxagoras – adds Aristotle[17] – brings in Nous and calls it a cause when he does not know how to overcome an obstacle, and he uses it almost like a *deus ex machina*. But it is clear that Anaxagoras could not do otherwise. His notion of Nous was reached through an intuition and not through logical reasoning. All those categories which, on the contrary, Plato and Aristotle firmly possess are lacking to him. These categories permit them to formulate the above-mentioned criticisms and make him incapable of doing the same. They were all categories which presuppose the results of the "second voyage," to which Plato will be forced, as he says in the *Phaedo*, after he tried to read the book of Anaxagoras.

III. The Atomists

1. The discovery of the atoms as principles

The atomistic doctrine, founded by Leucippus[1] and systematically developed and brought to completion by his follower Democritus,[2] signals the final attempt to respond, remaining within the Presocratic area of interest, to the aporias generated by Eleaticism. It tried to preserve the basic principle of Eleaticism without denying at the same time the phenomena (Leucippus grasped the Eleatic problematic perfectly; as we have previously stated, he was the disciple of Zeno and Melissus).[3]

Aristotle has already perfectly specified the relations between Eleaticism and Atomism and expressed it in an illuminating page which is worthwhile reading because it is one of the most outstanding documents for the reconstruction of the thought of the Atomists:

> The most systematic and consistent theory, however, and one that applied to all bodies, was advanced by Leucippus and Democritus: and, in maintaining it, they took as their starting-point what naturally comes first [*scil.*, the phenomena]. For some of the older philosophers [*scil.*, the Eleatics] thought that "what is" must of necessity be "one" and immovable. The void, they argue, "is not": but unless there is a void with a separate being of its own, "what is" cannot be moved—nor again can it be "many," since there is nothing to keep things apart. ... Leucippus, however, thought he had a theory which harmonized with sense-perception and would not abolish either coming-to-be and passing-away or motion and the multiplicity of things. He made these concessions to the facts of perception: on the other hand, he conceded to the monists that there could be no motion without a void. The result is a theory which he states as follows: "The void is 'not-being,' and no part of 'what is' is 'not-being'; for what 'is' in the strict sense of the term is an absolute *plenum*. This *plenum*, however, is not 'one': on the contrary, it is a 'many,' infinite in number, and invisible owing to the minuteness of the bulk. The 'many' move in the void (for there is a void): and by coming together they produce 'coming-to-be,' while by separating they produce 'passing-away.' Moreover, they act and suffer action wherever they chance to be in contact (for there they are not 'one'), and they generate by being put together and becoming intertwined. From the genuinely-one, on the other hand, there never could have come-to-be a multiplicity, nor from the genuinely-many a 'one': that is impossible. But (just as Empedocles and some of the other philosophers say that things suffered action through their pores, so) all 'alteration' and all 'passion' take place in the way that has been explained: breaking-up (i.e., passing-away) is effected by means of the void, and so too growth—solids creeping in to fill the void places. Empedocles too is practically bound to adopt the same theory as Leucippus. For he must say that there are certain solids which,

> however, are indivisible—unless there are continuous pores all through the body. But this last alternative is impossible: for then there will be nothing solid in the body (nothing besides the pores) but all of it will be void. It is necessary, therefore, for his 'contiguous discretes' to be indivisible, while the intervals between them—which he calls 'pores'— must be void. . . . From what has been said, generation and dissolution for Leucippus would be two processes which may be understood by means of the void and contact . . ."[4]

Aristotle speaks clearly and well; it will be sufficient to add some analyses to fill out the picture.

In a certain sense, the atoms of Leucippus are nearer to Eleatic being than the Empedoclean elements and the Anaxagorean *homoiomeries* because they are qualitatively undifferentiated. As we will see, they are only geometrically differentiated, and hence they maintain again the equality of Eleatic being of itself with itself (equality which is precisely an undifferentiated absolute). The atoms are shards of the Eleatic One-Being; as infinite One-Beings they try to hold on to as many of the characteristics as possible of the One-Being.

The fundamental intuition of the Leucippean system must be drawn chiefly from the great Fragment eight of Melissus: "If things were many," said Melissus, "they would have to be of the same kind as I say the One is";[5] and in so speaking he believed that he had reduced to absurdity the pluralism in which men believed. The many, in order to be, must be eternal because this is the status of being. To be enduring is not to change; instead, the many change continually and therefore do not exist. Leucippus pins the Melissean argument on its back, making what in the Eleatic system was an absurd conclusion the very foundation of his system. The many exist because they can exist as the Melissean One, they can endure always and be immutable, that is, be conformed to the supreme status of being. He is not speaking, therefore, of an empirical multiplicity given through the senses, but of a further multiplicity, not perceptible, the foundation and reason for the very being of the sensible multiple. Just as Empedoclean and Anaxagorean pluralism, as we saw, overturned in a positive sense the Melissean hypothesis of a multiplicity which kept its identical *qualities*, so also the pluralism of the atoms of Leucippus again more completely fulfilled in a positive sense the hypothesis of multiplicity which keeps its identity as a nature qualitatively undifferentiated, and which as such was the reason for the being of the qualitatively differentiated phenomenal multiplicity.[6]

Analogously, the themes of the void, of the plenum, of movement and its hypothetical conditions contained in Fragment seven of Melissus are the other immediate antecedents starting from which Leucippus could arrive at the doctrine of the atom. In Parmenides we met the theme of the plenum but not of the void. Melissus developed this notion, opposing dialectically the notion of the void and the plenum. Leucippus constructed his conception of the atom precisely in terms of the plenum and the void and connected the possibility of movement with the void, once again overturning the negative hypothesis of Melissus in a positive sense.[7]

But we must yet make clear one fundamental point. To modern ears the word "atom" evokes inevitably those meanings which the term has acquired in modern science, from Galileo to contemporary physics. So it is necessary that we strip the term of these associated connotations if we want to discover the original metaphysical meaning it had in the philosophy of the Abderites. The atom of the Abderites contains in itself the typical mark of Hellenic thought. The mark is the atom-shape, the differentiation from other atoms through shape, order, and position, eidetically thought and represented. Alfieri clarifies this point rather nicely, "...when the neuter term τὸ ἄτομον (the indivisible thing, or substance) is not used in a generic sense, the term ἄτομος is always feminine and not masculine; ἄτομος in this case does not imply οὐσία (substance), which would be an anachronistic notion, but rather ἰδέα (shape). This is positively attested to, since it is explicitly stated by lexicographers and doxographers, whom we have no reason not to believe in this case, that Democritus used the term ἰδέα often, if not always, to designate the atom. What does the term ἰδέα mean? Etymologically, especially at this historical stage of the development of the Greek language in which we find it with Democritus (also not to gratuitously attribute the use of the term 'idea' to Leucippus, who is a little before him), here there is no doubt that ἰδέα means the visible. But the atom, because of its smallness which has been asserted as a consequence of its indivisibility and because it is difficult to uphold as indivisible what is perceptible to the senses and thus can only be maintained as susceptible of being fragmented into parts, is invisible. Then in what sense is ἰδέα visible? It is visible evidently only to the vision of the intellect, the reasoning intellect, which begins from the visible corporeal things and moves far beyond what the senses can attain and ends in a quintessential and potentiated world which is analogous to the visible corporeal world. Shape, hence visual geometry, is what is visible to the intellect but again analogous to the sensible, and hence retaining the capacity to generate the concrete sensible. Such is the 'idea,' or form, which can be conceived by a materialistic philosophy which does not admit the immaterial except for the void but defines the void correctly as not-being. The affirmation of an immaterial reality is not encountered before Plato (and that is precisely Plato's greatness); before him there was no distinction of two levels of reality, the one material and the other immaterial. In atomism, in fact, the material and immaterial are on the same level, they are being and not-being, the two inseparable terms of the dialectic of reason, admitted now (unlike in Eleaticism) wholly for the purpose of providing experience with a logos. And then the form is visible to the intellect; it is material in nature simply insofar as it is individuated and quantitatively, but only quantitatively, differentiated. Before the Idea of Plato, which is a quality involving immateriality and finality, there was the *idea* of Democritus which is a quantity involving materiality and necessity. But it is unusual that as materialism so idealism, as Democritus so Plato defined 'idea' as the truest reality that exists beyond appearances and illusions of a-critical and a-problematic experience. Ἄτομος ἰδέα is the first affirmation of individuality, of the substantiality of individual being in Greek philosophy. That was the greatness of Democritus."[8]

2. Atoms, mechanical movement, and necessity

All the things which exist, all their affections, qualities, and states are derived from the qualitatively equal and quantitatively and geometrically differentiated atoms. Empedocles and Anaxagoras derived the visible qualities from the originating qualitatively differentiated seeds, the Atomists derived all the qualitatively differentiated phenomena from quantitatively determined geometricals. The first distinction thus arose between what will be said to be "primary qualities" and "secondary qualities," to speak in modern philosophical terms. The former are the geometrico-mechanistic qualities which characterize the atoms, the latter are manifestations of the phenomena derived from the collisions of the atoms as well as from the relation of things to our senses.

We have already seen that analogously to what Empedocles and Anaxagoras have said birth and death, generation and corruption are denied as such by the Atomists. Birth is the aggregation of atoms, death is their disaggregation or the destruction of the atomic composite, without anything being derived from nothing and nothing going into anything in the process. But then what makes the atoms congregate and then separate?

Empedocles and Anaxagoras, as we have seen above, have introduced a new "cause," which Aristotle will call the cause from which movement takes its origin, or the efficient cause: the former introduced Love and Hate as kinetic powers, the latter introduced instead Mind. Moreover—this we have also seen—whether the Physicists prior to Parmenides either could not expressly speak of this cause or could speak of it only in a vague way, that option was no longer possible after the drastic rejections of every form of motion by Eleaticism, especially by thinkers who made as their aim the rehabilitation of the phenomenal world of which movement is the most basic characteristic. So the response of the Atomists to the problem differs both from the response by Empodecles, still full of imaginative elements, and from the more novel (but only intuitively achieved) approach of Anaxagoras. Movement is derived from nothing else than movement itself in the sense that the atoms are from the beginning and forever in motion through their very nature.

But how is this movement of the atoms to be conceived in detail? Zeller has maintained an interpretation which has become canonic according to which the original movement of the atoms was that generated by their weight in falling. The swift swirling movement of a vortex would have originated from the falling weight of the atoms and from this then would the world have been generated.[9] But later studies than those of Zeller have brought to light that this is not the original view of the Abderites, but rather of the Epicureans.[10] *a*) The original movement of the atoms, the pre-cosmic one, must be conceived as a random movement in all directions, like atmospheric dust which we see randomly moving caught in the sun's rays as they filter through a window. *b*) The cosmogonic movement is thought to be different from the original movement. It brings on the production of the world and it is a vortex or swift swirling motion which "is produced when, by the presence of a void of considerable size, there is a flowing in and confluence of the atoms of various shapes and weights in free space. The running together of material elements of diverse weights produces a swirling movement in which, acting from the primary law of aggregation which is that of the attraction of like toward like, the vortex acts like a sifter, so that the heavier elements sink toward the center of the vortex, those more minute are disposed toward the void . . . ,"[11] and thus the cosmos is formed. *c*) Finally, there is also a movement of the atoms in the formed cosmos which consists in atoms liberated from the atomic aggregation and which form the effluvia (as for example, the effluvia of perfumes).

It is understandable that as the atoms are infinite so also necessarily are the worlds which are constituted by them. There are diverse worlds and identical worlds, both of which come-into-being, develop, and finally perish, and so on without end.

The cosmos and the things contained in it, all of them from the greatest to the smallest, according to the Atomists, are produced *only from the atoms and from their movement.* Hence everything is explained in a rigorously mechanistic and necessary fashion.

Curiously, both Leucippus and Democritus have gone down in history, as is well known, as among those who posit the world "by chance," contrary to what was not only their intention but also the actual meaning of their thought. Therefore it will be appropriate to give some time to the question. It has come down to us that Democritus habitually said that he preferred to discover one *causal explanation* of some phenomena than be crowned the king of the Persians.[12] There is no better witness to explain the mental attitude of the Abderites. For them everything is the precise result of a definite cause. Nothing happens and nothing is thinkable without a cause. Therefore all happens according to *strict necessity.*

Leucippus expressly proclaims universal causal necessity in the only textual fragment of the philosopher preserved by Aetius:

> Leucippus said that all happens in conformity with necessity and that this corresponds to destiny. In fact he states in his treatise *On Mind*: "Nothing happens at random; everything happens out of reason and

by necessity."[13]

The same concept is maintained by Democritus, as Diogenes Laertius writes:

> All things happen by virtue of necessity, the vortex being the cause of the creation of all things, and this he calls necessity.[14]

The nature of necessity for Democritus, according to what Aetius says, consisted:

> in the impenetrability, in movement and in the push of matter.[15]

Why, then, is Democritus judged as "positing the world by chance"? *Chance, in this context, does not mean the contrary of cause* in general, but *the contrary of a particular kind of cause*, or better still, of one of those which will be called the four causes by Aristotle, that is, *the contrary of the final cause.* The statement means, therefore, not that the Abderites had denied that the world has causes, but only that it has *final causes.* It is evident that it is a judgment based on presuppositions which will be acquired only through Plato and Aristotle.

But this clearly permits us to say something else. The Atomists did not deny the final cause because it was not yet discovered nor explicated (Anaxagoras, a contemporary of Leucippus, it is true, with his notion of Nous caught a glimpse of the problem of the cause of order, but he had not adequately brought it up to critical awareness). Hence, the final cause could not be consciously denied because it was not yet present in the speculations on a thematic level. In addition, the clear and rigorous deduction of the system of the Atomists in the attempt to wholly explain everything only with these two principles (atoms and movement) clearly enabled the following thinkers to grasp what was lacking in those two principles. It came clearly in view that from atomic *chaos* and from chaotic movement it is not structurally possible for a *cosmos*, an ordered whole, to arise except by admitting as principles intelligence and the intelligibles. The credit for this discovery will belong to Plato, but it is certain that Plato could affirm so rigorously the necessity for a teleological cause just because he benefited from the radical experience derived from his adversary Democritus.

3. Man, soul, and the Divine

As every form of mechanism, so also atomistic thought reveals its insufficiencies chiefly in its explanation of organisms and in a particular way the human organism, its life, and its knowledge. The human body, as all other things, is constituted from the clash of atoms, and so naturally even the soul. The soul, which is what gives life and hence movement to the body, is constituted of atoms which are finer than the others, smooth and spherical, of a fiery nature. These atoms are spread throughout the entire body and thus give it life. Because of their fineness they tend also to exit from the body, but with respiration all these fiery atoms which succeed in escaping are slowly re-integrated. When respiration ceases death ensues, and all the fiery atoms in the body disperse.

The soul is, hence, of the same nature as the body. It is difficult to explain its pre-eminence over the body, which Democritus maintained in various ways, including a warning, as we will see better later on, to care for the soul and not the body and to search for the goods of the soul which are divine and not those of the body which are only human. The atoms of the soul have, it is true, a more perfect form, but they are still *qualitatively* equal to all the other atoms. In any case, given the privileged position which is accorded the soul in the system of the Atomists, it is easy to explain how they are said to be *divine*, and how in them more than in any other things the divine is visible; "principia mentis quae sunt in eodem universo deos esse dicit" [the principles of mind which are in the universe itself are said to be gods], Cicero writes.[16] The "principles of mind" are the fiery atoms of the soul with which the mind and thought are identified. Like all their predecessors, therefore, the Atomists identified the divine with what exists in the highest way in their systems.[17]

4. Knowledge

Atoms and movement also explain knowledge. From things emanate, as we know already, the effluvia of the atoms, which attain contact with the senses and generate in this way sensation and cognition. The contact of the atoms, which through the effluvia arrive from things to the senses, permits similar atoms outside of us to be impressed on the atoms similar in us, like acting on like, as Empedocles has already stated.

Democritus, on the basis of his naturalism, could certainly not oppose *sensation* to *intellectual knowledge* and had difficulty distinguishing one from the other on the critical level. However he considered sensations as subjective and obscure and only intellectual knowledge as genuine knowledge, that is, capable of penetrating to the foundation of things. Fragment nine states it and the context relative to it is given by Sextus Empiricus:

> And Democritus in some places abolishes the things that appear to the senses and asserts that none of them appears in truth but only in opinion, the true fact in things existent being the existence of atoms and void; for "By convention," he says, "is sweet, by convention bitter, by convention hot, by convention cold, by convention color; but by truth atoms and void." This means: sensible objects are conventionally assumed and opined to exist, but they do not truly exist, but only the atoms and the void. And in his *Confirmations*, although he had promised to ascribe the confirmatory evidence to the senses, nonetheless he is found condemning them. For he says: "Now truly that we do not

comprehend what the nature of each thing is or is not, has been often made plain" (R. G. Bury, trans.).

In Fragment eleven, which we will quote with the relevant comments of Sextus Empiricus, we read:

> But in his *Canons* he [Democritus] says that there are two kinds of knowledge, one by means of the senses, the other by means of the intelligence; and of these he calls that by means of the intelligence "genuine," ascribing to it trustworthiness in the judgment of truth, but that by means of the senses he terms "bastard," denying it inerrancy in the distinguishing of what is true. He expressly declares— "Of knowledge there are two forms, the genuine and the bastard; and to the bastard belong all these—sight, hearing, smell, taste, touch; but the other form is distinct from this and genuine." Then, while thus preferring the genuine to the bastard, he proceeds: "Whenever the bastard kind is unable any longer to see what has become too small, or to hear or smell or taste or perceive it by touch <one must have recourse to> another and finer <instrument>." Thus, according to this man also, reason is the criterion, and he calls it "genuine knowledge" (R. G. Bury, trans.).

But these are distinctions which conform to interior experience; therefore, they are contrary to the principles of atomism. In fact, in order to be justified at the critical level, they need the categories that are only arrived at with Plato.

5. Democritean ethics

There have come down to us numerous fragments of an ethical nature. The particular presence of a moral thematic in Democritus, on the other hand, is easily explained if we keep in mind that he lived in the Socratic period. However, he was far from knowing how to ground moral discourse philosophically. He remained with respect to moral philosophy almost entirely within the intellectual position of the Presocratics.

Democritus considered happiness the goal of life, and happiness consisted not in pleasures of the body, but in those of the soul.

> Happiness, like unhappiness, is a property of the soul.[18]

> Happiness does not dwell in flocks of cattle or in gold. The soul is the dwelling place of the (good and evil) genius.[19]

> He who chooses the advantages of the soul chooses things more divine, but he who chooses those of the body, chooses things human.[20]

> Men find happiness neither by means of the body nor through possessions, but through uprightness and prudence.[21]

Therefore Democritus exalted the victory of man over his sensible desires, which he considered to be inferior, and exalted self-control:

> The brave man is not only he who overcomes the enemy, but he who is stronger than pleasures. Some men are masters of cities, but are enslaved to women.[22]

He exalted, in addition, not only justice and the good but likewise the will to the good:

> Virtue consists not in avoiding wrong-doing, but in having no wish thereto.[23]

He affirmed, consequently, that it is not fearing the loss of reputation among others that holds us back from evil, but the respect for oneself:

> One must not respect the opinion of other men more than one's own, nor must one be more ready to do wrong if no one will know than if all will know. One must respect one's own opinion most, and this must stand as the law of one's soul, preventing one from doing anything improper.[24]
>
> Refrain from crimes not through fear, but through duty.[25]
>
> Do not say or do what is base, even when you are alone. Learn to feel shame in your own eyes much more than before others.[26]

He warned against envy, hatred, and the vices in general. And if the following fragment is authentic, he also professed cosmopolitanism:

> To a wise man, the whole earth is open; for the native land of a good soul is the whole earth.[27]

This is a thought which the Sophists and the Socratics especially supported and disseminated.

As can be seen from these few citations, the moral thoughts of Democritus are not too far removed in form from the sententious pronouncements of the poets and the Seven Sages, and in substance they do not agree in any way with the basic idea of the system which makes of man a mere mechanical aggregation of material atoms. These thoughts are on this side of moral philosophy. Before moral philosophy could arise, speculation must first radically change the very axis of its problematic. This change will be produced only by the Sophists and Socrates in a way which we will see in detail shortly.

IV. The Eclectic Physicists

1. The phenomenon of the eclectic physicists and the decline of the philosophy of nature

The series of Physicists closes out with some thinkers which modern philosophical historiography has qualified as "eclectics." The qualification is only halfway adequate because it is true that they are thinkers who take up the elements of their thinking from more than one philosopher which we have examined and with the obvious intent of mediating and grounding their positions. However it is likewise true that they are thinkers who (at least insofar as they are referred to in the more ancient tradition) have escaped, almost entirely, the sense of the revolution produced by Parmenides and Eleaticism, and consequently even the meaning of the successive proposals of the Pluralists, which in different ways was intended to undo the aporias which Eleaticism had left as an inheritance for philosophic thought.

It is precisely this incomprehension of the Eleatic aporias and of the urgent necessity of resolving them which lead the eclectic Physicists to return to "monism," judging "pluralism" in a negative way. They wanted, in substance, to return to the position of Ionian speculation and hence *to the affirmation of unity and indeed the unicity of the Principle*, welcoming nevertheless further speculative results that therefore either do not corrode this fundamental principle, or that generally do not support pluralistic positions.

Thus Hippon of Samos[1] proposed a return to Thales and maintained that water is the principle of all things,[2] but he accepted the Heraclitean fire, which according to him is generated from water itself and then "conquered its parent to form the cosmos."[3] Others[4] instead posited as a generative principle "an element more dense than fire or more subtle than air,"[5] or "an element more subtle than water but more swift than air,"[6] and they conceived it, in the Ionian manner, as infinite.[7] Here the attempt is evident to mediate between Heraclitus and Anaximenes on the one hand, and Thales and Anaximander on the other.

But it was not these vain efforts at the mediation of positions already definitively surpassed that could return life to the philosophy of nature, which had by now nearly exhausted its strength. The ancients were well aware of the minor importance of Hippon, whom Aristotle judged in a decidedly negative manner,[8] and of the other Eclectics of whom we have spoken (to whom Aristotle himself has alluded without mentioning any names).[9]

Our interest in these Physicists is restricted, as a matter of fact, to only one thinker, that is, Diogenes of Apollonia (of whom there have come down to us, in addition to indirect testimonies, some important fragments); and not so much for his attempt to return to monism but rather for the systematic exploitation of the Anaxagorean discovery of the notion of Nous, of Intelligence, for reasons that we will immediately see.

2. Diogenes of Apollonia and his historical significance

The reasons that forced Diogenes[10] not to accept pluralism and to return to monism are well known from an extant fragment and from a testimony of Aristotle's. Diogenes thought that the elements were multiple and each in its proper nature were different from the others and not derivable from the others nor transformable into each other, so they (and the things derived from each of them) could not structurally (given their differences in nature) be mixed together with them, and none were subject to mutual changes. In others words, one could not either damage the others nor help the others nor, vice versa, receive benefit or damage from the others, and finally, it would likewise be unthinkable that from earth, plants and animals were born. So that all this may be possible, the element or originative principle must be single and everything must be derived from it through alteration or change of the principle itself. Here are the exact words of Diogenes:

> It seems to me, to sum up the whole matter, that all existing things are created by the alteration of the same thing and are the same thing. This is very obvious. For if the things now existing in this universe— water and earth and air and fire and all the other things which are seen to exist in this world: if any one of these were different in its own nature, and were not the same thing which was transformed in many ways and changed, in no way could things mix with one another, nor could there by any profit or damage which accrued from one thing to another, nor could any plant grow out of the earth, nor any animal or any other thing come into being, unless it were so compounded as to be the same. But all these things come into being in different forms at different times by change of the same substance and they return to the same.[11]

And here is the parallel Aristotelian testimony:

> And in this respect Diogenes is right when he argues that "unless all things were derived from one, reciprocal action and passion could not have occurred." The hot thing, e.g., would not be cooled and the cold thing in turn be warmed: for heat and cold do not change reciprocally into one another, but what changes, it is clear, is the substratum.[12]

This principle thus, for Diogenes, is not an *intermediate* between air and water or fire but, as for Anaximenes, it is *air*, as the testimonies and the fragments for the most part inform us, and precisely it is "infinite air."[13] The eclecticism of Diogenes is manifested therefore in other directions, and more precisely in the attempt to make coincide the air of Anaximenes with the Nous of Anaxagoras by affirming that this air-principle is "endowed with much intelligence."[14]

It was exactly this identification of mind with air that permitted Diogenes, although purely in a physical manner and for aporetic and problematic reasons, to explain with mind all the phenomena of the universe, which could not but be derived and hence be explained by a single air-principle, thus they could not but be derived and hence be explained by the coincidence of mind with air. Here are the words of Diogenes:

> Such a distribution would not have been possible without mind, that all things should have their measure: winter and summer and night and day and rains and winds and periods of fine weather; other things also, if one will study them closely, will be found to have the best possible arrangement.[15]

And in Fragment five we read:

> And it seems to me that that which has mind is that which is called air by mankind; and further, that by this all creatures are guided, and that it rules everything; for this in itself seems to me to be God and to reach everywhere and to arrange everything and to be in everything. And there is nothing which has no share of it; but the share of each thing is not the same as that of any other, but on the contrary there are many forms both of the air itself and of mind; for it is manifold in form: hotter and colder and dryer and wetter and more stationary or having a swifter motion; and there are many other differences inherent in it and infinite of taste and color. Also in all animals the soul is the same thing; it is air, warmer than that outside in which we move about but much colder than that nearer the sun. This degree of warmth is not the same in any of the animals (and indeed, it is not the same among different human beings), it differs, but not greatly, so as to be similar. But in fact, no one thing among things subject to change can possibly be exactly like any other thing without becoming the same thing. Since therefore change is manifold, animals also are manifold and many and not like one another either in form or in way of life or in intelligence because of the large number of changes. Nevertheless, all things live, see, and hear by the same thing (air), and all have the rest of mind also from the same.[16]

From this fragment it is clear that our souls, just as the first principle, are air-mind, insofar as they are a moment themselves of the principle, fragments so to speak of the principle which are derived from the principle and return to the principle. Our philosopher says:

> Further, in addition to these there are also the following important indications: men and all other animals live by means of air which they breathe in, and this for them is both soul and mind, as had been clearly demonstrated in this treatise; and if this is taken from them, mind also leaves them.[17]

The judgment made about Diogenes by philosophical historiography has been mostly negative and many times it has made canonical the following judgment of Zeller: "However much such an attempt can be worthy of consideration, still one cannot accord to it very high philosophical value; the principle merit of the Apollonian seems rather to be placed in the researches with which he tried to promote the empirical knowledge of nature and the empirical explanation of it; his philosophical hypotheses were, on the contrary, offered to him already defined by his predecessors, that is, by Anaxagoras and by the ancient Physicists. Greek philosophy as a whole would have by this time in the age of Diogenes taken a route which would lead it away more and more from the orientation belonging to ancient Ionian physics.[18]

Actually, the most recent research[19] has moved to a radical reorientation of Zeller's judgment for the following reasons. Anaxagoras had, it is true, introduced for the first time mind as a principle, but then (the ancients would be in complete agreement on this, as we have already recognized above) he did not make use basically of his discovery, and in the explanation of the world had recourse for the most part to the traditional physical causes and to mind he appealed rather rarely. Instead, Diogenes identified mind with the principle of all things and used it systematically, thus elevating that *teleological conception of the cosmos* which had commenced with Anaxagoras and carrying it to its extreme limits, the limits into which only those who would revolutionize the areas of interest of the philosophy of *physis* would be able to proceed.

But there is more. The teleological conception of Diogenes had a notable influence on the Athenian environment and is one of the starting points of that conception of God and of universal finality which Socrates made his own and developed in a non-physical sense, as we will see in its place, and as we will document. Diogenes signals hence a stage which we cannot avoid if we wish to understand the evolution of the theological and teleological thought of the Greeks.[20]

3. Archelaus of Athens

Let us conclude the treatment of the Eclectic Physicists with the mention of Archelaus of Athens.[21] Diogenes Laertius writes of him:

> Archelaus, the son of Apollodorus, or as some say of Midon, was a citizen of Athens or of Miletus; he was a pupil of Anaxagoras, who first brought natural philosophy from Ionia to Athens. Archelaus was the teacher of Socrates. He was called the physicist inasmuch as with him natural philosophy came to an end, as soon as Socrates had introduced ethics. It would seem that Archelaus himself also treated of ethics, for he has discussed laws and goodness and justice; Socrates took the subject from him and, having improved it to the utmost, was regarded as its inventor.[22]

Another ancient source thus summarizes the thought of Archelaus:

> Archelaus, was Athenian by birth, son of Apollodorus. He admitted the mixture of matter, similarly to Anaxagoras, and his first principles were the same. He said that innately there is a certain mixture in the mind. The mutual separation of hot and cold is the principle of movement; hot is in motion and cold is at rest. Water melts and flows to the center, where fiery air and earth are generated, from which the one is forced toward the height and the other is deposited at the bottom. The earth hence is immobile and has its origin through these causes. It lies then at the center, without being, so to speak, any part of the universe. The air rules everything, derived from combustion: at the very beginning it caught fire and produced the nature of the stars, among which the greatest is the sun, and in second place the moon, and of the others some are very small and some are very large. Archelaus says that the heavens are inclined and thus the sun diffused light on the earth and made the air transparent, the earth dry. In fact the earth at first was a marshy lake, being high around the rim and concave at the center. And as a sign of the concavity of the earth he adduced the fact that the sun does not rise on high at the same time in all places, which is contrary to what must occur if the surface of the earth were flat. Concerning animals, he says that the earth grew warm first of all in its lower part, where hot and cold are mixed, and thus many kinds of animals appeared, including man. They all had the same food, getting their nourishment from the ooze (and they were short-lived). Later on they were engendered from each other. Men then were distinguished from the other animals, and they created rulers, laws, arts, cities, and other institutions. He says in addition that in all the animals intellect is inborn equally, and also, that each animal uses intellect, some more quickly, others more slowly.[23]

Other sources insist again more emphatically on the air as principle, indeed on *infinite air* identified with *intellect*,[24] going back thus to a position very close to that of Diogenes of Apollonia.

The importance of this thinker is wholly in the role which has been attributed to him, not only by Diogenes Laertius (in the passage read above) but by numerous other sources, as the "teacher" of Socrates.[25] In addition Aristophanes himself, in some passages of the *Clouds*, puts in Socrates's mouth some statements that are clearly taken from Diogenes and from the eclectic followers of Anaxagoras.[26]

Hence, it will be necessary to start from Diogenes of Apollonia and from Archelaus, as well as from Sophistic philosophy in order to grasp in an adequate way the thought of Socrates and his revolutionary message. First, we must study in depth the phenomenon of Sophistry, whose spread and whose success coincided exactly with the moment of regression of the philosophy of the *physis* and indeed contributed in an essential way to putting in doubt definitively its very possibility or at the least the claims of the naturalistic type of thought.

Second Part

THE SOPHISTS: THE TRANSITION FROM THE PHILOSOPHY OF NATURE TO MORAL PHILOSOPHY

«πολλὰ τὰ δεινὰ
κοὐδὲν ἀνθρώπου δεινότερον πέλει.»

"The wonders of the world are many,
but there is none more wonderful than
man."

Sophocles *Antigone* 332

First Section

THE ORIGIN AND NATURE OF THE MORAL PROBLEM

«χαλεπὸν τὸ ἑαυτὸν γνῶναι.»

"It is difficult to know oneself."

Maxim attributed to the Seven Sages

I. Why the Philosophical Problem about Human Beings Does Not Arise Together with the Problem of the Cosmos

Philosophy with Thales arises as an attempt to rationally comprehend the cosmos, that is, as an attempt to find the "principle" that explains the whole, and it is focused through this perspective throughout the sixth century B.C. and for part of the fifth. Philosophy consistently concerned itself with the cosmos and with being, understood exclusively, or chiefly, as cosmos. In such a way it has obscured, or at least left in the shade, the *being of man* and it has not been concerned with the rational comprehension of the *specific nature of human beings*. Consequently, it did not know nor could it scientifically grasp *human excellence* [ἀρετή], that is, the virtue of man, nor did it know how to philosophically justify the laws, the rules, and prescriptions to which human beings try to conform themselves in their acts.

Naturally, even man is part of the cosmos, and as the *physis* sought by Thales and his followers explained all things, it also explained, in a certain sense, even man. But—and this is a point to which we need to bring attention—Thales explained it only as *a thing in relation to other things*, that is, as an *object* and not as a *subject*. In fact in the area of the philosophy of *physis* man was not assigned a privileged place, or better, such a privileged position was neither understood nor justified.

However strange what was said above can seem to modern man, who has gone a long way towards understanding the human subject, it is instead quite understandable and almost obvious if we go back to the situation of human thought at its origins. As the historians of philosophy have well noted, the condition that allows something to be or to become the object of systematic reflection is that this something constitute, or that it at least appears as, an organic unity and not as a disjointed plurality without visible connections. Now while the world and cosmic events appear even to immediate sensorial presentation as an organic unity, men and human events instead appear in a totally different guise. They appear precisely as a multiplicity in which there are no clear visible connections and in which, moreover, breaks and separations seem to prevail.

Zeller writes in an illuminating page: "The exterior world is presented even to sensible perception *as a whole*, that is as an edifice, the foot of which is the earth and the head the celestial vault; in the moral world, instead, sight is only used at first to see *just a swarm of individuals or small groups that move arbitrarily and confusedly*. In the one sphere, the *great relations* of the world edifice, the vast actions of celestial bodies, the alternate events on earth and the influence of the seasons, and in general the universal and regularly renewed phenomena are those which, above all others, attract attention; in the other sphere, it is *personal actions or events*. In the first, fantasy tries to integrate with a poetic cosmology the gaps in natural knowledge; in the other, the intellect tries to establish rules of practical conduct *for particular cases*. While cosmological reflection tried to make origins conceivable and right from the beginning was directed towards the whole, ethical reflection, on the contrary, was limited to *particular observations* and rules of life. Although ethical reflections offered homogeneous conceptions of moral relations, they did not directly and consciously lead to universal principles, except in the indeterminate and imagistic form of religious representations involving general considerations about the destiny of men, the destiny of souls in the hereafter, and the divine governance of the world."[1]

It is clear, hence, why a cosmogony was formed first, then a philosophical cosmology, and only subsequently ethical reflection, and finally moral philosophy. It is clear also why cosmogony was able to support the origins of philosophical cosmology much more effectively than pre-philosophical ethical reflections were able to support moral philosophy. Therefore it is not an anomalous fact that moral philosophy was established about a century and a half after the birth of philosophy (the philosophy of *physis*).

II. Some Terminological and Conceptual Distinctions That Are Essential to the Understanding of Ethical Problems

The antecedents of philosophical cosmology we know were theogonies, and these were the works of poets. So also the antecedents of moral philosophy, that is to say pre-philosophic ethical reflections, were expressed chiefly by poets and were in part also nourished by legislators.

But in order to examine, although briefly, the characteristics of pre-philosophic moral reflection, and in order to basically comprehend the difference that opposes it to moral philosophy and the meaning and character of the influence of the one on the other, it is necessary that we proceed to some terminological distinctions that are of crucial importance:[1]

    a) one thing is the notion of *morality*, or *moral conduct;*

    b) another and different thing is the *moral convictions* that men expressly profess;

    c) another too is moral *philosophy.*

a) *Morality*, or *moral conduct*, is possessed by all men indiscriminately, even the most primitive and uncivilized. In fact it is impossible to live without acting in determined ways, no matter how rough and primitive they are, and this is freely acknowledged in general.

b) *Moral convictions* are also an inheritance of all men. They are absorbed first from the nuclear family and then from the environment that is frequented and in general from the society in which we live. Primitive man also had moral convictions, although somewhat rough and unformed, in the measure in which he has, and knows that he must respect, rules of social living with the family and tribe, ways of acting toward enemies, etc. Little by little he becomes civilized and constructs his own civilization. Hence man determines and increases more and more the patrimony of these convictions, explicates them, and gives them their form as maxims and precepts, songs, encomiums, and then he proposes them to everyone's honor.

So while on the level of *moral conduct* reason may not even intervene (or it intervenes in a minimal way), as a kind of instinctive imitation, the imitation of examples or paradigms of life intuitively grasped, is sufficient. It is clear, on the contrary, that *in moral reflection there is an opening into the area of reason.* It is not possible to explain, determine, and express rules of life except by comparing, weighing, discriminating, and hence reasoning. But—and this is the point that we want to emphasize—this type of reflection and reasoning is still pre-philosophic because it depends on an intuition of the particulars and is anchored to it and almost dispersed in it. Thus, this kind of moral reflection does not go beyond intuition to universal principles.

c) Now all that remains to us is to clarify the nature of *moral philosophy.* At the level of moral philosophy, reason goes beyond the particular and tries to establish not only rules applicable in particular cases, but *in general it tries to establish nexuses and connections that are universal and necessary.* The point from which moral philosophy starts is naturally given in current moral convictions, just as the starting-point from which the philosophy of the cosmos moves is that which is furnished by the senses and experience. But moral philosophy immediately subjects these convictions to critical scrutiny, determining whether they are or are not false, that is, whether they are grounded or not, and hence if they are justifiable or unjustifiable. Just as the philosophy of the cosmos is constituted by bringing back various phenomena to their first principle and showing the connection that they have with the principle, so also moral philosophy is constituted by bringing back the norms of man's life to a principle.

What is this principle?

Anyone who has followed us to this point understands well that this principle could only be given by *the nature or the essence of man*. Therefore, the condition out of which a moral philosophy might arise was that it would previously determine, in an organic and precise way, what the essence or nature of man was, the reason why this nature was different from all other beings, and in what this difference consisted. Only on this basis will it be possible to establish the nature of the much praised human *arete*, that is, in what virtue consists. The *arete* permits us to fully realize the nature of man, that which makes man fully and completely a human being (one cannot in fact know what it is that perfectly completes a nature, except that one knows first of all, in what that nature consists). Only on this bases, that is, in connection with the nature of man and on his true *arete*, will it be possible to establish authentic values (the good, the just, the noble, the holy, etc.).

III. Moral Reflection Prior to the Birth of Moral Philosophy

But before moral philosophy arises how did the moral convictions of the Greeks develop and at what point did it become moral reflection?

A place to look for the answer about the formation of moral convictions and for the stimulation of ethical reflection would be, in the first place, the Homeric poems; but more through the characters and the human types that they represent than through the opinions and maxims put in the mouths of people. Actually people like Achilles, Hector, Ulysses, Agamemnon, Ajax, Nestor, Helen, Andromache, Penelope, Nausicaa, and all the others whom we met in the *Iliad* and the *Odyssey* were shaped with such suppleness and effectiveness, and in that way they answer well the needs of the ancient spirit and it is no wonder that they became and remained for such a long time authentic and proper paradigms and models of life, imaginary universals, to use a later term.

In the *Odyssey*, then, there would even seem to be outlined in a rudimentary fashion a very general conception of ethics according to which men who revere and obey the Gods also have advantages over men who are wicked and arrogant, those who cannot escape the divine wrath. It is generally certain that through the singing and emotional experiencing of the Homeric poems the Greeks were strongly impressed by the heroism of Achilles, the wisdom of Nestor, the daring and resourcefulness of Ulysses, the faithfulness of Penelope, and so on; and consequently, the Greek will wonder, nevertheless, which of these heroes is better and thus would ethical problems be sharpen little by little into moral awareness.

A notable step forward toward moral reflection is taken by Hesiod, not only because in his poem *Works and Days* he connects to the ideal of the heroic life of the *Iliad* and the *Odyssey* the ideal of the farmer's life, elevating the humble sacrifices of daily living, the daily toil without reward, hand-labor as such to the highest moral dignity, but especially because it contains precepts, maxims, and aphorisms. The ethico-religious conception of life is delineated in Hesiod in a clear manner. The evils from which human beings suffer are punishments inflicted by the Gods because of the arrogance of men themselves. The hard work is linked to human faults, but it is the unique way that man must stay on in order to live; anyone who does not work must have recourse to injustice which then calls down nemesis, punishment. Hesiod exhorts us to follow the way of virtue even if it is hard and difficult; he recommends simplicity, moderation, prudence, and benevolence. But although these concepts are noble, in Hesiod they are for the most part communicated through aphorisms or through reflections of an intuitive nature, and hence they are not justified or, at best, only motivated by the power of myth.

A further sharpening of ethical reflection belongs to the poets of the seventh century and especially the gnomic poets of the sixth century, like

Solon, Phocilydes, and Theognides. From the aphorisms of these poets there emerges clearly enough the norm of the *just measure*, of the *middle state*, of the *middle measure* as a foundation of living sensibly and happily. This norm we will see dominant in the ethics of Plato and Aristotle, and in the ethics of the post-Aristotelian philosophies. But—and this is a remark to consider carefully—while through the poets they are only learned and affirmed intuitively, through the philosophers they are instead grounded and justified theoretically.

Finally, we must mention the so-called *Seven Sages* (the list, as is known, is given by various sources in different ways), among whom Thales himself is to be counted. It is possible to say very little historically about these *Seven Sages*. Some of the aphorisms that are attributed to them are certainly not authentic, and further, it is difficult to accurately establish to which of them belong the authentic sayings. In any case, the *Seven Sages signal the moment of the emergence on the first level of moral interest prior to the emergence of moral philosophy.*[1] Plato[2] gives the following list: Thales of Miletus, Pittacus of Mytilene, Bias of Priene, Solon of Athens, Cleobulus of Lindus, Myson of Chen, and Chilon of Sparta. Stobaeus, following Demetrius of Phaleron in place of Myson of Chen, places the name of Periander, and gives us a richer account of the aphorisms attributed to these savants. Because these aphorisms sketch, so to speak, the map of moral wisdom of the Greeks prior to the rise of moral philosophy both in its positive and its negative aspect, it is appropriate to read them here in their entirety. These are attributed to Cleobulus of Lindus:

> 1. The measure is the better thing. 2. A father must be respected. 3. Esteem the body and the soul. 4. Be a lover a listening rather than speaking. 5. Be enamored of study rather than deprived of studies. 6. Do not be a foul-mouth. 7. Be intimate with virtue and a stranger to vice. 8. Hate injustice, do the right action. 9. Consult the best of your fellow-citizens. 10. Bridle pleasure. 11. Do nothing with violence. 12. Educate children. 13. Give offerings to fortune. 14. Make up with enemies. 15. The adversary of the people deal with as a foreign adversary. 16. Do not fight with a wife nor be proud in the presence of strangers; since the former is stupidity, the latter is silliness. 17. Do not punish a servant in the course of a banquet, otherwise it will seem to be from drunkenness. 18. Take as a wife one of equal condition to yourself, since if you take one of a higher position to your own, you will acquire some masters, not some relatives. 19. Do not deride those who are scorned by anyone, since you will gain the hatred of those scorned. 20. Do not be proud when things are going well, and when you are having difficult times do not lose heart.

These are attributed to Solon:

> 1. Nothing in excess. 2. Do not sit as a judge, if not, you will become the enemy of those who give way to judgment. 3. Avoid pleasures that

generate pain. 4. Preserve the probity of your dress more than the fidelity of your oaths. 5. Seal your discourses with silence, silence with time. 6. Do not lie but be truthful. 7. Get involved in serious matters. 8. Do not claim that there is something more just than parents. 9. Do not acquire friends quickly, but those that you have acquired, do not reject them quickly as unworthy. 10. When you have understood what it is to be under orders then you will know how to command. 11. If you value the report of the justice that others give, it will also be presented to you. 12. Consult with fellow-citizens not because it is more pleasant but because it is better. 13. Do not be foolhardy. 14. Do not join evildoers. 15. Have recourse to the Gods. 16. Be upright with friends. 17. That which you have <not> seen, do not speak of it. 18. Being aware, be silent. 19. Be gentle with yourself. 20. Guess at the things that do not appear to be so from those that do so appear.

These are attributed to Chilon:

1. Know yourself. 2. While drinking do not open your mouth, lest your foot be in it. 3. Do not threaten the free because it is not just. 4. Do not speak badly of those who are near, otherwise you might hear things that may upset you. 5. To the banquets of friends bring yourself slowly, to those of the unfortunate quickly. 6. Make a modest marriage. 7. He who is dead enjoys it. 8. Respect those who are older. 9. Hate those who get mixed up in the affairs of others. 10. Prefer more the damage than evil advantage because the former gives a pain only once, while the latter for always. 11. Do not scorn those who have suffered some misfortune. 12. If you are of a sour temperment, show yourself as calm, so that they will respect you rather than be threatened by you. 13. Be the master of your house. 14. Your tongue should not run ahead of your mind. 15. Conquer anger. 16. Do not desire the impossible. 17. Do not be in a hurry on the way. 18. Do not move your hands a lot, the way the unbalanced do. 19. Obey the laws. 20. If someone harms you, if someone is violent with you, seek revenge.

These are attributed to Thales:

1. Security values damage. 2. Remember present and absent friends. 3. Do not make your face beautiful, but in your clothes be beautiful. 4. Do not get wealthy through evils. 5. Do not place in a bad light your discourses near those who have relied on your words. 6. Do not waste time flattering your parents. 7. Do not accept that which is evil from your father. 8. Whatever are the contributions you give to your parents, such you will receive yourself in your old age from your children. 9. It is difficult to know oneself. 10. It is a sweet thing to achieve what one has desired. 11. Idleness is damaging. 12. Intemperance is dangerous. 13. A lack of culture is a serious thing. 14. Teaching and learning, which is better. 15. Not to be lazy, if not to be wealthy. 16. Dirty linen should be hidden. 17. Be envied rather than be commiserated. 18. Use moderation. 19. Do not give trust to everyone. 20. If you wish to govern,

first be subject to discipline yourself.

These are attributed to Pittacus:

1. Seize the opportunity. 2. What you have to do keep to yourself, do not talk about it, since if you fail, you will be subject to derision. 3. Preserve the things necessary to life. 4. What you blame in your neighbor, you should not do. 5. Do not insult those who are unfortunate, since for these occasions there are the nemesis of the Gods. 6. Give back the things that have been entrusted to you. 7. Accept the small damages which your neighbor inflicts on you. 8. Do not speak evil of a friend nor good of an enemy, since such a thing is illogical. 9. To know what is going to happen is terrible, but to know what has happened gives security. 10. The earth is trustworthy, but the sea is not. 11. Earnings do not satisfy. 12. Acquire your own things. 13. Cultivate piety, education, temperance, wisdom, truth, faith, skill, ability, friendship, diligence, frugality, and art.

These are attributed to Bias:

1. Men are for the most evil. 2. It is necessary, he said, to look at yourself in a mirror, and, if you appear handsome, do beautiful things, if instead you appear ugly, it is necessary to correct the defect of nature with honesty. 3. Be slow to begin an action, but once you have begun, carry it energetically to its conclusion. 4. Avoid speaking quickly, in order not to be mistaken, since regret about it will dog you. 5. Do not be a simpleton nor malicious. 6. Do not welcome rash action. 7. Love wisdom. 8. Concerning the Gods, you must say that they exist. 9. Reflect on what you have done. 10. Listen most of the time. 11. Talk about what is opportune. 12. Being poor, the wealthy do not criticize you, unless you take too much advantage of them. 13. Do not praise an unworthy man because of his wealth. 14. Take after having convinced, do not have recourse to force. 15. Whatever good things befall you attribute to the esteem of the Gods. 16. Happiness is acquired in youth, wisdom in old age. 17. With application you will have memory, with opportunity prudence, with character noble mindedness, with toil temperance, with religious fear piety, with riches friendship, with reasoning persuasion, with silence composure, with wisdom justice, with boldness courage, with action power, with good repute hegemony.

These are attributed to Periander:

1. Exercise is everything. 2. Tranquility is a beautiful thing. 3. Precipitateness is unsafe. 4. Profit is a shameful thing. 5. [. . .] accusation of nature. 6. Democracy is better than tyranny. 7. Pleasures are mortal, virtue is immortal. 8. When you have good fortune, be moderate, when instead bad luck, be prudent. 9. It is better to spare to die than by living to be in need. 10. Make yourself worthy of your parents. 11. When you live, be complimenting, when you are dead, your memory will be a blessing. 12. Be the same with your friends whether they are

in good fortune or in bad fortune. 13. The agreement that you have voluntarily entered, observe it, since it is wrong to break it. 14. Do not divulge secret conversations. 15. Blame as if you were to become friends (of those whom you blame). 16. Use the ancient norms, but use fresh bread. 17. Do not only punish those who transgress, but also detain those who are about to transgress. 18. When you have some misfortune, conceal it, so that your enemies will not be cheered.[3]

We can say that these aphorisms are truly exemplary in showing the qualities and limits of pre-philosophic moral reflection. They are the fruit of long experience and reflection but unconnected to one another. They are not supported by a principle nor grounded and hence *are not justified*. They are beyond philosophy.

The fact that Thales is numbered among the Seven Sages is particularly significant. He found philosophy (as cosmology), but not moral philosophy, and the reasons for this we know already quite well. On the other hand, not only Thales but all Presocratic philosophers, as moralists, did not go beyond the sphere of the intuitive aphorisms they taught and expressed, indeed *because they investigated the principle of the cosmos but not the nature of man as such*. Those philosophers who, like the Pythagoreans and Empedocles, go in a certain measure beyond this type of moral wisdom could do this on the basis of a vision of man and of life that they received from Orphic belief and not from their doctrine of the *physis*. But they still remained imprisoned in the aporias that we have examined above.

Hence, because moral philosophy arose *it was necessary that man as such become the object of philosophical reflection*. It was also necessary that his essence be determined as well as the meaning of man as man. It was necessary that from this essence be deduced the concept of *arete*. Finally, it was necessary that the table of traditional values be systematically tested and their theoretical consistency be determined.

This was the great work that the Sophists initiated and that Socrates will carry to completion, as we will see.

Second Section

THE SOPHISTS

«πάντων χρημάτων μέτρον ἐστὶν
ἄνθρωπος.»

"Man is the measure of all things."

Protagoras *Fragment* 1

I. The Origin, Nature, and Goals of the Sophistic Movement

1. The significance of the term "sophist"

Before beginning our discussion on the Sophists, it is necessary to clarify what was the original and authentic meaning of the term "sophist."

It is well known, in fact, that the term "sophist" currently has taken on a decidedly negative connotation. "Sophist" is said of those who make use of reason captiously in order to try to weaken and hide the truth, and others in order to attempt to strengthen false reasoning giving it the appearance of the truth. But this sense is not the original meaning of the term, which means simply "wise one," "expert in wisdom," "possessor of wisdom," and hence it means not only something positive, but something highly positive.[1]

The negative acceptation of the term "sophist" became current perhaps begun by Socrates and certainly it was used by the disciples of Socrates, Plato and Xenophon, who radicalized the ideological battle against the Sophists, and then by Aristotle, who canonized what Plato had said.

Here is Plato's definition of the Sophist in the dialogue of that name:

> First, I believe, he was found to be a *paid hunter after the young and wealthy*...secondly a kind of *merchant in articles of knowledge* for the soul...third did he not turn up as a *retailer* of these same articles of knowledge?...and in the fourth place we found he was *a seller* of his own productions of knowledge...and fifth he was *an athlete in contests of words*, who had taken for his own the art of disputation...the sixth case was doubtful, but nevertheless we agreed to consider him a purger of souls, who removes opinions that obstruct learning.[2]

Xenophon writes:

> For to offer one's beauty for money to all comers is called prostitution;...So it is with wisdom. Those who offer it to all comers for money are known as *sophists*, prostitutors of wisdom.[3]

And further on:

> The sophists speak in order to deceive, and they write for their own gain, and in no way to be of use to anyone...[4]

Aristotle concludes:

> The art of the sophist is the semblance of wisdom without the reality, and the sophist is one who makes money from an apparent but unreal wisdom.[5]

It is evident that the chief charges are twofold and of different natures; *a)* the sophistic art is an apparent but inauthentic wisdom and, in addition, *b*) it is professed for the purposes of profit and is not in any way a disinterested love of the truth.

To these chief charges alleged by philosophers there must also be added those facts circulating as public opinion. Public opinion sees in the Sophists a danger both for religion (as moreover had been seen in the final Physicists) and for traditional morals, since the Sophists had focused their attention on this area. The aristocrats in particular did not forgive the Sophists for having contributed to their loss of power and for having given a strong incentive to the formation of a new class that was not founded on nobility of birth, but rather on personal ability and natural endowment. This was precisely what the Sophists intended to create or, more generally, to systematically educate.

It is nevertheless true that the greatest responsibility for the discrediting of the Sophists was Plato's. It went beyond what he said to the particularly effective way in which he said it using his great literary skills. Because Plato is the most important source for the reconstruction of Sophistic thought, it is clear that, inevitably, historians have generally taken as accurate not only the information that he furnished us on the Sophists, but also the judgments that he made about them.

But we will immediately see that even if the reasons brought forward by Plato to discredit some Sophists in contemporary eyes appear grounded and beyond discussion, on the contrary (or they are only such in a minor way), they are not really so for a well-educated historian who is able to resist taking sides and give an objective judgment. Thus only from the end of the previous century has the refining of the historical method permitted us to slowly liberate the Sophists from that condemnation, and it has also permitted us an integral re-evaluation and a just placement of them in the history of ideas. All the most qualified scholars agree in affirming that "...the Sophists are a phenomena as necessary as Socrates or Plato, without whom in fact both of the latter would be unthinkable."[6]

2. The reasons for the rise of Sophistry

To say that without the Sophists Socrates and Plato are wholly inconceivable means that the Sophists produced something entirely new, and which in some way resulted in a revolution with respect to the philosophy of *physis*. This revolution, together with the reasons that produced it, must now be taken up.

In the first place, in order to grasp the rise and development of this phenomenon of the Sophistic art we need to consider the particular results at which naturalistic speculation had arrived. These results had now become such as to eliminate each other. The results of Eleaticism contradict those of Heracliteanism; the results of the Pluralists, those of the Monists; finally, the very solutions of the Pluralists excluded each other, if not in their basic thought at least in their further determinations. It would seem, then, that all the possible solutions had been proposed and that any others were inconceivable. The principles are one, many, infinite, or even do not exist (the Eleatics); everything is mobile, everything is immobile; everything depends on the ordering intelligence of Mind, everything is derived from a mechanical movement. Thus it is possible to proceed in the list of the antitheses that the philosophy of *physis* had achieved. The same attempt made by some thinkers to support again or rethink, with appropriate corrections, the thought of one or another of the ancient masters (for example, the attempt of Hippon to support Thales again, or that of Diogenes of Apollonia who went back to the doctrine of the air of Anaximenes) shows, as we have seen above, that by now all paths have been trodden and that the search for the principle of all things had exhausted all possibilities and had thus reached its own limits. It was inevitable, hence, that philosophical thought must put to the side *physis* and invest its interest in another objective.

The new objective was precisely that which the Naturalists had wholly passed by, or only marginally touched upon, namely, *man and all that which is typically human.* Nestle says it well, "for the Sophists man and his spiritual creations stand at the center of reflection. Also for them what Cicero[7] says of Socrates is true, 'he has made philosophy come down from heaven to earth, he has installed it in the city-state and has introduced into the household and has limited its reflection to its life and its customs, to its good and evil.' Man as an individual entity and as a member of society is that to which the attention of the Sophist has turned."[8] So it is not difficult to understand how the dominant themes of sophistic speculation would become ethics, politics, rhetoric, art, language, religion, and education, that is, all those things which we today call *humanistic culture.* With the Sophists, in short, begins what, with an effective expression, is known as *the humanistic period of ancient philosophy.*

We, therefore, cannot explain this radical shift of the orientation of philosophy if we limit ourselves to pointing out this negative factor, namely, the exhaustion of the resources of the philosophy of nature. In addition, the new historical conditions acted in a decisive way, slowly maturing in the course of the fifth century along with the new social, cultural, and even economic conditions that in part created and in part were created by the new historical conditions.[9]

Let us remember, above all, the slow but inevitable crises of the aristocracy, which went hand in hand with the always increasing power of the *demos,* of the people. These factors must also be kept in mind: the affluence in the cities, especially Athens, of an increasing number of merchants, the widening of opportunities for commerce that surpassed the limiting restrictions of individual cities bringing each of them in contact with a much wider world, and the widening of experience and knowledge of the voyagers who brought to the fore the inevitable comparison of Hellenic usages, customs, and laws in relation to wholly different usages, customs, and laws. All these elements contributed strongly to the rise of the sophistic problematic. The crisis of the aristocracy involved the crisis also of ancient *arete*, of traditional values that were precisely the values held as precious by the aristocracy. The growing confirmations of the power of the *demos* and the broadening of the vast circle of possibilities of acceding to power would destroy the conviction that *arete* was connected to birth, that is, that human excellence was inborn, and did not develop. They posed immediately the problem of how to acquire "political *arete*." The bridging of the restricted circle of the *polis* and the knowledge of different customs, usages, and laws must have constituted the first premise of relativism, causing the conviction that what was eternally stable and valid was instead lacking value in other circumstances and environments. The Sophists completely welcomed these attitudes of this period of turmoil in which they lived. And this explains why they achieved such a great success especially among the young. They answered to the real needs of the moment, they spoke to the young who were no longer satisfied with traditional values that their elders proposed nor with the manner in which they proposed them, and they gave the young the new language for which they were waiting.

3. The inductive method of sophistic inquiry

It is quite evident by now that by changing *the object of inquiry* of the Naturalists the Sophist had to change *the method of inquiry* as well. While the philosophers of nature established the primary principle, *they deduced* from it various conclusions, and thus they used a chiefly *deductive* method. Sophists, as has been brought to light by Nestle, followed a procedure chiefly *empirico-inductive*: "The sophistic art," writes the German scholar, "takes its point of departure from experience and attempts to reach the greatest amount of knowledge possible in every area of life, from them it draws some conclusions, in part theoretical, as for example, the possibility or impossibility of acquiring wisdom, about the origin, development, and goal of human culture, about the origin and structure of language, about the origin and essence of religion, about the difference between free-men and slaves, Hellenes and barbarians; in part, practical in nature, about the form of the life of the individual and of society. It proceeds therefore in an empirico-inductive manner."[10]

4. The practical goals of Sophistry

What we have analyzed up to this point will permit us to grasp those aspects of the sophistic art which in the past were hardly appreciated, or which were even considered as totally negative.

The *practical* and not the more purely *theoretical* goal of the sophistic art is, for example, much insisted on and this is considered as a speculative and moral decline. The philosophers of nature—they say—searched for the truth, for the truth itself, and the fact of having or not having pupils is purely accidental; vice versa, the Sophists did not search for truth itself, but had teaching as their aim, and having disciples instead for them was essential. In conclusion, the Sophists made an authentic *profession* of their wisdom. Now even if these judgments contain the truth, they will carry us away from a balanced judgment unless we take into account what follows. It is true that the Sophists compromised in part the theoretical aspect of philosophy; but it is likewise true that because the thematic that they treated was not concerned with *physis* but the life of men and concrete ethico-political problems so, contrary to the Naturalists, they were forced by the necessity of things to make their reflections practical. But the practical goal orientation of their doctrines also has a higher meaning. *The problem of education and the pedogogic task emerges with them on the primary level and assumes a new significance.* Against the claims of the nobility, who maintained that human excellence was a prerogative of blood and birth, the Sophists worked to propose the principle that everyone, instead, can acquire *arete*, and that this rather than nobility of blood is grounded *in wisdom*. In this light, the fact that the Sophists wanted to be the dispensers of that wisdom, and not simply as researchers but as educators, is best explained. (It has been correctly said that with the Sophists arises the Western notion of education, which indeed is structured and based on wisdom.[11]) If it is true that the Sophists did not extend their teaching to all, but only to that *elite* who must or wished to accept the guidance of the State, then it is still true that, with their principle, they at least broke the prejudice that saw *human excellence* necessarily linked to the nobility of blood.

5. The financial compensation demanded by the Sophists

We are now in a position to confront and resolve the thorny question of compensation which the Sophists required for their teaching, for their work of education. Plato and other ancients brand the venality of the Sophists and considered this custom of payment for teaching as an indisputable sign of moral baseness. But keep in mind that Plato was, in this judgment rather more than he believed, the victim of aristocratic prejudice (in general, the culture was the inheritance of the aristocrats and the wealthy who, having solved all the problems of life, devoted themselves to the culture as their sublime *otium* and considered the culture as wholly cut off from every thing that had relation with earnings and with money, and they supported it simply as the effect of a disinterested spiritual communion). But—and this is the point to be emphasized—the Sophists did not have a fixed residence and a fixed source of income, and hence, having imparted their wisdom and their work in the way explained above, it was necessary for them to make a job of it and to require money as compensation in order to live. The abuses of which they were guilty can certainly be condemned, but it is necessary in any case to guard against being too severe in our judgments. If Plato, in fact, in the *Meno*, says of Protagoras that "alone...amassed more for his wisdom than Phidias...or any ten other sculptors,"[12] he does not hesitate, in the dialogue entitled *Protagoras*, to place in the mouth of Protagoras himself this phrase, "I have arranged my charges on a particular plan, when anyone has had lessons from me, if he likes he pays the sum that I ask; if not, he goes to a temple, states on oath the value he sets on what he has learnt, and pays that amount."[13] On the basis of this source, not favorably inclined toward the Sophists, we can hence establish that they were not simply common and despicable profiteers of science, as has been said many times in the past. Because we have spoken about the notion of a profession, we would like to quote a passage of Gomperz, who is quite clear on this point, "The modern world does not present in any form a professional life that can be established as an exact term of a comparison with them. From professors of our day the Sophists are distinguished clearly by the absence of any relation...with the State just as much as by the fact that no specialization limited their activity. Inasmuch as they were men of science, for the most part at least, they were experts almost in everything that was knowable, as orators and writers then, ever-ready and disposed always as they were to engage in diatribe and polemics, the type today that is closest to them is rather the print journalist. *Half journalists and half professors*, here is the description perhaps which communicates to us moderns an idea approximate enough to what the sixth century Sophists were."[14] That is true, hence, only if we consider that the professor and the journalist are, *normally*, only vehicles of information and makers of opinion, but not creators, whereas the Sophists were also creators.

6. The pan-Hellenic spirit of Sophistry

The Sophists were, then, reproached for being vagabonds, for going from city to city and hence of breaking the allegiance to their city, and therefore of breaking that bond which the Greeks (who felt that they were rather more than private individuals, in fact that they were essentially citizens of a particular city-state) held as unbreakable. So, if for the men of that time the reproach is to be understood, it was overturned and became an advantage, by seeing it in a wider historical perspective. The Greeks, in order to preserve themselves politically and get out of the mortal struggles among city-states, would have to be anchored to a solid *pan-Hellenic ideal*. The Sophists were precisely expressing such an ideal. They felt that the narrow limits of the city-State were no longer justified. They no longer had a reason to be so limited and, further, the citizen of a given city-state is *a citizen of Hellas*. In this respect they went also beyond Plato and Aristotle, who continued to see in the *polis* the ideal model of the State.

7. The enlightenment of the Greek Sophists

Connected to the characteristics examined above, and even a minimum common denominator of all them, is the *liberty of spirit* that was typical of the Sophists. They overthrew the old conceptions of *physis* in which thought threatened to become solidified, criticizing traditional religion, eating away at the claims of the presupposed aristocracy on which the old politics was built, overrunning the malfunctioning institutions, contesting the traditional table of values, which by this time were defended without conviction. This liberty of spirit and this spiritual liberation from every tradition which was typical of the Sophists gives meaning to their epithet of "enlightened Greeks,"[15] an epithet which, if correctly understood, yields an adequate definition of them. In fact, the Sophists achieved this liberation on the basis of reason, and in reason and intelligence they had, just as the men of the Enlightenment, an unlimited faith. What they denied was the possibility of achieving what the Naturalists believed they had achieved in an absolute way, or in a way in which the tradition believed it had possessed a definitive understanding. "But to deny the absolute in thought," Saitta states clearly, "does not mean that the Sophists denied thought. Their dogged persistence in attacking the notion of the presentation which in its generality smothered sensations and particulars was the requirement of a critical thought that wishes to exercise its power and its dominion over all things, whence, in the depths itself of sophistic relativism, thought is shown as both building and destroying presentations and as such shows itself more as an unlimited power, circumscribed and finite. In fact, the concern of the Sophists was consistently focused on making men cultured, and that culture must be the result of a conscious criticism which centers again on its primary immediate objects, laws, customs, passions, and religion. The original attitude of sophistic thought did not believe, but investigated and criticized, and thus it constructed the concept of the productivity of the spirit that becomes aware of grasping only in full liberty, the fruit of each thing."[16]

8. The different currents of Sophistry

In order to conclude we will clarify a final point. A Sophistic system or a Sophistic doctrine does not exist in the sense that it is impossible to reduce the thought of various Sophists to propositions to which they would all agree. But it is nevertheless true that the doctrines of individual Sophists almost have a unity beyond their incommensurability. And it is, on the contrary, true that, as a French scholar has said, "...the sophistic art of the fifth century represents a complex of *independent forces* in order to satisfy, with *analogous means, identical needs*,"[17] and we might add implying a series of identical *problems*. What these needs are we will see fully. They are those of the society of the fifth century that evolved in a democratic direction, the themes and the identical problems that fully characterized them, those relative to man, to his *arete*, to the table of moral values, in short, they are ethico-political themes and problems.

Let us now see the independent efforts made by individual Sophists and examine the analogous method constructed by them. But before we proceed to this examination, it is necessary to point out that in order to understand and correctly evaluate the Sophists it is necessary distinguish individual Sophists from individual Sophists, without lumping all of them together. The sophistic art, in fact, was subject to an evolution, indeed a regression, which was rather marked; and among the masters of the first generation and the disciples of the second generation runs a noteworthy difference, as in part Plato himself had already noted. Therefore, it is necessary to distinguish at least three groups of Sophists; (1) the great and famous masters of the first generation, not lacking moral commitments and so, as Plato recognized, essentially worthy of respect; (2) the "eristics," those who, exploiting the sophistic method and elevating the formal aspect without any interest in the content and without maintaining the moral commitment of their masters, transformed sophistic dialectic into a sterile art of contending with words, into a real logomachic art; (3) finally, the "politico-sophists," politicians who aspired to political power, who without holding any moral commitment used, or better, abused certain sophistic principles to conceive of an authentic immorality which led to the rejection of "justice so-called," of every established law, of every moral principle. But those, more than the authentic spirit of the sophistic art, represent the pathological excrescence of the sophistic art itself.

Let us separately consider both individual figures and individual groups of Sophists.

II. Protagoras

1. The principle that "man is the measure"

The fundamental proposition of Protagoras, the greatest and most famous of the Sophists,[1] must be the axiom "man is the measure of all things, of the things that are that they are, and of the things that are not, that they are not."[2] And by "measure" Protagoras must have meant the norm of judgment, while by "the things" he must have meant all facts in general. The axiom has very quickly become famous and it is considered and is actually almost the *magna charta* of western relativism. Protagoras undoubtedly intended, by using the principle of *man-measure*, to deny that an absolute criterion exists by which to discriminate between being and not being, truth and falsity, and in general every value. The criterion is only relative, it is the man, *the individual man.*

Some scholars have tried to interpret the Protagorean principle to mean that the man about whom he is speaking is not the individual man, but the *generic* man, in this way making Protagoras a precursor of Kant.[3] But all our ancient sources directly exclude the possibility of this interpretation. The man of whom Protagoras speaks is *the concrete individual.* Plato, presenting the axiom, comments:

> Well, is not this about what he means, that individual things are for me such as they appear to me, and for you in turn such as they appear to you—you and I being "man"?...Is it not true that sometimes, when the same wind blows, one of us feels cold, and the other does not? or one feels slightly and the other exceedingly cold?...Then in that case, shall we say that the wind is in itself cold or not cold; or shall we accept Protagoras' saying that it is cold for him who feels cold, not for him who does not?[4]

That it is a question of single individuals is also confirmed by Aristotle,[5] and finally by Sextus Empiricus:

> And because Protagoras only admits that which appears *to single individuals*, and in that way he introduces the principle of relativity.[6]

In addition, Protagoras did not develop an epistemological doctrine in a systematic way, that is, a general doctrine of knowledge. The various epistemological values of the principle of *man-measure* raised by Plato and Aristotle are, more than anything else, explications and consequences drawn by these philosophers. And analogously, the systematic connection of this relativism with the Heracliteans' doctrine of the perennial flux of all things is almost certainly an explication of Plato and of Aristotle. Protagoras established his principle particularly in an empirical way, by generalizing from the observation of the opposed valuations that men give to all things and not from an outline of a systematic study of the nature of knowledge. In this way he (just as many Naturalists had also done) contributed notably to the birth of epistemology, but *he did not found this science* (in order to have done this he would have had to analyze systematically sensible and intellectual knowledge, to set out the problem of the epistemological nature of truth and, in general, cognitive processes; but these problems only come to the forefront with Plato and Aristotle). Furthermore, he did not systematically extend his principle to everything and he applied it, instead, as a fundamental canon for his teaching about *arete*, that is, for his educational work, as we will now see.

2. The principle of the twofold contradictory reasons and its application

The relativism expressed by the principle of *man-measure* was probably analyzed in the work entitled *Contradictory Arguments*. Diogenes Laertius writes that Protagoras maintained that "there are two sides to every question, opposed to each other,"[7] that is, that it is possible to speak for or against any issue, namely, to adduce reasons which mutually exclude each other. Aristotle writes that Protagoras tried to "make the stronger argument weaker."[8]

It is easy to reconstruct even from these simple pieces of information the target at which Protagoras aimed and how many imitated him. "Since their aim," writes Robin, "is that of arming the student for all conflicts of thought or of action of which the social life could be the occasion, their method will be hence essentially *antilogic* or controversy, the opposition of the various possible theses on a given theme, or hyptheses, conveniently defined or catalogued; it is a matter of teaching how *to criticize* and *discuss*, to organize a tournament of reasons against reasons."[9]

Protagoras, hence, based on these premises, taught that on each thing (and in particular on those things about which the ethico-political life is concerned) it is possible to adduce reasons pro and con, and he taught that it is possible to support the weaker argument. He certainly did not consider that he taught injustice and iniquity against justice and rectitude, *but simply that he taught the ways in which it was possible to support and carry to a successful conclusion an argument* (whatever the content might be), *that which in the discussion in a given circumstance might be the weaker argument.* An echo of this Protagorean procedure is very likely found in the anonymous work entitled *The Two-fold Reasonings*, which was concerned with ethical values, the teachability or unteachability of virtue, and the criterion of the choice of political obligations. This anonymous author writes:

> A twofold order of reasoning was practiced in Greece by the learned philosophers concerning *good* and *evil*. Some maintained that the good is other than evil; some, instead, that they are the same thing; what for some would be good, for others would be evil; and for the same

individual it would be at one moment good and at another evil. For me, I am closest to the last position; and I will look for its proof in human experience.[10]

After having adduced a series of reasons inspired by Protagorean relativism of which there is parallel testimony by Plato,[11] the anonymous author concludes:

And in this way I do not define what is good, but this I do my best to teach, that good and evil are not the same thing, but it is true that each of these two can be one or the other.[12]

The same thing is repeated by the author for the beautiful and the ugly, the just and the unjust, the true and the false, foolishness and wisdom. The essence of values is not defined, but a whole series of reasons is given that makes a thing appear good, beautiful, and so on, and the other series of reasons that make the same thing appear in the same way, the ugly, evil, and so on.

3. The teaching of "virtue" and the meaning of this term

We are now in a position to grasp what is the nature of the *arete*, of which Protagoras is the professed *teacher* and for the knowledge of which youths flock around him. In the dialogue of the same name Plato has our Sophist say:

That learning consists of *good judgment in his own affairs*, showing how best to order his own home; and *in the affairs of his city*, showing how he may have most influence on public affairs both in speech and in action.[13]

Now this "good judgment" (εὐβουλία) is the ability to speak, especially in public, before a tribunal or assembly, and *Protagoras maintained that it was teachable precisely by means of the technique of the* **antilogic** *and the consequent ability that enables a person to make any point of view whatsoever prevail over its opposite.*

It is clear, hence, that we are speaking of *arete* not in the Christian sense of *virtue*, but in the original sense of *ability* (the same sense that Machiavelli presented in speaking of the *virtue* of the Prince). In fact it is evident that to present oneself as a teacher of virtue understood in the former sense is ridiculous, while it is not so in the latter case. And if Socrates and Plato contested the possibility of teaching virtue, it will be because they are refuting virtue understood as mere ability, as we will see later on.

4. The limitation on the range of the principle that "man is the measure"

We have previously stated what are the limits and nature of the principle of "*man-measure*." These are again still further clarified by the examination of the strong reduction of the character of the principle produced by Protagoras with respect to its application in the field of praxis. If it is true that no absolute moral values exist, and hence no absolute good, it is likewise true nevertheless that *there exists something which is more useful, more convenient, and therefore more appropriate.* The wise man is not one who recognizes the absolutes which do not exist, but he is the one who recognizes this *relative* which is more useful, more convenient, and more appropriate, and knows how to carry it out and actually does carry it out. Here is a page of the Platonic dialogue the *Theaetetus* which describes in a splendid way this Protagorean attitude, which for good reasons we are able to call, in modern terminology, "pragmatic."

> For I maintain that the truth is as I have written; each one of us is the measure of the things that are and those that are not; but each person differs immeasurably from every other in just this, that to one person some things appear and are, and to another person other things. And I do not by any means say that wisdom and the wise man do not exist; on the contrary, I say that if bad things appear and are to any one of us, precisely that man is wise who causes a change and makes good things appear and be to him. And, moreover, do not lay too much stress upon the words of my argument, but get a clearer understanding of my meaning from what I am going to say. Recall to your mind what was said before, that his food appears and is bitter to the sick man, but appears and is the opposite of bitter to the man in health. Now neither of these two is to be made wiser than he is—that is not possible—nor should the claim be made that the sick man is ignorant because his opinions are ignorant, or the healthy man wise because his are different; but a change must be made from the one condition to the other, for the other is better. So, too, in education a change has to be made from a worse to a better condition; but the physician causes the change by means of drugs, and the teacher of wisdom by means of words. And yet, in fact, no one ever made anyone think truly who previously thought falsely, since it is impossible to think that which is not or to think any other things than those which one feels; and these are always true. But I believe that a man who, on account of a bad condition of soul thinks thoughts akin to that condition, is made by a good condition of soul to think correspondingly good thoughts; and some men, through inexperience, call these appearances true, whereas I call them better than the others, but in no wise truer. And the wise, my dear Socrates, I do not by any means call tadpoles; when they have to do with the human body, I call them physicians, and when they to do with plants, husbandmen; for I assert that these latter, when plants are sickly, instil into them good and healthy sensations, and true ones instead of bad sensations, and that the wise and good orators make the good, instead of the evil, seem to be right to their states. For I claim that whatever seems right and honorable to a state is really right and honorable to it, so long as it believes it to be so; *but the wise man causes*

the good, instead of that which is evil to them in each instance, to be and seem right and honorable. And on the same principle the teacher who is able to train his pupils in this manner is not only wise but is also entitle to receive high pay from them when their education is finished. And in this sense it is true that some men are wiser than others, and that no one thinks falsely, and that you, whether you will or no, must endure to be a measure. Upon these positions my doctrine stands firm.[14]

5. The utilitarian background of Protagorean philosophy

What clearly emerges from the page that we have just read is the following. If man (*each man* as a sentient and percipient being) is a measure of *truth* and *falsity*, he is not on the contrary a measure of the *useful* and *harmful*. In other words, it would seem that while man is *the measure* with respect to truth and falsity, he is instead *measured* by *utility*. It would seem then that we must ascribe an *objective validity* to utility (although not an absolute one). *Good and evil are respectively the useful and the harmful; the better and the worse are the most useful and the most harmful.*

That Protagoras did not notice any contrast between his epistemological relativism and his pragmatism based on utility (a contrast that instead many modern interpreters note) depends on the fact that the useful, at least on the experiential level, appears always and only in contexts of a series of correlations, to the point that it does not seem possible to determine it except by determining, at the same time, *the subject* to which the useful is referred, *the aim* for which it is useful, the *circumstances* in which it is useful, and so on.

A Platonic text, which pictures Socrates confronting Protagoras, is especially indicative in this respect:

Now do you say there are things that are good?

I do.

Then, I asked, are those things good which are useful to men?

Oh yes, to be sure, he replied, and also when they are not useful to men I call them good.

Here Protagoras seemed to me to be in a thoroughly provoked and harassed state, and to have set his face against answering: so when I saw him in this mood I grew wary and went gently with my questions. Do you mean, Protagoras, I asked, things that are useful to no human being, or things not useful in any way at all? Can you call such things as these good?

By no means, he replied; but I know a number of things that are useless to men, namely, foods, drinks, drugs, and countless others, and some that are profitable; some that are neither one nor the other to men, but are one or the other to horses; and some that are useful only to cattle, or again to dogs; some also that are not useful to any of those, but are to trees, but bad for its shoots—such as dung, which is a good thing when applied to the roots of all plants, whereas if you chose to cast it on the young twigs and branches, it will ruin all. And oil too is utterly bad for all plants, and most deadly for the hair of all animals save that of man, while to the hair of man it is helpful, also to the rest of his body. The good is such an elusive and diverse thing that in this instance it is good for the outward parts of man's body, but at the same time as bad as can be for the inward; and for this reason all doctors forbid the sick to take oil, except the smallest possible quantity, in what one is going to eat—just enough to quench the loathing that arises in the sensations of one's nostrils from food and its dressings.[15]

It is evident hence that Protagoras feels perfectly authorized to introduce again the concept of the wise (even after having eliminated the absolute notion of true and false) precisely on the basis of utility and in relation to utility. The farmer is wise insofar as he knows the good and useful thing for plants and procures it for them; the doctor insofar as he knows the good and useful for the body and procures it for it; the sophist or rhetorician is wise insofar as he knows the good and useful for the city-state and makes it appear so to the city-state (the just is not hence the true but the *public utility*), and educates the citizenry. It is likewise evident consequently that Protagoras, understood in this sense, must grant to the wise the right of supremacy, because "it is the wise man who causes the good, instead of that which is evil [= harmful] to the citizenry in each instance, to be and seem right [= useful] and honorable."[16]

This is a wisdom unconnected with ontological truth and, as is clear, it has assumed as its basis the experiential or, as we might say in modern terms, the phenomenological.[17]

It is hardly necessary to point out that Protagoras has moved in the phenomenological dimension purely through intuition. He, in fact, certainly did not have at his disposal the theoretical means which are necessary to distinguish the ontical from the phenomenological. And in the measure in which his position reaches the level of intuition it is not theoretically grounded and hence it is in a state of aporia with regard to the affirmation of the principle of *homo-mensura*. Moreover, the basic aporia emerges in working out the following counterproof. The useful for plants is determined by the farmer with respect to the criteria of growth and maturation of the plants; the useful for the human body is determined by the doctor with respect to the criteria of health, and so on. But what is useful for man (not understood as simply a body, but in his fullness), who determines that, and in reference to what? What is useful for the city-state with respect not to the simple material needs, but to the ethico-political living together of the citizenry, who determines that and in relation to what? So Protagoras does not hesitate to say that the one who determines it is precisely the Sophist; but then he does not say *in relation to what thing* does the Sophists proceed to this determination. In order to do that he would have had to penetrate more deeply into the nature of man to determine his essence. In that case, he would have had to realize that the reduction of man and his soul to a mere feeling and perceiving being[18] was in clear antithesis with the ethico-political vision that he drew from the phenomenological analysis. He would thus inevitably have had to change the former or the latter, but this would have involved an overturning of all his thought.

6. The attitude of Protagoras concerning the Gods

Our sources are in agreement in writing that Protagoras abstained from saying whether or not the Gods existed. Here are his words:

> As to the Gods I have no means of knowing either that they exist or that they do not exist.[19]

Probably, because of his method of setting up contradictory arguments, he must have shown *the arguments for and against the existence and the non-existence of the Gods.* But it is certainly inaccurate to say that by saying this Protagoras meant to deny the Gods, as some ancient authors do not hesitate to conclude. Diogenes of Enoanda, for example, writes:

> Protagoras of Abdera maintains, as a concept, the same opinion as Diagoras [who was an atheist]; but he expresses it in different words, almost in order to avoid excessive audacity; in fact, he says whether or not the Gods exist: which is just like saying that he knows that they do not exist.[20]

This inference surely cannot be attributed to Protagoras, since he did not deny the existence of the Gods nor even the belief in their existence *but only the knowledge of them.* Hence he was a *theological agnostic*, in great part counter-balanced by his practical attitude. In fact he must have, on the level of belief, admitted the existence of the Gods, as we know from Plato.[21]

But it is clear that as the principle of *man-measure* is strictly applied it inevitably leads to a more total scepticism and immoralism, and in this sense his attitude of marked agnosticism with respect to the Gods could have been carried to the point of denying the existence of the Gods. If Protagoras did not come to this conclusion, it only happened because he did not track out the consequences to which his premises through their internal logic ought or at least could lead.

III. Gorgias

1. The negation of truth

While Protagoras starts from *relativism* and on it bases his method of contradictory arguments, Gorgias,[1] somewhat inferior to him in reputation and ability, begins instead from a position of *nihilism*.

In a work of his—which must certainly have been the systematic over-turning of the philosophy of *physis* and especially of Eleaticism in the very way it had been presented by Melissus, and which is entitled *On the Nature of Not-Being* (which is the precise opposite title of the writing of Melissus)[2]—Gorgias maintained the interconnection and mutual dependency of these three theses: *a*) *being does not exist*, that is, nothing exists; *b*) if being exists, *it is inconceivable*; *c*) even if it were conceivable, it *would be incommunicable or inexplicable to others*.[3] The demonstration of the three propositions (which is accomplished through a series of dilemmas and using categories and techniques which are clearly Eleatic in origin), far from being an exhibition of rhetorical ability, as some have proposed,[4] has the clear purpose of rad-ically excluding the possibility of the existence, or the achievement, or generally of the expression of an objective truth.[5] Sextus Empiricus himself, who has recorded one of the two paraphrases extant of the work, thus concludes:

> Such, then, being the difficulties raised by Gorgias, *if we go by them the criterion of truth is swept away; for there can be no criterion of that which neither exists nor can be known nor is naturally capable of being explained to another person*.[6]

Therefore, if there existed a relative truth for Protagoras (in the sense that everything is true which seems to be so to man), on the contrary for Gorgias, *no truths exists and everything is false*.

Let us see in detail the principal arguments with which Gorgias reasoned to his three theses because they have had a considerable role in carrying to exasperating limits, so to speak, the crisis of the philosophy of *physis*.

2. Being does not exist

a) That being does not exist (that is, that nothing exists) Gorgias proves by mutually counterpositing the conceptions that the Physicists have main-tained about being and which as such mutually annihilate one another. Here is an anonymous author's summary of this part of Gorgias's work:

> Through combining the doctrines maintained by other philosophers who in their statements of the problem of beings support, as a result of their opinions—some with demonstrations of the unity of being instead of its multiplicity, others its multiplicity instead of its unity,

> some that it is ungenerated, others that it is generated—he argues for a principle antithetical to all of them that nothing exists. It follows logically, he affirms, that if anything exists, it must be either one or many, and either generated or ungenerated. If therefore, it cannot be either one or many, ungenerated or generated, it would be nothing at all. For if in fact anything were to exist, it would have to correspond to one of these alternatives.[7]

In short, the results of the speculations of the Physicists on being are cancelled and, self-destroying, they demonstrate the impossibility of the very being which is the object of their iniquity.[8]

Note, then, the type of procedure Gorgias adopted in order to destroy these alternatives, that is, on the basis of which being had been affirmed. He used, in fact, as we have already pointed out, the weapons of Eleatic logic. He wanted to show, by means of this procedure, that the very weapons which destroyed all the adversaries of Eleaticism could be used in turn against Eleaticism itself and destroy in this way the entire philosophy of *physis*, without any possibility of retrieval.

3. Even if being existed it would be inconceivable

b) The second thesis itself, which affirms that being is unknowable and inconceivable by man, is presented in the context of a anti-Eleatic argument. Parmenides, in fact, is the philosopher who stated that the link between *being and thought* is structurally unbreakable. Thought, he said, is always and only *the thought of being*. It is true that ultimately it can be said that *thought and being are the same thing*, in the sense that thought exists in the measure in which it returns to being (to think means nothing other than to grasp or to express being). Vice versa, not being is inconceivable and inexpressible because only being is conceivable and expressible.

So Gorgias overturned both capstones of Eleaticism. Against the principle that thought is always and only thought about being, Gorgias demonstrates that there are *things thought*, that is, *contents of thought* which do not have any reality and which therefore do not exist:

> And in fact, that the things thought are not existent is plain; for if the things thought are existent, all the things thought exist, and in this way, too, in which one has thought them. But this is contrary to sense. For if someone thinks of a man flying or of a chariot running over the sea, it does not follow at once that a man is flying or a chariot running over the sea. So that the things thought are not existent [= the thought is not a thought of being].[9]

Once the primary principle is destroyed the second is destroyed by that fact also, since it is nothing but an aspect of the first, as Gorgias himself clearly notes. So that not-being is *not* conceivable is once again refuted by the evidence because we can conceive of the Scylla, the Chimera, and many other things which do not exist:

> If "to be thought" is a property of the existent, "not to be thought"
> will most certainly be a property of the non-existent. But this is absurd;
> for Scylla and Chimera and many non-existent things are thought.[10]

Thus Sextus Empiricus summarizes the position of Gorgias. If it is true
that things thought do not exist, the contrary is also true, that is, that
being is not thought; stated again in more precise terms: "if the things
thought do not exist, being is not thought."[11]

The divorce between being and thought could not be worked out more
radically.[12]

4. Even if being were conceivable it would be inexpressible

c) The third thesis is demonstrated by Gorgias *in contesting the capability
of the word to signify, in a veridical way, things other than itself.* The page in
which our Sophist expresses this thought is worthwhile reading in its
entirety:

> For how, he says, could any one communicate by word of mouth that
> he has seen? And how could that which has been seen be indicated to
> a listener if he has not seen it? For just as the sight does not recognize
> sounds, so the hearing does not hear colors but sounds; and he who
> speaks, speaks, but does not speak a color or a thing. When, therefore,
> one has not a thing in the mind, how will he get it there from another
> person by word or any other token of the thing except by seeing it, if
> it is a color, or hearing it, if it is a noise? For he who speaks does not
> speak a noise at all, or a color, but a word; and so it is not possible to
> conceive a color, but only to see it, nor a noise, but only to hear it. But
> even if it is possible to know things, and to express whatever one
> knows in words, yet how can the hearer have in his mind the same
> thing as the speaker? For the same thing cannot be present simultane-
> ously in several separate people; for in that case the one would be two.
> But if, he argues, the same thing *could* be present in several persons,
> there is no reason why it should not appear dissimilar to them, if they
> are not themselves entirely similar and are not in the same place; for
> if they were in the same place they would be one and not two. But it
> appears that the objects which even one and the same man perceives
> at the same moment are not all similar, but he perceives different
> things by hearing and by sight, and differently now and on some
> former occasion; and so a man can scarcely perceive the same thing as
> someone else (trans. T. Loveday and E. S. Forster).[13]

Thus the divorce between being and thought becomes just as radical a
divorce as that between word, thought, and being.

What still remains for Gorgias after the negation of absolute being and
truth and the negation of thought as vehicle both of being and truth, and

after the negation of the word as revelatory of that being and that thought?

5. The refuge in the domain of the experiential and the reality of the situation

The possibility of achieving an absolute truth destroyed, that is, ἀλήθεια, it would seem that for Gorgias no other way remains except that of *opinions*, that is, δόξα, except that Gorgias expressly denies any validity to *doxa*, considering it "the most unfaithful of things."[14]

What has emerged from the most recent research is that Gorgias tried to find a third way between being and the deceptive appearance, between truth and *doxa*. It means that Gorgias rejected any *incontrovertible logos about being, but not the logos that is limited to the area of human experiences, that is, the logos which is limited to illuminating facts, circumstances, situations of the life of men and of the city-state.* M. Migliori has written, "It is thus possible to reinterpret the moral situation of the Greeks, by drawing forth more generally maintained valid principles or proposing an ideal of moderate eudaimonism and intellectualism."[15] And again: "This is not the science that permits definitions or absolute rules, nor the ever-wavering individualistic opinion. It is...an analysis of the situation, a description of what ought to be done or avoided. ... Gorgias is then one of the first representatives of *situation ethics*. The duties vary according to the moment, the age, the social characteristics; the same action can be good or evil according to whom the subject is. It is clear that this theoretical work, done without metaphysical bases and without absolute principles, involves the acceptance of much of current opinions. This explains that strange mixture of the new and the traditional which we find in Gorgias."[16]

Indeed, many extant testimonies do seem to confirm this interpretation. Gorgias, in the Platonic dialogue of that name, is not presented as a teacher who teaches in a specific and express way supreme moral values (this would be equivalent to teaching the unattainable absolute truth). He presupposes that his student already possesses the common knowledge of the moral values that all Greeks possess (if not he says that he will furnish them those knowledges, but on the basis of common convictions).[17]

We know from the Platonic dialogue *Meno* that he mocked those who promised to *teach virtue* and, more realistically, he proclaimed to desire and to know how to form only good orators.[18]

Analogously, we know from Aristotle that Gorgias did not define virtue (which would be equivalent to something absolute), but was limited to doing "an enumeration of the virtues."[19] More specifically, Meno, in the dialogue of that name, in a completely Gorgean manner characterized virtue phenomenologically in the following way:

First of all, if you take the virtue of a man it is easily stated that a man's virtue is this—that he be competent to manage the affairs of his city, and to manage them so as to benefit his friends and harm his enemies, and to take care to avoid suffering harm himself. Or to take a women's virtue: there is no difficulty in describing it as the duty of ordering the house well, looking after the property indoors, and obeying her husband. And the child has another virtue—one for the female and one for the male; and there is another for elderly men—one, if you like, for freemen, and yet another for slaves. And there are very many other virtues besides, so that one cannot be at a loss to explain what virtue is; for it is according to each activity and age that every one of us, in whatever we do, has his virtue; and the same, I take it, Socrates will hold also for vice.[20]

It is evident for anyone who has followed us thus far that this empirico-phenomenological way that Gorgias has tried to enter has a corresponding analogy also in Protagoras.[21] But it is likewise evident that just as for Protagoras's, so also for Gorgias's, this way does not receive adequate theoretical justification. In fact there is no sufficient ground on which to take a stand within the Gorgean position.

Given the elimination of the knowledge of being as incontrovertible, Gorgias must now demonstrate the theoretical possibility of a human wisdom which is not the science of the Physicists, not even that of *doxa*. But it is impossible to succeed in this matter because the theoretical categories at his disposal were Eleatic, which we have already seen are totally incapable of justifying the phenomena.[22] In addition, he had already demonstrated that the Eleatic categories are contradictory in nature and do not possess a constructive capacity that would enable him to construct a morality.

Hence, the phenomenological approach was only glimpsed by Gorgias and followed intuitively, but could not be theoretically justified.

Gorgias's thoughts about rhetoric reveal a much more solid consistency and lucidity.

6. Rhetoric and the omnipotence of words

Let us turn for a moment to the conclusions of the *Treatise on Not Being*. If an absolute truth does not exist (not even in a relative way, as Protagoras maintained), it is clear that *words acquire their own autonomy*, in fact an almost unlimited autonomy, because they are indeed not connected by the bonds of being to anything beyond themselves. In their ontic status as independent, words become (or can become) open to each and every meaning and hence become meaningless.

It is here then that Gorgias discovers on the properly theoretical level that *aspect of words which is the vehicle (putting aside all truths) of suggestion, persuasion, and belief*. Rhetoric is precisely the art of basically producing this aspect of words and can be said to be the *art of persuasion*.[23]

It is a persuasion that does not, as is evident on the basis of what we have said in detail, depend on any knowledge of incontrovertible truths but which is joined to pure belief. Therefore it is understandable that Gorgias, once the link between words and knowledge is broken and he has thus empowered the very great psychological effects of words, can now boast not only of being able to speak about everything and to convince anyone about anything whatever, but he is even able to conquer, by persuasive ability, technical experts in their own fields. Rhetoric is advantageous, for example, for surpassing the medical fraternity in persuading the sick to undertake a particular course of therapy. He used to boast, for example, of surpassing through rhetoric his brother, who was a doctor, in his ability to persuade a patient to undertake a particular course of therapy.

The social relevance and importance of these arts are clear; more so in fifth-century Athens, with its tribunals and assemblies, rhetoric could guarantee success to anyone who possessed it. It became, as has been accurately stated, "the true rudder in the hands of the statesman."[24] The structural connection to politics is so clear that politicians were called rhetoricians in the classical age. "Words," explains Jaeger, "do not have yet merely formal meanings as they do today, but include also an essential element: that the unique content of every public eloquence is the State and its affairs is in that time an obvious thing."[25]

Moreover, in the Platonic dialogue of the same name Gorgias expressly says about rhetoric:

> I call it the ability to persuade with speeches either judges in the law courts or statesmen in the council-chamber or the commons in the Assembly or an audience at any other meeting that may be held on public affairs.[26]

The enormous success that, as Protagoras, Gorgias achieved everywhere he went is explained by the thaumaturgic potency of the word capable of persuading all about all. It was through words that people thought they would be able to find the necessary instrument for domination.

But words not grounded in values, and in general any kind of objective truth, can become very dangerous indeed. Gorgias, as we have seen, admits the commonly admitted moral values of the Greeks and places his oratorical skills at their service.[27] Further, he blames those disciples who, on having learned rhetoric, go outside of and contrary to those values and he disassociates himself from any responsibility for them:

> If a man becomes a rhetorician and then uses this power and this art unfairly, we ought not to hate his teacher and cast him out of our cities. For he imparted that skill to be used in all fairness, whilst this man puts it to an opposite use. Thus it is the man who does not use it aright who deserves to be hated and expelled and put to death, and not his teacher.[28]

But after the divorce of truth from words situation ethics was certainly not sufficient to guarantee the correct use of rhetoric. Indeed it was typical of a changing situation to make rhetoric open to extreme vicissitudes, as we will see.

7. Words and poetic deception and illusion

The detailed analysis of the word and its capacities was to make Gorgias particularly sensitive to their poetic in addition to their rhetorical value. Our Sophist writes:

> All poetry can be called speech in meter. Its hearers shudder with terror, shed tears of pity, and yearn with sad longing; the soul, affected by the words, feels as its own an emotion aroused by the good and ill fortunes of other people's actions and lives.[29]

The arts, just as rhetoric, do not aim at truth but *at moving the emotions*. While rhetoric, by moving the emotions, pursues its practical end by aiming at generating persuasion and belief in relation to ethical, social, and political questions, the poetic art pursues ends which are both *theoretically and practically disinterested*.

What meaning, then, has that shudder, that fear, that sadness, that compassion that the arts produce through the effect of words, once both the theoretical or the practical end is eliminated? It is clear that here Gorgias not only glimpsed but in a certain way explicated the notion of *the aesthetic value of the emotions* and hence of the words that produce them. But there is more. In a testimony of Plutarch he writes:

> But tragedy blossomed forth and won great acclaim, becoming a wondrous entertainment for the ears and eyes of the men of that age and, by the mythological character of its plots and the vicissitudes which its characters undergo, it effected a *deception* wherein, as Gorgias remarks, *"he who deceives is more honest than he who does not deceive and he who is deceived is wiser than he who is not."*[30]

Here what the poetic words produce is even qualified as "deception" (ἀπάτη) and illusion. The deception, in our judgment, exactly defines the non-theoretic truth of that poetic sentiment which hence has it own precise character and (we will say with modern terminology) autonomy.

The positive character of poetic deception for Gorgias is evident. He does not hesitate to say that he who poetically deceives is "better" than he who does not deceive and that he who is deceived is "wiser" than he who is not. The former is better in his creative ability to produce poetic illusions, the latter because he has more ability to accept the message of this poetic creativity.

Both Plato and Aristotle touched on these questions, the former denied validity to art, the latter, on the contrary, discovered the cathartic power, the purifying quality of poetic emotions, as we will see.

IV. Prodicus of Keos

1. The invention of synonymy

The other Sophists, of whom there is extant testimony, are to be placed on a decidedly inferior level to Protagoras and Gorgias. However all of them are thinkers in different respects, interesting and indicative of the new tendencies.

In the first place there is Prodicus of Keos,[1] whom Socrates more than once jokingly referred to as his teacher.[2] Prodicus was also a teacher of the art of argumentation. But this art, which he taught to his disciples, was very expensive indeed and was based on something that claimed to be (and actually was) novel, that is, on *synonymy, on the distinction of the various synonyms, as well as on the precise determination of the shades of meaning of different synonyms.*[3] Thus the logos, after having experienced the possibility of the separation into opposed reasons with Protagoras and after having recognized in itself an all-powerful capacity for persuasion with Gorgias, now uncovers the innumerable nuances with which it can say things and hence discovers the properties of words and language.[4]

Naturally, Prodicus taught his students how to make the best of the play of synonymous distinctions from a practical viewpoint in speaking to judges in the tribunals or to people in the assembly. In the *Protagoras*, Plato describes with delicate humor the way in which the Sophists made use of such synonymical advantage. This art of synonymy, even though it was over-valued by its inventor and was often applied in an inappropriate way, certainly did not lack beneficial results and influences, as has been recognized by modern scholarship, on the Socratic method of searching for the "what-is" of things,[5] even if, evidently, the Socratic quest will aim at something far more profound than mere lexical definition.

2. Utilitarian ethics and the myth of the "uncertainty of Heracles"

In the field of moral reflection Prodicus became famous for his personal re-elaboration of the myth of the "uncertainty of Heracles" that is accurately recorded by Xenophon.[6] The myth, which only recently has been correctly understood,[7] is very interesting not only as a document of the thought of Prodicus, but likewise as evidence of the general tendency toward a utilitarian orientation of Sophistic ethics, and therefore it is worth careful consideration.

Heracles, who was passing from boyhood to adolescence, which is the time when the young become their own masters and chose a moral direction went to a quiet place in order to ponder. There appeared two women of great stature; one was fair to see and of reserved bearing; the other, on the contrary, plump and soft, with an exuberant disposition. The two women are symbols, one of depravity (or vice), the other of the virtues; their names, in Greek, are respectively *Arete* and *Kakia*. The woman who symbolizes depravity and vice says:

> Heracles, I see that you are in doubt which path to take towards life. Make me your friend; follow me, and I will lead you along the pleas- antest and easiest road. You shall taste all the sweets of life; and hardship you shall never know. First, of wars and worries you shall not think, but shall ever be considering what choice food or drink you can find, what sight or sound will delight you, what touch or perfume; what tender love can give you most joy, what bed the softest slumbers; and how to come by all these pleasures with the least trouble. And should there arise misgiving that lack of means may stint your enjoy- ments, never fear that I may lead you into winning them by toil and anguish of body and soul. Nay; you shall have the fruits of others' toil, and refrain from nothing that can bring you gain. For to my companions I give authority to pluck advantage where they will.[8]

As is evident, the type of life that *Kakia* proposes to Heracles is that of the most abandoned hedonism. Happiness is in the enjoyment of intense and easy pleasure, it is in draining the cup of pleasure to the full and what is useful and of service without scruples of any sort. Here instead is what *Arete* says:

> I, too, am come to you, Heracles: I know your parents and I have taken note of your character during the time of your education. Therefore I hope that, if you take the road that leads to me, you will turn out a right good doer of high and noble deeds, and I shall be yet more highly honored and more illustrious for the blessings I bestow. But I will not deceive you by a pleasant prelude: I will rather tell you truly the things that are, as the Gods have ordained them. *For of all things good and fair the Gods give nothing to man without toil and effort.* If you want the favor of the Gods, *you must worship the Gods: if you desire the love of friends*, you must do good to your friends: *if you covet honor from a city*, you must aid that city: *if you are fain to win the admiration of all Hellas for virtue*, you must strive to do good to Hellas: *if you want land to yield you fruits in abundance*, you must cultivate that land: *if you are resolved to get wealth from flocks*, you must care for those flocks: *if you essay to grow great* through war and want power to liberate your friends and subdue your foes, you must learn the arts of war from those who know them and must practice their right use: and *if you want your body to be strong*, you must accustom your body to be the servant of your mind, and train it with toil and sweat (E. C. Marchant trans.).[9]

Scholars have been deceived many times by the first phrase said by *Arete*, that is, by the emphasis on the concept that everything which is of value man must acquire only *at the price of toil* and they have not noted, first of all, that this was a commonplace which occurred often in the mouths of Sophists;[10] but especially they did not perceive that *Arete* speaks,

as is obvious, *in utilitarian terms.*[11] All her precepts are, to use Kantian
vocabulary, *from an hypothetical imperative aimed wholly at the attainment
of particular advantages* and precisely in order to obtain the friendship of
the Gods, the affection of friends, the honor of cities, the admiration of the
Greeks, to obtain the abundant fruits of the earth, wealth, and so on.
Virtue is only the most appropriate means for the obtaining of these advantages and these utilities.

If this is so, the basic contrast between *Kakia* and *Arete* does not turn on
pleasure as such which is the aim to be pursued but rather on the means
used to reach it.[12] In fact *Kakia* responds to *Arete*:

> Heracles, mark you how *hard and long* is that road to joy of which this
> women tells? but I will lead you by a *short and easy road* to happiness
> (E. C. Marchant trans.).[13]

To which *Arete* responds:

> What good thing is yours, poor wretch, or what pleasant thing do you
> know, if you will do nothing to win them? You do not even tarry for the
> desire of pleasant things, but fill yourself with all things before you
> desire them, eating before you are hungry, drinking before you are
> thirsty, getting cooks to give zest to eating, buying yourself costly
> wines and running to and fro in search of snow in summer to give zest
> to drinking; to soothe your slumbers it is not enough for you to buy
> soft coverlets, but you must have frames for your beds. For not toil, but
> the tedium of having nothing to do makes you long for sleep. You do
> rouse lust by many tricks when there is no need, using men as women:
> thus you train your friends, becoming wanton at night, consuming in
> sleep the best hours of the day. Immortal art you, yet the outcast of the
> Gods, the scorn of good men. Praise, sweetest of all things to hear, you
> hear not: the sweetest of all sights you behold not, for never yet have
> you beheld a good work done by yourself. Who will believe what you
> say? Who will grant what you ask? Or what sane man will dare join
> your throng? While your votaries are young their bodies are weak,
> when they wax old, their souls are without sense; idle and sleek they
> thrive in youth, withered and weary they journey through old age, and
> their past deeds bring them shame, their present deeds distress. Plea-
> sure they ran through in their youth: hardship they laid up for their
> old age. But I company with Gods and good men, *and no fair deed of
> God or man is done without my aid.* I am first in honor among the Gods
> and among men that are akin to me: to craftsmen a beloved fellow-
> worker, to masters a faithful guardian of the house, to servants a
> kindly protector: good helpmate in the toils of peace, staunch ally in
> the deeds of war, best partner in friendship. *To my friends meat and
> drink bring sweet and simple enjoyment*: for they wait until they crave
> them. *And a sweeter sleep falls on them than on idle folk*: they are not
> vexed at awaking from it, nor for its sake do they neglect to do their
> duties. *The young rejoice to win the praise of the old*; the elders are glad

to be honored by the young; *with joy* they recall their deeds past, and their present well-doing is joy to them, for though me they are dear to the Gods, lovely to friends, precious to their native land. And when comes the appointed end, they lie not forgotten and dishonored, but live on, sung and remembered for all time. O Heracles, you son of goodly parents, if you will labor earnestly on this wise *you may have for your own the most blessed happiness* (E. C. Marchant trans.).[14]

As can be seen, Prodicus dared to even put into the mouth of *Arete* a language which also assumes hedonistic advantages, although surely somewhat tempered. The best of all the studies concerned with this aspect of the thought of Prodicus is Zeppi, who writes: "In conclusion the contest between *Arete* and *Kakia*, which takes up the entire tale, turns on the means by which success is achieved, happiness-utility is considered by both questioners as the *acme* of human positivity...the disagreement is not about the ultimate ideals—it is not the case that to the identification of ἀρετή [virtue] and ἡδονή [pleasure] Prodicus opposes the identification ἀρετή [virtue] and πόνος [toil]—but in the choice of the means to attain them. Here is the core of the issue, Prodicus supports an activistic *utilitarian-eudaimonism* in the argument against a *sensistic-eudaimonism* but from the adversarial position he does not reject *tout-court* [wholly] the fundamental requirements by condemning them *in limine litis* [from the beginning]. It is instead true that he accepts and makes them true and hence presents his own doctrine as a non-deceptive hedonism."[15]

In short, we can conclude that for Prodicus virtue is the rational calculation of pleasures and of moral and material benefits, that is, a *reasoned utilitarianism*. The tale from this point of view of "the uncertainty of Heracles" can be taken as emblematic of the ethics of the Sophists (of the Sophists of the first generation), who see in utility the highest moral value.[16]

3. The Gods as deifications of utility

But there is more. Prodicus maintains that utility is not only a foundation of morality but also of theology. Here are some important testimonies:

> Perseus...in the work *Concerning the Gods*, maintains that through the demonstration by Prodicus it does not seem improbable that things from which benefits to human life have been derived have come to be considered as deities and, in addition, the related arts, such as Demeter and Dionysus.[17]

The testimony of Sextus Empiricus, who also reports a fragment with the original words of our Sophist, is even clearer:

> And Prodicus of Chios says: "The ancients accounted as Gods the sun and moon and rivers and springs and in general all the things that are

of benefit for our life, because of the benefit derived from them, even as the Egyptians deify the Nile." And he says that it was for this reason that bread was worshipped as Demeter, and wine as Dionysus, and water as Poseidon, and fire as Hephaestus, and so on with each of the things that are good for use.[18]

And again:

But Prodicus said that what benefits life is God, such as the sun and moon and rivers and lakes and meadows and crops and everything of that kind.[19]

This interpretation of the Gods and the divine given by Prodicus, which could be seen as an audacious anticipation of the Enlightenment, even expresses a key notion of the Sophists. While the Naturalist philosophers identified the divine with the Principle, that is with what according to them was more valued, Prodicus identified it with utility, which means with what for him (as for all the Sophists) was more valued.

V. Hippias and Antiphon

1. The naturalistic current of Sophistry

The statement that the Sophists opposed *nomos* and *physis*, that is, "law" and "nature," is commonplace among writers of potted histories of philosophy and is used to reduce "nomos" to pure convention. But this commonplace statement is only partially supportable. The opposition of law and nature is not present in Protagoras or in Gorgias or even in Prodicus.[1] It is found instead in Hippias and Antiphon, that is, in what has been correctly called *the naturalistic current of Sophism*, and then in the political Sophists, at a different level.[2]

2. The method of the "polymathia" of Hippias

Let us begin with Hippias.[3] This Sophist, who was very famous (Plato wrote two dialogues by that name),[4] shared the conception of the goal of teaching (political education) which was typical of all the other Sophists, but he differed in his method, which he argued was the only valid one. He did not value contradictory arguments, nor rhetoric, nor synonymity, but *polimathia*, that is, *encyclopedic knowledge* (and Hippias, in addition to *knowing* everything, was also led to boast of *being able to do everything*).[5] But in order to know and to learn many things a particular ability is necessary that makes it easy to memorize the various contents of knowledge, and with this in mind he taught the art of *mnemonics*.[6] His encyclopedic didacticism proposed mathematics among the disciplines, and the natural sciences were of great importance.[7] This makes understandable the fact that he maintained as necessary the teaching of the natural sciences, because he thought that *human life must conform to nature and to the laws of nature more than to human laws*.

3. The opposition between "law" and "nature"

And with this we enter into the lively theme of law versus nature. Faced with men from different cities and conditions, Hippias says what follows in the Platonic dialogue:

> O men who are present, I consider you blood relations, relatives, and fellow citizens *by nature*, not *by law*: in fact the similar is by nature relative of the similar, while the law, which is the tyranny of men, many times forces many things *against nature*.[8]

It is clear that here the sphere of *physis*, or nature and that of *nomos*, or law are not only clearly distinct but also radically opposed to each other. Nature is presented as that which *unites* men (the similar with the similar); law, on the contrary, is presented as that which *divides* men by coercing nature and hence going against nature. Nature is thus presented as that which alone constitutes the true base of human action, while law is rejected as the "tyranny of men" and hence is radically disvalued, *at least when and in the measure in which it is opposed to nature.* The distinction thus arises between *natural law* (a law of nature) and a *positive law* (a law proposed by men). The conviction follows that for the reasons mentioned above only the former is valid and eternal, while the latter is contingent and basically invalid. Thus *the premises are put down which lead to a total secularization of human laws,* which will thus be considered the product of simple convenience and to be arbitrary in character, and hence considered completely unworthy of the respect with which they had always been surrounded.

But Hippias draws more positive consequences from this distinction than negative ones. Since the nature of men is equal (at least the nature of the wise on whom he focuses in the context of the argument), neither the distinctions that divide the citizens of one city from those of another nor the distinctions that are internal to the city further divide citizen from citizen have any meaning. In this way arose *a cosmopolitan and egalitarian ideal that for the Greeks was not only quite novel but revolutionary as well.*

4. The radicalization of the contrast between "law" and "nature" in Antiphon

Probably Antiphon was able to proceed even further along the path opened by Hippias.[9] He also, in his teaching, must have elevated the natural sciences, for the reasons argued by Hippias, that is, because he saw the authentic norm of living only in *physis.* But he forced an even more radical split between nature and law to the point of a complete break by affirming with Eleatic terminology that nature is "truth" while positive law is pure "opinion." Therefore, the former is almost always in opposition with the latter and, consequently, one must break the laws of men in order to follow the laws of nature when one can do so without suffering any penalty:

> Justice, then, is not to transgress that which is the law of the city in which one is a citizen. A man therefore can best conduct himself in harmony with justice, if *when in the company of witnesses* he upholds the laws, and *when alone without witnesses he upholds the edicts of nature. For the edicts of nature are compulsory. And the edicts of the laws are arrived at by consent, not by natural growth, whereas those of nature are not a matter of consent.* So if the man who transgresses the legal code evades those who have agreed to these edicts, he avoids both disgrace and penalty; otherwise not. But if a man violates against possibility any of the laws which are implanted in nature, even if he evades all men's detection, the ill is no less, and even if all see it is no greater. *For he is not hurt on account of an opinion, but because of truth* (K. Freeman trans.).[10]

5. Cosmopolitanism and naturalistic egalitarianism

The egalitarian and cosmopolitan conceptions of man that Antiphon proposes are likewise more radical than those proposed by Hippias:

> We respect and honor he who is of noble origin, but he who is of obscure descent, we neither respect nor honor. In this, we behave toward each other like barbarians, *since by nature we are absolutely equals*, whether Greek or barbarian.[11]

The Sophistic Enlightenment has here dissolved not only the ancient prejudices of the aristocratic class and the traditional narrowness of the city-state, but also the most radical prejudice that was common among all the Greeks about their superiority to other peoples. All cities are equal to other cities, all social classes are equal to other social classes, all peoples are equal to other peoples, because all men are *by nature* equal to all others.

But what is this nature which unites all men? In what exactly does it consist?

From the extant fragments, it is undoubtedly true that Antiphon understood nature to mean *sensible nature*. That is the nature for which the good is *useful* and *pleasure*, and evil is *harmful* and *painful*. That is the nature which is spontaneous and instinctively free. And it is in the light of this concept of nature that the law is again seen—not that it could be otherwise—as unnatural because it compels sacrifice and hence pain, the result of the bridling and blocking of spontaneity. Here is a particularly important text:

> The majority of just acts according to law are prescribed contrary to nature. For there is legislation about the eyes, what they must see and what not; and about the ears, what they must hear and what not; and about the tongue, what it must speak and what not; and about the hands, what they must do and what not; and about the feet, where they must go and where not. And about the soul, what it must desire and what not. Now *the law's prohibitions are in nor way more agreeable to nature and more akin that the law's injunctions. But life belongs to nature, and death too, and life for them is derived from advantages, and death from disadvantages. And the advantages laid down by the laws are chains upon nature, but those laid down by nature are free. So that the things which hurt, according to true reasoning, do not benefit nature more than those which delight; and things which grieve are not more advantageous than those which please*; for things truly advantageous must not really harm, but must benefit (K. Freeman trans.).[12]

On the bases of these premises the equality of men is seen as nothing other than an equality of their structure and sensible necessity:

> It is enough to observe—he said—*the natural necessity proper to all men*...none of us can be defined neither as barbarian nor Greek: all in

fact breathe air by mouth, with nostrils, etc.[13]

This is extremely interesting because if the nature of man is restricted to the purely sensible sphere there is the illusion of eliminating all diversity among men, while in reality there is put in its place the premises to ground another kind of diversity and other kinds of distinctions, which from another perspective is even more serious. And thus is explained how by the same principle of sensible natures some could with ease deduce conclusions opposed to those deduced by Antiphon. Nature shows that men are *stronger* and men are *weaker*, and that hence *men are diverse, and that he who is stronger is naturally to rule over the weaker and impose on him his own will.* It likewise explains how on these bases that the law, understood as contrary to nature, must be lacking any objective foundation and hence is presented as unjustifiable. These conclusions were immediately reached by the political Sophists.

VI. Eristic and Political Sophistry

1. The characteristics of the Eristics

The relativism and antilogical method of Protagoras applied by the Sophists of the youngest generation produced *eristic*. If unconditioned truth does not exist and if it is possible to oppose any proposition to its contrary (and if it is possible to make the stronger argument the weaker), then it is always possible to refute any assertion. Thus the Eristics invented a series of questions that anticipate answers capable of being refuted; dilemmas that can always be resolved in both an affirmative and negative sense, bringing us back again to contradictory answers. They were able to construct a play on concepts through terms which were semantically ambiguous, and thus they ensnared the hearer and placed him in a position of checkmate and produced inferences which result again in absurd consequences. In short, the Eristics invented the whole range of capricious and deceptive arguments which came to be called "sophisms."

Let us record from the *Euthydemus*[1] a passage in proof of what we said and which demonstrates quite well the measure of the deterioration that Protagoreanism suffered on the level of eristics, reaching the point of denying capriciously the possibility of contradiction, that is, to speak falsely and to be deceived:

> On this Dionysodorus said: "As though there were such a thing as contradiction! Is that the way you argue, Ctesippus?"
>
> "Yes, to be sure," he replied, "indeed I do; and do you, Dionysodorus, hold that there is not?"
>
> "Well, you at any rate," he said, "could not prove that you had even heard a single person contradict another."
>
> "Is that so?" he replied: "well, let us hear now whether I can prove a case of it—Ctesippus[2] contradicting Dionysodorus."
>
> "Now, will you make that good?"
>
> "Certainly," he said.
>
> "Well then," proceeded the other, "each thing that is has its own description?"
>
> "Certainly."
>
> "Then do you mean, as each is, or as it is not?"
>
> "As it is."
>
> "Yes," he said, "for if you recollect, Ctesippus, we showed just now that no one speaks of a thing as it is not; since we saw that no one speaks what is not."
>
> "Well, what of that?" asked Ctesippus: "are you and I contradicting any the less?"

"Now tell me," he said, "could we contradict if we both spoke the description of the same thing? In this case should we not surely speak the same words?"

He agreed.

"But when neither of us speaks the description of the thing," he asked, "then we should contradict? Or in this case shall we say that neither of us touched on the matter at all?"

This also he admitted.

"Well now, when I for my part speak the description of the thing, while you give another of another thing, do we contradict then? Or do I describe the thing, while you do not describe it at all? How can he who does not describe contradict him who does?"[3]

We even find the Protagorean foundation of the doctrine placed in the mouth of Socrates in the immediately following passage:

At this Ctesippus was silent; but I, wondering at the argument, said: "How do you mean, Dionysodorus? For, to be plain with you, this argument, thought I have heard it from many people on various occasions, never fails to set me wondering—you know the followers of Protagoras made great use of it, as did others even before his time, but to me it always seems to have a wonderful way of upsetting not merely other views but itself also—and I believe I shall learn the truth of it from you far better than from anyone else. There is no such thing as speaking false—that is the substance of your statement, is it not? Either one must speak and speak the truth, or else not speak?"

He agreed.

"Then shall we say that speaking false 'is not,' but thinking false 'is?'"

"No, it is the same thing with thinking," he said.

"So neither is there any false opinion," I said, "at all."

"No," he said.

"Nor ignorance, nor ignorant men; or must not ignorance occur, if it ever can, when we put things falsely?"

"Certainly," he said.

"But there is no such thing as this," I said.

"No," he said.

"Is it merely to save your statement, Dionysodorus, that you state it so—just to say something startling—or is it really and truly your view that there is no such thing as an ignorant man?"

"But you," he replied, "are to refute me."

"Well, does your argument allow of such a thing as refutation, if there is nobody to speak false?"

"There is no such thing," said Euthydemus. "So neither did Dionysodorus just now bid me refute him?" I asked.

"No, for how can one bid something that is not?"[4]

It was clearly pointed out by Plato, through Socrates, that such a way of
reasoning destroys everything, the other persons reasoning and one's own
as well. This is certainly not the meaning of the Protagorean discovery,
which has its own truth and tragic stature, as we have seen above. Rather,
as we have emphasized, it is nothing other than the pathological excrescence
and parody of the Protagorean *antilogic*.

2. The theses maintained by the political Sophists

Instead, the Gorgean rhetoric and the deductions of the naturalistic
current of Sophistry were the roots of that phenomenon which has been
called political-Sophistry or sophistic-Politics. They made their devastating
incursions, proposing statements of almost total immoralism, in the ethico-
political sphere instead of in the logico-methodological field.

Critias,[5] more than any of the other Sophists, secularized the concept of
the Gods, considering them nothing more than a scarecrow introduced in
order to frighten the wicked and in order to gain respect for the laws that
in themselves do not have sufficient force to assert their authority. Sextus
writes:

And Critias, one of the Tyrants at Athens, seems to belong to the
company of the atheists when he says that the ancient lawgivers
invented God as a kind of overseer of the right and wrong actions of
men, in order to make sure that nobody injured his neighbors privily
through fear of vengeance at the hands of the Gods; and his statement
runs thus: "There was a time when the life of men was unordered,
bestial and the slave of force, when there was no reward for the virtuous
and not punishment for the wicked. Then, I think, men devised retrib-
utary laws, in order that Justice might be dictator and have arrogance
as its slave, and if anyone sinned, he was punished. Then, when the
laws forbade them to commit open crimes of violence, and they began
to do them in secret, a wise and clever man invented fear (of the Gods)
for mortals, that there might be some means of frightening the wicked,
even if they do anything or say or think it in secret. Hence he introduced
the Divine, saying that there is a God flourishing with immortal life,
hearing and seeing with his mind, and thinking of everything and
caring about these things, and having a divine nature, who will hear
everything said among mortals, and will be able to see all that is done.
And even if you plan anything evil in secret, you will not escape the
Gods in this; for they have surpassing intelligence. In saying these
words, he introduced the pleasantest of teachings, covering up the
truth with a false theory; and he said that the Gods dwelt there where
he could most frighten men by saying it, whence he knew that fears

exist for mortals and rewards for the hard life: in the upper periphery, where they saw lightnings and heard the dread rumblings of thunder, and the starry-faced body of heaven, the beautiful embroidery of Time the skilled craftsman, whence come forth the bright mass of the sun, and the wet shower upon the earth. With such fears did he surround mankind, through which he well established the deity with his argument, and in a fitting place, and quenched lawlessness among men. ... Thus, I think, for the first time did someone persuade mortals to believe in a race of deities (K. Freeman trans.).[6]

Thrasymachus of Chalcedon[7] stated that "justice is nothing other than the advantage of the stronger";[8] from which he deduced almost certainly, as Plato says in the first book of the *Republic*, that therefore justice is good for the powerful and bad for those under the rule of the powerful. So that the just man again has the disadvantage and the unjust the advantage.

Callicles,[9] in the *Gorgias* of Plato (which, even if he is not a real person or is just a mouthpiece for a real person, is in general a perfect expression of this current of thought), states:

But in my view nature herself makes it plain that it is right for the better [= stronger] to have the advantage over the worse [= the weaker], the more able over the less.[10]

Actually, among animals the stronger hunt the weaker, stronger men dominate weaker men, stronger states the weaker states. The law is again contrary to nature (this nature). It is made by the weaker in order to defend themselves against the stronger and in this sense it is wholly negative. Therefore Callicles exalts the man of strength, the superman who breaks the law and subjugates the weaker:

But if a man arises endowed with a nature sufficiently strong he will, I believe, shake off all these controls, burst his fetters, and break loose. And trampling upon our scraps of paper, our spells and incantations, and all our unnatural conventions, he rises up and reveals himself our master who was once our slave, and there shines forth nature's true justice.[11]

The "just life according to nature" also involves the satisfaction of all the instincts, because they are all in accord with nature. They involve the free release of the instincts, their satisfaction after being aroused, and thus to concede absolutely everything to them. It involves doing all this at the expense of the weaker and even exploiting the weaker to this end just because nature has made them different and has placed them at the mercy of the stronger. Here are the words that Plato has Callicles say, which perfectly capture this conception:

No, but the naturally noble and just is what I now describe to you with all frankness—namely that anyone who is to live aright should suffer his appetites to grow to the greatest extent and not check them, and through courage and intelligence should be competent to minister to them at their greatest and to satisfy every appetite with what it craves. But this, I imagine, is impossible for the many; hence they blame such men through a sense of shame to conceal their own impotence, and, as I remarked before, they claim that intemperance is shameful and they make slaves of those who are naturally better. And because they themselves are unable to procure satisfaction for their pleasures, they are led by their own cowardice to praise temperance and justice. For to those whose lot it has been from the beginning to be the sons of kings or whose natural gifts enable them to acquire some office or tyranny or supreme power, what in truth could be worse and more shameful than temperance and justice? For though at liberty without any hindrance to enjoy their blessings, they would themselves invite them. And surely this noble justice and temperance of theirs would make miserable wretches of them if they could bestow no more upon their friends than their enemies, and that too when they were rulers in their own states. But the truth, Socrates, which you profess to follow, is this. Luxury and intemperance and license, when they have sufficient backing, are virtue and happiness, and all the rest is tinsel, the unnatural catchwords of mankind, mere nonsense, and of no account.[12]

Thus the Protagorean *man-measure*, starting as a *criterion* becomes, in the hands of the Eristics, the *elimination of all criteria*. Even the Hippean and Antiphonean *physis*-criterion, which, on the contrary, grounded the equality of all men, ends by becoming with the political Sophists the criterion for grounding absolute inequality. By creating superman, it leads to more pointless immoralism.

But these currents are *a product* of sophistry, not the *only outcome*. They point out not the whole nature of sophistry, but only the negative face, as we have stressed before. The other face, the positive face, is the more authentic one, and it is revealed in Socrates. But before speaking about Socrates, we want to draw the conclusions which have arisen from all that we have said to this point.

VII. The Conclusions on Sophistry

As we have seen, both in various ways and at least apparently also in contrasting ways, the Sophists produced *a substantial re-alignment of the axis of philosophical inquiry in concentrating their problematic entirely on man.* The naturalistic current of Sophistry itself is concentrated on *physis* in a sense wholly different from the Naturalists, that is, not in order to know the cosmos as such but for a better understanding of man and his actions, for ethico-politico-educational aims.

So *in this re-orientation of the axis lies the essential value of Sophistry.* However, it cannot be said that Sophistry was in any way capable of *grounding moral philosophy.* All the Sophists aroused and variously analyzed moral problems and problems structurally connected with morality, but *they did not achieve, on the thematic level, the principle from which all could be derived.* This principle, as we know, consists in the *precise, conscious, and reasoned determination of the nature of man.* None of the Sophists has expressly stated, that is, thematically, what man is and consequently none of the Sophists was able to see consciously that the various doctrines that they professed united in a determined conception of man.

It is understandable, therefore, why some interpreters have exalted the Sophists as the greatest philosophers and, on the contrary, that other interpreters have accused the Sophists of superficiality or have even denied that they were philosophers. The former chiefly are concerned with the importance of the new philosophical problematic aroused by the Sophists, the latter have instead been concerned with the absence of a foundation that is discoverable in this new problematic.

The truth is somewhere in the middle. To the Sophists should be given credit for having given voice to the new exigencies of the historical moment and for having prepared the ground for the advent of moral philosophy, but we need at the same time to acknowledge that they did not take the final step. Notwithstanding that admission, it is still true to say that their contribution was decisive, for the reasons that we have amply explained.

The thought of the Sophists has been fruitful even in certain respects which many have seen as excessive if not downright iconoclastic. Actually, some things were to be totally destroyed by Sophistic thought in order to be more soundly reconstructed; old and narrow areas of interest were to be broken up so that other ones could be opened up. Let us illustrate.

The Naturalists criticized the old anthropomorphic conception of the Gods and they identified God with the principle. The Sophists rejected the old Gods, who after the naturalistic criticism were no longer believable; but they rejected likewise the conception of the Divine as the principle of things, having as a whole rejected cosmo-ontical research. Thus they drifted into the negation of every form of Divinity. Protagoras is an agnostic, Gorgias certainly goes beyond agnosticism to nihilism, Prodicus interpreted the Gods as human hypostatization of utility, Critias as the invention of an able and wise man for the enforcement of the laws, which of themselves were not binding. Certainly after these criticisms, which could not be turned around, *belief in the Divine must only be found by searching and looking in the highest sphere.*

Now let us move on from the Divine and consider the human dimension. We have already said that the Sophists did not arrive at any systematic determination of the nature of man. However from many hints it is not difficult to explain the meaning that they implicitly ended in giving to man. In this area the Sophists did not have to destroy what the Naturalists had said. They had to destroy instead, definitively, the vision that the tradition, chiefly transmitted by the poets and lawgivers, had constructed. But in the very moment in which they attempted to reconstruct a positive image of man it vanished in their hands. Protagoras understood man chiefly as a sentient being, relativizing sensation; Gorgias as the subject of changing emotions, subject to being fascinated by rhetoric in every way; and the Sophists themselves will appeal to nature, understanding this especially as biological and animal nature, from which they could deduce antithetical conclusions with absolute rigor either about the absolute equality or inequality of men. *Man, in order to be recognized, must be grounded on a more solid base.*

Finally, what about the issue of truth? Before the birth of philosophy, truth was not distinguished from appearances. The Naturalists opposed the *logos* to appearances, and only in it did they recognize truth. But Protagoras cut the *logos* up into "two-sided reasonings" and discovered that the *logos* speaks and contradicts; Gorgias rejected the *logos* as thought and preserved it only as a thaumaturgic word, but found again a word that could say everything and the contrary of everything and hence that would express nothing. These experiences, as has been said by an acute interpreter of the Sophists, are "tragic";[1] and we would add that they are found to be tragic just because thought and language have lost their object and their rule, they have lost being and truth. The naturalistic current of Sophistry, which even if in a confused way grasped this, was deluded in thinking it was able to find a content which would in some way be objectified in an encyclopedic knowledge. This encyclopedic knowledge as such is shown to be totally vain. *Language and thought must recover truth at its highest level.*

Although in order to recover the Divine and truth the metaphysical and logical discoveries of Plato and Aristotle are necessary, which are decidedly beyond the area of concern of Sophistry, nonetheless *in order to reconstruct a new image of man the resources available within the range of Sophistry were sufficient.* This was precisely the contribution that Socrates gave us, and thus with Socrates Sophistry ended and freed itself, as we will now see in detail.

Third Part

SOCRATES AND THE MINOR SOCRATICS: THE FOUNDATION OF MORAL PHILOSOPHY

«ἐγὼ γάρ, ὦ ἄνδρες Ἀθηναῖοι, δι᾽ οὐδὲν ἀλλ᾽ ἢ διὰ σοφίαν τινὰ τοῦτο τὸ ὄνομα ἔσχηκα. ποίαν δὴ σοφίαν ταύτην; ἥπερ ἐστὶν ἴσως ἀνθρωπίνη σοφία· τῷ ὄντι γὰρ κινδυνεύω ταύτην εἶναι σοφός.»

"I have gained this reputation, Athenians, from nothing more or less than a kind of wisdom. What kind of wisdom do I mean? Human wisdom I suppose. It seems that I am really wise in this limited way."

Plato *Apology* 20 D-E

First Section

SOCRATES AND THE DISCOVERY OF THE NATURE OF MAN

«ψυχὴν ἄρα ἡμᾶς κελεύει γνωρίσαι ὁ
ἐπιτάττων γνῶναι ἑαυτόν.»

"Then he who enjoins a knowledge of
oneself bids us become acquainted with
the soul."

Plato *Alcibiades* I 130 E

I. The Socratic Question and the Problem of the Sources

Before turning to any discussion of Socrates[1] it is necessary, although quite briefly, to trace in outline the so-called "Socratic question."

Socrates wrote nothing. In order to come to a knowledge of his thought and to evaluate its importance and quality, we must have recourse to the testimonies of his contemporaries, or the testimonies that are derived from them. But these testimonies (from which all the difficulties arise) *are profoundly in disagreement, and are in some cases even radically opposed, almost to the point of eliminating one another.* Therefore, some scholars are not mistaken when they say that despite all the statements that the ancients have made about Socrates, we can grasp with historical accuracy less about him than we can about the Presocratics. Their fragments have survived, even though they are relatively scarce. They are, however, sufficient to help us to listen to their authentic voice and the original tenor of their words and hence to communicate the meaning of their message.

The most ancient source regarding Socrates is Aristophanes in his comedy *The Clouds.*[2] *The Clouds* is not only a parody of philosophy, but also a vehement act of condemnation of Socrates's teaching and his pernicious influence on Athenian youth. Socrates is considered to be a Sophist and indeed, in a certain sense, the worst of the Sophists. At the same time he is considered a natural philosopher (professing doctrines that echo again those of Diogenes of Apollonia). For these reasons Aristophanes, for a long time, was not considered as important a source to use in finding the historical Socrates and *The Clouds* was also considered a work of pure imagination devoid of all historical value.

The second source, in chronological order, is Plato, who made Socrates the protagonist of the greater number of his dialogues and made Socrates the spokesperson of all his philosophical ideas which he then gradually unfolded with the exception of a part of the dialectical doctrine of the final dialogues, the cosmology of the *Timaeus*, and the doctrine of the *Laws.*[3] But the Platonic testimony is conditioned by two presuppositions which structurally compromise its historical credibility. In the first place, Plato systematically exalted his teacher and ended little by little in transfiguring him and transforming him into a symbol. Socrates is a moral hero, he is a secular saint, strong, temperate, wise, just, the most authentic educator of men, the only true statesman that Athens has ever possessed (it would be very difficult to think of two pictures of Socrates more antithetical than that described in *The Clouds* and that in the *Phaedo*, nevertheless both refer to the same man). In the second place, Plato places in Socrates's mouth almost all of his own doctrines, including those of his youth, those of his maturity, and some of those of his later years (*Philebus*), and it is fairly certain that, for the most part, these doctrines are *not* Socrates's, but are re-interpretations, amplifications, and even novel creations of Plato.

How then do we separate what is Socratic from what is Plato's in the writings of Plato? Is there any criterion which will permit us to do this? The answer is that the separation is, if not wholly impossible, at the very least most difficult. In fact such a criterion does not exist or, if it does exist, it is only very approximate because Plato, from the moment in which he began to write, did not objectively transcribe, but interpreted, rethought, revived, explicated, analyzed, reconstructed, and transposed Socrates. In brief, he projected himself, all of himself, into Socrates.

The third source is Xenophon, with his *Memorabilia* and other minor writings in which Socrates is a protagonist.[4] But Xenophon only knew Socrates for a very short time personally when he was young, whereas he composed his Socratic writings when he was much older. Furthermore, Xenophon lacks a certain speculative rigor and does not have the temperament of a thinker and as a result his Socrates is dessicated and lacks charisma. It would certainly be impossible to think that the Athenians would have bothered to put to death the kind of man that Xenophon depicted Socrates to have been.

The fourth source is found in Aristotle, who speaks of Socrates only occasionally;[5] but what he says of him is important. But Aristotle was not a contemporary. He could only confirm in various ways what was already written about Socrates. So Aristotle lacked the direct contact with the person himself for which, in the case of Socrates, there can be no substitute and the experience of whom cannot be recovered through any written sources.

Finally, there are various Socratics who founded the so-called Minor Socratic Schools who unfortunately have left little behind, or so little that each has left of the whole man only a ray filtered through a deforming prism.[6]

All of this is enough for the reader to comprehend the enormous difficulty which faces any attempt to reconstruct the thought of Socrates. The wide margin of the aleatory and hypothetical is inevitably destined to remain in all the reconstructions, given that the same sources from which each of them derives are not objective descriptions but rather interpretations.[7]

In the present work it is not possible to analytically dwell on the question. Let us only say that from the actual state of the scholarship it is now clear that, on the one hand, no sources can be considered privileged and that, on the other hand, no source can be neglected. Aristophanes himself, who for a long time was considered as wholly worthless as an historical source, instead when examined against the light is seen to contain numerous historical elements of great importance for understanding Socrates.[8] And vice versa with Aristotle, whom many consider as an impartial judge and the source capable of furnishing the criterion for the correct orientation of all the others. More recent studies have cast doubt on his impartiality and it has been demonstrated that he attributes to Socrates some things which we will see, on the contrary, were later acquisitions.[9] Therefore, a reconstruction of Socrates can be done only by taking into account all the sources, not only what they say, but likewise what they do not say, reading one in the light of the others and, vice versa, likewise standing each of them against the light and searching everything with a careful critical eye, in this way not getting lost in hyper-critical attitudes which unfortunately, in these previous decades, seem to have almost totally paralyzed Socratic scholars.[10]

It may be objected that in order to do this it would be necessary to propose a precise criterion without which any choice, any mediation, and any operation of filtering intended to apply to the sources will stand accused of being arbitrary.

We reply that as a matter of fact such a criterion exists and has already been used by some scholars,[11] even if not yet adequately stated on a methodologically reflective level. We bring to the readers attention the fact that beginning from first moment in which Socrates began to make his presence felt at Athens, literature in general, and the philosophical literature in particular *recorded a series of novelties of considerable enough nature* that then remain, in the sphere of Greek culture, an irreversible and a constant point of reference. But there is more; the sources about which we spoke above (as well as any others in addition to those mentioned) indicate an agreement that Socrates is the author of this novelty, both in an explicit way and in an implicit way, but not for this any less clearly. These two circumstances, that are mutually reinforced and validated, offer the thread of Ariadne which permits us to find our way through the labyrinth of the Socratic question. We can therefore proceed to consider Socratic, not with total certainty but with sufficient historical probability, the doctrines our sources attribute to Socrates as well as those which the documents in our possession confirm to be novel and which we find present in Greek culture beginning at the time Socrates was active. Moreover, it would not be difficult to demonstrate that to a greater or lesser degree, even if in a somewhat incomplete way, the greater part of the most qualified interpreters of Socrates have *as a matter of fact* applied this criterion from the beginning while noting the differences and the changes *before* and *after* Socrates, and then valuing highly those sources which give the reasons for the changes as the better ones. If what we said previously is correct, namely that we know historically less about Socrates than about any other Presocratic philosopher, it is because we possess fragments, at least, from the Presocratics which give us their original words, whereas we do not possess even one word of Socrates which can with certitude be said to be historically authentic and original. Therefore, this understanding, which makes a great difference in our procedure, is to some degree reversible. In fact the fragments of the Presocratics are like the pieces of a mosaic, which assume different meanings depending on the contextual design in which they are placed, and none of the Presocratics has transmitted the design with the fragments. We can only reconstruct on a strongly conjectural basis because of the fact that these fragments are texts taken from original *contexts* and were used and transmitted in doxographical contexts usually quite different from their original contexts as well as being quite distant in time from the originals. The context in which the individual doctrines are to be placed which are attributed to Socrates is reconstructible in a way that is much less conjectural, because his followers and his contemporaries are the ones who propose them (although they furnish us with evaluations of different weights, or in some cases that are even opposed). It is the abrupt change that occurred in philosophy after Socrates which confirms this in a manner which has no equal in preceding philosophers.

This long presentation of a methodological nature was necessary in order to justify the criteria that we follow in the reconstruction of the thought of Socrates as well as the ample space that we dedicated to it. In fact, read again with these criteria, Socratic philosophy will have decisive influence on the development of Greek thought, and in general western thought, as well as on its direction. Sadly, the philosophical historiography of the last century was not only rather far from recognizing this factor, but even of merely suspecting it.[12]

II. Socratic Ethics

1. Socrates in relationship to the philosophy of "nature"

We have seen what the attitude of the Sophists was in relation to the philosophy of *physis*. They have a totally negative attitude which attains paradigmatic shape in Gorgias in his treatise *On Nature or Not Being* (as we have seen above), in which he tried to demonstrate the *structural incommensurability* between being (*physis*), on the one hand, and thought and human speech on the other.[1]

The attitude of Socrates was analogous, but more complex and more articulated. It was not simply based on the dialectical deductions of the Gorgean type, but on the stress of the mutual contradictions of the various systems of the philosophies of nature which had been proposed at various times and which came to conclusions that cancelled each other and hence showed in this contradiction their incapacity to arrive at any valid conclusions.

The testimony of Xenophon is very clear in this regard and it is essentially confirmed by that of Plato. Xenophon states:

> He did not even discuss that topic so favored by other talkers, "the Nature of the Universe": and avoided speculation on the so-called "Cosmos" of the Professors, how it works, and on the laws that govern the phenomena of the heavens: indeed he would argue that to trouble one's mind with such problems is sheer folly. ... He marveled at their blindness in not seeing that man cannot solve these riddles; since even the most conceited talkers on these problems *did not agree in their theories, but behaved to one another like raving lunatics.*[2]

And here is how he characterized this "raving":

> So it is, he held, with those who worry with "Universal Nature." Some hold that being is *only one* [*scil.*, the Eleatics], others that is infinite in number [*scil.*, the Atomists]: some that *all things are in perpetual motion* [*scil.*, Heraclitus and his followers], others that *nothing can ever be moved* at any time [*scil.*, the Eleatics]: some that *all life is birth and decay*, others that *nothing can ever be born or ever die* [the statement is understood as being referred to the cosmos and not to the Principle or Principles, and the antithesis, this time, is between all the Physicists, on the one hand, and the Eleatics on the other].[3]

The confusion which was reached following the naturalistic inquiry, according to Socrates, is no less explicitly revealed in Plato, in some famous passages of the *Phaedo*.

Therefore, the science of the cosmos is inaccessible to man. Man dedicates his energies in vain attempts to acquire a knowledge which only a God could possess. Again Xenophon writes:

> In general, with regard to the phenomena of the heaven, he deprecated
> curiousity to learn how the deity contrives them: *he held that their*
> *secrets could not be discovered by man, and believed that any attempt to*
> *search out what the Gods had not chosen to reveal must be displeasing to*
> *them.* He said that he who meddles with these matters runs the risk
> of losing his sanity as completely as Anaxagoras, who took an insane
> pride in his research into the works of the Gods.[4]

Finally, according to Socrates, anyone who is concerned with these inquir-
ies becomes wholly absorbed in them, forgetting himself and what counts,
that is, man and the problems of man.[5]

We will speak about this further on, but first we must still show how
these precise conclusions of Socrates are not so much a point of departure,
but rather a troubled and laborious achievement which chronologically
can probably be located at the mid-point of his life.

We know with certainty that when he was about thirty Socrates was
linked to Archelaus (who, as we have seen, proposed again the doctrine of
Anaxagoras in a rather eclectic manner) and with him, as is attested by the
poet Ion of Keos,[6] he went to Samos. Theophrastus writes, analogously, as
we have already reported, that "...of Archelaus of Athens it is said that
Socrates was also his disciple."[7] Some hints in this direction can also be
seen in Plato[8] and in Xenophon (and in later authors there are consequently
many explicit confirmations).[9]

The length of time Socrates was exposed to these naturalistic doctrines
is impossible to establish with certitude. Aristophanes, whom as we have
said, presents Socrates in his forties, attributes to him again a series of
connections (sometimes even in some detail) with certain doctrines of the
Physicists. One thing, however, seems certain, or at least highly probable,
and it is that *Socrates was not very satisfied by this line of inquiry and*
consequently he never made it the major object of his own teaching, as all the
sources agree. At his trial Socrates can proudly affirm certainly with good
reason:

> But I, men of Athens, have had nothing to do with these things [the
> things which are the object of the philosophy of nature]. And I offer, as
> my chief witnesses, you; and I ask you to inform one another and to
> tell, all those of you who ever heard me conversing—and there are
> many such among you—now tell, if anyone ever heard me talking
> much or little about such matters.[10]

We do not know, in addition, whether Socrates had ceased to frequent
and to study with the Physicists gradually or as a result of a sudden crisis,
although the first possibility seems the most probable.[11] In any case, it is
certain (and this is a point that it is well to bear in mind) that Socrates at
a certain point of his spiritual development left behind those naturalistic
doctrines and all their connections in a clear break and without attempting

any mediation or overcoming of them, a task which was taken up instead by Plato, who will again consider these naturalistic doctrines exactly at the point at which Socrates had broken with them, in order to undertake, as we will see, his "second voyage."[12]

Socrates, therefore, entirely displaced all his interests from nature to man, and only on this point did he begin his teaching in Athens. In any case it is certain that when Xenophon and Plato began to frequent him he had already been established for many years in this precise position. After having communicated the criticism that Socrates leveled against the Naturalists, Xenophon notes:

> His own conversation was ever of human things (τῶν ἀνθρωπείων). The problems he discussed were, what is godly, what is ungodly; what is beautiful, what is ugly; what is just, what is unjust; what is prudence, what is folly; what is courage, what is cowardice; what is a state, what is a statesman; what is government, and what is a governor;—these and others like them, of which the knowledge made a man "humanly excellent," in his estimation, while ignorance should involve the reproach of "slavishness."[13]

The Platonic Socrates in the *Apology* makes this statement, which is an authentic plan:

> The fact is, men of Athens, that I have acquired this reputation *on account of nothing else than a sort of wisdom*. What kind of wisdom is this? Just that which is perhaps *human wisdom* (ἀνθρωπίνη σοφία). For perhaps I really am wise in this wisdom.[14]

Here we have finally come to the focal point; what is this "human wisdom," this ἀνθρωπίνη σοφία? Let us investigate it in more detail.

2. The discovery of the nature of man

Let us return to the current in the development of Sophistic thought that we had interrupted. We have seen that all the contradictions, aporias, and uncertainties of the Sophists, and finally the checkmate position to which they had come as a result of all their attempts, *essentially depended on having spoken about some problems of man without having inquired in an adequate way about the nature or essence of man or from having determined it in a wholly inadequate manner.* So then, unlike the Sophists, Socrates embarked on this task in a such a way as to give to the problematic of man a decisively novel significance.

What, therefore, is man? The Socratic reply is wholly unequivocal. *Man is his soul*, since it is the soul that distinguishes man from any other thing.

It may be objected that Greek literature and philosophy have for centuries made reference to *psyche*. Homer spoke about it, the Orphics spoke about it, the Physicists spoke about it, and likewise the lyric and tragic poets also.

But, as it has only recently come to light, no one prior to Socrates had understood by soul what Socrates understood by it, and after Socrates, the whole of the West.[15] For Homer, the soul is the spirit in the sense of the "ghostly appearance" which leaves a man at his death in order to go as a ghost, useless and unaware, to wander without purpose in Hades. For the Orphics it was instead the daimon which expiates its guilt and which was more itself when it was detached from our consciousness and was more active when our consciousness was weakened and fragmented (hence in dreams, faints, and death). For the Physicists it was instead the *principle* or an aspect of the principle (hence it was air, water, fire). Finally, for the poets, it is something indeterminate and in generally it was never theoretically defined.[16] On the contrary, the soul for Socrates was identified *with our consciousness when it thinks and acts with our reason and with the source of our thinking activity and our ethical activity.* In short, for Socrates the soul *is the conscious self, it is intellectual and moral personhood.*

With this is said all that is necessary to understand the revolution produced by this Socratic intuition. The life of man acquired its correct sense only now because the "Orphic life" itself and the "Pythagorean life" itself, with their doctrine of "purification," essentially tended to purify a soul-daimon which was beyond the self, beyond consciousness, beyond the subject, dividing man from himself and thus wounding the unity of man. The English scholar A. E. Taylor has said correctly: "Clearly, what is needed for the development of a 'spiritual' morality and religion is that the Orphic insistence on the supreme importance of 'concern for the interests of the *psyche*' shall be combined *with the identification of this supremely precious psyche with the seat of normal personal intelligence and character.* This is just the step which is taken in the doctrine of the soul taught by Socrates in both Plato and Xenophon, and it is by this breach with the Orphic tradition as much as by giving the conduct of life the central place which earlier thinkers had given to astronomy or biology that Socrates, in the hackneyed Ciceronian phrase, 'brought philosophy down from heaven to earth.' In other words, what Socrates did was to definitively create philosophy as something distinct from natural science [of the Physiologists] and from theosophy [of the Orphic-Pythagoreans], or any amalgam of the two, and to effect this result once for all."[17] So he can say, "It was Socrates who, so far as can be seen, created the conception of the *soul* which has ever since dominated European thinking."[18]

3. The determination of and documents relative to the new Socratic conception of "psyche"

But because the image of Socrates which we have presented is unusual and almost totally ignored by the historians of potted histories of philosophy, who as a rule remain some ten years behind with respect to the results of historiographic researches but who are the principal channels through which common opinion is formed, we must give an account of the assertions made above and we must document them in a more detailed manner.

First, let us say that the first restatement of the thesis discovered by Socrates about the soul understood as a conscious self has been made by the school of Scottish philologists who with delicate analyses noted that the conception of the soul, although almost absent prior to Socrates, is wide-spread in the literature immediately following Socrates and is common to Isocrates, Xenophon, and Plato. It is evident, therefore, that it must have had its origin either with Socrates or with some of his contemporaries; but we do not know of any contemporaries of Socrates to whom we might possibly attribute it, while we know from Plato and Xenophon that Socrates typically professed it in such a way that the attribution of the doctrine in question to Socrates becomes a practical necessity.[19]

Unfortunately, the manualists and scholars who are not specialists are perplexed faced with this originality. They do not perceive that it is a sound and documented conclusion and that it is not connected to the otherwise extreme theses professed by the Scottish school,[20] and so they do not accept it. But more attentive scholars have not been at a loss to accept it, and an historian of the caliber of Werner Jaeger, to cite a most distinguished example, used it as the very cornerstone of his reconstruction of Socrates in his famous work *Paideia*,[21] bringing to the fore quite well its religious aspect: "It is striking that, both in Plato and in the other Socratics, Socrates always uses the word *soul* with exceptional emphasis, a passionate, a beseeching urgency. No Greek before him ever said it in that tone. We can feel that this is the first appearance in the Western world of what we now, in certain connections, call the soul. . . . Because of the intellectual contexts in which the meaning of the word has developed, we always hear ethical or religious overtones in the word *soul*. Like his 'service of God' and 'care of the soul,' it sounds Christian. But it first acquired that lofty meaning in the protreptic preachings of Socrates."[22] Let us now look at some documentation.

All the Socratic doctrine can be summarized in these converging propositions: "know your self" [*viz.* psyche] and "take care of your self" [*viz.* psyche]. To know "your self" does not mean to know your own name, nor your own body, but rather to examine interiorly and to know your own soul, just as to care for your self does not mean to care for your body but for your soul. *To teach to men to know and to care for their souls is the supreme task that Socrates considered himself to have been given by God.*

On this point the Platonic testimony is most clear especially in the dialogues of his youthful period, which are those about Socrates and hence more worthy of belief historically. Here is the most important passage of the *Apology*:

> Men of Athens, I respect and love you, but I shall obey the God rather than you, and while I live and am able to continue, I shall never give

up philosophy or stop exhorting you and pointing out the truth to any one of you whom I may meet, saying in my accustomed way: "Most excellent man, are you who are a citizen of Athens, the greatest of cities and the most famous for wisdom and power, not ashamed to care for the acquisition of wealth and for reputation and honor, *when you neither care nor take thought for wisdom and truth and the perfection of your soul?*" And if any one of you argues the point, and says *he does care*, I shall not let him go at once, nor shall I go away, but I shall question and examine and cross-examine him, and if I find that he does not possess virtue, but says he does, I shall rebuke him for scorning the things that are of most importance and caring more for what is of less worth. This I shall do to whomever I meet, young and old, foreigner and citizen, but most to the citizens, inasmuch as you are more nearly related to me. For know that the God commands me to do this, and I believe that no greater good ever came to pass in the city than my service to the God. For I go about doing nothing else than urging you, young and old, *not to care for your persons or your property more than for the perfection of your souls, or even as much*; and I tell you that virtue does not come from money, but from virtue comes money and all other good things to man, both to the individual and to the state.[23]

But Plato returns to this concept again and again. Read the prologue of the *Protagoras*[24] where the difference between the Sophists and Socrates is pointed out in this way. The Sophists are hawkers selling food for the soul, but they do not know either food or the soul and hence they do not know whether it is helpful or not. While Socrates is clearly presented as one who knows these foods and knows the soul, and he is consequently presented as the "physician of the soul."[25]

In the *Laches*, the science of education is presented as the "...science that has as its goal the soul, and precisely that of the young."[26]

Here in the *Charmides* there is a clear depiction of this work of education:

Then Chaerephon called me and said, "How does the youth strike you, Socrates? Has he not a fine face?"

"Immensely so," I replied.

"Yet if he would consent to strip," he said, "you would think he had no face, he has such perfect beauty of form."

And these words of Chaerephon were repeated by the rest. "Then—by Heracles!" I said, "what an irresistible person you make him out to be, if he has but one more thing—a little thing—besides."

"What?" said Critias.

"*If in his soul*," I replied, "*he is of good grain*. And I should think, Critias, he ought to be, since he is of your house."

"Ah," he said, "he is right fair and good in that way also."

"Why then," I said, "*let us strip that very part of him and view it first, instead of his form*."[27]

But further, there is a more explicit passage in the *Alcibiades* I. After having affirmed that he needs, according to the oracle at Delphi, to know himself and to find the means to take care of himself, that is, the means which permit the best possible care that he can exercise, and after having, in the *Apology*, linked his own educational work to the will of the daimon, Socrates says:

> Come then, whatever kind of art can we use for taking pains over ourselves?
>
> I cannot say.
>
> Well, so much at least has been admitted that it is not on which would help us to make a single one of our possessions better, but one which would help to makes ourselves so?
>
> That is true.
>
> Now should we ever have known what art makes a shoe better, if we had not known a shoe?
>
> Impossible.
>
> Nor could we know what art makes rings better, if we had no cognizance of a ring?
>
> Well then, could we ever know what art makes the man himself better, *if we were ignorant of what we are ourselves?*
>
> Impossible.
>
> Well, and it is an easy thing *to know oneself*, and was it a mere scamp who inscribed these words on the temple at Delphi; or is it a hard thing, and not a task for anybody?
>
> I have often thought, Socrates, that it was for anybody; but often, too, that it was very hard.
>
> But, Alcibiades, whether it is easy or not, here is the fact for us all the same; *if we have that science, we are like to know what pains to take over ourselves; but if we have it not, we never can.*
>
> That is so.
>
> Come then, in what way can 'the same-in-itself' be discovered?

After having distinguished the subject who uses a given instrument from the instrument itself, and showing that this is the means and that is the user, the dialogue continues:

> And man uses his whole body too?
>
> To be sure.
>
> And we said that the user and what he uses are different?
>
> Yes
>
> So man is different from his own body?
>
> It seems so.

> Then whatever is man?
>
> I cannot say.
>
> Oh, but you can—that he is the user of the body.
>
> Yes.
>
> *And the user of it must be the soul?*
>
> It must...
>
> *The soul, hence, is ordered to know anyone who admonishes us: "Know your self."*[28]

Finally, let us remember that for his "swan-song," Plato has placed in Socrates's mouth his argument on the soul. Likewise as a final recommendation to his disciples, almost a spiritual final testament, Plato has placed in Socrates's mouth the message that the only thing that is worth doing is to take care of their selves, that is, that *they take care of their souls.*

But even Xenophon, in agreement in the final analysis with what Plato has said, affirms in fact that for Socrates the soul is that which in us participates in the Divine and that which in us rules.[29] He even states that Socrates explained to painters and sculptors that in order to adequately portray man they must not limit themselves to depicting his body, but they must also *achieve the picturing of his soul.* Let us read the two dialogues of Socrates with the painter Parrhasius and the sculptor Cleiton presented by Xenophon, because they are of exceptional importance in documenting this position. Here is the dialogue with the painter:

> Is painting a representation of things seen, Parrhasius? Anyhow, you painters with your colors represent and reproduce figures high and low, in light and in shadow, hard and soft, rough and smooth, young and old.
>
> True.
>
> And further, when you copy types of beauty, it is so difficult to find a perfect model that you combine the most beautiful details of several, and thus contrive to make the whole figure look beautiful.
>
> Yes, we do!
>
> Well now, do you also reproduce the character of the soul, the character that is in the highest degree captivating, delightful, friendly, fascinating, lovable? Or is it impossible to imitate that?
>
> Oh no, Socrates; for how could one imitate that which has neither shape nor color nor any of the qualities you mentioned just now and is not even visible?
>
> Do human beings commonly express the feelings of sympathy and aversion by their looks?
>
> I thinks so.
>
> Then cannot thus much be imitated in the eyes?
>
> Undoubtedly.

Do you think that the joys and sorrows of their friends produce the same expression on men's faces, whether they really care or not?

Oh no, of course not: they look radiant at their joys, downcast at their sorrows.

Then it is possible to represent these looks too?

Undoubtedly.

Moreover, nobility and dignity, self-abasement and servility, prudence and understanding, insolence and vulgarity, are reflected in the face and in the attitudes of the body whether still or in motion.

True.

Then these, too, can be imitated, can they not?

Undoubtedly.

Now which do you think the more pleasing sight, one whose features and bearing reflect a beautiful and good and lovable character, or one who is the embodiment of what is ugly and depraved and hateful?

No doubt there is a great difference, Socrates.[30]

Likewise explicit is the discussion of Socrates with the sculptor:

"Cleiton, that your statues of runners, wrestlers, boxers and fighters are beautiful I see and know. But how do you produce in them that illusion of life which is their most alluring charm to the beholder?"

As Cleiton was puzzled and did not reply at once, "Is it," he added, "by faithfully representing the form of living beings that you make your statues look as if they lived?"

"Undoubtedly."

"Then is it not by accurately representing the different parts of the body as they are affected by the pose—the flesh wrinkled or tense, the limbs compressed or outstretched, the muscles taut or loose—that you make them look more like real members and more convincing?"

"Yes, certainly."

"Does not the exact imitation of the feelings that affect bodies in action also produce a sense of satisfaction in the spectator?"

"Oh yes, presumably."

"Then must not the threatening look in the eyes of fighters be accurately represented, and the triumphant expression on the face of conquerors be imitated?"

"Most certainly."

"It follows, then, that *the sculptor must represent in his figures the activities of the soul*."[31]

Ample confirmation can be drawn likewise from the minor Socratics as well as from Isocrates, who in more than one respect shows traces of the doctrine of Socrates.

From all these testimonies it is therefore certain that for Socrates the essence of man is to be found in his *psyche*.

Let us linger awhile to document this point fully because, as we have stated at the beginning, it has not been accepted and yet it is a necessary prerequisite for the comprehension not only of Socrates, but likewise the relations of Socrates with preceding and subsequent philosophies and therefore for the comprehension of the precise place that Socrates occupies in the spiritual history of the West.[32]

4. The new meaning of *"arete"* and the revolution in the table of values

We have seen that the Sophists essentially did not achieve their aim because the technique of education which they intended to realize, when placed in the hands of their disciples, immediately degenerated, with the results that we have illustrated amply above. The reason was, to repeat it, that the Sophists did not know specifically what the nature of man was, and so they ignored the nature of his ultimate and authentic *end* and consequently the true *arete* of man. They had mistakenly identified their rhetorical methods with *arete* or they thought it was close to it. Due to this basic confusion, it is evident that the abilities and the techniques taught by Sophists would end by being ethically vacuous and deceptive; instead of being capable of educating, they ruined their students.

Plato understood and insistently emphasized that the superiority of Socrates over the Sophists consisted chiefly in this, having understood that man is distinguished from all other beings because of his soul. Socrates was thus enabled to determine the nature of human *arete*. *Arete cannot exist except as something that permits the soul to be good, that is, to be what it ought to be.* Thus to cultivate *arete* means to produce the best soul. It means to realize fully the spiritual self. It means to achieve the end which is proper to the interior man and at the same time to achieve happiness. But what is human excellence [*arete*]?

The reply of Socrates is well known. *Arete*, collectively and singly, is "science" or "knowledge." The contrary of virtue, that is vice, collectively and singly, is the privation of science or knowledge, that is, ignorance. All our sources agree completely on this point, and further on we will document it in a special way. Moreover, anyone who has followed us to this point will have noted the coherence of this affirmation with the premise on which it is based. If man is characterized through his soul, and if his soul is the conscious self, aware and intelligent, then *arete*, which is what fully actuates this awareness and intelligence, cannot be anything else except science and knowledge.

Therefore the supreme value for men is science, since it is precisely knowledge which makes the soul be what it ought to be and it brings to completion the man whose essence is his soul.

Socrates in this way revolutionized the traditional table of values to which all the Greeks had until then given allegiance, and which the Sophists themselves had not substantially altered. In fact the fundamental traditional values were principally those linked to the body: life, health, physical vivacity, beauty, or exterior goods or linked to the exteriority of man, such as wealth, power, fame, and similars. Moreover, the clear hierarchical superordination of the soul with respect to the body and the identification of authentic man with the soul and no longer with the body implies the shift to an inferior level, if not the annulment of those physical and external values, and the consequent emergence on an upper level of the interior values of the soul, especially of the value of science which sums them all up.

Plato, in the *Symposium*, has Alcibiades enunciate this judgment concerning Socrates:

> I tell you, all the *beauty* a man may have is nothing to him; he despises it more than any of you can believe; nor does *wealth* attract him, nor *any sort of honor that is the envied prize of the crowd*. All these possessions he values as nothing, and all of us as nothing, I assure you.[33]

The same judgment on these traditional values, in addition to numerous other passages of Plato, is found also in Xenophon, who referring to a conversation between Socrates and Euthydemus writes as follows:

> Happiness sees to be unquestionably a good, Socrates.
>
> It would be so, Euthydemus, were it not made up of goods that are questionable.
>
> But what elements in happiness can be called in question?
>
> None, *provided we don't include in it beauty or strength or wealth or glory or anything of this sort*.
>
> But of course we shall do that. For how can anyone be happy without them?
>
> Then of course we shall include the sources of much trouble to mankind. For many are ruined by admirers whose heads are turned at the sight of a pretty face; many are led by their strength to attempt tasks too heavy for them, and meet with serious evils; many by their wealth are corrupted, and fall victims to conspiracies; many through glory and political power have suffered great evils.[34]

The impression could be gathered from the reading of these passages that traditional values and goods were totally rejected by Socrates, but this is not the case. Only Plato will draw these consequences because he will not only distinguish and hierarchically subordinate soul and body but he will also oppose the one to the other and will even understand the body as a jail, a prison which encloses the soul. Instead, in a subordinate way and under the control and rule of the soul, Socrates again can give a certain standing to the traditional values, in the measure in which he does not understand the body as the antithesis of the soul. What was this standing and in what measure contained?

Socrates subordinated the actual validity of those things which the Greeks had traditional considered as goods to their *right use*, and he affirmed that the right use *depended exclusively on knowledge and science*. Here is the most compact and clear passage in this regard, taken from the dialogue *Euthydemus:*

> To sum up them, Cleinias, I proceeded, it seems that, as regards the whole of things which at first we termed goods, the discussion they demand is not on the question of *how they are in themselves and by nature goods*, but rather, I conceive, as follows: if they are guided by ignorance, they are greater evils than their opposites, according as they are more capable of ministering to their evil guides; whereas if *understanding and wisdom guide them, they are greater goods; but in themselves neither is of any worth.*
>
> I think the case appears, he replied, to be as you suggest.
>
> Now what results do we get from our statements? Is it not precisely that, of all the other things, not one is either good or bad, but of these two, *wisdom is good and ignorance bad?*[35]

With this we turn to the focal point of the Socratic reduction of *arete* to *science*, about which we will now speak in a more detailed way.

5. The "paradoxes" of Socratic ethics

The Socratic tenet of the identity of virtue and science implies in the first place the unification of the traditional virtues like wisdom, justice, temperance, fortitude into a single and unique virtue. The reason is that in the measure in which they are virtues each and every one of them is essentially reduced to knowledge. In addition, the unification of the virtues implies the reduction of vice, which is the contrary of virtue, to ignorance, which is the contrary of knowledge. Finally, it implies the conclusion that anyone who performs an evil act (which is through ignorance) does it, indeed, only through ignorance, and not, however, because he wills evil knowing that it is evil.

These tenets are splendidly developed in detail by Plato in the *Protagoras*[36] with the aid of a typically Socratic method which is often to be noted in the other dialogues. The other sources, on these points, are in complete agreement. Let us read Xenophon:

> Between wisdom and prudence he drew no distinction; but if a man knows and practices what is beautiful and good, knows and avoids what is base, that man he judged to be both wise and prudent. When asked further whether he thought that those who know what they ought to do and yet do the opposite are at once wise and vicious, he answered: "No; not so much that, as both unwise and vicious. For I

think that all men have choice between various courses, and choose and follow the one which they think conduces most to their advantage. Therefore I hold that those who follow the wrong course are neither wise nor prudent." He said that justice and every other form of virtue is wisdom. "For just actions and all forms of virtuous activity are beautiful and good. He who knows the beautiful and good will never choose anything else, he who is ignorant of them cannot do them, and even if he tries, will fail. Hence the wise do what is beautiful and good, the unwise cannot and fail if they try. Therefore since just actions and all other forms of beautiful and good activity are virtuous actions, it is clear that justice and every form of virtue is wisdom.[37]

Aristotle also writes:

Socrates believed that the virtues are principles, for he said that they are all of them forms of knowledge.[38]

It is strange...Socrates held, if when a man possessed knowledge, some other thing should overpower it, and "drag it about like a slave." In fact Socrates used to combat the view altogether, implying that there is no such thing as unrestraint, since no one, he held, acts contrary to what is best, believing what he does to be bad, but only through ignorance.[39]

These two Socratic principles, a) that *virtue is science* and b) that *no one voluntarily acts evilly,* which in various way condition all Greek ethical speculation, have been the subject of innumerable discussions and arguments. To many scholars it seemed that Socrates, having based his entire ethics on science and reason, fell into "intellectualism," and thus misunderstood almost entirely the role of the will in moral action, and in general, the significance of the a-logical and a-rational aspects which enter into play in human action. Others have tried, on the contrary, to show that given a detailed analysis, the accusation of intellectualism is incorrect and that actually the two Socratic principles are much less paradoxical than they appear to be at first glance.

In our judgment, there is soundness in both views, and therefore we will want to uncover the correct attitudes which will give an appropriate weight to both aspects of this difficulty.

In the first place, we say that not only is it correct, but it is an interpreters essential duty to find the point of view from which the affirmations of the author studied may appear the least paradoxical and intelligible as possible. Now certainly the affirmation that *virtue is science* and *vice is ignorance*, from the Christian viewpoint and in general to modern man—who in the inquiry as to the causes of human behavior has a more profound awareness than the ancients, and who understands "knowledge" and "science" in a wholly novel way—sound paradoxical. But it will sound less paradoxical if we try to divest ourselves a little of our habitual way of thinking and see these affirmations within the precise configurations of Socratic thought.

The common opinion and the Sophists themselves (who simply pretended to be teachers of virtue) saw in the diversity of virtues (justice, piety, prudence, temperance, and wisdom) a multiplicity, and they did not entirely grasp the nexus which is common to them. It is this nexus which precisely makes them virtues and which justifies them, and hence is their common denominator as virtues. And by virtue, the common man (and for the most part the Sophists themselves) understood what was understood by the tradition and the poets. Hence it was something based on *custom, the habits and convictions of Greek society, but not grounded on or justified on a strictly rational basis.* Now Socrates, with respect to virtue and the moral life of man, did exactly what the Presocratics had done in regard to nature (and which the Sophists had begun to do, but did not always succeed in doing, in relation to man). *Socrates attempted to subject human life to the rule of reason, just as they had subjected the external world to the rule of human reason.* For Socrates, virtue was not and could not be simply adapted to customs, to habits, and not even to generally accepted convictions. It must be something *rationally motivated and justified and grounded on the terrain of science.* It is in this sense that he undoubtedly says that *virtue is science.* Evidently, virtue is not any science (not, for example, the knowledge of the various technical or productive sciences), but it is the highest and most elevated science, the science of the nature of man and what is good and useful for him (today we would say: of the highest *ethical values*). This science of man and of his moral values Socrates did not have concretely grounded, but that is something which does not eliminate the value of his essential discovery. It will be left to Plato to provide the basis for the meaning of man and his goods; but Socrates had already pointed out clearly the indications, as we have seen in the preceding paragraph. Man's true self is his spirit, his soul. The soul is thus the seat of all those values which are most typically human, and hence the true values are the values of the soul. In this way, the proposition which states that virtue is *science* and vice is *ignorance* ceases to be that strident a paradox which at first glance it seems to be.

The justification of the second principle may seem to be more difficult. Man wills only the good and not evil and if anyone does evil he does it involuntarily, which means that no one does evil voluntarily. But are there not perhaps men, it will be said, who expressly admit that they do things which are evil? Is not the evidence undeniably stated in the famous maxim *video meliora proboque, sed deteriora sequor*? Certainly, we answer, but Socrates did not intend to deny it. Thus under all of these considerations there stands something more complex than what seems to be the case. A. E. Taylor explains it clearly: "'Moral weakness,' the fact that men do what they themselves confess to be wrong, and that they do it so without any forcing, is one of the most familiar facts of experience, and we are not to suppose that Socrates means to deny this. He means to say that the popular phrase we have just used gives an adequate analysis of the fact. A man often enough does evil *in spite of* the fact that it is evil; no man ever does evil simply *because* he sees it to be evil, as a man may do good simply because he sees it to be good. A man has temporarily to sophisticate himself into regarding evil as good before he will choose to do it. As it is put in the *Gorgias*, there is one fundamental desire which is ineradicable in all of us: the desire for *good* or *happiness*. It is possible, in the case of all other objects, to prefer the appearance to the reality, the outward show, e.g., of power or wealth, to the thing itself, but no one can wish for the show of good or happiness rather than the reality: this is the one case where the shadow cannot possibly be esteemed above the substance. To say that vice is involuntary means, therefore, that it never brings the vicious man that on which his heart, whether he knows it or not, like the heart of every one else, is really set.... Thus, if a man really knew as assured and certain truth, of which he can no more doubt than he can doubt of his own existence, that the so-called 'goods' of body and 'estate' are as nothing in comparison with the good of the soul, and knew what the good of the soul is, nothing would ever tempt him to do evil. Evil-doing always rests upon a false estimate of goods. A man does an evil deed because he falsely expects to gain good by it, to get wealth, or power, or enjoyment, and does not reckon with the fact that the guilt of soul contracted outweighs these supposed gains."[40]

But now that we have grasped the meaning of the apparently paradoxical affirmations of Socrates, we must nevertheless point out their onesidedness and inadequacy.

Socrates says in essence that it is not possible to be virtuous without knowledge, because one cannot do the good act without knowing what it is. Up to this point everything is fine; but he maintained likewise that it is not possible to know what the right act is unless one performs right actions. *This is the point which is incorrect.* The knowledge of the good, for Socrates, is not only a necessary condition, but is likewise a sufficient condition for being virtuous. Now, we say that it is true that knowledge of the good is necessary, but *we cannot admit that it is sufficient.*[41] In moral action, that is in the exercise of virtue, the *will* has a weight and a significance at least as important as the *knowledge* of the good. (Christianity has, in fact, shown that the will is determining, because in the ultimate analysis it is the will, the good will, which determines the moral character and value of man, that is, which saves or condemns him). Now this unlimited confidence in reason and in the intelligence and the emphasis, almost none, given to the will is exactly what has merited the accusation of intellectualism against Socratic ethics. And it is correct to speak of intellectualism, but only with the appropriate precisions. Actually, Socrates, as the historically educated scholar of today recognizes, did not distinguish among the various faculties of the human spirit and their complexity. Socrates, in sum, *has on his mind that same onesided vision of the human soul which Parmenides had with respect to being.* And it will be Plato who will accomplish the famous "parricide of Father Parmenides" by uncovering the undeniable character of not-being.[42] In the same way he will also discover the structural complexity of the human soul and he will show that, next to its rationality, there is in us the spirited and the visceral, and that moral action consists in a delicate equilibrium of these forces, which see the spirited (the will) in an alliance and cooperating with reason.[43] It is precisely by seeing Socrates in the light of these successive distinctions of the faculties of the human soul that the Socratic position can appear and seem to be intellectualistic. In the presence of these precisions, Socratic intellectualism can hence be spoken of in a correct manner.

Moreover, all of Greek ethics (even the Platonic, the Aristotelian, and their successors), if compared to Christian ethics, is, in its entirety, intellectualistic. It is not only Socrates, with his onesided discovery, but also succeeding philosophers who would not be able to explain that dramatic human experience which is moral evil. They tend always, more or less accentuatedly, to reduce moral evil to an error of reason, or generally to explain it chiefly in that sense. It will be Christianity, and only Christianity, which will reveal to Western man the upsetting significance of sin and moral evil.

6. Self-control, interior liberty, and autonomy

The things which we have said will receive further elucidation by means of the particular specifications of some concepts introduced by Socrates for the first time into the ethical problematic.

First, the concept of "self-control" is particularly revelatory because it is expressly declared to be the "highest good for man."[44] The creation of the concept with the related term ἐγκράτεια (*enkráteia*) certainly goes back to Socrates. We can affirm this conclusion on the basis of the same methodology which enabled us to attribute to him the new concept of *psyche*. In fact, as is well known,[45] the concept and term appear at the same time in Xenophon and in Plato, who attributes it to Socrates, as well as in Isocrates, who as we know absorbed many Socratic ideas. "The word," explains Jaeger, "derives from the adjective ἐγκρατής used of anyone having power or authority over anything. But the noun is found only in the meaning of moral self-mastery, and does not appear before this period; therefore, it was obviously created to express the new concept, and did not exist beforehand as a purely legal term."[46]

Enkráteia is the control of self in the presence of pleasure and pain, in tiredness, in the presence of urges and passions. In a word, it is *the control over one's own sentient nature*.[47] It is now possible to understand how Xenophon undoubtedly was made to say to Socrates:

> Should not every man hold self-control (*enkráteia*) to be the foundation of all virtue, and first lay this foundation firmly in his soul?[48]

To lay the foundation of *enkráteia* in the soul means to make the *soul the ruler over the body,* and *reason the ruler over the instincts.* This can be seen in all the examples which Xenophon uses and as it is very clearly confirmed by Plato, especially in the *Gorgias.*[49]

Contrarily, the absence of the self-control allows the body and its instincts to rule and hence to deprive a man of all virtue and become similar to the most savage beasts.

Xenophon writes, referring to a conversation of Socrates with Euthydemus:

> "Socrates," said Euthydemus, "I think you mean that he who is at the mercy of the bodily pleasures has no concern whatever with virtue in any form."
>
> "Yes, Euthydemus; for how can an incontinent man be any better than the dullest beast? How can he who fails to consider the things that matter most, and strives by every means to do the things that are most pleasant, be better than the stupidest of creatures?"[50]

This tenet was also expressed and carried to the ironic limit by Plato with a most effective analogy. He compared the man who has no control over himself to a *karadriou* [plover], which according to ancient lore was a savagely voracious bird which ate and evacuated at the same time.[51]

But there is more. Socrates has expressly identified *liberty* with *enkráteia.* By doing this he opened up a new perspective. In fact, before him liberty had an almost exclusively juridical and political meaning; with him it took on *the moral meaning of the control of rationality over animality.* Here is the passage of Xenophon which explains the equivalence between *self-control* and *liberty* (ἐλευθερία):

> "Tell me, Euthydemus," he said, "do you think that freedom is a noble and splendid possession both for individuals and for communities?"
>
> "Yes, I think it is, in the highest degree."
>
> "Then do you think that the man is free who is ruled by bodily pleasures and is unable to do what is best because of them?"
>
> "By no means."
>
> "Possibly, in fact, to do what is best appears to you to be freedom, and so you think that to have a master who will prevent such activity is bondage?"
>
> "I am sure of it."
>
> "You feel sure then that the incontinent are bond slaves?"
>
> "Of course, naturally."
>
> "And do you think that the incontinent are merely prevented from doing what is most honorable, or are also forced to do what is most dishonorable?"
>
> "I think that they are forced to do that just as much as they are

prevented from doing the other."

"What sort of masters are they, in your opinion, who prevent the best and enforce the worst?"

"The worst possible, of course."

"And what sort of slavery do you believe to be the worst?"

"Slavery to the worst masters, I think."

"The worst slavery, therefore, is the slavery endured by the incontinent?"

"I think so."[52]

In connection with these concepts of *enkráteia* and *eleuthería* Socrates must also have developed the concept of *autarcheia* (αὐτάρκεια), that is, the *autonomy of virtue and the virtuous man*. Maier writes that "the expression is perhaps somewhat foreign to Socrates; but the meaning was very clearly before his eyes."[53] Nevertheless it is to be noted that the adjective αὐτάρκης (autonomous, independent) is found in Xenophon.[54] The term *autarcheia* occurs in the later works of Plato in the definition of the good,[55] and it is also technical in Antisthenes.[56] In addition, we know that the teacher of the Sophist Hippias taught that the goal to be achieved was *techne autarcheia*, that is, the capacity of knowing how to do for oneself everything that is necessary for life. The same Hippias is represented by Plato as especially proud of this capacity of being able to do everything by himself, and by his own hands.[57] Therefore, it is logical to think that the interiorization of *autarcheia*, that is, the transformation from technical *autarcheia* into moral *autarcheia* was accomplished by Socrates, even if it then received special development within the circle of the Socratic schools.[58]

In the concept of *autarcheia* there are two characteristic features: *a)* autonomy with respect to physical needs and impulses through the control of reason (the *psyche*), and *b)* reason (the *psyche*), which alone is sufficient to achieve happiness. He who abandons himself to the satisfactions of his desires and impulses is forced to depend on things, on men, and on society, which are in various measures necessary in order to procure the objects which gratify the desires. He requires everything which is difficult to obtain and becomes victimized by forces beyond his control, loses his liberty, his tranquility, and his happiness.

> You seem, Antiphon, to imagine that happiness consists in luxury and extravagance. But my belief is that *to have no wants is divine; to have as few as possible comes next to the divine*; and as that which is divine is supreme so that which approaches nearest to its nature is nearest to the supreme.[59]

Werner Jaeger has interpreted in a holistic way the new Socratic connotation of the concept which we have been discussing: "The wise man, in his independence of the external world, re-creates, on the spiritual plane, a quality of the mythical heroes of old. The greatest of them, in Greek eyes, was the warrior Heracles with his labors (πόνοι), and the heroic quality was self-help. It began with the hero's power to 'make his hands keep his head' against enemies, monsters, and dangers of all kinds, and to come out victorious. Now this quality becomes a spiritual one. It can be attained only by man who conforms his wishes and endeavors to those things which are within his power to obtain. Only the wise man, who has tamed the wild desires in his own heart, is truly self sufficient. He is nearest to God: for God needs nothing."[60]

It would seem that with respect to these three concepts, which comprise the fundamental core of Socratic ethics as well as being fundamental for the comprehension of the succeeding ethics, scholars have not emphasized their basic intellectualistic parameters. In fact, self-control (*enkráteia*) is control not of the *will*, but of *reason and knowledge* over sensible impulses; liberty (*eleuthería*) is not free will, the freedom to choose, but *the liberty of the logos*, that is, the capacity of the reason to impose its own requirements onto the requirements of human animality. And *autarcheia*, as independence from animal needs, is in itself *the self-sufficiency of the human logos*. In conclusion, these concepts arise from the same matrix from which the doctrine of virtue-science and the omnipotence of science arise, and they are all of the same nature.

7. Pleasure, utility, and happiness

In the *Protagoras* the Platonic-Socrates affirms that *pleasure* and the *good* are identical, while in the other dialogues the Platonic-Socrates not only does not make this identification, but rejects the notion that pleasure is a good. Well then, the affirmation of the *Protagoras*, which some interpreters have absurdly taken as Socrates's own position, actually is part of the play of irony and the dialectic of this dialogue. It has no independent value but only that of a commonly held opinion, hence in context it means "granted but not conceded." In other words, following a method peculiar to him (about which we will speak at length), Socrates, in order to move the reader to admit his ethical paradoxes, starts his argument from the conviction that all commonly accept and none reject (*viz.*, that the good and pleasure are the same thing), and moving from this premise, on which in point of fact all are agreed, he shows in any case that happiness does not consist in abandoning themselves to pleasure, but rather in the use of a shrewd *calculus of pleasure*, a cunning *measuring of pleasure* which is able to adequately distinguish and weight them. And if this is so, the *art of measuring* pleasure emerges as the authentic criterion and salvation, which is or implies reason and science. Hence, beginning from this commonly held and presupposed hedonism, it also emerges that *virtue* (the highest human capacity) *is science.*[61]

Moreover, a text of Xenophon, which on the subject of this discussion is certainly not suspect, states the same thing:

> "Has it ever occurred to you, Euthydemus?" "What?" "That though pleasure is the one and only goal to which incontinence is thought to lead men, she herself cannot bring them to it, whereas nothing produces pleasure as surely as self-control?" "How so?" "Incontinence will not let them endure hunger or thirst or desire or lack of sleep, which are the sole causes of pleasure in eating and drinking and sexual indulgence, and in resting and sleeping, after a time of waiting and resistance until the moment comes when these will give the greatest possible satisfaction; and thus she prevents them from experiencing any pleasures worthy to be mentioned in the most elementary and recurrent forms of enjoyment. But self-control alone causes them to endure the sufferings I have named, and therefore she alone causes them to experience any pleasure worth mentioning in such enjoyments." "What you say is entirely true." "Moreover, the delights of learning something good and excellent, and of studying some of the means whereby a man knows how to regulate his body well and manage his household successfully, to be useful to his friends and city and to defeat his enemies—knowledge that yields not only very great benefits but very great pleasures—these are the delights of the self-controlled; but the incontinent have no part in them. For who should we say has less concern with these than he who has no power of cultivating them because all his serious purposes are centered in the pleasures that lie nearest?" "Socrates," said Euthydemus, "I think you mean that he who is at the mercy of the bodily pleasures has no concern whatever with virtue in any form?" "Yes Euthydemus," says Socrates...[62]

Thus the grave error committed by many scholars who have made Socrates into an hedonist is obvious as soon as one goes back to the doctrine of the *psyche* and to the new table of values based on the *psyche*. Like all the putative goods of the body and all exterior goods, Socrates does not say that pleasure is a good in itself, not that it is an evil in itself either, but everything depends on its use. If pleasure is placed under the care of *enkráteia* and science, it is positive. It is certain, therefore, that happiness does not depend on pleasure as such.

An analogous argument was made even for *utility*. Actually, anyone reading the Socratic writings of Xenophon would be left with the impression that Socrates identified the *good* with the *useful*. And even Plato, although for different reasons, attributed to Socrates the identification of the *good* with the *enjoyable*, and hence, with utility. This explains, therefore, how many interpreters considered the ethics of Socrates as *utilitarian* and how they came to give such disparate interpretations of his utilitarianism. But if the Socratic ethics were truly utilitarian, then the conclusion could not be avoided that, in the ultimate analysis, *the foundation of the moral life for Socrates is egoism*. Actually this is not at all the case. Once again, it is the concept of the *psyche* which straightens things out and cuts short the never-ending discussions on this question. In fact the utility about which Socrates speaks is always (or chiefly) the *utility of the soul*, and the utility of the body to him is of interest only *in function of the utility of the soul*. In addition, we could make it more precise by saying that the parameters of utility are given by nothing other than the *arete* of the soul, that is, by *science* and by *knowledge*. With respect to the modern meaning of utilitarianism, which is in some way always linked to empiricism and to positivism if not even to materialism, the Socratic "utilitarianism" involved the opposite meaning and can be correctly understood only in connection with the Socratic discovery of the essence of man as *psyche*.[63]

The discussion, however, which concerns happiness, the Greek *eudaimonia*, is different. That Socrates tended to the achievement of happiness and that his philosophy wants, in the ultimate analysis, to *teach men how to be truly happy* is beyond discussion. Socrates, therefore, is decisively an *eudaimonist*. All Greek philosophers, in addition, are *eudaimonists*. An ethical discussion which is not in some measure eudaimonistic is conceivable only beginning from Kant.

But to say that Socrates is an eudaimonist and that he teaches men how to achieve *eudaimonia* does not mean anything unless the nature of happiness is made precise and pointed out. Even in order to establish this, it is necessary to go back to the *psyche* and to its *arete*. Happiness is not given by exterior goods nor by goods of the body, but by goods of the soul, that is, by the perfecting of the soul through virtue which is knowledge and science. To perfect the soul with virtue (with knowledge) means, as we saw, for man *to realize his most authentic nature, to be fully himself*, to bring to completion the full accord of himself with himself, and it is precisely this which brings happiness.

Happiness is now *entirely interiorized* and is freed from what comes from the outside and finally from what comes from the body, and *it is located in the soul of human beings* and hence it is assigned to the self-dominion of man. Happiness depends not on things and good fortune, but on the human *logos* and on the *interior formation which the human logos can impart to a person*. Here are fragments taken from the dialogue *Gorgias* in which Socrates, arguing with the Sophist Polus, denies that the possession of power, wealth, and honor make a person happy:

> Then doubtless you will say, Socrates, that you do not know that even the Great King is happy. Yes, and I shall be speaking the truth; for I do not know how he stands *in point of interior formation* and justice. Why, does happiness entirely consist in that? Yes, by my account, Polus; for a good and honorable man or woman, I say, is happy, and an unjust and wicked one is wretched.[64]

Conversely, even unhappiness does not come from the outside, but from within us; not others, but we alone are able to do the greatest evils to ourselves. He who is good has the greatest defense against evil in his goodness, and no one can harm him. In the *Apology* we read:

> For I believe it is not God's will that a better man be injured by a worse. He might, however, perhaps kill me or banish me or disenfranchise me; and perhaps he thinks he would thus inflict great injuries upon me, and other may think so, but I do not; I think he does himself a much greater injury by doing what he is doing now—killing a man unjustly.[65]

No evil can come to a good man either in life or after death. . .[66]

Here is what is the good and happiness for Socrates:

> I say that to talk every day about virtue and the other things about which you hear me talking and examining myself and others is the greatest good to man, and that the unexamined life is not worth living.[67]

A final point must be clarified before we can conclude this discussion. Happiness not only has no need of anything *from the outside* of man, but not even *from above* man. Virtue is autarchic and has no need of a reward in the hereafter, having in itself its own reward which is happiness.

It is understandable hence why Socrates never felt the need to solve the question of the immortality of the soul on the theoretical level. He says in this regard:

> For the state of death is one of two things, either it is really the entrance to nothingness, so that the dead have no consciousness of anything, or it is, as people say, a change and migration of the soul from this to another place.[68]

On the level of reason the two hypothesis seem to be equally plausible, even if on the level of faith Socrates tends toward the second. On the level of reason Socrates cannot demonstrate the immortality of the soul because he lacks the necessary metaphysical categories. But what is important is that he declared, without benefit of the proper categories, *the possibility for man of being happy, prescinding from his fate after death, and the total autonomy of the moral life.*

To the virtuous man nothing evil can happen because virtue is a radical defense against all evils. With this conviction, he serenely drank the hemlock which brought him to his death, and he serenely drank it because he was convinced that death kills the body but not the virtue of man. Life is destroyed, but not the having lived well.

8. Friendship

With Socrates begins also the philosophical reflection on friendship, a problematic concerning which a whole literature has flourished that goes from the Platonic *Lysis* and *Symposium* to two entire books of the *Nicomachean Ethics* (touching on only the works which are the best known from antiquity), and which will have continued success in the Hellenistic Age.

To establish what Socrates thought about friendship is impossible, given the enormous disjunction between what the Xenophonean Socrates and what the Platonic Socrates say. It is certain that the Platonic treatises, in the measure in which they utilize metaphysical categories unknown to Socrates, cannot possibly be attributed to Socrates; but it is probable that Xenophon, in his turn, has overly simplified Socrates's position.

In any case, using Xenophon's testimony we can clearly say that Socrates contributed in a significant way to the refinement of the concept of friendship *by locating it among things having moral value*.[69]

True friends are undoubtedly a great blessing for human beings, and in order to acquire good friends a man must not spare any sacrifice.

But who is a good friend? It certainly is not someone who seeks exterior advantages from the relationship, for example, power, fame, or wealth. It is instead the virtuous man, the man, that is, who possesses those prerogatives connected with virtue which we have analyzed above, the man who is *capable of self-sufficiency (αὐτάρκης),* the man who controls himself (ἐγκρατής) and possesses the qualities connected to these virtues.

Naturally, the first condition for acquiring good friends is to become good ourselves. In fact only the good person can be a friend of a good person. The evil person can only have enemies or chiefly enemies; and friendship cannot even flourish between the good and the evil-doer, precisely because of this disparity.

In conclusion, even friendship is located within the confines of the *psyche* and is based on *arete*. In this precise direction Socrates cultivated his friendships, and his followers were not simply disciples but friends. It is easy to see that the art of love, in which he was especially gifted, is nothing other than the art of the "concern for souls."

9. Politics

Socrates had no sympathy for militant politics, in fact he felt a strong aversion for it. In the *Apology* he even affirms that he avoided active participation in political life because of his "divine sign" (which we shall discuss in detail further on).[70] He criticized the democratic practice which entrusted to a lottery the accomplishment of the various offices and functions, instead of distributing them on the basis of the competence and the worth of individuals. But he did not for this reason sympathize with the oligarchs, either. Actually, he was pursued by both the democrats and the oligarchs and for the same reason, that is, because he did not hesitate to criticize the evil actions of either one or the other; in fact in order to oppose injustice, he even went to the point of risking his life.

However, his teaching was far removed from being *politically neutral*. The Socratic area of interest remained centered on the Greek *polis* and even the Athenian *polis*. He conceived and placed all his teaching ability at the service of Athens.

There is no doubt that he tended to the education of men who could in a better way be concerned with the public welfare; and there is no doubt even over the fact that the greater part of his friends who frequented him also made this their aim. Moreover, both Xenophon and Plato agree in emphasizing the political nature (in the Greek sense, naturally) of the Socratic teaching.

It could be said that as the Socratic irony affirmed of itself that the God wished that he remain deprived of knowledge but that he would be capable of extracting it maieutically from the souls of others, so also could he affirm that the God wished that he not be militantly political, but that he wished him rather to have the capacity to make others political.

It is clear, from what we have said to this point, that the true politician for Socrates could not but be *the completely moral human being*; that is, the statesman must be *a politician within the parameters of the soul and capable of caring for the souls of others*. The Platonic Socrates would say that "the good politician" must be someone who *has a concern for the souls* of human beings.[71]

The disengagement of Socrates from militant political activity will become in the minor Socratics a strong disengagement from all political activity. Instead, Plato understood the meaning of the higher politics at which Socrates's teaching aimed. Socrates's message was received and taken to its extreme consequences. In fact in the *Gorgias* Plato appraised the nature of the educative work of Socrates, and realized that in comparison those who practised active politics were totally deprived of it, and so he did not hesitate to declare that Socrates was the only "authentic politician" that the Greeks had produced.[72]

10. The revolution of non-violence

There has been a good deal of controversy about the reasons for which Socrates was put to death. It is clear that on a strictly juridical basis the offense imputed to him was sustained. Socrates did not believe in the Gods of the city-state and, in addition, he induced others to believe likewise. But it is clear that, from the moral point of view, the judgment should have been overturned and the true offense imputed to the accusers and judges.

The fact remains in any case that *Socrates was a revolutionary* and that he was so *in every sense of the term*. But there are two ways that revolutions are realized; with the aid of force and *violence* and by means of *non-violence*. Now Socrates was involved in this second kind of revolution, so he likewise perfected its theory in a very clear way. The weapons of his revolution were not violent but were the weapons of *persuasion*, not only in relation to individuals but with the State as well. About to be put to death unjustly, he was offered the option of escape; he rejected this possibility in a categorical way because he judged that it would work a *violence* against the laws. Plato has him say:

> You must not give way or draw back or leave your post, but in war and in court and everywhere you must do whatever the state, your country commands, or must show her *by persuasion* what is really right, but that it is impious to use violence.[73]

Xenophon points out the same thing:

> He chose to die through his loyalty to the laws rather than to live through violating them.[74]

Only one higher form of non-violent revolution will be acknowledge by human beings after Socrates, that of love; but this was totally unknown to the Greeks. So the non-violent revolution of Socrates is the highest that the pagan world has known.

III. Socratic Theology and Its Significance

1. The position of Socrates in relation to the theological problem

The first charge made against Socrates in the trial, as we have already said, precisely concerned the anomalous attitude that the philosopher tenaciously maintained throughout his entire life with respect to the official belief in the Gods, and it went like this:

> Socrates is guilty of not believing in the Gods in which the State believes and of introducing other strange Divinities.[1]

Evidently this is not a charge of *atheism*, because one cannot be guilty of atheism if one is guilty of introducing strange Divinities and he is recognized as such; rather, to use modern terminology, the charge concerned *heresy* (heresy with respect to the official State religion).

The position of Socrates with respect to God and the Divine hence not only had something objectively in common with those of the Sophists, who went on (indirectly or directly) to atheism, but further, as we have seen above, this will be recognized even by those who dragged the philosopher before the seat of justice, who did not make any distinctions between the Sophists and Socrates in other respects.

But why did Socrates reject the State religion? Because he found the anthropomorphism with which it was infected, whether used descriptively or morally, deeply repugnant. Indirectly, from some testimonies of Antisthenes, we know that this philosopher was inspired in fact by Socrates, and he maintained that "God does not resemble anything and that therefore no one can know him by means of images"[2] and that "he cannot be seen with the eyes."[3] This means to precisely contest any possibility of depicting God in human form or in any physically apparent form whatever. In Plato's *Euthyphro*, to the priest who tells him (to support his own claim to wisdom about divine things) about the fights, the contests, and the furious wrath of the Gods against the other Gods, Socrates expressly says:

> Is not this, Euthyphro, the reason why I am being prosecuted, because when people tell such stories about the Gods *I find it hard to accept them?*[4]

So it means that Socrates maintained that moral anthropomorphism was also absurd, and denied that passions, sentiments, and human habits could be attributed to the Gods.

Up to this point, Socrates said nothing original, because Xenophanes previously had denounced the anthropomorphic error of the traditional conception of the Gods, in all its forms, in a very clear manner.[5]

In addition, it would seem to be possible to derive from various hints in the sources, that Socrates, even in this case, was reacting against the exaggerated polytheism of the popular religion, and had affirmed a unitary conception of divinity, even if he did not exclude the multiplicity of its manifestations. Maier writes in this regard: "That he ended with considering as unique the dominant power of the universe...is certain; and it is probable that on occasion he opposed this unique divinity to the many Gods of popular belief. ...At any rate, we cannot attribute to Socrates a monotheism similar to that which has become familiar to us through the advent of Christian theology and that modern philosophy determined by it. For the cultivated person, in the area of the Divine there did not exist any opposition between unity and plurality. Behind the many the one God is sensed, however they did not even begin to imagine this unity except in the vivid variety of plurality. Philosophy could only confirm this way of seeing it. Even the monistic philosophers of divinity admitted below divinity a plurality of natural forces, considering them equal to divinity and for the most part placing them in a determined relation with the Gods of popular religion. A strictly monotheistic presentation of God is possible only when God is posited qualitatively and dynamically as entirely beyond this world, which notion did not occur to the Greeks at all. The true and proper dualism between God and the world was extraneous both to the Greek religion and to their philosophy. Thus a divinization through the hypostatization of natural forces, of realities, of ethico-cultural ideals was so much more possible insofar as the enriched and emphasized concept of personhood, of which we are aware, on the contrary, was completely absent from the Greeks. Certainly Socrates did not reject such a polytheism."[6]

But also in this tendency to unify the divine, although maintaining the multiplicity of its manifestations, Socrates had a precursor in Xenophanes. The difference is only in the fact that Xenophanes conceived God in a cosmological manner, Socrates, as we will immediately see, thought of God, rather, in an ethical manner.

But—and this is the most delicate problem to resolve for the purpose of understanding the nature of Socratic theology—does Socrates try, on the basis of the philosophical categories at his disposal, to *theoretically ground* a conception of God? The Physicists, as we saw, identified the Divine with the cosmogonic Principle and, in any case, they interpreted it in function of their cosmological categories; but Socrates, who had rejected as a whole the philosophy of *physis*, could hardly use any categories that might be taken from such a philosophy. On the other hand, he did not have at his disposal any later metaphysical categories, which were acquired only after the Platonic "second voyage," thus Socrates was fated to be able to speak of God (if not exclusively, at the least prevalently) *on the intuitive level*. With respect to the problem of God, in the ultimate analysis Socrates came back to the same problem which he had already encountered in dealing with the problem of the soul. Just as in order to define the soul, he could not say what it was metaphysically, but he could only define it in terms of its operations, so also the same thing was involved in speaking about God and the Divine.

He took from Anaxagoras and from Diogenes of Apollonia (and perhaps also from Archelaus) the notion of God as *intelligent orderer, disengaging it*, therefore, from the physics on which it is based in these philosophers, and focused his argument on the works of God, substituting for the physical-metaphysical reasons reasons of a chiefly ethical nature or generally reasons coming from a precisely moral source.

Let us see in a detailed way what our sources say in this regard, since it is a question of a conception which, although it was achieved chiefly on an intuitive level, is important enough both in itself and because of the remarkable developments which it received in succeeding periods of time.

2. God as purposeful and providential mind

Xenophon is our best source of information concerning the Socratic conception of God. It is found in some passages of the *Memorabilia* (especially in two chapters of great pre-eminence) which scholars have distorted, in an unbelievable way, particularly by casting doubt on their truthfulness and trustworthiness. But, if adequately read and interpreted, they clearly leave clues by means of which the genuine thought of Socrates can be reconstructed.

A first passage, from a dialogue which Xenophon wrote that he personally heard between Socrates and Aristodemus, is a real demonstration of the existence of God hinging on the following concepts: 1) what is not simply the work of chance but is able to achieve a goal or end requires an intelligence which produced it after due consideration; 2) especially, if we observe man, we note that each and every organ is purposeful in such a way that it cannot be explained except as the work of an intelligence (of an intelligence which has expressly willed this work); 3) against this reasoning it is no use objecting that this intelligence is not visible while the artificer in this world is proximate to his works; in fact, our soul also, that is, our intelligence, is not seen, and no one states that for this reason we do not make anything by reflection, but everything by chance; 4) in addition, it is possible to establish, on the basis of the status that man has with respect to all the other beings (he possesses the most complete physical structure, chiefly the possession of soul, that is, intelligence), that the divine artificer had a concern for man in a way which is wholly special; 5) Xenophon draws a final confirmation of this tenet, finally, from divination (and this probably is one of his personal additions).[7]

Two characteristics reveal the typical features of Socraticism: in the first place, the nexus that is instituted between God and the *psyche*, that is, between the divine Mind and human mind; in the second place, the strong anthropocentrism (everything used to prove teleology is taken from the structure of the body, while any consideration of a cosmological kind is missing; man is seen as the most remarkable work of God and as the being for which he has the most concern). But let us read the passages which take up the first point:

> Do you think that you have any intelligence yourself?
>
> Oh! Ask me a question and judge from my answer.
>
> And do you suppose that wisdom is nowhere else to be found, although you know that you have a mere speck of all the earth in your body and a mere drop of all the water, and that of all the other mighty elements you received, I suppose, just a scrap towards the fashioning of your body? But as for intelligence, which alone, it seems, is without mass, do you think that you snapped it up by a lucky accident, and that the orderly ranks of all these masses, infinite in number, are due, actually, to a non-intelligent power?
>
> Yes; for I don't see the master hand, whereas I see the makers of things in this world.
>
> Neither do you see *your own soul*, which has the mastery of the body; so that, as far as that goes, you may say that you do nothing by design, but everything by chance.[8]

There follows a list of the privileges that man has with respect to all the other animals, and as a final argument we read:

> Nor was the Deity content to care for man's body. What is of yet higher moment, *he has implanted in him the noblest type of soul*. For in the first place what other creature's soul has apprehended the existence of Gods who set in order the universe, greatest and fairest of things? And what race of living things other than man worships Gods? And what soul is more apt than man's to make provision against hunger and thirst, cold and heat, to relieve sickness and promote health, to acquire knowledge by toil, and to remember accurately all that is heard, seen, or learned? For is it not obvious to you that, in comparison with the other animals, men live like Gods, by nature peerless both in body and in soul?[9]

And at the end of the whole discussion he writes:

> Be well assured, my good friend, that the intelligence within you directs your body according to its will; and equally you must think that wisdom in dwelling in the universe disposes all things according to its pleasure. For think not that your eye cannot see the whole world at once; that your soul can ponder on things in Egypt and in Sicily, and God's thought is not sufficient to pay heed to the whole world at once.[10]

Both characteristics (anthropocentrism and the analogy of God with the human soul) return to and are also developed in another passage of the *Memorabilia*. It is worthwhile reading the passage in its entirety because, in addition to being a document essential to the understanding of Socratic thought, it is also an essential document for the comprehension of the development of Greek thought. Here it follows a route the inverse of its basic tendency, which is fundamentally cosmocentric, and hence it reveals the presence of a somewhat hidden turn.

Skill in speaking and efficiency in affairs, therefore, and ingenuity were not the qualities that he was eager to foster in his companions. He held that they needed first to acquire prudence. For he believed that those faculties, unless accompanied by prudence, increased in the possessors injustice and power for mischief. In the first, then, he tried to make his companions prudent towards the Gods. Accordingly he discoursed on this topic at various times, as those who were present used to relate. The following conversation between him and Euthydemus I heard myself:

"Tell me, Euthydemus," he began, "has it ever occurred to you to reflect on the care the Gods have taken to furnish man with what he needs?"

"No, indeed it has not," replied Euthydemus.

"Well, no doubt you know that our first and foremost need is light, which is supplied to us by the Gods?"

"Of course; since without light our eyes would be as useless as if we were blind."

"And again, we need rest; and therefore the Gods grant us the welcome respite of night."

"Yes, for that too we owe them thanks."

"And since the night by reason of her darkness is dim, whereas the sun by his brightness illuminates the hours of the day and all things else, have they not made stars to shine in the night, that mark the watches of night for us, and do we not thereby satisfy many of our needs?"

"Moreover, the moon reveals to us not only the divisions of the night, but of the month too."

"Certainly."

"Now, seeing that we need food, think how they make the earth to yield it, and provide to that end appropriate seasons which furnish in abundance the diverse things that minister not only to our wants but to our enjoyment."

"Truly these things too show loving-kindness."

"Think again of their precious gift of water that aids the earth and the seasons to give birth and increase to all things useful to us and itself helps to nourish our bodies, and mingling with all that sustains us make it more digestible, more wholesome, and more palatable: and how, because we need so much of it, they supply it without stint."

"That too shows design at work."

"Think again of the blessing of fire, our defense against cold and against darkness, our helpmate in every art and all that man contrives for his service. In fact, to put it shortly, nothing of any account that is useful to the life of man is contrived without the aid of fire."

"This too is a signal token of loving-kindness."

"Think again how the sun, when past the winter solstice, approaches, ripening some things and withering others, whose time is over; and having accomplished this, approaches no nearer, but turns away, careful not to harm us by excess of heat; and when once again in his retreat he reaches the point where it is clear to us that if he goes further away we shall be frozen with the cold, back he turns once more and draws near and revolves in that region of the heavens where he can best serve us."

"Yes, truly, these things do seem to be done for the sake of mankind."

"And again, since it is evident that we could not endure the heat or the cold if it came suddenly, the sun's approach and retreat are so gradual that we arrive at one or the other extreme imperceptibly."

"For me," exclaimed Euthydemus, "I begin to doubt whether after all the Gods are occupied in any other work than the service of man. The one difficulty I feel is that the lower animals also enjoy these blessings."

"Yes," replied Socrates, "and is it not evident that they too receive life and food for the sake of man? For what creature reaps so many benefits as man from goats and sheep and horses and oxen and asses and the other animals? He owes more to them, in my opinion, than to the fruits of the earth. At the least they are not less valuable to him for food and commerce; in fact a large portion of mankind does not use the products of the earth for food, but lives on the milk and cheese and flesh they get from livestock. Moreover, all men tame and domesticate the useful kinds of animals, and make them their fellow-workers in war and many other undertakings."

"There too I agree with you, seeing that animals far stronger than man become so entirely subject to him that he puts them to any use he chooses."

"Think again of the multitude of things beautiful and useful and their infinite variety, and how the Gods have endowed man with sense adapted for the perception of every kind, so that there is nothing good that we cannot enjoy; and again, how they have implanted in us the faculty of reasoning whereby we are able to reason about the objects of our perceptions and to commit them to memory, and so come to know what advantage every kind can yield and devise many means of enjoying the good and driving away the bad; and think of the power of expression, which enables us to impart to one another all good things by teaching and to take our share of them, to enact laws, and to administer states."

"Truly, Socrates, it does appear that the Gods devote much care to man."

"Yet again, insofar as we are powerless of ourselves to foresee what is expedient for the future, the Gods lend us their aid, revealing the issues by divination to inquirers, and teaching them how to obtain the best results."

"With you, Socrates, they seem to deal even more friendly than with other men, if it is true that, even unasked, they warn you by signs what to do and what not to do."

"Yes, and you will realize the truth of what I say if, instead of waiting for the Gods to appear to you in bodily presence, you are content to praise and worship them because you see their works. Mark that the Gods themselves give the reason for doing so; for when they bestow on us their good gifts, not one of them ever appears before us gift in hand; and especially he who coordinates and holds together the universe, wherein all things are fair and good, and presents them ever unimpaired and sound and ageless for our use, and quicker than thought to serve us unerringly, is manifest in his supreme works and yet is unseen by us in the ordering of them. Mark that even the sun, who seems to reveal himself to all, permits not man to behold him closely but if any attempt to gaze recklessly upon him blinds their eyes. And the God's ministers too you will find to be invisible. That the thunderbolt is hurled from heaven, and that he overwhelms all on whom he falls is evident, but he is seen neither coming nor striking nor going. And the winds are themselves invisible, yet their deeds are manifest to us, and we perceive their approach. Moreover, the soul of man, which more than all else that is human partakes of the divine, reigns manifestly within us, and yet is itself unseen."

"For these reasons it behoves us not to despise the things that are unseen but, realizing their power in their manifestations, to honor the Godhead."[11]

Now, it is almost certain that the substance of this exposition is actually derived from Socrates because Plato and even Aristotle himself give us detailed proof thereof.[12] Moreover, in this case also the relation between before and after Socrates is illuminating. Before Socrates only Diogenes of Apollonia (developing the basic thought of Anaxagoras) had maintained a teleological conception of the universe, as we have seen above. However for Diogenes the ordering Intelligence which governs everything was the *air* (and the soul itself was air) and all of his discussion was of a physico-cosmological character. Socrates, undoubtedly inspired by the discussion of Diogenes but radically eliminating from the discussion the physico-cosmological foundation, impressed on it a new direction, as we have seen. He speaks of God simply in terms of intelligent, purposeful, and providential activity, proceeding in his discussion in a purely intuitive manner or by means of analogy. But what the mind is in itself Socrates was not in a position to explain, nor was he in position to establish the precise ontological status of the goal, nor could he consequently give a meaning, except a generic one, to that Divine concern or providence which God has for human beings. The work of Plato and Aristotle, as we will see, will consist precisely in providing a foundation for these intuitions and consequently in their reorientation. Socrates represents hence the positive aspect of the crisis he induced in the *physical*[13] inquiry about the Gods and the preliminary statement to such a theological inquiry in a metaphysical key.

3. The *daimonion* of Socrates

Again, in the principal charge made against Socrates at the trial (in connection, that is, to the charge of not believing in the Gods of the State, and also as proof of it), as we previously stated, it is asserted that Socrates introduced "new *daimonia*," which the accusers certainly understood as new "divinities."

The terminology (τὰ δαιμόνια) indicates in a clear way that the accusers are referring to the fact that Socrates repeatedly had spoken about a kind of internal admonition, in certain circumstances a divine and supernatural phenomenon, which he, as a matter of fact, called his δαιμόνιον.

What is this *daimonion*? Here is what the Platonic Socrates says in the *Apology*:

> But the reason for this [*scil.*, of the fact that Socrates has kept far away from militant politics], as you have heard me say at many times and places, is that *something divine and daimonionic comes to me*, the very thing which Meletus ridiculed in his indictment. *I have had this from my childhood; it is a sort of voice that comes to me, and when it comes it always holds me back from what I am thinking of doing, but never urges me forward.*[14]

Plato constantly repeated this every time he mentioned the Socratic *daimonion*. It is a "sign" (σημεῖον) or a "voice" (φωνή) which Socrates expressly said was the voice of God (τοῦ θεοῦ), that is, a voice which came to him from God. Xenophon says the same thing, and disagrees with Plato only insofar as he maintained that the *daimonion* communicated to Socrates not only what he ought *not* do, but likewise, positively, what he ought to do.

It is clear that the *daimonion* was judged by Socrates to be a kind of *divine revelation* granted to him, a privilege lavished on him by Divinity which was totally exceptional and hence an experience which in some way transcended human limitations.

The interpreters are for the most part somewhat baffled and have given widely differing interpretations of the Socratic *daimonion*. Some have tried to nip the question in the bud by explaining the matter of the *daimonion* entirely within the context of Socratic irony and his inventiveness. Others have understood this most peculiar Socratic experience, so to speak, using a psychiatric model, and therefore as an indication of a psychopathology. Others, in a not so extreme vein, reduced it to *the voice of conscience*, or *to a suitable feeling,* or to *the feeling associated with genius.* Examples can be multiplied to include modern interpretations in a psycho-analytic mode or inspired by psycho-analysis. Actually, these interpretations result from the position of scholars who do not give credence to religious phenomena and resolve or dissolve them in a positivistic or rationalistic or psychologistic or psycho-analytical manner and who consequently misrepresent, in an irreparable way, what is unique about the experience of the Socratic *daimonion.*

It is important and necessary to point out that the *daimonion* (τὸ δαιμόνιον) is a neuter grammatical form, and that hence (and the interpreters of a positivistic or rationalistic bent have insisted on this fact) it does not indicate a daimon-person, that is, a personal being (a sort of angel or genie), but rather a divine *fact* or *event* or *phenomenon*; actually never, either in Plato or in Xenophon, is the *daimonion* said to be a *daimon*, but it is always described as a "sign," a "divine voice."

After having gone into some detail on this issue it is necessary to emphasize what follows; *a)* Socrates, in the *Apology,* expressly allies the "divine sign" in relation to the *daimons,* explaining that in the measure in which he believes in "daimoniacal things" does he also believe in *daimons* and hence in the Gods from whom the *daimons* are derived.[15] *b)* In addition, likewise, he expressly connects the "divine sign" with God himself, saying without any possibility of equivocation that the sign and the voice which he senses inside himself were the sign and the voice of God.[16] Moreover, all the Greeks maintained that there are *daimons* who are intermediaries between the Gods and human beings and it is highly probable, if not to say certain, that this was also the belief of Socrates. For the Greeks, it was not easy to conceive of an immediate contact or relation between God and human beings. The pluralistic conception of the divine which, as we have seen, even Socrates shared, by its internal dynamism brought about the conception of the relation between God and man through the intermediary of *daimons.*

The "divine sign" must therefore come to Socrates through a *daimon.* However he avoided this word and it is incorrect to transliterate and substitute *daimon* for *daimonion* (as many do), because in doing this, what for Socrates was purposefully left unexplicit would be made explicit. He, in fact, preferred to cling to the internal experience and to qualify it as this divine phenomenon without going on to analyze the way it came or through what means.

In conclusion, the *daimonion* was understood by Socrates as a fact outside of the ordinary and of a superhuman character. In order to understand this it is necessary to consider two factors; firstly, the Socratic religious spirit which was of exceptional intensity; secondly, the Socratic conception of a providential-God.[17] From Xenophon, according to Socrates, as we have seen in the preceding section, we understood that God has disposed the organs of man in function of the good of man, and that he has ordered the entire universe and its parts in function, once again, of man's good. In addition, we draw from Plato that God, according to Socrates, beyond a generic concern for all mankind, has a particular concern for the *good-man*[18] (note, not for every individual man indiscriminately—this tenet was always foreign to the Greek understanding—but only for the individual virtuous man). It is natural, hence, that in the context of this belief Socrates located his own experience of the *daimonion*. In his judgment, it was a very special sign given on certain occasions to one who aimed at the good with all his strength; thus the *daimonion* was a providential Divinity pointing out the just way of living.

But there is again an essential point to be clarified in order to gain a correct understanding of the *daimonion*, and that is the context in which its influence is to be located.

What exactly did the divine voice reveal?

In the first place, it is to be emphasized that the *daimonion* reveals nothing within the sphere of philosophic truth. The "divine voice" does not reveal anything about "human wisdom" to Socrates, nor does it suggest to him any general or particular propositions about his ethics. For Socrates philosophical principles derive their validity entirely from the *logos* and not from divine revelation. The prophetic attitudes of Pythagoras, Empedocles, as well as Parmenides, are almost wholly foreign to our philosopher.

Moreover, no matter how odd it seems to appear to us, Socrates does not immediately connect the *daimonion* to his conviction that he has received from God a special mission, the task of spurring the Athenians to concern themselves with the soul and virtue. In the Platonic *Apology* we read:

> But, as I believe, I have been commanded by God [note: ὑπὸ τοῦ θεοῦ], through *oracles* and *dreams* and in every way in which any man was ever commanded by divine power (θεία μοῖρα) to do anything whatsoever.[19]

If we exclude the *daimonion* from the ambit of philosophy and likewise exclude it from the sphere of ethical choice basic to the life of Socrates, then the only possibility which remains is the area of the *actions and particular events of the life of Socrates*. And it is exactly to this area that all the texts on the Socratic *daimonion* at our disposal refer. The divine sign, time after time, impedes the performance of specific actions (whether to leave a place, to cross a river, to accept in his circle particular persons), and not to do these actions is to have a great advantage. The most consistent and certain of the prohibitions given to Socrates by the divine voice, about which we have already hinted, is not to concern himself with being active politically. The advantage that Socrates would gain by obeying the voice is expressly revealed in the *Apology*:

> For you may be quite sure, men of Athens, that if I had undertaken to go into politics, I should have been put to death long ago and should

have done no good to you or to myself.[20]

A passage of Xenophon helps us in locating this point quite well and in concluding:

> For the craft of carpenter, smith, farmer or ruler, and the theory of such crafts, and arithmetic and economics and generalship might be learned and mastered by the application of human powers; *but the deepest secrets of these matters the Gods reserved to themselves; they were dark to men.* You may plant a field well; but you know not who shall gather the fruits; you may build a house well; but you know not who shall dwell in it; able to command, you cannot know whether it is profitable to command; versed in statecraft, you know not whether it is profitable to guide the state; though, for your delight, you marry a pretty woman, you cannot tell whether she will bring you sorrow; though you form a party among men mighty in the state, you know not whether they will cause you to be driven from the state. If any man thinks that these matters are wholly within the grasp of the human mind and nothing in them is beyond our reason, that man, he said, is irrational. But it is no less irrational to seek the guidance of heaven in matters which men are permitted by the Gods to decide for themselves by study...so too with what we may know by reckoning, measurement, or weighing.[21]

So then the *daimonion*, with its prohibitions, makes clear to Socrates exactly what the Gods reserved for themselves and what they sometimes reveal by means of the oracles,[22] and hence it was undoubtedly understood by Socrates as a kind of *interior oracle*, with all those implications which we pointed out above.

4. The relations between the theology and ethics of Socrates

We have seen that the phenomenon of the *daimonion*, which is of a clearly religious character, leaves intact the sphere of Socratic philosophy. The same must be said with respect to the relations between religious faith and the theology professed in general by Socrates and his ethics.

Socratic ethics is not a *theonomy*, and hence its validity does not spring from being a divine command or rule. It is instead based, as we have seen above amply, on the total autonomy of the soul, that is, on the *psyche*, which for Socrates constitutes the nature of man. We have also seen that Socratic ethics has maintained its autonomy even in relation to the question of the immortality of the soul. Moral values are imposed of themselves, and prescind from whether or not the soul endures after the death of the body. It is understandable, therefore, that for Socrates, since the Gods do not intervene in the foundation of ethics, neither do they intervene with rewards or punishments, either in this world or in the next. In this respect Maier emphasizes the point quite well, "...the task of securing a congruence between moral merit and happiness does not belong to divinity nor to initiate the means from the outside. Happiness is, in fact, for Socrates something profoundly interior which has its origin and its source in the human soul. It resides in the moral life itself. The good man receives from himself his own reward, the evil his own punishment."[23]

But then—the reader will ask—how is it possible to reconcile, on the one hand, all this with the Socratic conception of Divinity, which is conceived and interpreted essentially as providential mind? And, on the other hand, how does it avoid contradicting the firm Socratic conviction that God has a special concern with regard to the good man, and beyond that, that he goes so far as to send him his *diamonionic* sign?

The response is not difficult to make. Moral values are not created nor imposed by Divinity, but are *the highest values* because they are the values of the spirit and *as such are acknowledged also by Divinity*. Therefore, it is possible to point out that God, although not the *author* of moral values, may be their *protector*. In conclusion, moral values are not such *because they are willed* by God, but they have their own intrinsic value, objective perfection, and so merit maximum consideration by God. This means, as someone has correctly pointed out, that Socrates, in a certain sense, grants to moral values ultimate importance for cosmic reality (and it is by taking up this intuition and grounding it on the metaphysical level that Euclid and Plato, as we will see, would make of the Good the highest universal reality).

All the aforementioned should explain the thought of Socrates satisfactorily (which, as we have seen, at first glance seemed to be anomalous and contradictory), namely, that the Divinity is concerned *in general* with all men, but that he is also concerned *in a particular way only about virtuous men*. Socrates says to his judges in the *Apology* of Plato:

> But you also, judges, must regard death hopefully and must bear in mind this one truth, that no evil can come to a *good man* either in life or after death, and *the Gods do not neglect him.*[24]

In no text at our disposal is it emphasized, on the contrary, that the Gods are concerned or interested in every single individual person, even less so that the individual person who walks outside the right way will find Gods who are concerned to lead him back to the right way. So then Divinity intervenes only in favor of individuals who live lives of virtue, because they are attracted, so to speak, by the absolute value which they instantiate, as though through a law of the community of like with like. But they do not intervene through an act of love which is directed to the person as such, like that intended by the Christian God, which indeed has no proportion to the value of our actions and hence is characterized by the total gratuity of a pure gift.

If this is so, if Divinity is concerned in a special way with individual persons not insofar as they are individual persons precisely, but insofar as they are good, the reverse is also true. It is true, therefore, that man has no need of Divine assistance in order to be good. The special concern of Divinity for the good man is a consequence (that is, an effect) and it is not an antecedent (that is, a condition) of his being good. Therefore, Maier is quite right in saying, "For Socrates moral *autarcheia* continues to be the ultimate anchor of every aspect of happiness and every confidence in life; he does not think in the least of searching in the religious attitude towards divinity and in the divine assistance for a solid support for the man in need of liberation and salvation. The moral life is itself health and liberation. The Socratic optimism, there is no need to forget it, is based entirely on moral attitudes, and Socratic faith is in its most profound foundation a moral faith. In conclusion, the 'philosophy' of Socrates is and remains a 'gospel' of the here and now."[25]

IV. Socratic Dialectic

1. The protreptic function of the dialogical method

Even for the correct interpretation of the Socratic "method" of philosophizing it is necessary to refer to the new concept of *psyche*. The dialectic of Socrates with all the complex means which support it, in fact, consciously points without deviation toward the soul and toward the concern for the soul.

In the first place, it is the reference to the new concept of *psyche* which explains the drastic split with and the overturning of the method of the Sophists. Common to all the Sophists without exception was the system of teaching their doctrine by means of *pompous discourses*, a truly verbal defense which could be protracted at will which dazzled the hearer with the charm of a flow of words that seemed inexhaustible. And in these discussions logical proof and the citation of the testimony of the poets were often mixed together, and contrarily, the citation of the poets was often substituted for logical proof with an effect (deliberately calculated) which was readily and securely impressed on the public.

But what did Sophists aim at with all this display? Their goal was to fascinate and seduce their hearers. Unfortunately, the display did not at all furnish the hearers with nourishing food for their souls. Thus the Sophists did not care for the souls of their listeners, nor did they aim at making them as good as possible but, on the contrary, *they caused harm to the souls of their hearers in an irreparable way.*[1] The soul of man is not cared for by being harangued amidst a throng of listeners in which the individuality of the hearer is as such almost wholly obscured and ignored, and it is not cared for by listening only to what the teachers, or so-called teachers, said. The soul, the individual soul, is cared for only through *dia-logue*, that is, a conversation through or with the logos which proceeds by question and answer, actively involving both the teacher and the student in a single spiritual experience, the mutual search for the truth. Thus, the "short discussion," which is precisely the open dialogue, as Socrates called it, is substituted for the pretentious "long discussion," which is a closed monologue. The open dialogue corresponds more closely to the most profound needs of those who inquire together. It thus places them in a relationship, so to speak, soul with soul. It is not difficult to understand why there is no room of any kind in this dialogue for the voice of the poets. For Socrates, the summoning of the testimonies of the poets in philosophical discussions was in total disharmony with and wholly extraneous to the logos from which the dialogue arose and through which it was nourished.

Therefore it is evident, on the basis of what has been said, that the goal of the dialogical Socratic method is *fundamentally of an educative and ethical nature* and only *secondarily and indirectly of a logical and epistemo-*

logical nature. Socratic dialectic aims at exhorting man to virtue. It aims at convincing human beings that the soul and the care of the soul are the maximum good for man. It aims at purifying the soul by basically testing it precisely through questions and answers in order to liberate it from errors and to dispose it towards the truth.[2] Let us now read some documents which confirm the assertions we have made.

In this passage from the Platonic dialogue *Laches*, the notion that the Socratic dialogical method aims at testing the soul and making it reveal itself is clearly present:

> Lysimachus, it looks to me in very truth as though you only knew Socrates at second hand – through his father – and had not conversed with him personally except in his childhood, when you may have chanced to meet him among the people of his district accompanying his father at the temple or at some local gathering. But you have evidently not yet had to do with him since he has reached maturer years.
>
> How are you so sure of that, Nicias?
>
> You strike me as not being aware that whoever comes into close contact with Socrates and has any talk with him face to face *is bound to be drawn round and round by him in the course of the argument – though it may have started at first on a quite different theme – and cannot stop until he is led into giving an account of himself, of the manner in which he now spends his days, and of the kind of life he has lived hitherto*; and when once he has been led into that, Socrates will never let him go until he has thoroughly and properly put all his ways to the test. Now I am accustomed to him, and so I know that *one is bound to be thus treated by him*, and further, that I myself shall certainly get the same treatment also. For I delight, Lysimachus, in conversing with the man, and see no harm *in our being reminded of any past or present misdoing*: nay, one must needs take more careful thought for the rest of one's life if one does not fly from his words but is willing, as Solon said, and zealous to learn as long as one lives, and does not expect to get good sense by the mere arrival of old age. So to me there is nothing unusual, or unpleasant either, *in being tried and tested by Socrates*; in fact, I knew pretty well all the time that our argument *would not be about the boys if Socrates were present, but about ourselves*.[3]

In the *Charmides* the dialectical discussion through a very clear image is represented as a "stripping," an "undressing," and a "contemplation" of the soul.[4]

Socrates speaks about his philosophy to the judges in the *Apology*, he tells them that he goes about asking questions, testing and refuting the Athenians one by one as an exhortation and an incitement and an aid to "taking care of the soul," thus as an inexorable goad to "giving an account of their lives."[5] As a matter of fact, he pointed out in this description the ultimate reason why he was condemned to death. To condemn Socrates to death, for many, meant to free themselves from the obligation of *laying bare their soul*. But the process begun by Socrates was by now irreversible and the physical suppression of his person would do nothing to arrest that process. So Plato can rightly have Socrates condemned to death and have him voice this prophecy:

> I say to you, you men who have slain me, that punishment will come upon you straightway after my death far more grievous in fact than the punishment of death which you have meted out to me. For now you have done this to me *because you hoped that you would be relieved from rendering an account of your lives*, but I say that you will find the result far different. *Those who will force you to give an account will be more numerous than heretofore*; men whom I restrained, though you knew it not; and they will be harsher, inasmuch as they are younger, and you will be more annoyed. For if you think that by putting me to death you will prevent anyone from reproaching you because you do not act as you should, you are mistaken. That mode of escape is neither possible at all nor honorable, but the easiest and most honorable escape for you is not by suppressing others, *but by making yourselves as good as possible.*[6]

Since the goal of Socratic dialectic has been ascertained, we must now indicate its two basic characteristics, as well as examining in what ways it is practiced, and lay out in detail the essential conditions within which it arose.

2. Socratic ignorance

In the measure in which the goal of Socratic dialectic is revolutionary, so also is its point of departure. Socrates always began from the affirmation of his *ignorance*, placing himself in relation to the interlocutor as someone who has to learn everything, and not as someone who is going to teach. But it is precisely this initial affirmation of ignorance which overturns the "pompous discourse," that is, the sophistic monologue, and opens up the possibility of true dialogue.

There is a good deal of ambiguity about this Socratic ignorance; some even go as far as seeing in it the expression of a sceptical principle. Actually, it is to be understood in an entirely different manner, that is, primarily as a statement "affirming" the hiatus present when the knowledge and speculation of the Physicists, the Sophists, as well as the traditional culture in general are compared, and then as an opening to that new form of wisdom that Socrates himself called "human wisdom" and which he expressly admitted that he possessed.

The Socratic affirmation of ignorance in relation to the wisdom of the Physicists means, as we have already seen, the rejection of the desire to engage in undertakings that go beyond human capacities and powers. The desire to know the *physis* of the cosmos is the useless attempt to know the secret laws of the cosmos. It is useless because it neglects man and so in the vain search for what is different from man it forgets man himself.

In relation to the Sophists, it means instead the rejection of a presumed wisdom which they almost always cannot justify. Gorgias affirmed, with a boldness which borders on impudence, that he was able to respond to anything asked of him, although no one actually asked him anything truly novel.[7] Protagoras, likewise, with a patrician arrogance claimed that he could make those who frequented him better every day by teaching them political virtue.[8] Hippias boasted of being wise and of knowing how to do everything,[9] and so the examples can be multiplied.

In relation to traditional wisdom belonging to the politicians and the poets and the cultivators of the various arts, finally, the Socratic affirmation of ignorance involved the rejection of them as being almost totally inconsistent. They are rejected because they skate on the surface of problems and proceed only by intuition and natural disposition or from a claim to know everything solely based on their domination of a single art form.[10] But there is more.

The meaning of the Socratic ignorance can be gauged exactly only if it is placed in relation, beyond the wisdom of men, to the wisdom of God. As we have already seen above, for Socrates God is omniscient, his knowledge extends from the universe to man without restriction of any kind right to the point of the most hidden thoughts of man. Well then, it is properly only in comparison to the stature of this divine wisdom that human wisdom is shown in all its fragility and narrowness, and not only that illusory wisdom which we have discussed above but even Socratic *human wisdom* itself is an unknowing. Moreover, in the *Apology,* it is Socrates himself who, interpreting the dictum pronounced by the Delphic Oracle according to which no one was more wise than Socrates, explicated this concept:

> God is really wise and by his oracle means this: "Human wisdom is of little or no value." And it appears that he does not really say this of Socrates, but merely uses my name, and makes me an example, as if he were to say: "This one of you, O human beings, is wisest who, like Socrates, recognizes that he is in truth of no account in respect to wisdom."[11]

Finally, the value and the *ironic function* which the affirmation of ignorance plays within the Socratic method is to be noted. Not only when the affirmation of the principle is involved with the precise implications examined above, but also when it is involved in particular questions to which Socrates knows well the answers *he is feigning* being "ignorant." But this "feigning" in each individual situation provokes the analogous effect of the proclamation of the general principle. It provokes the helpful irritation and conflict in the hearer from which the spark of dialogue begins and gathers strength.

So we have now reached a point which will not allow us to put off any longer a consideration of the Socratic use of "irony" which constitutes the most characteristic element of the Socratic method.

3. Socratic irony

Irony (εἰρωνεία) means, in general, *dissimulation*, and in this specific case it indicates the multiple play and variety of disguises and deceptions that Socrates used in order to constrain his interlocutor to give an account of himself. Here is how Maier describes it, "Its fundamental tenor is the teasing of men with a sense of superiority, a capricious humor which, however, allows a glimpse of a certain displeasure in the interlocutor [it would be better to say, of the pride in the interlocutor] or at least the intention of moderating the high opinion which such a person can have of himself, and making sport of him. In the jocular context, Socrates dons some mask, showing that he is a passionate friend of the interlocutor, admiring his capacities and talents, seeking advice or training and so on. But at the same time he is concerned that to those who observe more closely the pretence be transparent; nor in this play is there ever absent the undertone of seriousness, although frequently the quiet undertone of seriousness is found only in the goal which the humor is destined to serve. But this goal is always serious. In fact, in substance it is nothing other than the identical goal of all Socratic action. The irony of Socrates is a necessary means for a moral dialectic."[12] We might add that the ironic play of Socrates is used even more basically. In its dissimulation he even feigns taking on as his own the ideas and methods of the interlocutor (especially if they are cultivated men, and especially if they are Sophists) in order to proceed to the very edge of caricature, or in order to throw them into confusion using their own logic and thus ensnaring them in contradiction.

The trait of unknowing or ignorance, the principal disguise that Socrates sometimes takes on, is always visible under the various masks. Indeed it can also be said that basically the multi-colored masks of Socratic irony are nothing more than variants on Socratic unknowing, with its multiform dissolving play always ending in Socratic ignorance.

It will be precisely this claim to ignorance which sends his adversaries into rages;[13] the mask of ignorance which Socrates assumed was always a most effective means to unmask the apparent wisdom of others and to reveal their basic ignorance. But it was likewise Socratic ignorance that in a most effective way assisted those who trusted Socrates's teaching and accepted the invitation to reveal themselves.

Since irony in the sense clarified is a necessary accompaniment to the Socratic method and entirely pervades it, it can undoubtedly be said that Socratic dialectic, as such, can be called "ironic." And because for Socrates there is no philosophy without dialogue

But there still remains something to say about the two necessary moments in which dialectic, and hence irony, are explicated, that is, "refutation" and "maieutic."

4. Refutation (the *elenchos*) and the maieutic art

The first moment of the ironic method is, so to speak, a *destructive one*, a moment (as we said above) in which Socrates began with those with whom he dialogued to uncover their presumed claim to wisdom, that is, their ignorance. He forces them to define the subject on which the inquiry turns; then he digs in various ways into their definition, revealing the imperfections and contradictions to which it brings the interlocutor; then he moves him to attempt successive definitions and refutes them with the same technique, and thus he continues until that moment when the interlocutor acknowledges his ignorance. Here is how Plato described this moment of the method in the *Sophist*:

> They question a man about the things about which he thinks he is talking sense when he is talking nonsense; then they easily discover that his opinions are like those of men who wander, and in their discussions they collect those opinions and compare them with one another, and by the comparison they show that they contradict one another about the same things, in relation to the same things, and in respect to the same things. But those who see this grow angry with themselves and gentle towards others, and this is the way in which they are freed from their high and obstinate opinions about themselves. The process of freeing them, moreover, affords the greatest pleasure to the listeners and the most lasting benefit to him who is subjected to it. ...Those who purge the soul believe that the soul can receive no benefit from any teachings offered to it until someone by refutation reduces him who is refuted to an attitude of modesty, by removing the opinions that obstruct the teachings, and thus purges him and makes him think that he knows only what he knows, and no more. ...For all these reasons...*we must assert that refutation is the greatest and most efficacious of all purifications, and that he who is not refuted, even though he be the Great King, has not been purified of the greatest taints, and is therefore uneducated and deformed in those things in which he who is truly happy ought to be most pure and beautiful.*[14]

It was because of the stage of *refutation* which belonged to his method that Socrates was the victim of the most lively aversion and the most harsh emnity, which, in the end, resulted in his condemnation to death. It is clear that the mediocre must always react negatively to this refutation. They begin from an acritical certitude and trust in their wisdom; they are so pained at the exhaustion of all of their resources, consequently, a crisis is produced in them which is derived, on the one hand, from the sudden befuddlement about what they had previously maintained with such certainty and, on the other hand, from the absence of new certitudes on which they can depend. Hence pride prevents them from admitting that they do not actually know. They accuse Socrates of confusing them and their ideas and of benumbing them. From this experience is derived the accusation against Socrates that he is a sower of doubts and hence a corrupter. The best illustration of this attitude is Meno, in the Platonic dialogue of that name:

> Socrates, I used to be told, before I began to meet with you, that yours was just a case of being in doubt yourself and making others doubt also; and so now I find you are merely bewitching me with your spells and incantations, which have reduced me to utter perplexity. And if I am indeed to have my jest, I consider that both in your appearance and in other respects you are extremely like the flat torpedo sea-fish; for it benumbs anyone who approaches and touches it, and something of the sort is what I find you have done to me now. For in truth I feel my soul and my tongue quite benumbed, and I am at a loss what answer to give you. And yet on countless occasions I have made abundant speeches on virtue to various people – and very good speeches they were, so I thought – You are well advised, I consider, in not voyaging or taking a trip away from home; for if you went on like this as a stranger in any other city you would very likely be taken up for a wizard.[15]

But if this was the effect produced by Socratic refutation on the mediocre, who did not admit to being ignorant, the effect it produced on the best was quite different. As we have seen in the passage of the *Sophist*, the best are *purified* not insofar as any authentic certitudes have been destroyed but only apparent and false certitudes. Hence they are lead not to a loss but to a gain. And the achievement, once again, the *Sophist* has said, consists in this; *as long as there are false opinions and false certitudes in the soul it is impossible to reach the truth; these eliminated, on the contrary, the soul is purified and is ready to attain, if it is pregnant, the truth.*

We may now go on to the second moment of the ironic method.

We have said that for Socrates the soul can achieve the truth only "if it is pregnant"; he in fact, as we have seen, professed ignorance and hence precisely rejected being in a condition to communicate wisdom to others, or at least a wisdom with a specific content. But as the physically pregnant woman needs the services of a midwife in order to give birth, so also the disciple whose soul is pregnant with truth needs a kind of spiritual midwifery which assists this truth to come to light, and this is precisely the Socratic "midwifery."

Plato has described it in an exemplary page which can neither be summarized nor paraphrased if all the many allusions and nuanced subtleties it involves are to be maintained and hence it should be read in its entirety:

> Yes, you are suffering the pangs of labor, Theaetetus, because you are

not empty, but pregnant.

I do not know, Socrates; I merely tell you what I feel.

Have you then not heard, you absurd boy, that I am the son of a noble and burly midwife, Phaenarete?

Yes, I have heard that.

And have also heard that I practice the same art?

No, never.

But I assure you it is true; only do not tell on me to the others; for it is not known that I possess this art. But other people, since they do not know it, do not say this of me, but say that I am a most eccentric person and drive men to distraction. Have you heard that also?

Yes, I have.

Shall I tell you the reason then?

Oh yes, do.

Just take into consideration the whole business of the midwives, and you will understand more easily what I mean. For you know, I suppose, that no one of them attends other women while she is still capable of conceiving and bearing, but only those do so who have become too old to bear.

Yes, certainly.

They say the cause of this is Artemis, because she, a childless Goddess, has had childbirth allotted to her as her special province. Now it would seem she did not allow barren women to be midwives, because human nature is too weak to acquire an art which deals with matters of which it has no experience, but she gave the office to those who on account of age were not bearing children, honoring them for their likeness to herself.

Very likely.

Is it not, then, also like and even necessary, that midwives should know better than anyone else who are pregnant and who are not?

Certainly.

And furthermore, the midwives, by means of drugs and incantations, are able to arouse the pangs of labor and, if they wish, to make them milder, and to cause those to bear who have difficulty in bearing; and they cause miscarriages if they think them desirable.

That is true.

Well, have you noticed this also about them, that they are the most skillful of matchmakers, since they are very wise in knowing what union of man and woman will produce the best possible children?

I do not know that at all.

But be assured that they are prouder of this than of their skill in cutting the umbilical cord. Just consider. Do you think the knowledge of what soil is best for each plant or seed belongs to the same art as the tending and harvesting of the fruits of the earth, or to another?

To the same art.

And in the case of a woman, do you think, my friend, that there is one art of sowing and another for the harvesting?

It is not likely.

No; but because there is a wrongful and unscientific way of bringing men and women together, which is called pandering, the midwives, since they are women of dignity and worth avoid match-making, through fear of falling under a charge of pandering. And yet the true midwife is the only proper match-maker.

It seems so.

So great, then, is the importance of midwives; but their function is less important than mine. For women do not, like my patients, bring forth at one time real children and at another mere images which it is difficult to distinguish from the real. For if they did, the greatest and noblest part of the work of the midwives would be in distinguishing between the real and the false. Do you not think so?

Yes, I do.

All that is true of the art of midwifery is true also of mine, but mine differs from theirs in being practiced upon men, not women, and in tending their souls in labor, not their bodies. But the greatest thing about my art is this, that it can test in every way whether the mind of the young man is bringing forth a mere image, an imposture, or a real and genuine offspring. For I have this in common with the midwives: I am sterile in point of wisdom, and the reproach which has often been brought against me, that I question others but make no reply myself about anything, because I have no wisdom in me, is a true reproach; and the reason of it is this: the God compels me to act as midwife, but has never allowed me to bring forth. I am, then, not at all a wise person myself, nor have I any wise invention, the offspring born of my own soul; but those who associate with me, although at first some of them seem very ignorant, yet, as our acquaintance advances, all of them to whom the God is gracious make wonderful progress, not only in their own opinion, but in that of others as well. And it is clear that they do this not because they have ever learned anything from me, but because they have found in themselves many fair things and have brought them forth. But the delivery is due to the God and me. And the proof of it is this: many before now, being ignorant of this fact and thinking that they were themselves the cause of their success, but despising me, have gone away from me sooner than they ought, whether of their own accord or because others persuaded them to do so. Then, after they have gone away, they have miscarried thenceforth on account of evil companionship, and the offspring which they have brought forth through my assistance they have reared so badly that they have lost it; they have considered impostures and images of more importance than the truth, and at last it was evident to them, as well as to others, that they were ignorant. One of these was Aristeides, the son of Lysimachus, and there are very many more. When such men come back and beg me, as they do, with wonderful eagerness to let them join me again, the spiritual *daimonion* that comes to me forbids me to associate with some of them, but allows me to converse with others, and these again make progress. Now those who associate with me are in this matter also like women in childbirth; they are in pain and are full of trouble night and day, much more than are the women; and my art can arouse this pain and cause it to cease. Well, that is what happens to them. But in some cases, Theaetetus, when they do not seem to me to be exactly pregnant, since I see that they have no need of me, I act with perfect goodwill as match-maker and, under God, I guess very successfully with whom they can associate profitably, and I have handed over many of them to Prodicus, and many to other wise and inspired men.

Now I have said all this to you at such length, my dear boy, because I suspect that you, as you yourself believe, are in pain because you are pregnant with something within you. Apply, then, to me, remembering that I am the son of a midwife and have myself a midwife's gifts, and do your best to answer the questions I ask as I ask them. And if, when I have examined any of the things you say, it should prove that I think it is a mere image and not real, and therefore quietly take it from you and throw it away, do not be angry as women are when they are deprived of their first offspring. For many, my dear friend, before this have got into such a state of mind towards me that they are actually ready to bite me if I take some foolish notion away from them, and they do not believe that I do this in kindness, since they are far from knowing that no God is unkind to mortals and that I do nothing of this sort from unkindness either, and that it is quite out of the question for me to allow an imposture or to destroy the true. And so, Theaetetus, begin again and try to tell us what knowledge is. And never say that you are unable to do so; for if God wills it and gives you courage, you will be able.[16]

The maieutic art involves the *psyche*, which is exactly how Socrates defines his ironic-maieutic art; it cannot be stated better, nor can the central role of the *soul* in Socratic dialectic be presented better.

5. Socrates, founder of Logic?

The assertion that Socrates is *the inventor or the discoverer of the concept* and consequently the founder of western logic has been for a long time commonplace. However the elements which we have brought to light on occasion and the Platonic passages which we have reported in order to illustrate the Socratic ironic method would be sufficient of themselves to destroy any plausibility in this assertion. The Socratic dialogical method has in fact an essentially ethico-pedagogic and even religious goal (given that Socrates says that he began it *by the command of the God*) and the singular logical value of the method, which is simply undeniable, has not been placed in the forefront by Socrates. However, since this interpretation of Socrates as the discoverer of the concept has been maintained by authoritative interpreters and is now wholly accepted by the manualists, it is necessary that we subject it to critical examination and that we demonstrate its lack of substance.

Moreover, Schleiermacher has seen in the Socratic thought the awakening of the idea of science and the birth of the first forms of science.[17] Zeller gave to this interpretation its most complete form, writing that "it is the idea of science which is at the foundation of the philosophy of Socrates,"[18] in the sense that Socrates not only did science like the other philosophers, but he was the first who came to the awareness of the idea of science as such, both its conditions and the procedures which make it possible. The condition of doing science is summarizable in this principle, nothing can be asserted of an object until its *concept* is known, its universal and permanent essence. Consequently, the procedure followed by Socrates in order to achieve the concept was *induction*, the logical movement from particular instances to the universal.

At this point, then, these interpretations begin which go beyond the evidence, and they make Socrates the founder of a rationalistic culture and a precursor of modern rationalism.

It is true that the basic source of these interpretations which see in Socrates the discoverer of the concept and of western logic is taken from some passages of the *Metaphysics* of Aristotle, which we should now read:

> And when Socrates, disregarding the physical universe and confining his study to moral questions, sought in this sphere for the *universal* and was the first to concentrate on *definition*, Plato followed him because of the conviction that he accepted from the Heracliteans [that is the doctrine according to which everything is in perpetual flux] and assumed that the problem of definition is concerned not with any kind of sensible thing but with entities of another kind; for the reason that there can be no general definition of sensible things which are always changing; he called these other entities Ideas and he held that sensible things exist in virtue of their relationship to them.[19]

> Socrates...naturally inquired into the essence of things; for he was trying to reason logically, and the starting-point of all logical reasoning is the essence.... Actually there are two innovations which may fairly be ascribed to Socrates: *inductive reasoning* and *universal definition*. Both of these are associated with the starting-point of scientific knowledge.[20]

> This way of thinking [belonging to the Platonists], as we have said in an earlier passage, was initiated by Socrates as a result of his definitions, but he did not separate universals from particulars.[21]

Now scholars of these last decades have brought to light that Aristotle always is to be taken with extreme caution as an historical source, for when he speaks of the thought of other philosophers he interprets them and systematizes them in function of his own categories.[22] Especially, in the passages we have read, he says two things that are accurate and objective remarks, that is, that Socrates was concerned with ethical questions and that the doctrine of the Ideas is Platonic and not Socratic. But the third thing that Aristotle says, which specifically is about Socrates, is that Socrates discovered the universal, the definition, and inductive procedure, but this statement *cannot in any way be true*, for the simple reason that such discoveries postulate a whole series of logical and metaphysical categories (universal-particular, essence-concept, deduction-induction) which not only were not at Socrates's disposal, but were not even present in the early Plato. Only at the time of the *Republic* are these categories established and even then only with Aristotle do they take the shape of logical structures which he would like to attribute to Socrates.

In the question "what-is-it?" with which Socrates hammered at his interlocutors and which is increasingly recognized today in specialized studies, "theoretical knowledge of the logical essence of the universal concept was not already absolutely contained."[23] In fact with his question *he wanted to start the ironic-maieutic process and did not wish at all to reach logical definitions*. Socrates opened the way that must lead to the discovery of the essence (of the Platonic *eidos*); he exercised a marked tendency in this direction but he does not by that fact establish the structure of the concept and the definition, since he lacked all the necessary means to achieve this goal which, as we have already stated, is a subsequent discovery.

The same remark is true of induction, which Socrates for the most part used with his constant bringing of his interlocutors from particular cases to general ones, especially by using examples and analogies, but which in spite of this did not reach a theoretical level and which hence did not theorize on the issue in a reflective way. Moreover, the terminology "inductive reasoning" is not only not Socratic, but it does not even belong to Plato. It is typically Aristotelian [*epagoge*], and presupposes the acquisitions of the *Analytics*.

We are forced to conclude then that Aristotle, from a purely theoretical concern, is involved in an error of historical perspective by claiming to find in Socrates some discoveries which he alone achieved; and modern scholars, with Zeller at their head, who base their views on Aristotle's report have been dragged along into an analogous error of perspective. Because Zeller, as we know, has been the immediate and indirect source of modern potted histories, the thesis, simply by being repeated, became the *communis opinio*, and only the most rigorous and up-to-date contemporary technique of historical research demonstrates its lack of foundation.

The assertions that we read in the following passages of Xenophon do not seem too distant from the historical truth:

I will try also to show how he encouraged his companions to become skilled in discussion. Socrates held that those who know *what any given thing is* can also expound it to others; on the other hand, those who do not know are misled themselves and mislead others. For this reason, he never gave up considering with his companions what any given thing is.[24]

The very word "discussion," according to him, owes its name to the practice of meeting together for common deliberation, *sorting and discussing things after their kind*: and therefore one should be ready and prepared for this and be zealous for it; for it makes for excellence, leadership, and skill in discussion.[25]

Whenever he himself argued out a question, *he advanced by steps that gained general assent*, holding this to be the only sure method. Accordingly, whenever he argued, he gained a greater measure of assent from his hearers than any other man I have known. He said that Homer gave Odysseus the credit of being a "safe speaker" because he had a way of leading the discussion from one acknowledged truth to another.[26]

Well then, of the three logical criteria that we can derive from these passages none sound suspect nor show signs of subsequent doctrines, and all are confirmed by Platonic dialogues in which we see Socrates in the concrete actually acting according to them.

a) Socrates searched for the "what-it-is" of things and was accustomed to do so. Although this is correct, it does not at all mean that he discovered the ontological nature of the essence or, as Aristotle says, the logical nature of the *universal* and the *definition* (the concept). It does not even mean necessarily that Socrates discovered and pointed out the "what-it-is," given that the goal of his method was protreptic, and that what his philosophy, primarily and before all [*in primis et ante omnia*], wants to obtain is the examination of the *psyche* of the interlocutor.

b) Socrates taught that dialectic proceeded "by distinguishing by kind" or "classifying by kind." This is also, or can be, true (provided that the term "kind" [genus] is understood not in the late Platonic or Aristotelian sense), since the classification by kind enters into the procedure which aims at specifying the "what-it-is" of a thing.

c) Socrates, when he wished to resolve a question, proceeded by discussion on the basis of principles that all the hearers could accept (even if eventually Socrates did not agree to them), and he began from them in order to draw his conclusions. This is completely confirmed by the Platonic dialogues. The most eloquent example is the *Protagoras*, where Socrates, in order to demonstrate that *virtue is knowledge*, as we have seen already, began from principles admitted by all that the good and pleasure are identical (which is a principle not personally accepted by him) and drawing from it a series of conclusions on which again he was concerned to guarantee the assent of his hearers in order to draw his own conclusion.

This method of proceeding by Socrates completely explains only the protreptic function of his dialectic. And the same can be said also for all these artifices, some obviously arbitrary, which we find especially in the first Platonic dialogues, which receive their correct interpretation only from the aforementioned perspective.[27]

In conclusion, Socrates had a formidable, clever logic but he did not elaborate a logic on the theoretical level; in his dialectic the germs are to be found which will end up in future important logical discoveries, but he did not discover nor consciously formulate a logic.

On the basis of this interpretation only is it possible to explain the different positions taken by the disciples of Socrates and the opposed directions arising from the Socratic Schools. Some, in fact, pointing exclusively to the ethical goals of the Socratic method, put aside any logical details and reject the attempt of those who understand it in this sense. Plato developed, instead, the logical and metaphysical seeds of Socratic dialectic in order to elaborate a magnificent speculative system. Euclid and the Megaric school, finally, develop that aspect of Socratic dialectic which focuses on eristic, as we will shortly see.

V. The Aporias and Structural Limitations of Socraticism

Let us conclude with an examination of the principal aporias and structural limits of Socratic philosophy, recalling some of the observations already made, and developing others which will help us to better understand the further developments of Greek thought.

We have seen that the whole Socratic inquiry, his ironic-maieutic method, his protreptic, the entire circle of his thematic, revolves around the axis of the problem of the soul understood in the new sense that we have indicated. Yet, Socrates does not determine the nature of the soul and he is limited to defining it in a manner, as we would say today, which is purely operational. A. E. Taylor grasps this point quite clearly (denying here, for the sake of the truth, his own general position according to which everything that Plato says comes from Socrates),[1] "[*viz.*, Socrates] tells us nothing on the question what *is* the nature of the soul except that it is 'that in us, whatever it is, in virtue of which we are denominated wise and foolish, good and evil,' and that it cannot be seen or apprehended by any of the senses. It is not a doctrine of the 'faculties' of the soul, any more than of its 'substance.' The thought is that the 'work' or 'function' of this divine constituent in man is just to *know* good and evil, and to *direct* or *govern* a man's acts so that they lead to a life in which evil is avoided and good achieved."[2] At best Socrates wants to say that the soul, as no other thing, participates in the Divine; but then he cannot know nor determine the nature of the Divine. In order to determine the concept of the soul further, he would have to make use of metaphysical concepts which were not available to him. And it is hence wholly natural that he could not *philosophically* justify the immortality of the soul. Some (as we have said already) thought therefore that Socrates doubted the immortality of the soul and the beyond, but the text of the *Apology* does not suggest this at all, it merely shows that he did not have the means to solve the problem with certitude in any of the proper ways, and that the only option remaining was to maintain the thesis of immortality as worthy of belief.

In order to ground this thesis, just as to theoretically determine the nature of the soul, it is necessary to possess metaphysical categories without which the Socratic "concern for the soul" could not have the meaning which Socrates had pointed out. And, in fact, the Socratics (about whom we will immediately speak) who did not achieve these categories, bent and turned the message of Socrates in other directions to the point of distorting it in some essential points; while Plato, who will achieve these metaphysical categories, will explicate it in its most authentic meaning.

An analogous remark, as we have hinted previously, may be made about the Socratic conception of God and the Divine. He took up important notions from the Naturalists, emptying them therefore of their presupposed physics, but without knowing how to give them further foundations he thus limited himself in his arguments to intuitions and analogies. Just as from the works of the soul intelligence is attributed to the soul, so also from the works of God intelligence and providence are attributed to God. In order to go beyond these analogies he would have to have grasped the metaphysical categories of the intelligible.

The same structural limits are revealed in Socratic teleology. The conception of universal teleology which Socrates had taken from Diogenes of Apollonia did not have at its base a specific conception of *physis*, but it cannot give itself, however, any other theoretical basis. Socrates came to identify the good with the goal, "For all things are good and beautiful in relation to those purposes for which they are well adapted, bad and ugly in relation to those for which they are ill adapted";[3] but also in this case he is at the experiential and intuitive level. His proof of the thesis does not go beyond examples and analogies. To give a metaphysical foundation to the intuitive teleology of Socrates will require the Platonic "second voyage," that is, his theory of Ideas, and/or the Aristotelian metaphysical doctrine of the four causes.

We have already spoken rather fully about the aporias of Socratic intellectualism. Here we must only complete what has already been said, showing the final aporias implicit in the doctrine of virtue-knowledge. It is clear that Socratic *wisdom* is not empty, as some have claimed, since it has as its object the *psyche* and the concern for the *psyche* and given that the *psyche* is cared for by *simply destroying its pretensions to wisdom and bringing it to the acknowledgement of its unknowing.* However, it is likewise certain that the Socratic discussion leaves the impression, at a certain point, of escaping or at least of stopping halfway. And it is likewise true that, as it was thus formulated, Socratic discourse makes sense only in the hands of Socrates, derived from the indomitable force of his personality. In the hands of his disciples that method of discussion necessarily must either be reduced with a sacrifice of some of the basic positions of which it was the vehicle or, being completed, through the deepening of those demands into its metaphysical foundation. Against the simplifications produced by the minor Socratic schools once again it will be Plato who will attempt to give a precise content to that wisdom by pointing out, at first generically, the supreme object in the good, and then more specifically he will attempt to give to this good a metaphysical significance once again through the "second voyage."

Also, the unbounded Socratic confidence in wisdom, in the *logos* in general (not only in its particular content), receives a rather severe jolt, chiefly in the problematic results of the maieutic method. The Socratic *logos*, in the ultimate analysis, is not a condition for the arousal of knowledge in every soul, but *only in those who are pregnant.* It is a confession full of many implications, but since Socrates did not know about them he could not draw them forth. The *logos* and the dialogical structure on which the logos is entirely based is not sufficient to produce or at least not sufficient to help anyone *to recognize the truth and to live in accordance with that truth*. Many have turned their backs away from the Socratic logos because they were not "pregnant," says the philosopher. But then who fecundates the soul, who makes it pregnant? This is a question which Socrates did not pose and which in any case he could not have answered. It is well to notice that the source of this difficulty is the same as that which was present in the case of the actions of the man who sees and knows the better thing but does the worse. And if, put in this way, Socrates believed that he could avoid this difficulty with his intellectualism, put in another way he cannot avoid it and even the analogy with pregnancy, although beautiful and suggestive, does not solve the difficulty. It will be Plato also, in this case, who attempts to go beyond, but—we will see—not even Plato will emerge totally victorious. Between the knowledge of the good and the will to do it, that is, to make one's life agree with itself, there is a qualitative leap because in this process there is the entry of choice, that is of liberty, which structurally does not allow itself to be reduced to knowledge and wisdom. There is at this point the presence of a mystery, of the most profound mystery about man, who can accept but then can also absurdly reject the truth, *who can turn his back on the truth*. Socrates steadfastly refused to believe that this state of affairs was possible.

Leaving aside the basic aporias of Socratic dialectic about which we have already spoken above, let us come to the most fundamental aporia inherent in the Socratic doctrine itself, and hence ultimately grounded in his very existence itself. We previously showed that although Socratic dialectic carries in itself the germs of future great discoveries, nevertheless it suffers from a basic ambiguity, which makes it susceptible to being developed both in the eristical and logical scientific senses.

Our philosopher presented his doctrine as valid *in particular for the Athenians* and hence enclosed it in the narrow limits of a *polis*. It is, note, not given to the *polis* in general, but to that particular *polis* which was Athens. *He did not wish, then, to be a messenger for all the Greeks, much less for the whole of humanity*. On this point, evidently, Socrates was conditioned by the socio-cultural structure of the time to the point of not being aware that his message went well beyond the walls of the city of Athens. But it is not only that the message went beyond the walls of Athens, but it even went all the way to the limits of the Greek *polis*, in the cosmo-political sense. The pointing out of the essence of man in the *psyche*, in the *logos*, and having anchored the *logos* to *enkrateia*, to *liberty*, and to *autarcheia* carried, as a logical consequence, to the distinction between the *citizen* of a polis and *individual* human beings in general and finally to the declaration of the *autonomy of the individual*. But this conclusion will be explicated in part by the minor Socratics and more fully by the philosophers of the Hellenistic Age.

Socrates may be called a two-faced Herma; on the one hand his unknowing seems to move toward the negation of science, and on the other it seems to be a way of getting to an authentic higher science. On the one hand his message can be read as a mere moral exhortation, on the other as an opening toward the Platonic "second voyage." On the one hand his dialectic can appear to be sophistic and eristic in character, and on the other the foundation of scientific logic. On the one hand his message seems to be circumscribed by the walls of the Athenian *polis*, on the other it opens out into the cosmopolis, into the whole world.

Actually, the minor Socratics develop one side of this Herma, and Plato the opposite one. Discriminating between the two interpretations involves once again the Platonic "second voyage." But before we speak of this "second voyage," which signals a milestone for ancient speculation, we must discuss the minor Socratic schools, which not only remain on this side of the area of interest opened by it but which likewise lose a part of the Socratic area of interest itself.

Second Section

THE MINOR SOCRATICS

«πλείους ἔσονται ὑμᾶς οἱ ἐλέγχοντες,
οὓς νῦν ἐγὼ κατεῖχον, ὑμεῖς δὲ οὐκ
ᾐσθάνεσθε· καὶ χαλεπώτεροι ἔσονται
ὅσῳ νεώτεροί εἰσιν.»

"Those who will force you to give an
account will be more numerous than
heretofore; men whom I have
restrained, though you knew it not;
and they will be harsher, inasmuch as
they are younger, and you will be
more annoyed."

Plato *Apology* 39 C-D

I. The Circle of the Socratics and the Socratic Schools

In the *Apology* the Platonic Socrates makes an assertion directed at the judges who have condemned him (in a passage we have previously quoted) which was prophetic at the moment of the trial, but which was already a reality at the time Plato wrote it. Here is the entire passage:

> And now I wish to prophesy to you, you who have condemned me; for I am now at the time when men most do prophesy, the time just before death. And I say to you, you men who have slain me, that punishment will come upon you straightway after my death, far more grievous in fact than the punishment of death which you have meted out to me. For now you have done this to me because you hoped that you would be relieved from rendering an account of your lives, but I say that you will find the result far different. Those who will force you to give an account will be more numerous than heretofore; men whom I have restrained, though you knew it not; and they will be harsher, inasmuch as they are younger, and you will be more annoyed. For if you think that by putting me to death you will prevent anyone from reproaching you because you do not act as you should, you are mistaken. That mode of escape is neither possible at all nor honorable, but the easiest and most honorable escape for you is not by suppressing others, but by making yourselves as good as possible. So with this prophecy to you who condemned me I take my leave.[1]

Actually, not only is it true that the disciples who continued the Socratic work by subjecting to *examination* the life of men and *refuting* their false opinions were many and intrepid and were such as to overturn, with their doctrines, all the schemas of the moral tradition to which the accusers of Socrates clung; but it is also true that no philosopher before or after Socrates would have so many immediate disciples of such wealth and variety of orientation formed by his teaching.

Already the ancient doxographers were aware of this, and even connected almost all the succeeding philosophical Schools comprising those of the Hellenistic Age[2] to Socrates. We will see that this is substantially true and that Socrates had been in a certain sense the father also of Epicureanism and Stoicism (and in a certain sense even Pyrrhonism); but what actually happened afterwards is a complex series of phenomena, and hence Socrates is only *indirectly* their source. However even if prescinding from the indirect influence of Socraticism, what we asserted above is still true; Socrates was surrounded by men of uncommon genius and character who were in many ways exceptional.

Among all the friends of Socrates, Diogenes Laertius[3] points to seven as most representative and illustrious: Xenophon, Aeschines, Antisthenes, Aristippus, Euclid, Phaedo, and the greatest of all, Plato. And if Xenophon and Aeschines are excepted, who were not very philosophically inclined (the former was chiefly an historian and the latter a literary figure), the five others were all founders of philosophical schools.

The meaning and influence of each of these five schools are very diverse and even more diverse are the results to which they came, as we will see in a detailed manner. However, each of the founders felt himself to be an authentic (if not the sole authentic) heir of Socrates. The exceptional attachment to the teacher of all these disciples is attested to in a clear way; indeed the history of the relations of each of them with him (whether in the beginning or in its development) is an exceptional record. Here is how it is recorded by Xenophon:

> Xenophon, the son of Gryllus, was a citizen of Athens and belonged to the deme Erchia; he was a man of rare modesty and extremely handsome. The story goes that Socrates met him in a narrow passage, and that he stretched out his stick to bar the way while he inquired where every kind of food was sold. Upon receiving a reply, he put another question, "And where do men become good and honorable?" Xenophon was fairly puzzled; "Then follow me," said Socrates, "and learn." From that time onward he was a pupil of Socrates. He was the first to take notes of, and to give to the world, the conversation of Socrates, under the title of *Memorabilia*. Moreover, he was the first to write a history of philosophers.[4]

This amazing anecdote is told of Aeschines which illustrates his total attachment to Socrates:

> Aeschines said to him, "I am a poor man and have nothing else to give, but I offer you myself," and Socrates answered, "Nay, do you not see that you are offering me the greatest gift of all?"[5]

Of Antisthenes it is told that he knew and heard Socrates after he had already founded his School,

> he derived so much benefit from him that he used to advise his own disciples to become fellow-pupils of Socrates.[6]

And even this quite suggestive fact is recorded:

> He lived in the Peiraeus, and every day would tramp the five miles to Athens in order to hear Socrates.[7]

Of Aristippus it is said that after having gone on the occasion of the Olympic games to speak to Socrates he was seized by such turmoil that even his health was affected and he did not revive until, from far away Cyrene, he came to Athens and became a hearer of Socrates.[8]

Euclid of Megara, it is said, simply in order to continue to hear Socrates did not hesitate to put his life in jeopardy. In fact, afterwards there developed an emnity between Athens and Megara and the Athenians decreed the penalty of death for the Megarians who entered their city, and Euclid, in spite of this fact, continued to regularly travel from Megara to Athens, at night, camouflaged in women's clothes.[9]

The affection which joined Phaedo to Socrates is attested by Plato in the dialogue by that name, chiefly in the interlude, in the reference precisely "to the hairs of Phaedo," which is well known.[10] Moreover, we know that Socrates had liberated Phaedo, in a surprising way, from a double servitude, material as well as moral.[11] And here is finally what Diogenes Laertius says about Plato:

> It is stated that Socrates in a dream saw a cygnet on his knees, which all at once put forth plumage, and flew away after uttering a loud sweet note. And the next day Plato was introduced as a pupil, and thereupon he recognized in him the swan of his dream.[12]

> Afterwards, when he was about to compete for the prize with a tragedy, he listened to Socrates in front of the theater of Dionysius, and then consigned his poems to the flames with the words, "Come here, O fire-God, Plato now has need of you." From that time onward, having reached his twentieth year, he was the pupil of Socrates until his death.[13]

Many of these stories are perhaps legends, or are amplified in the style of legends; in any case, they represent clearly enough the different temperaments and characteristics of these persons who will be seen from the detailed examination that we will now make. Let us leave aside, naturally, Xenophon and Aeschines of Sphettus, who, as we have said above, are not properly philosophers and are of more interest to history and literature than to the history of philosophy. We will next study Antisthenes, Aristippus, Euclid, Phaedo, and their schools, which we will also consider, for many reasons, the minor Socratic Schools. Plato, on the other hand, because of the remarkable achievements of his speculation, will require half of the second volume. The story of the swan who flew from the lap of Socrates in order to sing its message appropriately illustrates, in a pregnant image, the distance which separates Plato from all the other Socratics.[14]

II. Antisthenes and the Foundation of the Cynic School

1. The relationship of Antisthenes to Socrates

Antisthenes[1] was certainly the person of major importance among the "minor" Socratics, insofar as, by filtering Socraticism in a one-sided manner, he gathered, interpreted, and basically revived one of its fundamental aspects. He revised the precise aspect which reveals the face of the two-faced Socratic Herma, which is exactly opposed to that revealed by Plato. It is not strange, therefore, that there would be a contrasting approach between Plato and Antisthenes, which, as is proved by some testimonies, nearly verged on emnity.[2]

Antisthenes especially admired the extraordinary capacity of Socrates for self-determination, his power of spirit, his wonderful tolerance for tiring labor, his capacity to be self-sufficient, in a word, *his total liberty*. He understood Socraticism as fundamentally a message of liberty and liberation and, as we will immediately see, as such he proclaimed it to others.[3]

Antisthenes took the central Socratic doctrine of the *psyche* and stated some corollaries,[4] but as positions already acquired, and as such needing no further development. He also affirmed the central thesis of Socratic intellectualism, but attenuated it theoretically, saying "virtue is sufficient for happiness,"[5] "virtue can be taught,"[6] and "it cannot be lost once acquired,"[7] insofar as it is "a weapon that cannot be taken away."[8] These theses presuppose the total identification of virtue with knowledge. So Antisthenes showed that he accepted this identification in its strongest form, as the following assertions demonstrate:

> Wisdom is a most sure stronghold which never crumbles away nor is betrayed.[9]
>
> Walls of defense must be constructed in our own impregnable reasonings.[10]
>
> Those who wish to become virtuous men must exercise their bodies with athletic exercises, and the soul with reasoned arguments.[11]

However, he limited not a little the bearing of these assertions, maintaining for a time what follows:

> Virtue has no need of anything else except the force of Socrates.[12]
>
> Virtue is an affair of deeds and does not need a store of words or learning.[13]

The negative attitude of Antisthenes with respect to science must be understood in this sense. Even the so-called "logic" of Antisthenes has no other aim than to limit to a necessary minimum what wisdom needs to know, and especially to deny the necessity and even the very possibility of those logico-metaphysical developments that Plato had impressed on Socraticism.[14]

The Platonic Ideas for him are absurd. It is written that he raised this objection against Plato, "I see the horse but not equinity,"[15] an assertion that means precisely that I see the particular experienced sensible thing, not the universal intelligible (not the Idea or essence). The definition, for him, states "what it was or what a thing is,"[16] but the "what it was or is" is understood in a way which is antithetical to Plato's understanding.[17] The simple or elementary things we know through sensorial perceptions and it is not therefore possible to furnish a definition and it is only possible, at best, to furnish a description by means of analogies of them. If, for example, we want to describe to someone who has never seen silver what silver is, we will say that it is "a metal like tin."[18] Instead, the definition of the "what-is" of complex things consists in the enumeration of the simple elements of which it is composed.[19]

The reasons for the nominalism of Antisthenes, then, are clear. "The principle of instruction—he says—is the inquiry into names."[20] This emphasis on the name more than on the essence means to give an account according to the Sophistic (remember especially Prodicus) more than in accordance with the Socratic position.[21] The individual thing is expressed by its proper name, and hence no other name can properly be attributed to it other than its very own. For example, it can be said that *man is man*, or even that *good is good*, but not that *man is good*.[22] The possibility of joining different terms is eliminated, that is, the possibility of formulating judgments which are not *tautologies*, and with that, every possibility of constructing a logic and a metaphysics of a Platonic type is also eliminated.[23]

In conclusion, for Antisthenes the true Socratic position was that—and only that—revealed by his practical wisdom which regulates living; the message of Socrates was a purely existential message.

2. The message of liberation and liberty

The Socratic overturning of the table of values, as we have seen, is based on the discovery of the *psyche* as the essence of man, and on the consequent assertion that the highest values are the values of the soul. Antisthenes revived this revolution, chiefly using its destructive aspect with respect to the traditional values, and the consequent sense of being freed and liberated from all those things which men have always considered good and indispensible for being happy and which, instead, are revealed as neither good nor necessary, but obstacles to happiness. The secret of happiness is wholly within ourselves. It is in our soul. It is in *our self-sufficiency*. It is in our *not being dependent on things and man*. It is in our *not-having-need-of-anything* (τὸ μηδενὸς προσδεῖσθαι). Here is how Xenophon describes this liberty of Antisthenes:

"And you, Antisthenes," Socrates asked, "tell us how it is that simply by possessing so little, you are thus proud of your wealth."

"Because, in my view, friends, men have *wealth and poverty not in their homes but in their soul.* I see much deprivation in those who by possessing many things are maintained in poverty to the point of enduring every labor, every risk in order to achieve more: I know some brothers who have the same inheritance, but one has the wherewithal for the necessary expenses and even above that while the other brother lacks everything: and I know certain tyrants so starved by wealth that they commit many more horrendous evils than the most desperate of men: such a one, in fact, robs the needy, others pillage homes, others make men into slaves: there are tyrants who destroy entire families, they kill enmasse and frequently they reduce entire cities to servitude for the money. These I pity and many others for their tragic obsession. It seems to me that they are in the same position, insofar as having much they eat much, never being satisfied. For my part, my possessions are such that I tire trying to find them: or they permit me to fully appease my hunger when I eat, to quench my thirst when I drink, and to shelter myself; finally, it is true by enduring the cold when I am outside I am better off than our very wealthy Callias: then when I stay home, the walls seem to me like a cold cloak, the hood of a thick cloak; finally I sleep, sheltered thus by the covers, which are a weighty matter lightened by the bed. And if in turn my body has need of love, what I have is enough for me because with the greatest joy they receive me, those to whom I go wishing nothing other than to be near them. And all these things seem thus pleasing from which, while I understand them one by one, I would never desire to receive a great joy, but instead a minor one, however pleasant some of them may seem to be! *But what I value more than my wealth is that if now everything I have were taken from me I would not see work as so ignoble that it would not offer me sufficient nourishment.* If, in fact, I wished to indulge my desires a little, I would not buy expensive bread—that which costs too much—but I would curb my appetite, because to be waiting a long time for satisfaction contributes much more to the achievement of pleasure than to be able to use things of great price, as now, for example, with this wine of Taso at hand, which I drink without being thirsty. In addition, it is *natural that there are many more just, than those who seek the frugality which is very expensive: in fact, he who is content with what he has does not long for other things.* It is good then to reflect that this wealth also make for liberality. Our Socrates, from whom I have acquired it, did not measure it nor weigh it with respect to me, but gave me as much as I could take, and now I am not envious of anyone and I share it with all my friends without jealousy. I share the wealth of my soul with anyone who asks for it. And, what is even better, guarding *my absolute liberty, through which I can observe what is worthwhile observing, to listen to what is worthwhile hearing and—what interests me more—to be in full possession of liberty from morning till night together with Socrates.* What I do not admire is one who esteems a lot of money, and spends time together with those who please them."[24]

A few lines after this ideal of liberty is mentioned it is identified with the expression *not-having-need-of-anything*.[25]

Here is how Epictetus brings back to life this ideal of Antisthenes in a neo-Stoic manner in this passage in which he speaks of Diogenes, a disciple of Antisthenes:

> That is how freedom is achieved. That is why he used to say, "From the time that Antisthenes set me free, I have ceased to be a slave." How did Antisthenes set him free? Listen to what Diogenes says. "He taught me what was mine; kinsmen, members of my household, friends, reputation, familiar places, converse with men—all these are not my own. 'What, then, is yours?' Power to deal with external impressions.' He showed me that I possess this beyond all hindrance and constraint; no one can hamper me; no one can force me to deal with them otherwise than as I will. Who, then, has authority over me? Philip or Alexander, or Perdiccas, or the Great King? Where can they get it? For the man who is destined to be overpowered by a man must long before that have been overpowered by things." Therefore, the man over whom pleasure has no power, nor evil, nor fame, nor wealth, and who, whenever it seems good to him, can spit his whole paltry body into some oppressor's face and depart from this life—whose slave can he any longer be, whose subject?[26]

The two passages read are two extreme examples of the way of Antisthenes, the first moderates it in an almost reactionary way (this was the Xenophonean thought), the second exacerbates it in the sense proper to Diogenes, with the further additions proper to the neo-Stoicism of Epictetus, however, and because of this, they fit together by correcting each other.

But we will now see in the concrete what is the precise significance of the liberty of Antisthenes.

3. The liberation of the appetites and pleasure

The passage of Xenophon speaks of the liberation from men and things (wealth and friends are *in the soul!*), while the passage of Epictetus, at the end, speaks also of total liberation from pleasures and hence from desire. It is this first point in which Antisthenes goes beyond Socrates, and radicalizes him.

Socrates did not maintain that pleasure was an *evil*, nor did he maintain that it was a good, either. Everything depends on the use which is made of it. Instead Antisthenes, as has been attested to by many sources, condemned in a categorical way every pleasure, considering them intrinsic evils, and with an astounding panache he said:

I would rather be insane than to have pleasures.[27]

He inveighed against sexual pleasure with a profane and (for a Greek) almost a blasphemous image:

If I could have Aphrodite in my hands, I would shoot arrows at her.[28]

Why this struggle with pleasure? Because pleasure, in any case in the moment in which it is being sought, makes slaves of man, making him dependent on the object from which it is derived. Especially, then, is this verified in erotic pleasure which is accompanied by sexual passion, for it puts man at the mercy of the person who gives that pleasure.[29]

The struggle against pleasure and passion—it is to be noted—in Antisthenes has a significance which is of an exactly contrary nature to that which the exactly parallel affirmation has for Plato. We will see, in fact, that Plato's condemnation of pleasure and passions depends on his metaphysical dualism and his religious (Orphic) conception of the body understood not only as totally other than the soul, but also as a tomb or prison-house of the soul.[30] Instead, in the materialist Antisthenes the condemnation of pleasure is proclaimed only *in order to safeguard the total liberty of man, because in order to obtain the objects of pleasure man loses his independence and autonomy and thus does not maintain absolute mastery over himself.*

4. The liberation from the illusions created by society and the exaltation of manual labor

The view of Antisthenes on wealth can be seen in the above mentioned passage of Xenophon and it is confirmed again by other sources: "no one who loves money—he says—is good: neither king, nor private citizen".[31] In fact for him "without virtue wealth does not bring joy."[32] And a life of luxury, he said, was something to be wished "only for the sons of one's enemies."[33]

But not even honor, reputation, and glory have any significance. But they have negative importance because society honors and praises that which is opposed to what the philosopher holds in esteem. To someone who said to Antisthenes, "Many men praise you," he sharply replied, "Why, what wrong have I done?"[34] This expresses very well an attitude which is charged with his accurate and precise disapproval of society. But he added even that "the absence of glory and reputation (ἀδοξία) is a good."[35]

And with *adoxia* he affirmed that the "ultimate goal" was *atuphia* (ἀτυφία), which means the *absence of illusion*, that is, all those fallacious opinions which come from society.[36]

This was also a further radicalization of Socratic thought. It was a radicalization which must necessarily lead to a rupture with law, with the *nomos* of the City-State and, in fact, Antisthenes expressly affirmed it:

> That the wise man will be guided in his public acts not by the estab-
> lished laws but by the law of virtue.[37]

Finally, Antisthenes also assumed an attitude of radical antithesis
towards the Gods of the City-State, which he declared existed as "many"
only "by law," while God is one "by nature," "similar to nothing," and
"cannot be known through images."[38] And even in respect to the hereafter
he did not hesitate to declare his opinion negatively, as can be surmized
from this delightful but irreverent riposte which he jauntily delivered:

> When he was being initiated into the Orphic mysteries, the priest said
> that those admitted into these rites would be partakers of many good
> things in Hades. "Why then," said he, "don't you die?"[39]

It is clear that the ethics of Antisthenes implies continual *power* and
labor on the part of man; labor in the combat against pleasure and impulse,
labor in detaching oneself from wealth and from things, labor in the renunciation of reputation, labor in the opposition to the laws of the State. And
the *toil*, indeed, *is said to be good* and strictly connected to virtue. But
Antisthenes, in order to underline his exalted concept of toil, of *ponos*
(πόνος), consecrated his School to Heracles, the hero of legendary and
apparently impossible labors. This notion of burdensome labor also meant
a drastic rupture with the common sentiment, because it elevated to the
highest dignity and value that which most men flee from.[40]

5. Antisthenes, the founder of Cynicism

Antisthenes was from ancient times acknowledged as the founder of
Cynicism and the head of the Cynic School.[41] The term "Cynic" was
derived from the term for "dog" (κύων), and probably has a two-fold origin.
Diogenes Laertius writes: "[Antisthenes] used to converse in the gymnasium of Cynosarges [Κυνόσαργες = *quick dog*], at no great distance from the
gates [of Athens], and some think that the Cynic school derived its name
from Cynosarges. Later he writes that Antisthenes was nicknamed
Ἁπλοκύων that is, *a dog, pure and simple*.[42] The disciple of Antisthenes,
Diogenes, was self-nicknamed "Diogenes the Dog."[43] It is probable that,
exploiting the coincidence between the name of the gymnasium in which
the School had arisen with the name which was given commonly to the
type of life that they loved, which was that of a dog, these philosophers
called themselves precisely "Cynics," a name which symbolized a break
with the past. It is also possible that in the dog they saw an totemic emblem
of their vigilance, of that vigilance which the dog has for his master and the
Cynic philosopher has for his doctrine.
Diogenes of Sinope carried the Cynicism of Antisthenes to its extreme
consequences, even reaching the negation of society and its structures, and
he proposed the suppression not only of social classes, but also the institu-

tion of marriage and of the State. He will open thus a new phase of Cynicism which endures with alternating vicissitudes until the Christian epoch (about which we will speak in succeeding volumes); however it is beyond doubt that the spirit and the premises of Cynicism are already quite clear in Antisthenes.[44]

The semi-barbaric origin that Antisthenes conceived with a sense of pride, overturning polemically the typically Attic mode of thinking,[45] and the consequent choice of the Cynosarges, which was a gymnasium reserved to Athenians who were bastards, simply of themselves are suggestive enough of the direction of the School.

But more suggestive than the aforementioned is his systematic distortion of Socratic thought. While Socrates wished with his philosophy to revitalize society, to purify the life of the State, to strengthen the vigor of the law, to stimulate, in short, the whole civic life with his logos, Antisthenes, on the contrary, disengaged the Socratic message from the pursuit of these goals and emphasized the individualistic, anti-social, and anti-political aspects, taking the concept of *not-having-need-of-anything* down to that precise plane on which later Cynicism will be played out.

Finally, even in his choice of the audience for his philosophical message Antisthenes corrected Socrates and opened up the Cynic perspective; Socrates, in fact, addressed himself not only to the Athenians, but fundamentally to the Athenian *elite*. Antisthenes proposed his message to the "evil-doers" too even beyond this *elite*, for which he was expressly reproached; but it is a matter of the precise choice of the break that Antisthenes had produced with full awareness to the point that he could undoubtedly respond: "Well, physicians are in attendance on their patients without getting the fever themselves,"[46] an affirmation which gives an impression analogous to the words of Christ, "It is not those who are well who have need of the doctor, but the sick; I have not come to call the just, but sinners."[47] It has correctly been observed, "The Cynics, in determining the mission of the philosopher and its object anticipated, hence, the overturning of the values which Christianity accomplished in determining its mission of redemption and its object. But Cynicism had already offered a kind of spiritual redemption; with this difference, however, that the Cynics were concerned only with the present life, whereas Christianity was concerned with the future life."[48]

III. Aristippus and the Cyrenaic School

1. The relationship of Aristippus to Socrates

From the distant and wealthy Cyrene, a city founded by Greek colonists on the coast of Africa, Aristippus[1] came to Athens irresistibly attracted by what he had heard recounted of Socrates by those that he had met at the Olympic games:

> Aristippus, when he met Ischomachus at Olympia, asked him by what manner of conversation Socrates succeeded in so affecting the young men. And when Aristippus had gleaned a few odd seeds and samples of Socrates's talk, he was so moved that he suffered a physical collapse and became quite pale and thin. Finally he sailed for Athens and slaked his burning thirst with draughts from the fountain-head, and engaged in a study of the man and his words and his philosophy, of which the end and aim was to come to recognize one's own vices and so rid oneself of them.[2]

His curiousity was certainly not disappointed. Nevertheless, on the basis of the elements which are in our possession, it is possible to affirm without fear of straying from the truth that Aristippus, among the number of Socratics, was the most independent from Socrates both in his activities and in his thinking. But it was an independence which bordered on unfaithfulness.[3]

Undoubtedly Aristippus maintained as almost second nature his own way of evaluating, which he had absorbed through the wealthy life-style of his family in Cyrene. This was certainly an obstacle to the comprehension and acceptance of the Socratic message.

In the first place, the conviction is so rooted in him that physical benefits are the highest good that he considered pleasure, as we will see, the principal motive of living. Socrates, as we have seen, does not condemn pleasure as an evil (as, on the contrary, Antisthenes did), but he did not consider it a good simply in itself; only *science and virtue* are good, and pleasure can also be good, but only if it is appropriately present in a life supported by knowledge. Instead, Aristippus, completely unbalancing the equilibrium of the Socratic position, affirmed that *pleasure is always a good* from whatever source it is derived. Aristippus was, in sum, a true and authentic hedonist, in sharp contrast with the Socratic message.[4]

In the second place, and again for the same reasons, Aristippus took an attitude with respect to money that for a Socratic was completely open-minded. He was, in fact, paid for his lectures just as the Sophists were, which is undoubtedly why the ancients dubbed him a "Sophist" (for the ancients the Sophists were those who, in point of fact, gave their teaching in exchange for money). Diogenes Laertius writes that Aristippus "was the first among the Socratics to charge fees,"[5] and that he even sent money to Socrates with the results that one can well imagine:

> And on one occasion the sum of twenty minas which he had sent was returned to him, Socrates declaring that the supernatural sign would not let him take it; the very offer, in fact, annoyed him.[6]

Even Xenophon branded Aristippus as follows:

> Some [this is clearly an allusion to our philosopher] indeed, after getting from him [Socrates] a few trifles for nothing, became vendors of them at a great price to others, and showed none of his sympathy with the people, refusing to talk with those who had no money to give them.[7]

It is not that Aristippus viewed money as a goal, but that he necessarily considered it as *an indispensible means for the leading of that kind of life demanded by his hedonism.*[8]

It is possible to understand, therefore, that the Socratic argument on the soul with its corollaries made little sense to Aristippus, and that the paradoxes of the Socratic ethics had lost much of their bite. Virtue ended for him in being the art of moving correctly within a life of pleasure, *the art of having pleasures without allowing oneself to be possessed or victimized by them.*[9]

It may be asked, at this point, how could Aristippus admire Socrates and what opinions could they possibly share. The answer is that Aristippus learned from Socrates precisely this ability to place himself beyond things and events without ever becoming their victims, this having without being possessed, this rejection of the superfluous, and finally this marvelous art of being concerned with all men. Diogenes writes:

> He was capable of adapting himself to place, time, and person, and of playing his part appropriately under whatever circumstances.[10]

> Being asked what he had gained from philosophy, he replied, "The ability to feel at ease in any company."[11]

And it is written that he educated his daughter "to reject the superfluous."[12]

It is difficult, in fact impossible, owing to the testimonies which have been handed down to us, to distinguish the thought of Aristippus from that of his immediate successors. His daughter Arete assembled the spiritual inheritance of her father in Cyrene and communicated it to her son, who was given the same name as his grandfather (and hence he is called Aristippus the Younger). It is probable that the essential nucleus of the Cyrenaic doctrine was laid down precisely during the period covered by the Aristippean triad of the elder Aristippus, Arete the daughter, and her son Aristippus the Younger, after which we may say that the School broke up into different currents. Here we will consider only those doctrines which we can with some probability trace to the original Cyrenaicism.[13]

2. The theoretical presuppositions of Cyrenaicism

Just as Socrates before them denied any usefulness to the inquiry into nature, so did the Cyrenaics. Diogenes Laertius writes:

> They abandoned the study of nature because of its apparent uncertainty...the Cyrenaics consider dialectic and physics to be useless.[14]

The Pseudo-Plutarch also writes:

> Aristippus the Cyrenaic...rejected all the other sciences of nature, saying that the only thing useful is to search "for things evil and good which are to be found existing in things."[15]

What Eusebius writes, bringing together the Cyrenaic and Socratic positions, is better:

> After him [Socrates] Aristippus the Cyrenaic and Ariston of Ceos were forced to affirm that philosophy ought *to argue only ethical issues*: these, in fact, are things that are useful to our nature; all reasoning about nature, contrarily, because it is incomprehensible, even in the case in which it were done profoundly, would not be of any use. Nor would there be anything useful for us, not even if we succeeded in flying higher than Perseus "above the waves of the sea and beyond the Pleiades," and thus we might observe with our own eyes the whole universe and the nature of things. It would not be certain, thanks to that, that we would be wiser, more just, or more courageous, or more judicious, or stronger, or more beautiful, or wealthier without which it is impossible to be happy. So Socrates justly said that things are partly above us and are partly not for us. Natural things are, in fact, beyond us like the things after death are not for us, while for us there are only human things available. Because of this he bid farewell to the naturalistic inquiry of Anaxagoras and Archelaus, and he said of their inquiry, "that things evil and things good are to be found existing in things."[16]

Mathematics itself was held to be wholly superfluous because it did not have anything to say about what was good and what was evil and hence it was not concerned with happiness, as Aristotle writes:

> And so for this reason some of the Sophists, e.g., Aristippus, spurned mathematics on the ground that in the other arts, even the mechanical ones such as carpentry and shoemaking, all explanation is of the kind "because it is better or worse," while mathematics *takes no account of good and bad*.[17]

Some sources tell us that the Cyrenaics also neglected logic,[18] while

Diogenes Laertius says that they applied themselves to it "because of its usefulness."[19] But between the two sources there is only an apparent inconsistency, because the Cyrenaic logic was nothing other than an elementary doctrine of the criterion of truth which, as we will immediately see, is reduced to a *phenomenological sensism* inspired in a certain measure by Protagoras and likewise not lacking some points of contact with Gorgean doctrines.

For the Cyrenaics only our sensible affections are cognizable, namely our subjective *states*, but never the object which provoked them. Here are some testimonies from Diogenes Laertius on this point:

> Only our affections are knowable, and not the things from which they come.[20]

Plutarch writes:

> [The Cyrenaics,] placing all experiences and impressions within themselves, thought that evidence derived from them was insufficient warrant for certainty about reality and withdrew as in a siege from the world about them and shut themselves up in their responses – admitting that external objects "appear," but refusing to venture further and pronounce the word "are."[21]

The testimony of Sextus Empiricus is superior to all others:

> Therefore the Cyrenaics say that the affections are the criteria and that they alone are apprehended and are infallible, but of the things that have caused the affections none is apprehensible or infallible. For, they say, we feel whiteness or sweetness is a thing we can state infallibly and incontrovertibly: but that the object productive of the affection is white or is sweet it is impossible to affirm.[22]

> Hence we must posit as apparent either the affections or the things productive of the affections. And if we assert that the affections are apparent, we must declare that all apparent things are true and apprehensible; but if we term the things productive of the affections apparent, all the apparent things are false and all non-apprehensible. For the affection which takes place in us reveals to us nothing more than itself. Hence too (if one must speak the truth), our affection alone is apparent to us and the external object which is productive of the affection, though it is perhaps existent, is not apparent to us. And in this way, whereas we are all unerring about our own affections, as regards the external real object we all err; and whereas the former are apprehensible, the latter is non-apprehensible, the soul being far too weak to discern it, owing to the positions, the intervals, the motions, the changes, and a host of other causes. Hence they assert that there exists no criterion common to mankind, but common names are given to the objects. For all in common use the terms "white" or "sweet," but they do not possess in common anything white or sweet. For each

man perceives his own particular affection, but as to whether this affection is produced by a white object both in himself and in his neighbor neither the man himself can affirm without experiencing his neighbors affection nor can the neighbor without experiencing that of the man. But since there is no affection which is common to us all, it is rash to assert that the thing which appears of this kind to me appears to be of this kind to the man next to me as well. For possibly while I am so constituted as to get a feeling of whiteness for that which impresses me from without, the other man has his sense so constructed as to be otherwise affected. So what appears to us is not always common to all.[23]

Hence the Cyrenaics are *phenomenalists* not in the modern Humean sense, in the sense which resolves the thing itself into its sensations,[24] but in the sense which maintains that sensations do not reveal their object (sensation does not reveal but conceals the object), and in addition, they maintain that sensations, which are subjective affections, are intra-subjectively incommunicable. Names, which are common, are conventions and cannot be objectively expressed except as *my* sensations, which are incapable of being compared with those of others.[25]

It is this precise premise, which is the basis of the uniqueness of *Cyrenaic hedonism*, which we will now examine more closely.

3. Cyrenaic hedonism

The fact that Aristippus already had a vision of a totally hedonistic life is certain, as Xenophon said:

But myself, I classify with those who wish for a life *of the greatest ease and pleasure that can be had.*[26]

Throughout his life he exemplified the doctrine that only (or chiefly) physical pleasure is valid, the pleasure of the moment, and as such it is to be cultivated and enjoyed.[27] Moreover, here is how the School settled this point:

Corresponding to the statements made by these men [Cyrenaics] regarding criteria [that is, they assert that only our affections are truly knowable] are, as it seems, their statements regarding ends. For the affections reach even as far as the ends. For of the affections some are *pleasant*, some *painful*, some *intermediate*; and *the painful*, they say, *are evils*, whereof the end is pain, and *the pleasant are goods*, whereof the infallible end is pleasure, and *the intermediate are neither goods nor evils*, whereof the end is neither good nor evil, this being an affection intermediate between pleasure and pain. Of all things therefore that exist, the affections are the criteria and ends, and we live, they say, by following these, paying attention to evidence and to approval – to evidence in respect of the other affections, but to approval in respect to pleasure.[28]

The fact that pleasure is the goal of action is shown from the fact that all animals seek it as well as flee pain. And we also behave in this way:

> That pleasure is the goal is proved by the fact that from our youth up we are instinctively attracted to it and when we obtain it seek for nothing more and shun nothing so much as its opposite, pain.[29]

But the Cyrenaics deepened the discussion further by explaining that pleasures are the sensations which imply a "gentle movement" while pains are sensations which imply a "violent movement"; the absence of pleasure and pain is, on the contrary, lacking movement or rest, and it is "similar to the state of one who is asleep."[30]

It is evident that once pleasure is reduced to a "gentle movement" there disappears any possibility of distinguishing one pleasure from another pleasure and of erecting any hierarchy of pleasures. Pleasures considered just as pleasures are completely equal because they are all "gentle movements," and all are goods even if they arise from things which are considered "indecent."[31]

In addition, it is evident that for the Cyrenaics pleasure essentially can only be "the pleasures of the body" and that only in subordination to them are those of the soul or intelligence to be considered pleasures:

> However, they insist that bodily pleasures are far better than mental pleasures, and bodily pains far worse than mental pains, and that this is the reason why offenders are punished with the former.[32]

It is likewise evident, on the bases of these premises that we have clarified, that for the Cyrenaics pleasure must be uniquely *that which takes place in an instant*, in the actual present, in the moment which passes. Elianus writes:

> Aristippus, it would seem, spoke with great vehemence and force, inviting men not to be anxious about things in the past, nor to be preoccupied by that which was yet to come: this is, in fact, a sign of the good disposition of the soul and a demonstration of a serene mind. He exhorted men to think about today and, further, to that part of today in which one acts or thinks something. He said, in fact, that only the present is ours and not that which is already accomplished or which has not as yet come: the former, in fact, is already determined and the latter is uncertain in terms of what it will be.[33]

Athenaeus adds:

> [Aristippus] maintained again that it [= the sensation of pleasure in which happiness consists] is instantaneous, putting it thus on the same level [as the sensation] of the dissolute, maintaining that the

memory of past pleasures was of no value, nor the hope of those in the future; but, making the good consist only in the present, he considered as without any value for him what had been enjoyed and what was to be enjoyed, since the former is no longer and the latter is not yet or is obscure. Similarly, those who are dedicated to dissoluteness live only in the present, believing they behave properly.[34]

But it is clear that the reduction of the good to pleasure and this to "gentle movement" can only result in the following consequence, since the "gentle movement" cannot exist either in the past (which is no longer) or in the future (which is not yet present); it can only be located in the present.[35]

Finally, it is evident that the Cyrenaics must prefer pleasures of the moment to happiness itself, which in their view has lost its concreteness:

They also hold that there is a difference between "goal" and "happiness." Our goal is particular pleasure, whereas happiness is the sum total of all particular pleasures in which are included both past [which are no longer] and future [which do not yet exist] pleasures. Particular pleasure is desirable for its own sake, whereas happiness is desirable not for its own sake, but for the sake of particular pleasures.[36]

In order to place happiness above momentary pleasures, the Cyrenaics would have had to overturn their conception of pleasure and thus give priority to spiritual pleasure.

If we compare the Cyrenaics with some of the Sophists and try to determine which is of Socratic origin, we find that the Cyrenaics transformed only the Socratic principle of self-control into control over the life of the instincts, and self-control over the desire for pleasure into control *within the* pleasure. Pleasure is not depraved, but to be victimized by it is depraved; the satisfaction of a passion is not evil, but to be satisfied by it is, or to allow oneself to be swept away by it; the enjoyment is not to be condemned, but every excess which insinuates itself into it.[37]

There is no doubt that *arete* and wisdom for the Cyrenaics would be reduced to this properly conducted life of pleasure, appropriately apportioning moment by moment the joys of life, and therefore would be considered only as a way to pleasure. Cicero writes:

The Cyrenaics...find all good to consist in pleasure and consider virtue praiseworthy only *because it is productive of pleasure.*[38]

And Diogenes Laertius writes:

They say that practical wisdom is a good, though desirable not in itself but *on account of its consequences.*[39]

After what we have said, there can be no doubt that Cyrenaicism represents a semi-Sophistic School, although the Socratic teachings present in it are no more than skin-deep and not very substantial. Cicero writes:

> Aristippus was only concerned with the body, as though we did not somehow have a soul.[40]

This judgment is rather cutting, but it is correct and we know, rather more than Cicero knew, about what the exaltation of pleasure and the obliteration of the *psyche* mean, namely, a damaging fall into inconsistency. In fact, hedonism and the Socratic principle of self-control and liberty cannot fit together because hedonism does not allow for drawing from pleasure the necessity of clinging to something which is stronger than pleasure itself; but once lost, the meaning of the discussion on the *psyche* and its value to us becomes simply the impossibility itself of finding any further support. As we will see in the third volume on the Hellenistic Age, it was this very aporia which provoked a schism within the Cyrenaic School and the rise within its very interior of a current inspired by a leadened pessimism. This current represented the clear antithesis of the high level of joyousness which was symbolic of the period within which the School began with Aristippus.

4. The breakdown of the "ethos" of the city-state

A further point which deserves to be mentioned, that is, the position of the break which Aristippus had produced in the *ethos* of the *polis*. Socrates was still entirely wrapped up in the ideal of the Greek *polis*, in which there are those who order and those who take orders, and consequently he imposed his educative discussion as if no other possibility existed except that of forming persons to act, to command, or to obey. In the conversation between Socrates and Aristippus reported by Xenophon in which he explains to Socrates that the life of one who controls (and which Aristippus rejects because it is only a source of concerns and contrasted with his ideal hedonism) is by far preferable to that of one who is controlled, Aristippus responds that there is a third possibility, which breaks this schema, being located entirely outside of the two possibilities:

> "No," replied Aristippus, "for my part I am no candidate for slavery; but there is, as I hold, a middle path in which I am desirous of walking. That way leads neither through control nor slavery, but through liberty, which is the royal road to happiness."
>
> "Ah," said Socrates, "if only that path can avoid the world as well as control and slavery there may be something in what you say. But, since you are in this world, if you intend neither to control nor to be controlled and do not choose to truckle to rulers—I think you must see that the stronger have a way of making the weaker rue their fate both in public and in private life and treating them like slaves..."
>
> "Yes, but my plan for avoiding such treatment is this. I do not shut

myself up within a city-state, but am a stranger in every land."[41]

The succeeding assertions in the Cyrenaic cosmo-political meaning are precisely involved in these premises, which are actually more negative than not positive, because the breakdown of the schemas of the *polis* occurs because of egoism and hedonistic utilitarianism, that is, because a participation in public life does not leave room for the individual's full enjoyment of life.

With respect to the position of Socrates, who placed his philosophy at the service of the City-State and died in order to remain faithful to the *ethos* of the *polis*, the position of Aristippus and of the Cyrenaics could not be in more strident contrast.[42]

IV. Euclid and the Megaric School

1. The philosophy of Euclid as a tentative synthesis of Eleaticism and Socraticism

Even the notices which have come down to us about Euclid[1] (who opened a school at Megara, his native city, from which his School took its name) and his followers are scarce.[2] The School is known to have enjoyed great success for a time,[3] but it was of short duration, and its message seems not to have been inscribed in an important way on the development of Greek thought. But we can also say that its message was somewhat ambiguous, or at least badly defined, from the uncertainties of the extant testimonies, which do not say in what sense and in what respect it was to be understood as Socratic, but instead insisted on elements which, as we will see, are of Eleatic extraction. The perplexity and uncertainties of the modern historical reconstructions are understandable; either they have heavily accented the Eleatic element thus risking making the connection with Socrates incomprehensible, or more recently, in order to clarify the relationship with Socrates, they have even denied the connection of the Megaric School with the Eleatic, contrary to the very evidence of the texts.[4] The truth is in the middle position; Euclid, as we will now see, had attempted the first synthesis between Socratic ethics and the Eleatic metaphysics, trying to give to the their axiology, as some have correctly stated, a metaphysical foundation.[5] But let us see in what precise way this synthesis was attempted and proposed.

2. The Eleatic component

First, the link of Euclid with Eleaticism is expressly established by Diogenes Laertius, who writes that he "applied himself to the writings of Parmenides."[6] Cicero, on the basis of more ancient testimonies, presents Megaric philosophy as the direct descendent of the Eleatic, expressly joining Euclid (who Cicero pointed out as a disciple of Socrates) to Xenophanes, Parmenides, and Zeno.[7] Another testimony also states:

> They maintained that we ought to deny validity to sensations and representations, while having confidence only in pure reason. Assertions of this kind were maintained in a more ancient era by Xenophanes, Parmenides, Melissus, and more recently by Stilpo, by the Megarics, and their followers. Consequently they are those who affirm that being is one, while one thing is not identical with another, and deny in an absolute way generation, corruption, and the movement of any thing.[8]

That these testimonies are veracious is shown by the history of the School itself, which argued vigorously against Plato and Aristotle, precisely about those points in which they had overcome the Eleatic views, as we will see in the third volume.[9]

In particular, in what concerns the thought of Euclid, the doctrinal points which confirm that he is inspired by Eleatic tenets are the following.

First, Euclid and his immediate successors reduced the good to the One (*id bonum solum esse dicebant quod esset unum*),[10] [they said that that which is good is solely being and it would be One] and this One is conceived as having Eleatic qualities of being absolute and immobile, *identical with itself and equal to itself (simile et idem semper)*.[11] That this One-Good is again identical with the Eleatic One-Being (Socratically reformed) is confirmed by the fact that it does not admit in any way on par with it, not-being, in the same way the Euclidean One-Good does not admit that its contrary exists:

> [Euclid] eliminated things contrary to the Good, maintaining that they are non-existent.[12]

This postulates likewise the Eleatic negation of generation, corruption, and becoming, in addition to multiplicity, because the existence of anything which is opposed to the One-Good has been neglected, and once the One-Good has been proclaimed to be always identical with itself there is no room left for multiplicity and becoming, which always take place between contraries.[13]

In the second place, it is expressly attested to that Euclid rejected the type of procedure based on analogies:

> He rejected the argument from analogy, declaring that it must be taken either from similars or from dissimilars. If it were drawn from similars, it is with these and not with their analogies that their arguments should deal; if from dissimilars, it is gratuitous to set them side by side.[14]

Analogy was one of the typical moments of the Socratic dialectical procedure (as the proto-Platonic dialogues show abundantly), and Euclid rejected it because it broke up the schema of the Eleatic dialectic, which conceives argument only in terms of absolute identity or absolute alterity.[15] The same source states:

> [Euclid] in demonstrations did not attack the premises, but the conclusions.[16]

Euclid, in other words, preferred to uphold dialectic in the purely Eleatic version, and more precisely the Zenonean, which aimed to demolish the adversary by attacking the conclusions and showing their absurdity.[17]

3. The Socratic component

Also the link of Euclid to Socrates is clear, if we keep in mind the particular reconstruction which we proposed above with respect to Socrates.

First, the Eleatic One-Being is identified with the Good which was the goal of the whole Socratic inquiry.[18] In addition, a series of attributes of exactly Socratic derivation was given by Euclid to the notion of the Good:

> Euclid asserted that the one is the Good and is called by many names: now wisdom, now God, now mind, and so on.[19]

Well then, the wisdom (φρόνησις) of which the above fragment speaks here is precisely that knowledge which Socrates also identified with the Good. God and mind are equally typical names in Socratic theology, as we have seen above. Finally, the Euclidean denial of the contrary of the Good as not-being corresponds to the essential Socratic denial of evil reduced to a pure ignorance of the Good.[20]

Virtue, for Euclid as for Socrates, was also one thing under different names,[21] and must coincide with the knowledge of the One-Good.

Moreover, the clear break which Euclidean Megaricism made between false opinion and truth identified with the One-Good-God, which seems to be so Eleatic in character, actually is in similar measure Socratic, as the following passage of the *Crito* demonstrates:

> Then, most excellent friend, we must not consider at all what the many will say of us, but what he who knows about right and wrong, the one man, *and truth herself will say.*[22]

And here truth is understood properly of God, as the interpreters of the *Crito* agree.

4. The integration of Eleaticism and Socraticism and its importance

If the situation is as we indicated above, then it is clear that Euclid, by mediating Eleaticism and Socraticism, had intended to provide the metaphysical foundation which was lacking in Socraticism.

Levi has nicely expressed in detail the sense of this Euclidean attempt at mediation. He writes: "The metaphysics of Euclid aimed at liberating man from the preoccupation with all particular things by showing that the value that he attributed to them with respect to this life is a pure illusion. Such things do not possess any reality. He who would be really convinced that Being-One, the Good, God are the only existents must be liberated from all thoughts which do not refer to them and must tend with all his energy toward that unique object, in order to have it present constantly in his mind. So science, conceived as ethics and religion together, becomes the highest virtue because it brings to man every perfection of which his soul is capable and thus makes him happy insofar as it liberates him from erroneous opinions about non-existent realities, consequently his spirit is purified from the turmoil which this false belief produces."[23] Actually, this explanation of Levi states explicitly many things which the text suggests but does not say expressly. Its focal point is completely confirmed by Cicero, who informs us that for the Megarics the human good is precisely the knowledge of the Truth, that is, of the One-Good-God.[24]

In sum, we are confronted with a somewhat clumsy attempt to do what on a higher level will be done by Plato, namely, the furnishing of a metaphysical foundation for Socraticism.[25]

The distance between the one and the other of these attempts is in fact that the former looked to the past philosophy of *physis* for a ground for Socraticism with uncertain results because it was a past which was rejected by Socrates for the reasons seen above; the latter discovered the ground, instead, in the overcoming of the philosophy of the *physis*, more precisely in the discovery of metaphysics, by means of the "second voyage," as we will see.[26]

5. The Megaric eristic and Socratic dialectic

The Megarics are well-known for having given a great deal of room in their speculations to eristic and dialectic, to the point that they were called, at certain times, Eristics, and then Dialecticians.[27] We will have to wait for the third volume to see the developments of the School in these directions, and to examine some famous eristic-dialectical arguments which support, at the same time, the Greek admiration for and irritation with their successful combative ways.

It is appropriate to note here that Euclid himself adopted this way, thus meriting the satiric slings of the satirist Timon, who wrote:

> But I care not for these babblers, nor anyone besides, not for Phaedo whoever he be, nor wrangling Euclid, who inspired the Megarians with a frenzied love of controversy.[28]

Actually, the method used by Euclid, that is, the method of the refutation of the conclusions of an adversary and their reduction to absurdity, is precisely a dialectical method which only with difficulty is freed from lapsing into cheap eristics.[29]

We saw that such a method was derived from Eleaticism and chiefly from Zeno; but we also saw that it was used a great deal by Socrates, so also in this Euclid was not unfaithful to his teacher simply by not accepting the procedure by analogy.

Finally, Euclid (and with him his successors) very probably attributed to dialectic a moral aim. This also has been well stated by Levi: "The Megarics assigned to their destructive criticism of the opinions of their adversaries the task of purifying both ethically and religiously their spirit of darkness and error, from passions, from suffering, and raising it to the vision of the true Good, which is both the highest knowledge and highest virtue and necessary source of happiness."[30] We will add that in addition the premises of the system completely agree with the character of Socratic dialectic itself which, as we have seen, had a protreptic and ethical goal more than a logico-epistemological one.[31]

The successors of Euclid and especially Eubulides, Alexinus, Diodorus Cronos, and Stilpo, as we have already hinted, acquired a reputation chiefly for their refining of dialectical arguments (which they used against their adversaries, but which they used likewise in empty exhibitions of eristic skill); but, as we will see, they did not forget the original ethical goal of these arguments. If antiquity did not pay a good deal of attention to this aspect and instead had preserved the record of the other, it was chiefly because in the ethical area the teachings of the new School were of such an innovative character as to make unimportant the message which came from Megara, although it continued to use eristic-dialectic, which for the Greeks was a very strong allurement and an intellectual stimulant.[32]

V. Phaedo and the School at Elis

Among the minor Socratics Phaedo (to whom Plato had dedicated a very beautiful dialogue) was, at least to judge from what little has come down to us about him, the least original. He founded a school in his native Elis.[1]

The testimonies indicate clearly enough that he followed two paths in his thinking.

The satirist Timon groups him with Euclid and seems to consider him, as Euclid, an eristic-dialectician.[2]

Instead, other sources indicate in a more specific manner that Phaedo was concerned chiefly with ethics.[3]

In his *Zopyrus*, he developed the concept that the *logos* (the Socratic *logos*) had no obstacle in the nature of man, in the sense that it is a condition for control of even the most rebellious natures and the most passionate temperaments. Zopyrus was a "physiognomist," that is, one who claims to be able to intuit from the appearance of men their moral character. Based on the appearance of Socrates, he opined that the philosopher must be a dissolute, arousing the rest of those present to ridicule him; but Socrates defended Zopyrus, explaining that he truly had those tendencies before his philosophical *logos* had changed him. Undoubtedly what Cicero writes in the *Tusculan Disputations* is derived from Phaedo although indirectly:

> Moreover, men who are described as naturally irascible or compassionate or envious or anything of the kind have an unhealthy constitution of soul, yet all the same are curable, as is said to have been the case with Socrates. Zopyrus, who claimed to discern every man's nature from his appearance, accused Socrates in company of a number of vices which he enumerated, and when he was ridiculed by the rest who said that they failed to recognize such vices in Socrates, Socrates himself came to his rescue by saying that he was naturally inclined to the vices named, but had cast them out of him by the help of reason (*ratione*).[4]

And again in the *De fato*:

> Again, do we not read how Socrates was stigmatized by the physiognomist Zopyrus, who professed to be able to discover men's entire character and natures from their body, eyes, face, and brow? He said that Socrates was stupid and dull-witted because he did not have hollows in the neck above the collar-bone – he used to say that these portions of his anatomy were blocked and stopped up; he also added that he was addicted to women – at which Alcibiades is said to have given a loud laugh! But it is possible that these defects may be due to natural causes; but their eradication and entire removal, recalling the man himself from the serious vices to which he was inclined, does not rest with natural causes, but will, effort, education (*in voluntate studio disciplina*).[5]

A confirmation that such was the basic thesis maintained by Phaedo is found in a letter of the Emperor Julian:

> Phaedo maintained that anything could be cured by philosophy, and that in virtue of it all could detach themselves from all kinds of lives, from all habits, from all passions, and from all the things of this kind. Now if philosophy had power only over well-born men and the well-educated, there would be nothing extraordinary in this; but that it can bring into the light men who lie in such a condition [an allusion to the condition of abasement into which Phaedo had fallen], it seems to me to be truly prodigious.[6]

Finally, from Seneca we derive a further proof of the centrality of this thematic in Phaedo's thought:

> Nothing is more successful in bringing honorable influences to bear upon the mind, or in straightening out the wavering spirit that is prone to evil, than association with good men. For the frequent seeing, the frequent hearing of them little by little sinks into the heart and acquires the force of precepts. We are indeed uplifted merely by meeting wise men; and one can be helped by a great man even when he is silent. I could not easily tell you how it helps us, though I am certain of the fact that I have received help in that way. Phaedo says: "Certain tiny animals do not leave any pain when they sting us; so subtle is their power, so deceptive for purposes of harm. The bite is disclosed by a swelling, and even in the swelling there is no visible wound. That will also be your experience when dealing with wise men: you will not discover how or when the benefit comes to you, but you will discover that you have received it."[7]

It is evident that Phaedo has deepened a point of Socratic philosophy of which he had directly experienced the efficacy (as we have seen, the *logos* of Socrates had the capacity to liberate him from the abasement into which he had fallen, imprisoned in a brothel with a prostitute);[8] but it was also a point that reflected well enough one of the most typical traits of Socratic intellectualism, that is to say, *the conviction of the omnipotence of the logos and of knowledge within the ambit of the moral life.*

The school at Elis was of brief duration. Phaedo was succeeded by Plistenus, a native of that same city. But already a generation later, Menedemus, coming from the Megaric School of Stilpo,[9] having grasped the tenets of the School of Elis, transplanted it to Eretria together with Asclepiades of Phlius,[10] settling on a direction analogous to that of the Megaric School.

VI. Conclusions about the Minor Socratics

Whatever we said about the Socratic circle should have of itself persuaded the reader that the various qualifications given to them of "minor," "semi-Socratics," "onesided Socratics," are adequate. Some scholars, as for example Robin,[1] have attempted to reject them, but they are incorrect.

These Socratics are called "minor" if the extant results they achieved are considered and if we compare these results with those of Plato, which are undeniably rather more remarkable, as our exposition of Plato will demonstrate in detail.

They may be said to be "semi-Socratics" because the Cynics and the Cyrenaics are half-Sophists and the Megarics are half-Eleatics; in addition, they did not produce a true and proper synthesis between Socrates and their other sources of inspiration but are to be found oscillating back and forth because they did not give their teaching a new foundation.

They are called "one-sided Socratics" because they filter through their prism a single ray, so to speak, of the light springing from Socrates, that is, they raise up to the heights one aspect of the doctrine or of the figure of the teacher to the detriment of the others and hence inevitably deform it.

Instead, Robin is right when he points out that in the minor Socratics "the influence of the Orient which was always counter-balanced up to now in the Greek spirit by the rationalistic tendency, crudely affirmed in the thought of Antisthenes, the son of the Thracian slave, and by Aristippus, the African Greek."[2] He is also correct in asserting that these Socratics "are already among the Hellenistic [philosophers]";[3] the Cynics precede the Stoics, the Cyrenaics the Epicureans, the Megarics, paradoxically, furnish abundant weapons for the Sceptics.

The theoretical discovery which distinguishes the speculative area of interest of these Schools from the later Platonic area of interest is that to which we have many times made reference and which Plato himself in the *Phaedo*, as we know, called the "second voyage." It is the metaphysical discovery of the supersensible; and it is exactly this discovery which, grounding the Socratic intuitions, will raise them up, enlarge their scope, enrich them, and bring them to very unique and fruitful results, about which we will speak in great detail in the second volume.

First Appendix

Orphism and the Novelty of Its Message

«Χαῖρε παθὼν τὸ πάθημα· τὸ δ᾽ οὔπω
πρόσθε ἐπεπόνθεις.»

«θεὸς ἐγένου ἐξ ἀνθρώπου.»

"Cheer up you who suffer passion: this
you do not have to suffer anymore."

"By being a man you are born a God."

Orphic Gold Plates found at Thuri,
4; Frag. 32f Kern; Frag. 4A67 Colli

1. The extant Orphic literature and its value

Modern scholars of Orphism have reached contrary conclusions. One position, which is overly dogmatic, holds that it can reconstruct the phenomenon of Orphism in its various dimensions. They even maintained that by using Orphism as a source they could explain not only most of the spiritual life of the Greeks, but most of its philosophical thought as well (which consequently, has been appropriately called the "pan-Orphic" interpretation). The other, and contrary, position, which is overly critical, has not only systematically put in doubt the foundation of a series of commonly held opinions about Orphism, but it has radically reduced the influence of Orphism as a source almost to the point of denying it by maintaining that certain typically Orphic theses are, on the contrary, to be considered inventions of the philosophers; firstly of Pythagoras and then of Empedocles and finally of Plato. Between these two extreme positions scholars today are trying to find a correct balance, avoiding not only the assertions that are not sufficiently critical but also those that are hypercritical and sceptical in the extreme.[1]

Actually, to reach an equilibrium in this matter is quite difficult given the very problematic state of the extant Orphic literature.

It is especially to be noted that whole works which have come down to us as Orphic are forgeries of a much later period, probably arising from the Neoplatonic period, and hence about a thousand years after the original Orphism. These works are: 1) 87 hymns (preceded by an introduction) which total 1133 verses dedicated to various divinities and distributed according to a precise conceptual arrangement; 2) a poem entitled *Argonauts*, composed of 1376 epic hexameters; 3) a small poem of 774 verses in epic hexameters entitled *Rocks*. In the *Hymns* are contained, in addition to Orphic ideas, conceptions taken from the Stoa and even echoes of Philo of Alexandria; in the *Argonauts* (dedicated to a mythical voyage of these famous heroes) the Orphic positions are rather limited, while in the *Rocks* (which is concerned with the magical properties of stones) there is almost nothing of Orphism. It is evident, therefore, that such works only serve to embrace the positions of latter descendants of Orphism.[2]

In order to reconstruct the positions of primitive Orphism about which we are concerned in this work, we have only testimonies and fragments at our disposal. Otto Kern, in his collection of 1921 which is still canonical, presents 262 indirect testimonies and 363 fragments, for a total amount a little beyond 600 verses.[3] But even the value of this material is very heterogeneous. In fact, among the testimonies, only one is of the sixth century, a few come from the fifth and fourth centuries BCE, while the major portion come from later antiquity. It is very difficult to ascertain the authenticity and antiquity of the fragments, since they have been handed down in the greater number of cases by authors belonging to the period of late antiquity.

The perplexity of scholars has serious foundations, and it is undoubtedly correct to use great critical caution in considering Orphism, although extreme scepticism does not seem to be warranted.

First it is to be noted that the poet Ibycus of Rhegium in the sixth century BCE speaks of "Orpheus, famous by name," attesting thus to the great notoriety of Orpheus at this period which is explainable only by supposing the existence and wide diffusion of the religious movement which goes back to him.[4] Euripides and Plato also attest in their period that a great number of writings surfaced under the name of Orpheus concerning the Orphic rites and purifications.[5] Herodotus and Aristophanes also speak about the Orphic rites and initiations.[6] But perhaps the most interesting testimony of all is Aristotle's, according to whom Onomacritus had put into verse form the doctrines attributed to Orpheus.[7] Now since Onomacritus lived in the sixth century BCE, we have a firm and secure point of reference. In the sixth century BCE there were certainly writings composed in verse under the name of the mythic poet, and hence there existed a spiritual movement which recognized in Orpheus their own patron and source of inspiration.[8]

The situation with respect to the doctrine is more difficult, since on the one hand certain beliefs, which as we will see cannot but be Orphic, are not always expressly specified as such by our sources, and on the other hand the direct fragments when ascertainable are often undatable. However, as we will see by considering some testimonies in parallel, a higher probability can be achieved in attributing certain doctrines to the Orphics. With respect, then, to the numerous Orphic verses belonging to the so-called rhapsodic theogony (*Sacred Discussions in Twenty-Four Rhapsodies*), at first held to be genuine then considered to be forgeries of late antiquity, they have come to be looked at in a new light today. The author of the rhapsodic theogony seems to have used ancient material, systematizing and completing it.[9] But a particularly important event has demonstrated recently how hypercriticism may be detrimental. A fragment of the theogony, a typical expression of the "pantheistic" Orphic position, reported in the *Treatise on the Cosmos for Alexander* attributed to Aristotle, considered to be composed in the Hellenistic Age just as the *Treatise* is supposed to have been, instead, because of a discovery of a papyrus by Derveni in 1962, is now considered to be much older. The papyrus, in fact, comes from the Socratic period, but since the poem was subjected to a commentary it means that at this period it already enjoyed considerable authority and notoriety and that therefore it goes back to a even more ancient period.[10]

These precisions are indispensible in order to clarify the real complexity of the situation as well as forcing us to furnish an abundant documentation, especially in a work of synthesis such as our own.

2. The basic novelty of Orphism

In the Greek literary documents which have come down to us there is in Pindar for the first time a conception of the nature and destiny of man almost entirely unknown to the Greeks of the preceding age and expressing a revolutionary belief in many respects which may correctly be considered as an *element for a new outline of civilization*. In fact they speak of the presence in man of something divine, and not mortal, which comes from the Gods and lodges in the body. It has a nature antithetical to the body, so that it is truly itself when the body sleeps or is about to die, hence when the bonds with the body are loosened it is let free. Here is the famous fragment of Pindar:

> The body of all obeys all-powerful death, but there is yet left alive this image, for it alone is from the Gods. It sleeps when the limbs are active, but to men asleep it reveals in many a dream the pleasant or painful issue of things to come.[11]

Scholars[12] have at present emphasized that this conception has exact parallels, both terminological and conceptual, in Xenophon at the end of the *Cyropaedia*, and in an extant fragment of the exoteric work of Aristotle, *On Philosophy*. Here is the passage of Xenophon:

> I, for my account, Son, am not persuaded of this: that the soul, as long as it is found in a mortal body, lives; when it is thus liberated it dies. I see in fact that the soul makes mortal bodies live for the whole time that it resides within. And I will never be convinced that the soul is insensible when it is separated from the body, which is insensible. Since, when the spirit is separated from the body then it is free from any mixture and pure, it is logically more sensible as it was before. When the body of a man dissolves, the individual parts join the elements of the same nature, but not the soul: it alone, present or absent, flees to the vision. Consider then—he continued—that there is nothing in the world more nearly like death than sleep; and the soul of man is then revealed in its divine nature more clearly and better, then it foresees the future without doubt because then it is more than ever free of the body.[13]

Here is the Aristotelian fragment:

> Aristotle used to say that men's thought of Gods sprang from two sources—the experiences of the soul and the phenomena of the heavens. To the first head belonged the inspiration and prophetic power of the soul in dreams. For when (he says) the soul is isolated in sleep, it assumes its true nature and foresees and foretells the future. So is it with the soul, when at death it is severed from the body. At all events, Aristotle accepts even Homer as having observed this; for Homer represented Patroclus, in the moment of his death, as foretelling the death of Hector, and Hector as foretelling the end of Achilles. It was from such events (he says) that men came to suspect the existence of

something divine, of that which is in its nature akin to the soul and of all things most full of knowledge.[14]

The new schema of belief consists, therefore, in a dualistic conception of man which opposes the immortal soul to the mortal body and considers the former as the authentic man, or better, that which truly counts and is of value in man. This is a conception, as is well known, that inserts into European civilization *a new interpretation of human existence.*[15]

That this conception is of Orphic origin does not seem to be in doubt. In fact, Plato presents a conception strictly connected in an express way to the Orphics in this passage of the *Cratylus*:

> I think that this admits of many explanations if a little, even very little, change is made; for some say it is the tomb [σῆμα] of the soul, their notion being that the soul is buried in the present life, and again, because by its means the soul gives any signs which it gives [σημαί-νει]; it is for this reason also properly called "sign" [σῆμα]. But I think it most likely that the Orphic poets gave this name with the idea that the soul is undergoing punishment for something; they think it has the body as an enclosure [σῴζηται] to keep it safe, like a prison, and this is, as the name denotes, the safe [σῶμα] for the soul until the penalty is paid, and not even a letter needs to be changed.[16]

The concept of the *divinity of the soul* is also central in "the golden plates" found in some ancient tombs, from which have been recovered that which constitutes the focal point of Orphic belief. Here is what is said on one of the golden plates found at Thuri:

> I come from the pure purities, O queen of the underworld,
> Eucles and Eubuleus and you other immortal Gods,
> because I have the advantage of belonging to your happy stock;
> but Moira rules over me, and the other immortal Gods...
> and the thunderbolt crashes down from the stars.
> I want a way out of the circle of troublesome burdening pain,
> and to rise and go up to the longed for crown with flying feet,
> then to surrender myself in the bosom of the Women, queen of the underworld,
> and descend from the longed for crown with flying feet.
> "O Happy and Most Blessed, you will be Gods though mortal."
> Sheep fallen into the milk.[17]

This solemn proclamation that the soul belongs to the lineage of the Gods is to be a consistent theme also in other golden plates and is even expressed with the same formula or with a wholly analogous meaning: "I am the daughter of the earth and of the star-spangled heaven."[18] But we will return again to this issue.

This new schema of belief, as we said, was destined to revolutionize the ancient conception of life and death, as a famous fragment of Euripides states in a paradigmatic way:

> Who knows if the living are not dead and the dead instead live?[19]

Plato, in the *Gorgias*, beginning from this idea shows all the revolutionary consequences of the new message. It postulates a new outline of the whole of existence, and in particular it postulates a mortification of the body and of all that which belongs to the body, and a life in relation to the soul and that which belongs to the soul.[20]

3. Orphism and the belief in metempsychosis

We have already emphasized the fact that the most widely held and diffused belief of scholars is that in Greece the Orphics defended the belief in metempsychosis. Zeller, who was unwilling to admit that the mysteries had an important impact on philosophy, writes, "...in any case it appears secure that among the Greeks the doctrine of the transmigration of souls did not go from philosophers to the priests, but from the priests to the philosophers."[21] However, since some scholars have contested this point it is well to be specific about it, because among the dissenting voices (which were not many) there was the authoritative and important one of Wilamowitz-Moellendorff.[22]

No ancient source expressly states that it was the Orphics who introduced the belief in metempsychosis; some late sources even say that it was Pythagoras.

Nevertheless, what follows is to be noted: *a*) Pindar knew this belief and it cannot be demonstrated that he derived it from the Pythagoreans and not from the Orphics. *b*) The ancient sources, in addition, when they speak of metempsychosis refer to it as a doctrine revealed by "ancient theologians," "prophets," and "priests," or they use expressions which generally allude to the Orphics. *c*) In a passage of the *Cratylus*, Plato expressly mentions the Orphics, attributing to them the doctrine of the body as the place of expiation of the original fault of the soul, which necessarily presupposes metempsychosis; finally even Aristotle writes expressly that the Orphic doctrines imply metempsychosis. *d*) Some ancient sources have made Pythagoras depend on Orpheus and not vice versa. Now let us take up these matters in detail.

a) Here are two fragments of Pindar, whose tone is itself quite significant insofar as they do not seem to refer to Pythagoreanism:

> For from whomsoever Persephone shall accept requital for ancient wrong, the souls of these she restores in the ninth year to the upper sun again; from them arise glorious kings and men of splendid might and surpassing wisdom, and for all remaining time are they called holy heroes amongst mankind.[23]

And if, possessing it, one knows what must befall—
that of those who die here, the arrogant
are punished without delay,
for someone under the earth
weighs transgressions in this realm of Zeus,
and there is iron compulsion in his word.

But with equal nights
and equal days,
possessing the sun forever,
the noble enjoy an easy existence, troubling
neither earth nor the sea's waters
in might of hand
for an empty living,
but with the gods they honored, all
who delight in oath-keeping
abide free of affliction, while the others
go through pain not to be looked at.

And those who have endured
three times in either realm
to keep their souls untainted
Zeus' road to the tower of Kronos,
where ocean-born breezes blow around
the island of the blest....
and sprays of gold flowers
from the earth and from the sea—
with these they wreathe their hands
and crown their heads...[24]

b) Previously the Pythagorean Philolaus—and this is very significant—
had written:

> *The ancient theologians and prophets* also attest that the soul is joined
> to the body in order to expiate some punishment; and it is almost
> buried in a tomb.[25]

Plato, in the *Meno*, while quoting the first passage of Pindar read above,
writes:

> They say that the soul of man is immortal, and at one time comes to
> an end, which is called dying, and at another is born again, but never
> perishes. Consequently one ought to live all one's life in the utmost
> holiness.[26]

In other passages as well he makes use of analogous expressions and in
particular the expression "ancient discourse," which could have no other
meaning than the sacred discourse of the Orphics.

Analogous conclusions can be drawn from the following fragment of the
Aristotelian *Protrepticus*:

By considering these errors and tribulations of human life it would seem sometimes that *these ancients, whether prophets or interpreters of the divine plans in the stories accompanying the sacred ceremonies and initiations, have seen something; these stories have said that we were born in order to expiate a crime of some fault committed in a prior life* and it would seem that what is mentioned by Aristotle is true, that is, *that we are punished much as those who once in earlier times, when they had fallen into the hands of Etruscan robbers, were killed with studied cruelty; their bodies, the living with the dead, were bound exactly as possible one against another: so our minds, bound together with our bodies, are the living joined with the dead.*[27]

c) We have read above the Platonic passage in the *Cratylus* in which the Orphics are expressly mentioned. But no less interesting is the following passage from Aristotle taken from the work *De Anima*, where clearly it is said that the Orphics admit the pre-existence of the soul:

The same error is met in the tenet found in the so-called Orphic poetry: there it is said that the soul enters into beings from the whole when they breathe, being carried in upon the winds. Now this cannot take place in the case of plants, nor indeed in the case of certain classes of animals, for not all animals breathe. This fact has escaped those who hold this doctrine.[28]

d) The fact, then, that the ancient sources affirm that Pythagoras put into poetic form doctrines and attributed them to Orpheus, even if they are not to be taken literally, is testimony, however, which was the most ancient conviction about the relations between the two of them.[29]

Metempsychosis has a fundamentally moral significance which is well emphasized by Plato, in addition to the well-known passages of the *Phaedo*[30], in two other passages of the *Laws* which we will present here:

Concerning all these matters, the preludes mentioned shall be pronounced, and, in addition to them, that story which is believed by many when they hear it from the lips of those who seriously related such things at their mystic rites, - that vengeance for such acts is exacted in Hades, and that those who return again to this earth are bound to pay the natural penalty,—each culprit the same, that is, which he inflicted on his victim,—and that their life on earth must end in their meeting a like fate at the hands of another.[31]

The myth or story (or whatever one should call it) has been clearly stated, as derived from ancient priests, to the effect that justice, the avenger of kindred blood, acting as overseer, employs the law just mentioned, and has ordained that the doer of such a deed must of necessity suffer the same as he has done: if even a man has slain his father, he must endure to suffer the same violent fate at his own children's hands in days to come; or if he has slain his mother, he must of necessity come to birth sharing in the female nature, and when thus born be removed from life by the hands of his offspring in after-days; for of the pollution of common blood there is no other purification, nor does the stain of pollution admit of being washed off before the soul which committed the act pays back murder for murder, like for like, and thus by propitiation lays to rest the wrath of all the kindred.[32]

Among modern scholars the meaning of these passages has been clarified best of all by E. R. Dodds in the following way, "But the post-mortem punishment did not explain why the Gods tolerated so much human sufferings, and in particular the unmerited suffering of the innocent. Reincarnation did. On that view no human soul is innocent: all were paying, in various degrees, for crimes of varying atrocity committed in former lives. And all that squalid mass of suffering, whether in this world or in another, was but a part of the soul's long education—an education that would culminate at last in its release from the cycle of birth and return to its divine origin. Only in this way, and on this cosmic time-scale, could justice in its full archaic sense—the justice of the law that 'the Doer shall suffer'—be completely realized for every soul."[33]

4. The final end of the soul according to Orphism

If the body is the prison of the soul, that is, the place where it expiates the punishment of an ancient fault, and if reincarnation is the continuation of this penalty, it is clear that the soul ought to be liberated from the body and that this is its ultimate end, the "reward" which belongs to it.

Greek literature prior to the sixth century BCE speaks of sufferings and rewards in the beyond, but only in a very restricted sense. They are, in fact, penalties for some exceptionally grave faults and rewards for some exceptionally meritorious acts. In both cases it is the destiny which falls *exclusively on some individuals*, few in number, and moreover on individuals of past epochs. According to Homer, as has been pointed out, neither rewards nor punishments are dispensed to the men of the present.[34]

The revolution of Orphism is hence evident, and it is a mistake to overestimate these antecedents about which we have spoken; in fact according to the new conception a reward or punishment belongs to all men without exception according to how they have lived their lives. Thus what was an exception is now the rule, *what was a privileged situation becomes everyone's destiny.*

Once again, Pindar offers us the first finished expression of this new belief. In the second Olympic *Ode* he speaks expressly of a beyond in which evil-doers will be implacably judged for their misdeeds and consequently condemned, while the good will be rewarded:

For them the sun's power refulgent
while here below is night;
the nearby city is their home, in the courtyard of the red rose,

of the shadowy plants <...> and it is burdened
<with trees> with fruits of gold; and some ride horses and
exercise the body,
others play chess; others with the sound of the lyre, and among
them prospers abundance in full flower: a pleasant odor is
diffused over that earth from what they carry again onto the
fire, offerings of every kind on the altars of the Gods is seen
from afar.[35]

Pindar actually makes the beyond vivid with his bright images, increasing in strength some of the colors of the here and now (as is known, scholars maintain that this is not the personal belief of the poet, rather it is that of the person to whom the poet has directed his poetry). Pindar, especially, does not tell us what is the supreme destiny of the souls of the good. This is, instead, stated with complete clarity in the Orphic gold plates found at Thuri.

In the plates dedicated to Hipponius, they say that the purified soul in the beyond will go on many journeys along the ways which the other initiates and those possessed by Dionysus also follow. In those found at Petelia, they state that the purified soul will rule together with the other Heroes. In one plate found at Thuri it is said that the purified soul, because it originally belonged to the stock of the Gods will be a God rather than a mortal. Finally, in another plate from Thuri, it states that from a man he will become a God. Here is the text of this beautiful plate:

But hardly had the soul abandoned the light of the sun, to the right...picking up, you that know the all together. Rejoice, you that have suffered from passions: this you have not suffered before.

From man you are born a God: a lamb you have fallen into milk. Rejoice, rejoice, take the path to the right toward the sacred grassy slopes and forests of Persephone.[36]

That "God will be reborn from man, because man comes from the divine" is the most upsetting novelty of the new schema of belief, the acceptance of which was destined to change their most ancient meaning of life and death.

5. Orphic theogony, the myth of Dionysus and of the Titans and the cause of the original fault that the soul must expiate

It is not our task in this work to go into the question of the reconstruction of Orphic theogony, because we are only interested indirectly in it in terms of our principal theme. That task would be nevertheless complex and uncertain enough, since the theogony is presented in different variants. Let us remember that late antiquity[37] distinguished three different Orphic theogonies: *a*) that referred to by Eudemus, a follower of Aristotle, *b*) the so-called theogony of Hieronymous and Ellanicus, and *c*) that of the *Sacred*

Discourses in Twenty-Four Rhapsodies (the so-called *Rhapsodic Theogony*) which we have previously mentioned. From a few hints of Plato and Aristotle joined with that which is extant of Eudemus, we can only obtain a few wholly insufficient passages;[38] of the theogony of Hieronymous and Ellanicus we possess a brief summary preserved by Damascius.[39] Concerning the *Rhapsodic Theogony*, we have numerous fragments on which, therefore, the weight of the hypotheses fall about which we spoke at the beginning of our presentation.

The basic idea of the Orphic theogony is for the most part the same as that of the theogony of Hesiod. In it the nature of the principle of everything, how the various Gods are born, how their various reigns began, and the generation of the whole universe are explained mythologically, through poetry and imagery.

With respect to the Hesiodic theogony, however, there seem to be two differences, both of considerable importance.

In the first place, it would seem more conceptual under the mythic covering, as Rodhe has noticed previously, "With unmistakable allusion to the oldest Greek theological system—that which had been committed to writing in the Hesiodic poem—these Orphic Theogonies described the origin and the development of the world from obscure primordial impulses to the clear and distinct variety-in-unity of the organized cosmos, and it described it as the history of a long series of divine powers and figures which issue from each other (each new one overcoming the last) and succeed each other in the task of building and organizing the world until they have absorbed the whole universe into themselves in order to bring it forth anew, animated with one spirit and, with all its infinite variety, a unity. These gods are certainly no longer deities of the familiar Greek type. Not merely the new gods evolved by the creative fancy of Orphism—creatures which had almost entirely lost all symbolical meaning—but even the figures actually borrowed from the Greek world of divinities are turned into little more than mere personified abstractions. Who would recognize the Zeus of Homer in the Orphic Zeus who, after he has devoured the World-God and 'taken to himself the power of Erikapaios,' has become himself the Universe and the Whole? 'Zeus the Beginning, Zeus the Middle, in Zeus all things are completed.' The concept so stretches the personality that it threatens to break it down altogether; the outlines of the individual figures are lost and are merged into an intentional 'confusion of deities.' "[40]

Moreover, what Rodhe said, in our judgment, acquires even more importance today, since the fragment of the theogony, or generally the poem, in which Zeus is said to be the beginning, middle and end, and in which his mythical appearances seem lost in order to become the Whole and the foundation of the Whole, is perhaps due to the fifth century BCE, as we have previously noted. Here is the fragment:

Zeus first-born, Zeus shimmering thunderbolt is last;

Zeus is the head, Zeus is means: from Zeus all is complete;
Zeus is the base of the earth and the starry heaven;
Zeus born masculine, Zeus immortal was a baby;
Zeus is the breath of all things, Zeus is the ardor of the
unquenchable fire.
Zeus is the root of the sea, Zeus is the sun and moon;
Zeus is the king, Zeus shimmering thunderbolt is the ruler of all
things: in fact, after having concealed everything, from the begin-
ning of the sacred heart it arises to the full light of joy, complete
ruin.[41]

In the second place, as Guthrie has chiefly emphasized, the Orphic theogony is different from Hesiod's; it ended with the myth of Dionysus and the
Titans (about which we will immediately speak) and the explanation of the
origins of men, as well as of the good and the evil which is in them.
Consequently, while "the one [that is, Hesiod's Theogony] could never
become a doctrinal basis of the spiritual life, the other [that is, the Orphic
theogony] could have constituted this doctrine, and actually did constitute
it."[42]

Now the basic idea of the final part of the theogony was the following.
Dionysus, son of Zeus, was cut up in pieces and eaten by the Titans, who,
for punishment, were burned up and reduced to ashes by Zeus himself, and
from their ashes human beings were born.[43]

It is evident in what sense and in what measure this myth constitutes
the basis of an ethic. It explains the consistent tendency toward good and
evil present in human beings; the Dionysiac part is the soul (and to it is
linked the tendency to the good), that which is Titanic is the body (and
linked to it is the tendency to evil), from which is derived the new moral
task of liberating the Dionysiac element (the soul) from the Titanic (the
body). Reincarnation and the cycle of rebirths are, hence, the punishment
of this fault and are destined to continue until man liberates himself from
this fault.

Some scholars have doubted the antiquity of this myth, not holding as
sufficient the testimony of Pausanius, who connected it to Onomacritus
(hence to the sixth century BCE), and noted that the connection of the
Dionysiac element with the soul is found only in Neoplatonists. But, to the
contrary, the archaic nature of the myth and some hints of Plato (which
cannot be explained without supposing that he alludes to the myth) have
been shown to guarantee its authenticity.[44]

The mystery of man, his sense of being a mixture of the divine and the
bestial with their opposed tendencies and impulses were thus explained in
a truly radical way. Plato will draw on this intuition for inspiration and
transpose and ground it on a metaphysical level; he will construe that
vision of humanity "in two dimensions," about which we will speak fully[45]
and which has largely conditioned all of Western thought.

6. Initiations and Orphic purifications

In order to conclude, we must still allude to the practices that the Orphics annexed to these beliefs and to which they attributed major importance.

We can distinguish two moments in these practices, one which involves the participation in rites and ceremonies and the other in which an adhesion to a certain type of life belongs in which the fundamental rule was to abstain from eating flesh meat.[46]

The killing and dismemberment of Dionysus on the part of the Titans was probably represented and imitated in the ceremonies of initiation; accompanying the rites, formulas of a magical character were uttered.[47]

The purification from the fault, in sum, was in large measure entrusted to the a-rational element or, as we said, the magical.[48]

Pythagoras and the Pythagoreans, though preserving many elements of this kind, began to point to the means of purification in music and then in science, as we have seen above.[49]

But the great revolution was accomplished by Plato, who in a famous passage of the *Phaedo*, theorized in a splendid way that the true purifying power is in philosophy and he presented his assertion as the ancient Orphic intuition taken to a higher level of truth. Here is the famous passage:

> And I fancy that those men who established the mysteries were not unenlightened, but in reality had a hidden meaning when they said long ago that whoever goes uninitiated and unpurified to the other world will lie in the mire, but he who arrives their initiated and purified will dwell with the Gods. For as they say in the mysteries, "the thyrsus-bearers are many, but the mystics few"; and these Bacchants are, I believe, those who have been true philosophers.[50]

Second Appendix

DETERMINATIONS OF THE FUNDAMENTAL CHARACTERISTICS OF THE GREEK CONCEPT OF PHILOSOPHY

«μάλα γὰρ φιλοσόφου τοῦτο τὸ πάθος, τὸ
θαυμάζειν· οὐ γὰρ ἄλλη ἀρχὴ φιλοσοφίας
ἢ αὕτη.»

"For this feeling of wonder shows that you
are a philosopher, since wonder is the only
beginning of philosophy."

Plato *Theaetetus* 155D

«διὰ γὰρ τὸ θαυμάζειν οἱ ἄνθρωποι καὶ νῦν
καὶ τὸ πρῶτον ἤρξαντο φιλοσοφεῖν.»

"Men had begun to philosophize, now as in
the beginning, because of wonder."

Aristotle *Metaphysics* A 2.982b12

1. The object of ancient philosophy as the "totality" of being

We have already stated, in the *Preface* and the *Introduction*, that one of the essential characteristics of Greek philosophy—and thus, in a certain respect, the characteristic upon which depends in large measure all the others— is in the claim alleged from its beginning (and maintained in the course of well over twelve centuries) that it concerns itself with the totality of things, that is, with *the whole of being.*

We wish here to furnish a complement to what we have said, documentation that will be able to illustrate in an essential manner this principal concept and some corollaries directly connected to it.

The aspiration to measure with the whole as such constitutes what we may call the metaphysical key to ancient speculation. It is on this key that we ought first of all to spend some time.

What exactly is understood when we speak of the "totality of things" or "the totality of reality" as the object of philosophy, and hence of the whole?

The *totality* is not just the consideration of every single thing together, which means that the *whole is not merely the sum of the parts.* In brief, in the problem of the whole the *quantity* of realities which philosophy claims to range over is not in question. Rather, it is the *quality of the approach to this reality,* that is, the angle in function of which it claims to range over reality. When it is said that "the philosopher desires to know all things insofar as it is possible"—Aristotle explains—he does not mean to say that the philosopher aspires to the knowledge of each and every individual thing or that he aims at knowing the *universal* in which all particular things are subsumed, that is, that universal which gives meaning to the particulars, unifying them.[1] The universal about which we are speaking is therefore not the logical universal, a mere abstraction, but a supreme and unconditioned principle (or some principles), always equal to itself, from which all things are derived and to which they are all subject and to which they all tend.

The question of the whole, then, coincides with the question about the grounding principle and hence that which unifies the multiplicity of things. We could also say that the question about the whole coincides with the question concerning the ultimate why of things on condition that the question of the whole belongs to this ultimate why insofar as it explains everything; in this way the ultimate why would constitute the area of interest for the comprehension of all things.

In fact, the Presocratic Naturalists had begun, even the first of them, that is from Thales onward, to follow this concept of philosophy, as is largely confirmed by the fragments and from the extant testimonies and as Aristotle has previously pointed out in clear critical awareness in a famous page of his *Metaphysics*:

Most of the earliest philosophers conceived only of material *principles as underlying all things.* That of which all things consist, from which they first come and into which on their destruction they are ultimately resolved, of which *the essence persists although modified by its affections*—this, they say, is an element and principle of existing things. Hence they believe that nothing is either generated or destroyed, since this kind of primary entity always persists. Similarly, we do not say that Socrates comes into being *absolutely* when he becomes handsome or cultured, nor that he is destroyed when he loses these qualities because the substrate, Socrates himself, persists. In the same way, nothing else is generated or destroyed, *for there is some one entity* (or more than one) *which always persists and from which all other things are generated.*[2]

In this passage Aristotle attributes to the Naturalists the search which concerns itself with the whole. He, however, emphasized the limitations of the solution they proposed, pointing out that the principles at which they aimed were *material*. Likewise, he fixed the limits that could denominate the *physicalistic* nature of these thinkers as consisting in the fact that they did not achieve a vision of super-physical realities. Stated in more precise terms, the limits of the Naturalists for Aristotle (as, moreover, also for Plato), consisted: *a*) in their having believed that only physical being exists and *b*) in there having consequently believed in their ability to explain this physical being with physical principles.[3]

In what sense, then, can it be equally affirmed that owing to these limits the inquiry for the Naturalists constitutes a true and proper inquiry into the whole of reality?

Aristotle himself has posed and correctly solved the question, pointing out that the Naturalists were limited, it is true, to *physis* but they maintained that this *physis* was the whole of reality and the whole of being, and consequently that it was the inquiry into the whole of reality and into the whole of being. Hence the inquiry of the Naturalists was an inquiry into the whole in the measure in which it is presented as embracing the whole of being.[4]

Yet Aristotle, in order to determine in an adequate way the whole, has coined the expression "being qua being" (ὂν ᾗ ὄν). All the special arts and sciences have to do with some beings, but none of them inquires into these beings *simply from the viewpoint of their being.* Hence the particular sciences study, each of them, only a part, a portion, a sector of being, and furthermore, not in the special area of their being. Consequently, the inquiry into the causes and principles of the special sciences has value only for those determined portions of being which they have as their object, while the causes and principles which the philosopher seeks in the area of pure being are those which unify and explain every being without exception. *This is precisely the meaning of the question concerning the whole of reality.*

Here are two passages of the *Metaphysics* which are exemplary in this respect:

There is a science which studies being qua being and the properties inherent in it in virtue of its own nature. This science is not the same as any of the so-called particular sciences, for none of the others contemplates being generally qua being; they divide off some portion of it and study the attribute of this portion, as do for example the mathematical sciences.[5]

It is the principle and causes of the things which are that we are seeking, and clearly of the things which are qua being. There is a cause of health and physical fitness; and mathematics has principles and elements and causes; and in general every intellectual science or science which involves intellect deals with causes and principles, more or less exactly or simply considered. But all these sciences single out some existent thing or class and concern themselves with that, not with being unqualified, nor qua being.[6]

Let us go on to the necessary documentation intended to prove the perduring character of the problem which we have illustrated in the whole range of Greek thought, in its variety, import, and beauty throughout the various formulas used by various thinkers.

Thales, as we know, did not write anything, and therefore about him we have only an indirect tradition. But previously Aristotle qualified him, without compromise, as "the initiator of this kind of philosophy,"[7] that is, of the philosophy which, surpassing myth, looks into the whole with pure reason.

Here is how the problem of the totality is faced in the very first fragments of philosophy that we possess, that is, those of Anaximander and Anaximenes:

[The principle]. . .comprehends in itself *all things* and to *all things* it is a guide. . .and it is divine. . .and it is immortal and imperishable.[8]

As our soul, being air, holds us together, so do breath and air surround *the whole universe*.[9]

The following three fragments of Heraclitus, in which the problem of the whole as the unity of the all already takes on a truly exceptional clarity, are even more interesting:

Things taken together are whole and not whole, something which is being brought together and brought apart, which is in tune and out of tune; *out of all things there comes a unity and out of a unity all things*.[10]

That which is wise is one: to understand *the purpose which steers all things through all things*.[11]

When you have listened, not to me but to the logos, it is wise to agree that *all things are one*.[12]

In Parmenides then, the vision of the totality emerges even in the act of denying any validity to the "opinions of mortals" (who, as we have seen, have partial or make partial sightings of being). In addition, in Parmenides the whole assumes the almost quasi-material connotations of the sphere. The whole of being is a being which "is like the mass of a well-rounded sphere," which is equal to itself (ὁμοῖον). Being is the eternal quietude of the atemporal instant which absorbs not only the *past* and the *future*, but coming-into-being and passing-away, change, and movement as well, and in its absolute identity absorbs every difference and ultimately destroys or annuls the multiple.

On the other hand, the preliminary discourse of the revelatory Goddess is much more eloquent:

> You will inquire into everything:
>
> [1] both the unshaken heart of well-rounded truth
>
> [2] and also the opinions of mortals, in which there is no true reliability;
>
> [3] but nevertheless you shall learn these things also: how one should go through all the things-that-appear, without exception, and test them (trans. Freeman with modifications).[13]

Leaving aside the Pluralists, who again propose unchanged this same kind of thinking, let us go on to Plato, who makes some assertions especially important and stimulating on this theme.

In the *Republic*, for example, he defines the nature of the philosopher as that of men who are lovers of the science which demonstrates to them the being which is always what it is and never changes through being born or dying. It shows being which embraces *all beings whatsoever* and does not wish to renounce any part of it, whether great or small. The philosopher is hence *the seeker of the science of the totality of being*.[14] Plato further states that the soul of the true philosopher

> ...is ever to seek integrity and wholeness in all things human and divine.[15]

Finally, he points out that the philosopher must have a mind

> which possesses the contemplation for all time *of all being*.[16]

The *contemplation of all being* is the most pregnant definition which can be given of the philosophy of the Greeks.

All the successive philosophical currents inspired by Plato and Aristotle naturally repeat these concepts and even in certain respects will amplify them. For Plotinus, for example, and for the Neoplatonists, not only must the philosopher contemplate the whole, but as we will see, he must even identify with it ecstatically and thus make himself one with the all.

> You grow yet you are the same, after having started on your way you remain: and you are present after such renunciation, *the whole*.[17]

But, one may object, how can the Sophists and Socrates, who explicitly rejected the claims of the Physicists in order to restrict the inquiry to human beings, or even the great philosophers of the Hellenistic Age, who rejected Platonic-Aristotelian metaphysics and centered their interests around ethics, be located within the outline which has now been traced? Did they not abandon, perhaps, the whole in favor of one of its parts, however privileged, that is, in favor of the inquiry into human affairs?

We reply that thus understood and posited the problem is stated in a grossly equivocal fashion.

First, it would not be very difficult to show that in the famous Protagorean tag-line "man is the measure of all things, of those that are insofar as they are and of those that are not insofar as they are not,"[18] that the interest in the whole is even thematically expressed in the very title of one of the principal works of Gorgias, which states, *On Nature or on Not-Being.*"[19]

That which changes, one could say, is not therefore the requirement of the whole, but simply the perspective according to which it is confronted.

What we are saying will be much clearer from some reflections on the position of Socrates.

Socrates opposed to the philosophy of the *physis* a "human wisdom,"[20] which means a wisdom which instead of focusing on the cosmos concentrated on man himself. But if the cosmos and *physis* for the Presocratics was the whole of things, how can man, which was the object of the Socratic inquiry, not be included within it as a part, and hence how can "Socratic wisdom" itself become a part in any way different from the preceding inquiry?

In order to solve this difficulty, let us ask in the first place what type of question did Socrates pose about man and what kind of response did he receive?

In that case, all the extant testimonies permit us with confidence to establish that Socrates has simply posed that type of question about man which the Naturalists had posed about the cosmos. They tried to explain *all things* relative to the universe, reducing them to the unity of a principle (or of some principles); Socrates tried, instead, to explain all things relative to man and his life by reducing them to the unity of a principle. He wanted to arrive at the essence of man and in function of this reinterpreted the entire life of man. Therefore the Socratic inquiry has nothing in common with all the other "special" sciences concerning man, for example medical science or sport science. These sciences are only concerned *with a part*, that is *with an aspect of man*, and not about *the whole man* in the sense which has been clarified. After the rise of the numerous human sciences at the end of the previous century and in our own century like sociology, psychology, and others, the examples could be multiplied at will. What these sciences of man avoid in principle is the whole man which was of interest to Socrates and which in the ultimate analysis is specific to philosophy even today.[21] With this consideration there is a corollary, then, which can be reached on which we do not insist, insofar as it serves simply as a reinforcement of the previous point. We also know from the *Memorabilia* of Xenophon—whose truthfulness on this point there is no reason to doubt—that Socrates was also concerned with God and had searched out some rational "proof" to support his existence with a method and openness which even prefigured the metaphysics of Plato and Aristotle, as we have seen.[22]

The problem relative to the philosophers of the Hellenistic Age, then, is resolved precisely by the consideration of the fact that they concentrated their efforts on ethics, *but they located their ethics in a very precise vision of being and the cosmos, even on the thematic level.*[23]

Finally, this problem did not arise for the philosophers of the Imperial Age because they went back to the metaphysical tenets of Plato and Aristotle.

Consequently, the fact ought not surprise us that Marcus Aurelius and Plotinus are, as a result, very distant indeed from the philosophers of the Hellenistic Age and in mutual agreement can write that the philosopher

...must be concerned with the whole.[24]

In conclusion, from beginning to end the Greeks considered philosophy as the attempt to comprehend the totality of things bringing them back to their ultimate foundation, that is, the attempt to grasp it as a whole.

Therefore, the following Platonic assertion can be truly considered as bearing the imprint of this conception:

He who has the capacity to see the whole is a philosopher, who does not is not.[25]

2. Philosophy as a primary need of the human spirit

Since man is submerged by so many other problems, why on earth should he take up the problem of the whole? Is it not possible that this problem is simply a luxury? Or worse—perhaps some modern readers may think—is it not possibly a problem that has been overcome, made irredeemably archaic by the new sciences of man mentioned above, and hence today not even able to be proposed?

Even the response to this question comes to us from Aristotle, who communicates the basic results of the message of his predecessors. Precisely at the beginning of the *Metaphysics* he writes:

All men *by nature* desire to know.[26]

This concept is expressed also in the *Protrepticus* in the following way:

The exercise of wisdom and knowledge for men is desirable for its own sake: it is not possible for human beings to live without these things.[27]

The "desire" for knowledge is impressed, therefore, on the very essence of man himself, revealing itself in such way that if we take it away the nature of man himself is compromised.

It is to be noted that this is not simply a desire for knowledge in general, but it is a desire to achieve *that particular kind of knowledge* which we mentioned above.

The demonstration of this assertion may be made by means of a phenomenological analysis and even by means of the exploitation of the common opinions of all men.

That the desire to know is an essential characteristic of the nature of man is evident from the fact that all men take pleasure in sensations and in a particular way in vision, *because it is that which helps them to know more.* And just as among the various sensations none is loved more than vision, so analogously, among the various forms of knowledge which are beyond sensation, we greatly prize that which makes us know more. In addition to sensation then, there is memory, experience, and then science. But all men prize the arts and sciences more than experience, even if those who have experience sometimes (or often) function more expeditiously in the area of practical activity than those who possess science. This is confirmed by the fact that experience only yields a knowledge of the *fact*, that is, of particulars and their empirical connections, while science allows us reach the *why* of the facts, that is, the causes and principles which determine the facts. And again, among the sciences we prize more those which place us in a condition for knowing not just some things but of coming to know all things, or better, not the cause of only some things, since the cause of all things, that is, "wisdom," grasps things as a whole.[28]

In an analogous way, in the *Protrepticus* Aristotle explains that we love life because of sensation, and further that we love sensation for its use in knowing; but because wisdom helps us to know the truth (the whole) in the highest measure in which it is possible for man, then it is right that we tend *naturally* toward that goal:

> Now living is distinguished from not living by reason of sensation and it is defined through the presence of this power. If this is taken away life is not worth living; it is as though life itself were extinguished by the loss of sensation. Among the senses, the power of sight is distinguished by being the clearest, and it is for this reason that we prefer it to the other senses; but every sense is a power of knowing by means of the body, as hearing senses sound by means of the ears. Therefore, if living is desirable because of sense, and sense is a form of knowledge and we love it because through it the soul has the power to know, and in the preceeding we have said that among two things the most desirable is always that which possesses the same attribute in greater measure, then among the senses sight will be the most desirable and appreciated. But wisdom is more desirable than living itself and all the other powers because it enjoys a greater power with respect to the

truth, so that all men aim chiefly at knowing. For in loving life they love thinking and knowing; they value life for no other reason than for the sake of sensation, and above all for the sake of sight; they evidently love this faculty in the highest degree because it is, in comparison with the other senses, simply a kind of knowledge.[29]

This desire to know in man is expressed in a particular way in the feeling of wonder. Plato previously had written:

It belongs to the philosopher: to be full of wonder; there is no other beginning of philosophy than this *being full of wonder.*[30]

Aristotle repeats and develops this concept:

It is through wonder that men now begin and originally began to philosophize, wondering in the first place at obvious perplexities, and then by gradual progression raising questions about the greater matters too, as the problems about the changes of the moon and of the sun, about the stars, and about the origin of the whole universe.[31]

We propose two considerations in this regard. One looks to the meaning of wonder. Considered in itself it implies an ignorance in relation to the difficulties which it progressively encounters; but at the same time it implies something further, that is, the awareness of a defect or the absence of something, and hence the aspiration to be freed of ignorance itself. Wonder, therefore, is a kind of absence of knowledge and hence it is also the need to satisfy that emptiness created by ignorance itself.

The second consideration concerns the progressive growth in the awareness of wonder, which—Aristotle says—first arises in relation to the most elementary phenomena and then in relation to more complex celestial phenomena and finally turns to problems concerning the "origin of the universe," and therefore to problems concerning the whole.

Indeed this wondering, which arises in man who posits himself in relation to the whole and asks about its origin and its foundation, is the root of philosophy. And if this is so, philosophy is structurally irradicable, *indeed because wonder about being is irradicable just as the need to satisfy it is so.*

Why is there this whole? From what has it come? What is its reason for being? These are the problems which are equivalent to the following: why is there being and not nothingness? And likewise a particular moment of such a general problem is the following: Why is there man? Why do any of us exist?

These are problems, evidently, that man cannot not pose, or generally, they are questions that, in the measure in which they are rejected, diminish those who reject them. Hence these questions cannot be renounced, and further, they are questions which even after the rise of the modern natural sciences and of the contemporary human sciences still remain pertinent in relation to their demands and their value, indeed because no one of these natural sciences nor those concerned with human affairs regards the whole of being, that is, the ultimate causes of reality and man.

For these reasons, hence, we can repeat with Aristotle that not only in the beginning but also now the time-honored question about the whole makes sense, and it will continue to make sense while men still manifest "wonder" in relation to the being of things and to their own being.

3. The aim of philosophy as the contemplation of being

Once the origin of philosophy is explained, the goal, that is, the aim of philosophy according to the Greeks, is easily explained as well. If the origin of "philo"—"sophia" is a desire to know, the goal must indeed be the satisfaction, or at the very least the tendency to gratify this need, as we have previously said, and hence *it is the pursuit of knowledge for its own sake and not for any further goal.* In short, the goal is knowledge for the sake of knowledge, or as the Greek would say, *theorein* (θεωρεῖν), knowledge as the pure contemplation of the truth.

Also, in order to grasp this point fully, the comparison with the particular or special sciences is illuminating. The special arts and sciences are directed by norms to the realization of their empirical goals and to the realization of their pragmatic ends. They have undoubtedly *also* a cognitive value, however, this is not primary for them insofar as it does not constitute their goal, as we have said, which consists in the production of a particular benefit in the practical order (for medicine it is health, for architecture the building, and so on). Since therefore the achievement of the practical goal is essential for the particular sciences, they do not value the science only for itself but rather (or at least chiefly) in the measure in which it is a condition for achieving the goal itself. On the contrary, philosophy values its own theorizing (rational nature), precisely *for its cognitive nature and value.*

The ancient tradition recognized this especially in the rational attitude of the first Greek philosophers, that is, in Thales. But Aristotle recognized as well a certain rational-theoretic nature also in the creators themselves of theogonic and cosmogonic myths, in which the myths answer (on a purely imagistic and poetic level) to that very need from which philosophy itself arises.[32]

Here is a passage of Plato in which Thales is proposed as a symbol of the "rational-theoretic life":

> And all these things [which concern the nitty-gritty of daily living] the philosopher does not even know that he does not know; for he does not keep aloof from them for the sake of gaining reputation, but really it is only his body that has its place and home in the city; his mind, considering all these things petty and of no account, disdains them and is taken in all directions, as Pindar says, "both below the earth," and measuring the surface of the earth, and, "above the sky," studying the stars, and investigating the universal nature of every thing that is,

each in its entirety, never lowering itself to anything close to hand.

What do you mean by this, Socrates.

Why, take the case of Thales, Theodorus. While he was studying the stars and looking upwards, he fell into a pit, and a neat, witty Thracian servant girl jeered at him, they say, because he was so eager to know the things in the sky that he could not see what was there before at his very feet. The same jest applies to all who pass their lives in philosophy. For really such a man pays no attention to his next door neighbor; he is not only ignorant of what he is doing, but he hardly knows whether he is a human being or some other kind of creature; but what a human being is and what is proper for such a nature to do or bear different from any other, this he inquires and exerts himself to find out. Do you understand, Theodorus, or not?[33]

The ancient tradition refers to an analogous attitude of Pythagoras and Anaxagoras, as we read in a fragment from the *Protrepticus* of Aristotle:

What is it, then, for the sake of which nature and God have brought us into being. Pythagoras, when asked what this goal is, said, "to observe the heavens," and used to say he was an observer of nature and it was for this that he had come into being. They say that Anaxagoras, when asked what the aim would be in view of which one could desire to come into being and to live, replied: "to observe heaven, and the stars and that which is about it, the moon and sun," everything else being worth nothing.[34]

It is scarcely necessary to point out that "heaven" and "world," in this context, mean the whole in the sense that we have already discussed; in the sense, that is, lacking a knowledge of the transcendent, for these philosophers the area of interest of the cosmos coincides with the area of interest of the whole.[35]

The Platonic conception, then, is expressed in a paradigmatic manner in the passage of the *Theaetetus* we read above, but which was used in writing again a rather short but effective passage of the *Republic*:

And the true philosopher. . .who are they for you? Those who love to contemplate the truth.[36]

And with *the contemplation of the truth* Plato means the *contemplation of the Absolute*.

In Aristotle the disinterested contemplation as the key activity of the philosopher is expressed, in addition to an exemplary page of the *Metaphysics*, previously read (as well as in the famous section of the *Nicomachean Ethics* which we will read further on),[37] in a fragment of the *Protrepticus* worth reading in its entirety:

To seek from all knowledge a result other than itself, and to demand that knowledge must be useful, is the act of one completely ignorant of the distance that from the start separates things good from things necessary; they stand at opposite extremes. For of the things without which life is impossible those that are loved for the sake of something else must be called necessities and contributing causes, but those that are loved for themselves even if nothing follows must be called goods in the strict sense. This is not desirable for the sake of that, and that for the sake of something else, and so *ad infinitum*; there is a stop somewhere. It is completely ridiculous, therefore, to demand from everything some benefit other than the thing itself, and to ask "What then is the gain to us?" and "What is the use?" For in truth, as we maintain, he who asks this is in no way like one who knows the noble and good, or who distinguishes causes from accompanying conditions. One would see the supreme truth of what we are saying if someone carried us in thought to the islands of the blest. There would be need of nothing, no profit from anything; there remain only thought and contemplation, which even now we describe as the free life. If this be true, would not any of us be rightly ashamed if, when the chance was given us to live in the islands of the blest, he were by his own fault unable to do so? Not to be despised, therefore, is the reward that knowledge brings to men, nor slight the good that comes from it. For as, according to the wise among the poets, we receive the gifts of justice in Hades, so (it seems) we gain those of wisdom in the islands of the blest. It is nowise strange, then, if wisdom does not show itself useful or advantageous; we call it not advantageous but good, it should be chosen not for the sake of anything else, but for itself. For as we travel to Olympia for the sake of the spectacle itself, even if nothing were to follow from it (for the spectacle itself is worth more than much wealth), and as we view the Dionysia not in order to gain anything from the actors (indeed we spend money on them), and as there are many other spectacles we should prefer to much wealth, so too the contemplation of the universe is to be honored above all the things that are thought useful. For surely it cannot be right that we should take great pains to go to see men imitating women and slaves, or fighting and running, just for the sake of the spectacle, and not think it right to view without payment the nature and reality of things.[38]

This, some reader will object, is of value for the Greek classical philosopher, but the philosophers of the Hellenistic Age and those of the Imperial Age, do they not reject perhaps the nature of pure contemplation or, at the very least, do they not perhaps reorient it radically?

We have answered this objection above briefly. However, given its great importance, we must repropose and resolve it by filling out the discussion with the acquisitions of further elements.

4. The practical-moral ramifications of philosophy: Greek "theorein" is not abstract thinking, but a thinking that is profoundly immersed in the ethico-political life

Only recently has it been discovered (but this point is still far from being admitted at the level of common opinion) that Greek "contemplation" *structurally implies a precise practical attitude with respect to living life*. This means that the Greek notion of *theoria* is not only a doctrine of an intellectual and abstract character, but is likewise always a doctrine for living life, or to say it in another way it is a doctrine which necessarily postulates an existential activity and, as a rule, is matched to it.

Cornelia de Vogel has recently and appropriately pointed it out in what follows: "To say that 'philosophy' for the Greeks meant 'rational reflection on the whole of things' is correct enough as far as it goes. But if we are to complete the definition, we must add that 'by virtue of the loftiness of its object *this reflection implied a very definite moral attitude and way of life which were held to be essential both by the philosophers themselves and by their contemporaries*.' This simply means that philosophy was never merely an intellectual affair. It is just as great an error to hold that in the classical period the manner of life had no bearing on philosophy as to maintain that in the later Hellenistic-Roman period *theoria* yielded to *praxis*. This much can be admitted: there is a certain shift of emphasis in the later period from the theoretical to the practical aspects of philosophy, not by everyone, but at least in some cases." The conclusions of de Vogel are the following: "In older Greek philosophy we find a *theoria* which necessarily implies a certain moral attitude and style of life; in later Greek philosophy we find, not always, but more often than not, a moral attitude and style of life which necessarily supposes *theoria*."[39]

We can, in conclusion, say that the constant in Greek philosophy is *theorein*, now emphasized in its speculative value, now in its moral value, *but always in a way that the two values reciprocally are involved in a structural way*. Moreover, a proof of this is in fact previously expressed by C. de Vogel, that the Greeks always maintained that true philosophers are only those who know how to exemplify a coherence of thought and living, and hence are those who are teachers not only of thinking but of living.

We maintain, however, that we can proceed beyond the conclusions affirmed by de Vogel.

First, that the meeting with the absolute and the whole places a gap between things that men have commonly prized—for example, wealth, honors, power, and similars—and hence requires a kind of life, let us call it ascetic, is not difficult to grasp, given that *contemplating the whole necessarily changes all the usual perspectives and in this global vision the meaning of life for man changes and imposes a new hierarchy of values*.

But the point that we have discussed is further clarified again by comparing "contemplation" and "politics," concepts which for us moderns are antithetical, and which, instead, the Greek philosophers coupled as essentially joined to one another, showing in this way the peculiar nature of their notion of *theorein*.

The ancient sources bear witness to political activity by many Presocratics. They do not involve themselves in militancy, but rather in the higher activities of making laws and giving counsel to the City-State. And again the same sources confirm expressly that the laws and counsels given by these philosophers were good laws and good counsels.[40] Up to this point, therefore, it is a question of the indirect tradition, which does not permit us to grasp the precise nexus existing between *theoria* and politics.

The Sophists as well, as we know, through their philosophy wanted to be involved in political activity. However even in their case the nature of the connection between the two activities does not appear from the extant testimonies.[41]

But in Socrates this connection emerges with total clarity. Socrates, as we have seen, rejected politics in the sense of daily militant activity, but understood completely and declared that his philosophical activity constituted a kind of higher political activity insofar as *it was formative of moral consciences in the measure in which it uncovered true values.* Having achieved a clear vision of the whole of man as *psyche* and having seen in the *psyche* what in man is like the divine involves not only a new statement of the individual's existence, which he in a paradigmatic way exemplified, but also involved others, all the others, including the entire City-State.[42] Plato saw in a very lucid manner the enormous practical energy of the Socratic "wisdom," which is why he has his Socrates say:

> I think I am one of few, not to say the only one, in Athens who attempts the true art of politics, and the only man of the present time who manages affairs of state.[43]

From his account in the *Republic* Plato carries these premises to their extreme consequences by pointing out those philosophers who have become kings (and those kings who have become philosophers) as the salvation of governments and States, as well as individual men:

> ...neither city nor polity nor man either will ever be perfected until...this uncorrupted remnant of philosophers, who now bear the stigma of uselessness, takes charge of the state whether they wish it or not, and constrains the citizens to obey them or else until by some divine inspiration a genuine passion for philosophy takes possession either of the sons of men now in power and sovereignty or of themselves.[44]

On what basis does Plato affirm this notion?

For our philosopher, we will see, the Good is the foundation of everything; not only of being and knowledge, but also of private and public activities.

> But at any rate, my dream as it appears to me is that in the region of the known the last thing to be seen and hardly seen is the idea of the good, and that when seen it must needs point us to the conclusion that this is indeed the cause for all things of all that is right and beautiful,

giving birth in the visible world to light, and the author of light and itself in the intelligible world being the authentic source of truth and reason, and *that anyone who is to act wisely in private or public must have caught sight of this.*[45]

But Plato has more to say. He reveals, in fact, the reason for which contemplation has practical and political value. Anyone whose thought turns to beings—he says—to those beings which are always self-identical and perfectly unified, will not allow himself to go astray owing to the useless concerns of men which fill up souls with envy and evils, but rather he will tend to "imitate" those beings and "to make himself as much like them as possible." And having done this, that is, lingering over what is "divine and unified" the philosopher himself becomes "as far as possible unified and divine." Consequently, the philosopher not only transforms his private life in this way but in case he must be concerned with the public welfare he thereby makes the State itself become, as far as possible, unified and divine, that is, structured according to virtue.[46]

In conclusion, the knowledge of the whole and the absolute, which for our philosopher is the Divine and the Transcendent, *involves also the imitation of the divine and the assimilation to the divine of each individual who contemplates it. This knowledge, then, also comprises the right to involve others in such an imitation, precisely in the political arena.*

Two particular points merit being emphasized again.

Plato has stressed a further point that knowledge of the whole leads to the "release from chains," an "ascent," and even "a turning around of the whole person," that is, a change of life, a conversion.[47]

Besides that he has also energetically pointed out—and this has only recently come to light—the necessity that those who have seen the absolute, return into the "cave," and "liberate," that is "convert" the others, even if this may cost their life, as it did with Socrates.[48]

No less explicit is the thematization of the practico-salvific power of "contemplation" in the *Phaedrus*. The souls—it is said in the famous myth of this dialogue—when they are beyond this world with the Gods, rotating around the heavens, reach the plain of truth, where they contemplate pure being (the world of the Ideas). And insofar as they succeed in contemplating, so much will they be reincarnated and returned to earth, and they will be rich in spiritual and moral energy. The best men will be those whose souls "have seen" more, the worst men will be those whose souls "have seen" less.[49] This means that the moral life depends in a structural way on contemplation: *the "doing" is so much more rich insofar as the "contemplation" has been so.*

Not a few of these concepts are to be found in the *Protrepticus* of Aristotle, from which we present a section concerned with the discussion of the relations between philosophy and the practical life:

This knowledge is theoretical indeed, but it enables us to frame all our practice in accordance with it. For as sight makes and shapes nothing (since its only work is to judge and to show us everything that can be seen), and yet it enables us to act as it directs, and gives us the greatest assistance towards action (for we should be almost entirely motionless if deprived of it), so it is clear that, though knowledge is theoretical, yet we do a host of things in accordance with it, choose some actions and avoid others, and in general gain as a result of it all the goods we possess.[50]

And again in the *Eudemian Ethics* Aristotle declares expressly that the "contemplation of God" is the "cornerstone" of the practical life.[51]

Having said this it is not necessary to linger for long on the philosophers of the Hellenistic Age. They did nothing other than to bring to completion as far as possible the moral energy, the ethico-salvific power of philosophizing, already perfectly specified, as is clear from the evidences that we have presented, by Plato and Aristotle. And because, as we will see in the third volume, the destruction of the polis brought Greek man to focus himself on himself and to discover the individual area and to close himself in it, it is not difficult to understand as the philosophic thematic which must be taken—consequently—this new perspective, proclaimed by philosophy as the "art of living."

We will see that in the creation of the great ethical systems of the Hellenistic Age many philosophers used intuition and emotionally circumscribed situations in the marking out of new areas of philosophical interest. But we will see concomitantly that all the new discoveries have always been disclosed through the consideration of the whole of man. Moreover, within what concerns the various philosophers, we can *locate this vision of the whole of man in a more general vision of the cosmo-ontological whole and with what urgency they pointed out in the knowledge of physis and being the true foundation of the "art of living."*[52]

We will use only one piece of evidence to document this point, taken from Pyrrho, the founder of Scepticism, who is the person whom we would least expect to adopt a position of this kind and who, instead, is no less explicit than the other philosophers. Timon asks in his *Images:*

O Pyrrho, this my heart desires to know, how is it that you, being simply a man, so easily lead a tranquil life, that you alone are a guide for humankind.[53]

Pyrrho replies:

I tell you in truth as it appears to me that it is, taking as a correct canon this word of truth: *a nature of the divine which lives eternally, from which the most equal life proceeds to man.*[54]

5. Philosophy and "eudaimonia"

Eudaimonia, the Greek word which we translate with the word happiness, means literally to have a good Daimon protector on whom to depend, consequently a prosperous life.

But this Daimon has been interiorized in philosophical reflection and placed in strict relation with the depths in man. Previously, Heraclitus affirmed:

> Character for man is the Daimon.[55]

And again, Heraclitus affirms that the eu-daimonia is not found in corporeal things:

> If happiness lay in bodily pleasures, we would call oxen happy when they find some thing to eat.[56]

This means, at least implicitly, that happiness lies in the area of the *psyche.* And Democritus explicitly stated this concept already, as we know, in a memorable way:

> Happiness does not dwell in flocks of cattle or in gold. The soul is the dwelling-place of our destiny.[57]

This concept was precisely incorporated into Socrates's activities and then ruled uncontested for the entire course of ancient philosophy. It is, of course, *theorein,* as a cognitive and moral activity, which matures the soul and makes it achieve virtue, that is, goodness. It is evident that if the Daimon is our soul (or is in our soul), the goodness or virtue of the soul structurally coincides precisely with eu-daimonia.

Therefore, happiness lies in the education and formation of the soul and spirit of man. Philosophy, therefore, more than any other knowledge, forms the soul.

In a passage of the *Gorgias,* the Platonic-Socrates expressly says that happiness consists in interior formation and virtue:

> Then doubtless you will say, Socrates, that you do not know that even the Great King is happy.
>
> Yes, and I shall be speaking the truth; for I do not know how he stands in point of education and justice.
>
> Why, does happiness entirely consist in that?
>
> Yes, by my account, Polus; for a good and honorable man or woman, I say, is happy, and an unjust and wicked one is wretched.[58]

This is a thesis which is the foundation of the whole complex construction of the *Republic* and in general of the whole Platonic ethics.

Further developments of this theme are achieved by Aristotle, who shows that living is linked to pleasure, and following that, to the highest form of life which is the thinking activity of the soul, which is the highest way and is found in philosophizing and is joined to the highest pleasure and hence to happiness.

In the *Nicomachean Ethics*, then, we will see[59] demonstrated the thesis that the culmination of happiness is in contemplation. The God himself of Aristotle is a self-contemplator.[60]

In the Hellenistic Age the nexus between philosophy and happiness is further emphasized. Moreover, a philosophy which proposes to be an art of living, a way leading to ataraxy, to peace of soul cannot not but identify happiness as its *telos*. A text of Epicurus will stand in as an example for all the above:

> Let no one be slow to seek wisdom when he is young, nor weary in the search thereof when he is grown old. For no age is too early or too late for the health of the soul. And to say that the season for studying philosophy has not yet come, or that it is past and gone, is like saying that the season for happiness is not yet or that it is now no more.[61]

6. The radical faith of Greek philosophy in the possibility of achieving the truth and of living in accordance with it

Approaching on the surface the history of Greek thought, it is possible to find in it two opposed tendencies in the determination of the relation between man and truth; one which is pessimistic and the second optimistic.

Xenophanes would seem to illustrate the sceptical or pessimistic tendency:

> And as for certain truth, no man has seen it, nor will there ever be a man who knows about the Gods and about all the things I mention. For if he succeeds to the full in saying what is completely true, he himself is nevertheless unaware of it; and opinion is fixed by fate upon all things.[62]

Heraclitus also writes:

> Truth loves to hide itself.[63]

Democritus writes:

> Truth is in the Abyss.[64]

Socrates's famous declaration *that he knew that he did not know*[65] is a further example.

The Sceptics even erected a system around the unreachability of truth.[66]

But in reality—and we have seen this in the course of this volume—Xenophanes, Heraclitus, Democritus, and Socrates, notwithstanding these assertions, maintain that truth is attainable. The Sceptics, as we will see, are nothing if not the exception, in addition a very partial one, that confirms the general rule.

On the contrary, Parmenides declared the identity between being and thought:

> For thinking and being are identical.[67]

This affirmation expresses in a most pregnant way the faith that human thinkers achieve truth (being is truth).

Plato developed these concepts establishing the following equation. Whatever is fully being is fully conceptualizable, what is mixed with being and not-being is only partially conceptualizable, that is, opinable; of not being there is only nescience.[68] In conclusion, being structurally involves its own conceivability. And because, for the Greeks, Being is truth, truth involves structurally its conceivability.

Aristotle also pointed out this fact, with different formulations. There is a proportion between being and conceivability *quoad se* [in itself], even if not *quoad nos* [for us]. In itself, the thing which has more being is more cognizable; for us, it is the reverse, the more cognizable to us a thing is, the more it lacks being. However it is possible for man (and this is, indeed, the task for philosophy) to make that which is more cognizable in itself *to become more cognizable to us*.[69]

Unshakable faith in the possibility of achieving truth is found also in the Epicureans and the Stoics; the one points it out in sensation (and we will see in its place what the reason is), the others in the cataleptic presentation, the bearer of incontrovertible evidence.[70]

The Neoplatonists, as we will see, feed not only on the conviction that the human spirit can achieve truth but even that it can be ecstatically unified with the absolute.[71]

Moreover, even the philosophers of the Hellenistic Age, as certain as they are of attaining the truth, are equally certain of the power to live in the truth a life of happiness which can vie with the life of Zeus.[72]

On the other hand, it is also to be pointed out that even in the maieutic of Socrates there is implicit the conception that the truth is in some way a structural condition of the human soul.[73] The conviction, as we will see, grasps and carries to extreme consequences the Platonic doctrine of anamnesis according to which the soul is such precisely because it has an original vision of the truth which, upon being born, it forgets but does not entirely lose and which can be revived.[74] The Middle Platonists and the Neoplatonists will seize upon and further develop this doctrine.[75]

But Aristotle himself, who rejects the doctrine of anamnesis, not only maintained the idea of the human spirit as a positive capacity to attain the truth, but developed a series of reflections upon the truth itself which are, in many respects, truly amazing. He writes, for example, in the *Rhetoric*:

> Men are sufficiently endowed for the truth and they achieve the truth for the most part.[76]

In the *Metaphysics*, he says that the inquiry into the truth is on the one hand difficult and on the other easy. It is difficult because it is impossible to grasp all truths; it is easy because it is not possible to miss all of them. But the most important affirmation in this regard is the following:

> However since the difficulty also can be accounted for in two ways, its cause may exist not in the objects of our study but *in us: just as it is with bats' eyes in respect of daylight, so it is with our minds in respect of those things which are by nature most obvious.*[77]

Truth is therefore always before us and we are hence surrounded and bound to it. Our minds must be habituated to seeing it; they, as our eyes, must be habituated to seeing the light which surrounds and inundates us.

This is a thought which Plotinus develops further, in a metaphysical and theological way, with truly extraordinary audacity.

7. The method of ancient philosophy

We have said that the method of ancient philosophy is based on the Logos and on reason. In order to determine this statement in detail, we must recall and anticipate many elements which could only be grasped in a section that looks into the details.

We say only that by *reason* we do not understand *the scientific reason* of today confined within the ambit of experience and mathematics. In fact, on the basis of the convictions stated above, Greek philosophical reason has wider play and is more mobile in approaching and analyzing the whole.

Experience, phenomenological analysis, the consent of all men, the convictions of the knowledgeable, inductive and deductive reasoning are all in a variety of ways intertwined in philosophical reason.

Some philosophers elaborate their teaching, it is true, by using logic. The most famous example is certainly that of Aristotle, which is based on the syllogism.[78] But these logical procedures end by becoming instruments of control *a-posteriori* rather than true guides through which the systems are constructed and which as a rule decisively arise from the logical relations expressly elaborated, as we will see.

Many philosophers had made explicit appeals to intuition as to that which constitutes, in some way, the principle of philosophy, since the primary principles cannot be further deduced and mediated and hence cannot be grasped except immediately, that is, intuitively.[79]

This recourse to intuition does not have anything of the aspect of the irrational which belongs to certain types of modern intuitionism precisely because of the presupposed conviction involving the equation of thought and being which is the base of Greek thought. Intuition means, in this context, a vision of how things stand in a certain way, that is it means *evidence*, and evidence is a rational criterion.

But ancient philosophy has detailed at least one type of procedure which is in some way privileged. It is the *elenchos*, chiefly used by the Eleatics, by Socrates, and by Plato and which is explained in detail by Aristotle in the *Metaphysics* Book Gamma with respect to his treatment of the principle of contradiction [Aristotle speaks of the principle of demonstration as "being contradicts non-being," *Met.* Γ 3.1005b25ff., in later terminology, the "principle of contradiction"].

Moreover, says Aristotle, the principle of contradiction, insofar as it is a primary principle, cannot be demonstrated. It is immediately evident, but it can in a certain sense be demonstrated through refutation (*elenchos*), precisely of anyone who denies it. The famous *elenchos* is hence in *showing the contradictory statements into which anyone falls who denies the principle in the act of denying it*. Actually, anyone who denies the principle of contradiction contradicts himself, because in the very statement in which he asserts the denial he surreptitiously makes use of the principle. And the same is true for all primary truths.[80]

From the point of view of method this discovery is probably the most important one for ancient philosophy. The highest truths which cannot be renounced are those which in the very moment itself in which they are denied constrain us to make surreptitious use of them, and hence we affirm them again by denying them.

This is an authentic "snare" in which primary truths, the truths from which a human being cannot flee, place us.

ABBREVIATIONS

EGP	Burnet, J. *Early Greek Philosophy* (London: A.&C. Black, 1930⁴).
D-K	Diels, H. and Kranz, W. *Die Fragmente der Vorsokratiker* (Berlin: Weidemann, 1952⁶).
DL	Diogenes Laertius, *Lives of Eminent Philosophers,* trans. R. D. Hicks (London-Cambridge, 1958)
DPG	Zeller, E. *Die Philosophie der Griechen in ihrer geschichtlichen Entwicklung,* 3 vols. (1844-52); ed. W. Nestle (Leipzig, 1920⁶; Hildesheim: G. Olms, 1963). Referred to as Zeller-Nestle.
La metaphysica	Reale, G. *Aristotele, La metafisica. Traduzione introduzione e commento* 2 vols. (Naples: Loffredo Editore, 1968; reprinted 1978)
LCL	The Loeb Classical Library (Cambridge-London: Heinemann-Harvard University Press) various dates and translators.
LFG	Zeller, E. – Mondolfo, R. *La filosofia dei Greci nel suo sviluppo storico I.1.* (Florence, 1943²). Also *Zeller-Reale* a revision of the above by G. Reale (Florence: La Nuova Italia Editrice, 1967) vol. 3 *Eleati.* Also Zeller-Capizzi.
Melisso	Reale, G. *Melisso, testimonianze e frammenti* (Florence, 1970)
Paideia	Jaeger, W. *Paideia. Die Formung des griechischen Menschen (Berlin and Leipzig, 1936²);* English translation 3 vols. Oxford, 1954 by Gilbert Highet; the references are by volume and page number.
PG	Gomperz, T. *Griechische Denker* (Leipzig, 1896). English version *Greek Thinkers. A History of Ancient Philosophy* trans. L. Magnus and G. G. Berry, 4 vols. (London: J. Murray, 1906-1912).
Pitagorici	Cardini, Timpanaro M. *Pitagorici. Testimonianze e frammenti* 1. (Florence, 1958); 2. (Florence, 1962); 3. (Florence, 1964); references given by volume and page.
Reale	Reale, G. *Storia della filosofia antica* 5 vols. (Milan: Vita e Pensiero) various dates and editions, the third volume of which has been translated in 1985. For the volumes which have not been published, a somewhat lengthy reference is given so that when the series is complete the reader will be able to locate the reference.
SR	Giannantoni, G. *Socraticorum reliquiae* (Rome-Naples, 1983).

Theology   Jaeger, W. *Die Theologie der frühen griechischen Denker* (Stuttgart, 1953) trans. E.S. Robinson *The Theology of the Early Greek Philosophers (Oxford at the Clarendon Press, 1947)* often reprinted.

NOTES

(pages 6-10) (1-10)

1. The drastic position taken by E. Zeller in his monumental work, *Die Philosophie der Griechen in ihrer geschichtlichen Entwicklung.* I. 1. (Leipzig, 1919⁶) 21ff. is very illustrative. For the later literature consult the note in Mondolfo's revision (Italian edition, E. Zeller and R. Mondolfo *La filosofia dei Greci nel suo sviluppo storico* I. 1. (Florence, 1943²) 35-63 and 63-99). The presentation of J. Burnet, *Early Greek Philosophy* (London: A.& C. Black, 1930⁴) section 10 is excellent. Later reprints are of this edition. The first edition was published in 1892. However section ten had the advantage of the preceding outline of Zeller. See now also W.K.C. Guthrie *A History of Greek Philosophy* vol. 1, Cambridge 1962, 30-38. In the course of our entire work, the results which Zeller reached will be constantly before us, because they are the unavoidable starting point of any analysis or of any synthesis regarding ancient thought. In these first chapters we frequently agree with them, in the remaining chapters, instead we dissent from them rather frequently. Or rather, one of the essential goals of the present work is to make a contribution to the breakdown of certain schemas of Zeller because new research has shown that they are no longer acceptable and because they have been taken up by the *manualists* as comfortable *clichés*, and they have frequently become such in time, and thus they have made rigid the lines of inquiry.
2. Cf. Suda under the name Numenius; Clem. Alex. *Stromata* 1.22 (93, 11 Stählin); Eusebius *Praep. Evang.* 11.10.14 (28.10ff. Mras).
3. Cf. Plato *Republic* 4.435Cff.; *Laws* 5.747B-C; *Timaeus* 22B.
4. Aristotle *Metaphysics* A1.981b23ff.
5. Cf. Bibliographical information in Zeller-Mondolfo *LFG* 1.1.49, note 1.
6. Zeller-Mondolfo *LFG* 1.1.62ff.
7. J. Burnet *EGP* sec. 10.
8. J. Burnet *EGP* sec. 11.
9. Herodotus 2.109.
10. Zeller-Mondolfo *LFG* 1.1.99.

(pages 11-16) (1-10)

1. W. Jaeger, *Paideia. Die Formung des griechischen Menschen* (Berlin and Leipzig: 1936²); English translation, vol. 1 Oxford, 1954. We will be citing the English translation of Gilbert Highet by volume and page number, *Paideia* 1.51.
2. W. Jaeger *Paideia* 1.429, note 34.
3. W. F. Otto *Die Götter Griechenlands* (Frankfurt am Main, 1956⁴).
4. Zeller-Mondolfo *LFG* 1.1.105ff.

5. Zeller-Mondolfo *LFG* 1.1.106.
6. Herodotus 2.123.
7. Zeller-Mondolfo *LFG* 1.1.139.
8. Zeller-Mondolfo *LFG* 1.1.139.
9. Zeller-Mondolfo *LFG* 1.1.174.
10. Zeller-Mondolfo *LFG* 1.1.175.

(pages 18-19) (1-2)

1. Aristotle *Met.* A 2.982b11-28.
2. The passage referred to [982b29-983a11] is a little further on, as follows:
   "Hence also the possession of it might be justly regarded as beyond
   human power; for in many ways human nature is in bondage, so that
   according to Simonides 'God alone can have this privilege,' and it is
   unfitting that man should not be content to seek the knowledge that is
   suited to him. If, then, there is something in what the poets say, and
   jealousy is natural to the divine power, it would probably occur in this
   case above all, and all who excelled in this knowledge would be unfortunate. But the divine power cannot be jealous (nay, according to the
   proverb, 'bards tell many a lie'), *nor should any other science be thought
   to be more honorable than one of this sort. For the most divine science is
   also most honorable*; and this science alone must be, in two ways, most
   divine. For *the science which it would be most meet for God to have is a
   divine science*, and so is *any science that deals with divine objects*; and this
   science alone has both these qualities; for (1) God is thought to be
   among the causes of all things and to be a first principle, and (2) such
   a science either God alone can have, or God above all others. All the
   sciences, indeed, are more necessary than this, but none is better."

(pages 29-30) (1-4)

1. Aristotle *Met.* A 2.982b18ff.
2. Aristotle *Met.* A 2.982b18ff.
3. W. Jaeger *Paideia* 1.151-2.
4. W. Jaeger, *Die Theologie des frühen griechischen Denker* (Stuttgart, 1953)
   English translation by Edward S. Robinson with the title *The Theology
   of the Early Greek Philosophers* [Gifford Lectures 1936] (Oxford at the
   Clarendon Press, 1947; reprinted 1948, 1952, 1960, 1964) 14.

(pages 35-37) (1-15)

1. Thales was a native of Miletus. We do not know the exact dates of his
   birth or death (moreover, the chronology of all the Presocratics is uncertain). He would seem to have been a contemporary of Solon and of
   Croesus. Because Thales predicted a solar eclipse, there are attempts to

determine its date and thus to determine from it also Thales's chronology. Unfortunately the results are uncertain, some have thought that it was the eclipse of 610 CE; a few today think instead is the one of 585 CE. If this were so, it would be plausible to locate the birth of our philosopher in the last decade of the seventh century and his death toward the first half of the sixth century. He was, in addition to being a scientist and philosopher, a judicious statesman. Almost all the Presocratics were involved in some political activity. Diogenes Laertius 1.25; *LCL* 1:27 tells us: "Thales is also credited with having given excellent advice on political matters." Cf. 11.A.1 *D-K* 1:67.

N.B. For all the Presocratics the collection of the testimonies and fragments edited first by Hermann Diels, *Die Fragmente der Vorsokratiker* (Berlin: Weidmann, 1903) and then systematically elaborated by Walter Kranz (Berlin: Weidmann, 1934-37⁵) is used. The 6th to the 8th editions (1951-56) by Kranz are reprints, with added *Nachträge* or appendices. An English translation of the fragments that are considered to be the original words of a Presocratic philosopher (given under section B in Diels) is to be had in Kathleen Freeman's *Ancilla to the Pre-Socratic Philosophers* (Oxford: B. Blackwell, 1948). The information contained in the other fragments (given under section A in Diels) is summarized and discussed by Miss Freeman in the *Pre-Socratic Philosophers, A Companion to Diels* (Oxford: B. Blackwells, 1946). General bibliography will be found in the fifth volume.

The reader will find that in the citations of Diels the first number indicates the section (which corresponds also to the number given to the philosopher by Diels), the capital letter (A) immediately following indicates the indirect testimonies, or (B) the direct fragments, as we said above. The number which follows the capital letter is the number of the testimony or the fragment assigned in the collection of Diels. The editor has also included the volume and page number from the seventh edition immediately following the abbreviation (*D-K*). We used the Freeman translation of the fragments unless otherwise noted. The detailed references to the sources are a constant invitation to the reader to go to the original text in order to hear the words of the philosopher in their original formulation.

2. Aristotle *Metaphysics* A3.983b6ff.; cf. 11.A.12 *D-K* 1:76-77.

3. Aristotle *De anima* A5.411a7; cf. 11.A.22 *D-K* 1:79.

4. Aristotle *De anima* A2.405a19ff.; cf. 11.A.22 *D-K* 1:79.

5. A. Maddalena *Ionici. Testimonianze e frammenti* (Florence, 1963; repr. 1970) 4.

6. Aristotle *Metaphysics* A3.983b9ff.; cf. 11.A.12.*D-K* 1:76-77.

7. J. Burnet *EGP* section 7.

8. Aristotle *Metaphysics* A3.983b20-27; cf. 11.A.12 *D-K* 1:76-77.

9. Aristotle *Metaphysics* A3.984a1-3.
10. Simplicius *In Arist. Phys.* 23.29; cf. 11.B.1 *D-K* 1:80.
11. Aristotle *De anima* A5.411a7ff.; cf. 11.A.22 *D-K* 1:79.
12. Cf. Plato *Laws* 10.899B; Aetius 1.7.11; cf. 11.A.23 *D-K* 1:79.
13. *DL* 1.35; *LCL* 1:37; cf. 11.A.1 *D-K* 1:67.
14. Aristotle *De anima* A2.405a19ff.; 11.A.22 *D-K* 1:79.
15. *DL* 1.24; *LCL* 1:25,27; cf. 11.A.1 *D-K* 1:67.

(pages 39-43) (1-14)

1. Anaximander was very probably a disciple of Thales (cf. 12.A.2, 9, 11, 12 *D-K* 1:82, 83, 83-84, 84). According to the testimony of Apollodorus quotes by Diogenes Laertius 2.2; *LCL* 1:131,133; 12.A.1 *D-K* 1:81 the philosopher was 64 years old in the second year of the 58th Olympiad (= 547-546 BCE) and died soon after; therefore, he was born in 611 BCE. He composed a treatise which, according to the ancient testimonies, was called *On Nature* (of which there is extant one fragment), and which is the first philosophical writing of the Greeks and the West. Anaximander was even more active politically than Thales. Elianus (*Var. Hist.* 3.17; *D-K* 12.A.3 *D-K* 1:82) writes: "Anaximander headed the colony which migrated from Miletus to Apollonia"; and in the archeological excavations at Miletus a statue has been discovered which the citizens dedicated to him, surely as a reward for his political activity.
2. Simplicius *In Arist. Phys.* 24.13; Theophrastus *The Opinions of the Physicists* frag. 2; 12.A.9 *D-K* 1:83.
3. Aristotle *Physics* Γ4.203b6ff.; 12.A.15 *D-K* 1:85.
4. W. Jaeger *Theology* 32-33.
5. Aetius 1.7.12; 12.A.17 *D-K* 1:86.
6. Cf. Simplicius *In Arist. Phys.* 150.24ff.; 12.A.9 *D-K* 1:83); Aristotle *Physics* A4.187a20ff.; *D-K* 12.A.9 *D-K* 1:83); Ps. Plutarch *Stromata* 2; 12.A.10 *D-K* 1:83).
7. The fragments given by Simplicius *In Arist. Phys.* 24.13ff.; *D-K* 12.B.1 *D-K* 1:89).
8. R. Mondolfo, in Zeller-Mondolfo *LFG* 1.2.204.
9. Cf. 12.A.10, A.11, A.18, A.21, A.22 *D-K* 1:83, 83-84, 86, 87, 87.
10. Alexander of Aphrodisias *Meteorol.* 67.3; 12.A.27 *D-K* 1:86.
11. Hippolytus *Ref.* 1.6.3; 12.A.11 *D-K* 1:84); cf. also Aristotle *De Caelo* B13.295b10ff.; 12.A.26 *D-K* 1:88.
12. Aetius 5.19.4; 12.A.30 *D-K* 1:88-89; cf. also the other testimonies collected under 12.A.30 *D-K* 1:88-89.
13. R. Mondolfo *Il pensiero antico* (Florence, 1950²) 39.
14. R. Mondolfo *Il pensiero antico* 50.

(pages 45-47) (1-12)

1. Anaximenes was a native of Miletus, disciple and successor of Anaximander. From the indications of the ancient sources no secure chronology can be derived, but it can be conjectured that he was born in the first decade of the sixth century BCE and died in the last decade of the same century. He wrote a book entitled *On Nature* which Diogenes Laertius says (*DL* 2.3; 13.A.1 *D-K* 1:90) was composed "in simple and unaffected writing in the Ionic dialect," of which three fragments remain.

2. Theophrastus *The Opinions of the Physicists* frag. 2; quoted in Simplicius *In Arist. Phys.* 24, 26; 13.A.5 *D-K* 1:91); See also Hippolytus *Ref.* 1.7; 13.A.7 *D-K* 1:92.

3. Simplicius *De caelo* 615.18ff. Heiberg.

4. Quoted by Aetius 1.3.4; 13.B.2 *D-K* 1:95.

5. Cf. Zeller-Mondolfo *LFG* 1.2.213ff.

6. Hippolytus *Ref.* 1.7.2; 13.A.7 *D-K* 1:92.

7. The fragment was reported by Olympiodorus *de arte sacra lapidis philosophorum* 25; 13.B.3 *D-K* 1:96 it is considered inauthentic, but without sufficient evidence (cf. what is said in Zeller-Mondolfo *LFG* 1.2.228ff.).

8. Cf. Cicero *De nat. deorum* 1.10.26; 13.A.10 *D-K* 1:93.

9. St. Augustine *The City of God* 8.2; 13.A.10 *D-K* 1:93.

10. Plutarch *De prim. frig.* 7.947F; 13.B.1 *D-K* 1:95.

11. Cf. J. Burnet, *EGP* sec. 31.

12. Cf. further on pp. 187-196.

(pages 49-54) (1-26)

1. Heraclitus was born at Ephesus and lived between the sixth and the fifth centuries BCE. Diogenes Laertius (*DL* 9.1; *LCL* 2:409; 22.A.1 *D-K* 1:139), undoubtedly following Apollodorus Chronicus, places the acme of the life of Heraclitus in the sixty-ninth Olympiad, that is, in 504-501 BCE; all the attempts of modern scholars to determine more exactly the dates of his birth and death have been aleatory. Again Diogenes informs us that Heraclitus was "high-minded and haughty beyond all other men." He did not participate in public life: "And when he was requested by them [again Diogenes writes] to make laws, he scorned the request because the state was already in the grip of a bad constitution" (*DL* 9.3; *LCL* 2:411). He lived a solitary life, and did not tolerate the company of his fellow-men. He did not have any direct teachers and boasted that he discovered his own wisdom. The work that he wrote, like the other philosophers we have looked at so far, is entitled *On Nature*; it was composed in an original, daring, and even obscure style. Again Diogenes tells us that "Heraclitus deposited this book [*On Nature*]

in the temple of Artemis and, according to some, he deliberately made it the more obscure in order that none but adepts should approach it, and lest familiarity should breed contempt" (*DL* 9.6; *LCL* 2:413). Heraclitus was for this reason called "the obscure." It is not improbable that the writing rather than having a specific structure had an aphoristic form, that is, it was a collection of reflective sayings which were linked more by concept than by formal structure. The numerous fragments which we possess, at least the ones which are extant, leave a good deal of room for this conjecture. Diogenes says that "Theophrastus puts it down to a melancholy temperament [*scil.*, to Heraclitus] that some parts of his work are half-finished, while other parts make a strange medley" (*DL* 9.6; *LCL* 2:413); hence unless, it was written in an aphoristic way, the scroll of Heraclitus appears generally to readers as having a decidedly amorphous structure. The large number of fragments which we include, in any case, give a sufficient idea of the inimitable style of this highly individualistic philosophy. Bibliography will be found in the fifth volume.

2. 22.B.12 *D-K* 1:154.

3. 22.B.91 *D-K* 1:171.

4. 22.B.49a *D-K* 1:161.

5. Aristotle *Metaphysics* Γ5.1010a10ff.

6. 22.B.126 *D-K* 1:179.

7. 22.B.53 *D-K* 1:162.

8. 22.B.111 *D-K* 1:175.

9. 22.B.23 *D-K* 1:156.

10. 22.B.60 *D-K* 1:164.

11. 22.B.103 *D-K* 1:174.

12. 22.B.88 *D-K* 1:170.

13. 22.B.10 *D-K* 1:152-3.

14. 22.B.50 *D-K* 1:161.

15. F. Hegel *Vorlesungen über die Geschichte der Philosophie*.

16. J. Burnet *EGP* sect. 68.

17. For a contrasting view of Heraclitus as a moralist, consult J. Owens, "The Interpretation of the Heraclitean Fragments" in *An Etienne Gilson Tribute* Milwaukee: The Marquette University Press, 1959 ed. Charles J. O'Neil, 148-68, esp. 160-66.

18. 22.B.90 *D-K* 1:171.

19. 22.B.30 *D-K* 1:157-58.

20. 22.B.31 *D-K* 1:158.

21. 22.B.67 *D-K* 1:165.

22. 22.B.66 *D-K* 1:165.

23. Zeller-Mondolfo *LFG* 4.161, note 82.

24. On the significance of the *logos* of Heraclitus see the note of Mondolfo "Il logos eracliteo e le sue interpretazioni" in Zeller-Mondolfo *LFG* vol.1.4.152ff.; see also G. Calogero, *Storia della logica antica* vol 1. *L'età arcaica* (Bari, 1967) 65ff.

25. Cf. 22.B.117, 118 *D-K* 1:177.

26. B. Snell, *Die Entdeckung des Geistes. Studien zur Entstehung des europäischen Denkens bei den Griechen* (Hamburg, 1946).

(pages 59-60) (1-7)

1. Cf. Diogenes Laertius 9.21; *LCL* 2:429; 28.A.1 *D-K* 1:217.

2. Pythagoras, scholars agree, is a native of Samos. On the basis of the testimonies we possess his acme seems to be around 532-531 BCE, and his death perhaps in the first years of the fifth century. Of the late books on *Life of Pythagoras* it is not possible to obtain almost anything that is historically well-founded. It seem that from Samos Pythagoras went to Italy, where in the city of Croton he found a School, which was very successful since, as we will see fully, the Pythagorean message contained a new vision of the mystical and ascetic life. It seems that the School acquired very rapidly a remarkable political position which would provoke a violent response from the opposition, who seem to have assaulted the buildings in which the School was located and to execute for treason almost all the most important members of the brotherhood. Pythagoras was saved and fled to Locri; from there he successively went to Tarantum and then to Metapontum, where he died. Of the numerous trips to the East and West that the tradition ascribed to Pythagoras none have any solid foundation. The *Three Books* and the *Golden Verses* which are attributed to Pythagoras are almost certainly forgeries which arose at the end of the ancient period or the first centuries of the Christian era. Pythagoras instead was probably interested in oral teaching. The veneration that the followers held for Pythagoras went on to the creation of many stories about him which make the historical dimension of his person impossible to recover. For the documents and sources with respect to the life of Pythagoras and the Pythagorean philosophy cf. Zeller-Mondolfo *LFG* 1.2 and the revision of Mondolfo 288ff. In English see J. E. Raven, *Pythagoreans and Eleatics* (Cambridge at the University Press, 1948); Peter Gorman, *Pythagoras: A Life* (Routledge & Kegan Paul, 1979) with a Select Bibliography 209, 210. For those who wish to deepen their knowledge of Pythagoreanism we suggest as an essential starting point E. Frank, *Platon und die sogenannten Pythagoreer* (Halle, 1923) which is onesided but very stimulating; W. Burkert, *Weisheit und Wissenschaft: Studien zu Pythagoras, Philolaos und Platon* (Nurnberg, 1962) English translation *Lore and Science in Ancient Pythagoreanism* (Cambridge, Mass.: Harvard

University Press, 1972); C. de Vogel, *Pythagoras and Early Pythagore-anism* (Assen: Van Gorcum, 1966; W. K. C. Guthrie *A History of Greek Philosophy* (Cambridge: at the University Press, 1962) 1:146-340. Further bibliography will be found in the fifth volume.

3. That Philolaus was a contemporary of Socrates is clearly taken from the *Phaedo* (61E; 44.A.1a *D-K* 1:398). Diogenes Laertius (9.38; *LCL* 2:447, 449; 44.A.2 *D-K* 1:398) makes him a contemporary of Democritus. That he was the first Pythagorean who made public the Pythagorean doctrines by writing them down seems beyond doubt. Iamblichus says (*Life of Pythagoras* 199): "The rigor of the secret was also a wonder; in fact in the course of so many years no one seems to have put into writing the doctrines of Pythagoras before the era of Philolaus. These first people fell on very hard times and divulged those famous three books, which it is said could be purchased for one hundred minas by Dion of Syracuse on behalf of Plato..." (14.A.17 *D-K* 1:104). Diogenes Laertius writes: "Some authorities, amongst them Satyrus, say that he wrote to Dion in Sicily instructing him to purchase three Pythagorean books from Philolaus for one hundred minas" (*DL* 3.9; *LCL* 1:285; 44.A.8 *D-K* 1:400). That, then, the books were three in number and not rather a book divided into three parts (Ethics, Politics, and Physics) is a secondary question. On the problem cf. M. Timpanaro Cardini, *Pitagorici, testimonianze e frammenti* vol. 2 (Florence, 1962) 84ff.; also see note 6 below.

4. One of the most famous recent attempts to distinguish ancient Pythagoreanism from the more recent is undoubtedly that of John Burnet *EGP* sections 37ff. and 88ff. The reader can personally judge whether the attempt of Burnet is successful by reading the sections indicated.

5. Cf. Aristotle *Metaphysics* A.5.985b23; 58.B.4 *D-K* 1:451.

6. M. Timpanaro Cardini has translated and commented on all the testimonies and fragments of Pythagoras in the bilingual collection of the "Biblioteca di Studi Superiori" of the La Nuova Italia Editrice (*Pitagorici. Testimonianze e frammenti* 1. (Florence, 1958); 2. (Florence, 1962); 3. (Florence, 1964). The reader who knows Italian has at his disposal an excellent instrument for orienting himself in the mass of problems which are aroused by Pythagorean thought.

7. M. Timpanaro Cardini, *Pitagorici* 3.12ff.

(pages 61-66) (1-14)

1. Aristotle *Metaphysics* A5.985b23-986a3; 58.B.4 *D-K* 1:451ff.

2. See for the explanation of this point, our commentary on Aristotle's Metaphysics *La metafisica* 1.165ff.

3. Aristotle *Metaphysics* A5.986b4ff.

4. Zeller-Mondolfo *LFG* 1.2.443.

5. 44.B.5 *D-K* 1:408.

6. 44.B.2 *D-K* 1:407.

7. M. Timpanaro Cardini *Pitagorici* 2.200.

8. Stobaeus *Anthol*.1.22.19; also Plutarch *De E apud Delphos* 388a-b; *LCL* 5:217, 219.

9. A. Rey, *La jeunesse de la science grecque* (Paris, 1933) 270ff.; also J. Burnet, *EGP* sect. 67ff.

10. Cf. Aristotle *Physics* Δ.6.213b22ff.; 58.B.30 *D-K* 1:459-60.

11. Cf. M. Timpanaro Cardini, *Pitagorici* 2.97ff.

12. Plato *Gorgias* 507E-508A.

13. 44.B.4 *D-K* 1:408.

14. 44.B.11 *D-K* 1:411-12.

(pages 67-68) (1-6)

1. Cf. 21.B.7 *D-K* 1:130-31.

2. Cf. 14.A.1., A.8a *D-K* 1:96 and 100.

3. Cf. U. von Wilamowitz-Möllendorff *Der Glaube der Hellenen* (Darmstadt, 1959³) 2:185ff.

4. Cf. J. Burnet *EGP* sect. 45; Zeller-Mondolfo *LFG* 1.2.646ff.

5. Zeller-Mondolfo *LFG* 1.2.404ff.

6. See the comments of R. Mondolfo in Zeller-Mondolfo *LFG* 1.2.645ff.

(pages 71-72) (1-5)

1. Zeller-Mondolfo *LFG* 1.2.573.

2. 44.B.11 *D-K* 1:411-12.

3. 44.B.11 *D-K* 1:411-12.

4. 44.B.20 *D-K* 1:416.

5. Reported again in 44.B.20 *D-K* 1:416.

(pages 77-82) (1-27)

1. Xenophanes was born in Colophon, probably around 570 BCE. From the fragments of his work we know that around the age of twenty-five he left his native city (scholars thinks in all probability that this happened around 545 BCE because the city was captured by Arpagus in the name of Cyrus the Persian king). From Ionia he went to Sicily and lower Italy and continued to wander around for the rest of his life, reciting his poetic compositions. He died quite old (perhaps he was beyond one hundred years of age). Among his very numerous compositions we can cite the *Elegies* and the *Silloi* (satirical poetry). His properly philosophical thinking perhaps was contained in a doctrinal poem, which is mentioned in our sources under the title *On Nature*, to which Diels assigns numer-

ous extant fragments. (Some modern scholars doubt the existence of a Xenophean doctrinal poem so entitled, but perhaps they are being excessively critical.) On the various questions concerning the chronology, life, and works of Xenophanes cf. Zeller-Mondolfo *LFG* 1.3.58-71 (this volume with the title *La filosofia dei greci nel suo sviluppo storico* Prima Parte, I Presocratici, vol. 3 [Florence: "La Nuova Italia" Editrice, 1967] has been systematically edited and revised by us from the text of the 5th German edition entitled *Die Philosophie der Griechen in ihrer geschichtlichen Entwicklung*[Leipzig: G. R. Reisland, 1892] trans. Rodolfo Mondolfo. We will cite it with the abbreviation Zeller-Reale *LFG*).

2. 21.B.8 *D-K* 1:131.

3. Cf. Plato *Sophist* 242C-D; 21.A.29 *D-K* 1:121.

4. Zeller-Reale *LFG* 162ff.

5. 21.B.15 *D-K* 1:132-33.

6. 21.B.16 *D-K* 1:133.

7. 21.B.11 *D-K* 1:132.

8. 21.B.14 *D-K* 1:132.

9. 21.B.26 *D-K* 1:135.

10. 21.B.32 *D-K* 1:136.

11. For a contrasting interpretation of the fragment see Zeller-Reale *LFG* 84-88.

12. Cf. Zeller-Reale *LFG* 93ff.

13. It is reported by Clement of Alexandria *Stromata* 5.109; 399.16 Stählin.

14. Aristotle *Metaphysics* A5.986b21ff.; 21.A.30 *D-K* 1:121.

15. Cf. Zeller-Reale *LFG* 87ff.

16. Cf. Zeller-Reale *LFG* 79ff.

17. 21.B.25 *D-K* 1:135; on the various interpretations of the fragment, cf. Zeller-Reale *LFG* 80ff.

18. 21.B.26 *D-K* 1:135.

19. Cf. Zeller-Reale *LFG* 104ff.

20. Cf. Zeller-Reale *LFG* 111ff.

21. Cf. Zeller-Reale *LFG* 111ff.

22. 21.B.27 *D-K* 1:135.

23. 21.B.29 *D-K* 1:136.

24. 21.B.33 *D-K* 1:136.

25. Cf. below, pp. 127-30; for the questions concerning the Xenophean physics cf. Zeller-Reale *LFG* 128-36.

26. M. Untersteiner *Senofane. Testimonianze e frammenti* (Florence, 1956).

27. 21.B.2 *D-K* 1:128-29.

(pages 83-90) (1-23)

1. Parmenides was born at Elea in Magna Graecia. From contrasting chronological indications in the ancient sources we can legitimately say only that he was born in the second half of the sixth century and died toward the first half of the fifth century BCE. At Elea he founded a School called by that name *Eleatic* which was destined to have a great influence on all Greek thought. Our sources say that he was initiated into the philosophy of the Pythagorean Ameinias (cf. *DL* 9.23; *LCL* 2:429; 28.A.1 *D-K* 1:217), and actually the religious and mystical is clearly present in the Parmenidean poem entitled *On Nature*, chiefly in the stately prologue. As were most of his predecessors, Parmenides was concerned also with politics. It is recorded, in fact, that he provided good laws for the Eleatics (cf. *DL* 9.23; *LCL* 2:429; 28.A.1 *D-K* 1:217; cf. also the testimonies of Strabo and Plutarch in 28.A.12 *D-K* 1:220). We have the complete prologue of the poem of Parmenides, almost all the first part, and only pieces of the second part. Traditionally, Parmenides is seen as a rival to Heraclitus, and it is claimed that there is an emphatic *anti-Heracliteanism* to be found in the poem; but more recent studies have cast doubt decisively on this notion. On the other problems regarding the chronology, life, work, and the presumed relations of Parmenides with Heraclitus, cf. Zeller-Reale *LFG* 165-183. [An up-to-date bibliography of works on Parmenides will be provided in the final (fifth volume) of the American edition. JRC]

2. Parmenides presents, therefore, his philosophical teaching as a revelation from the Goddess. On the authentically religious nature of the Goddess and of the "revelation," cf. Zeller-Reale *LFG* 320-34.

3. 28.B.1 *D-K* 1:230, vv.28-32.

4. On 28.B.2 *D-K* 1:231, cf. Zeller-Reale *LFG* 184ff.

5. The Parmenidean assertion, the great principle of the Eleatic school, is in the original: «ἔστι γὰρ εἶναι, μηδὲν δ᾽ οὐκ ἔστι.»

6. 28.B.1 *D-K* 1:228, vv.1-2.

7. 28.B.8 *D-K* 1:238 vv.34ff.; for the interpretation cf. Zeller-Reale *LFG* 318-31.

8. 28.B.8 *D-K* 1:235-37 vv.1-21. (There are some points in which we depart considerably from the reading of Diels-Kranz; for the justification of the reading which we have adopted see Zeller-Reale *LFG* 195-210.)

9. 28.B.8 *D-K* 1:237-38, vv.26-33.

10. 28.B.8 *D-K* 1:237, vv.22-25.

11. 28.B.8 *D-K* 1:239, vv.46-49.

12. 28.B.8 *D-K* 1:238, vv.42-44.

13. 28.B.8 *D-K* 1:235, v.6.

14. 28.B.8 *D-K* 1:238, vv.38-41.

15. 28.B.8 *D-K* 1:237, v.24.

16. See in this regard our *Nota sulle interpretazioni della doxa parmenidea*, Zeller-Reale *LFG* 292-319.

17. 28.B.1 *D-K* 1: 237ff., vv.31ff.

18. 28.B.8 *D-K* 1: 240, vv.60ff.

19. The re-evaluation of the *doxa* of Parmenides was initiated by Reinhardt *Parmenides und die Geschichte der griechischen Philosophie* (Bonn, 1916); but the new interpretative perspective which in part inspired us was started by H. Schwabl ("Sein und Doxa bei Parmenides" *Weiner Studien* 66 (1953) 50-75 and by M. Untersteiner "La Doxa di Parmenide" *Dianoia* 2 (1956) 203-221 and now in *Parmenide. Testimonianze e frammenti* (Florence, 1958) 165.

20. 28.B.8 *D-K* 1:239, vv.53ff. On these verses cf. what it said in Zeller-Reale *LFG* 244ff. The exegesis which we propose is not close to the traditional interpretations; see the reasons for the position in the place cited above.

21. On this fragment cf. Zeller-Reale *LFG* 250ff.; 313ff.

22. Theophrastus *De sensu* 1ff.; 28.A.46 *D-K* 1:226.

23. It is petrified like the eye of the Gorgon says G. Calogero with a very beautiful image, in his *Studi sull'eleatismo* (Rome, 1932) 82 [new edition Florence, 1977] speaking of Melissus; the same can be said for Parmenides.

(pages 91-96) (1-18)

1. Zeno was born at Elea toward the end of the sixth century or the beginning of the fifth century BCE. He was a follower of Parmenides and certainly his successor in the School. He is described as a very courageous man. Here is one of the variants of the episode in which Zeno, imprisoned in an attempt to overturn a tyrant, is made a mockery by the tyrant himself, an episode which tells us a great deal about his character: "Zeno was a truly noble character both as a philosopher and as a politician; at all events, his extant books are brimful of intellect. Again, he plotted to overthrow Nearchus the tyrant (or, according to others, Diomedon) but was arrested: so Heraclides in his epitome of Satyrus. On that occasion he was cross-examined as to his accomplices and about the arms which he was conveying to Lipara; he denounced all the tyrant's own friends, wishing to make him destitute of supporters. Then, saying that he had something private to tell him about certain people in his private ear, he laid hold of it with his teeth and did not let go until stabbed to death . . ." (*DL* 9.25; *LCL* 2:435,437; 29.A.1 *D-K* 1:247). Another version (*DL* 9.27) states, instead, that he bit off his tongue and spat it at him. Hence, he was as caustic as his irresistable dialectic. He probably wrote a single book, which can be gleaned from the Platonic *Parmenides*, in which he says that he wrote a work when

he was very young. For further discussion of the chronology and bibliography of Arabic sources concerning our philosopher see Zeller-Reale *LFG* 338-343 note 2. See the bibliography in the fifth volume.

2. Plato *Parmenides* 128B; 29.A.12 *D-K* 1:250.

3. Plato *Phaedrus* 261D; 29.A.13 *D-K* 1:250.

4. Cf. *DL* 8.57; *LCL* 2:373; *DL* 9.25; *LCL* 2:435 and Sextus Empiricus *Adv. math.* 7.7; *LCL* 2:5; 29.A.10 *D-K* 1:250. On the meaning and value of the Zenonean dialectic cf. Zeller-Reale *LFG* 349ff.

5. Simplicius *In Arist. Phys.* 1013.4ff. See further texts and interpretations in Zeller-Reale *LFG* 378ff.

6. Aristotle *Physics* Z9.239b14ff.; partially reported in 29.A.26 *D-K* 1:253.

7. Aristotle *Physics* Z9.239b30ff.; 28.A.27 *D-K* 1:222.

8. Simplicius *In Arist. Phys.* 1015.19ff. See further texts and interpretations in Zeller-Reale *LFG* 383ff.

9. See further texts and interpretations in Zeller-Reale *LFG* 391ff.

10. Cf. H. D. P. Lee, *Zeno of Elea* (Cambridge, 1936, 1967²) 42 and 46.

11. Many scholars do not consider it an independent argument, but only a "piece" of the third. But see also Epiphanius *Adv. haeres.* 3.11 in Diels *DG* 590.20.

12. For a detailed exposition of the arguments with a review of the various interpretations cf. Zeller-Reale *LFG* 354-375.

13. Philoponus *In Arist. Phys.* 42,9ff.; 29.A.21 *D-K* 1:252.

14. 29.B.1 *D-K* 1:255.

15. Cf. Zeller-Reale *LFG* 354ff.

16. 29.B.3 *D-K* 1:257-58. For the different interpretations of this argument cf. Zeller-Reale *LFG* 360ff.

17. Simplicius *In Arist. Phys.* 562.1ff.; Zeller-Reale *LFG* 368ff.

18. Simplicius *In Arist. Phys.* 1108.181ff.; 29.A.29 *D-K* 1:254-55; cf. Zeller-Reale *LFG* 374ff.

(pages 97-100) (1-11)

1. Melissus of Samos was born toward the end of the sixth century or in the very first years of the fifth century BCE (as we have recently shown in our examination of the sources: cf. G. Reale, *Melisso, testimonianze e frammenti* (Florence, 1970) chapt. 1 passim). He was an expert seaman and a valiant politician. In 442 BCE he was nominated strategos by his fellow-citizens, later as a result of a quarrel with Athens, he fought against the fleet of Pericles and was defeated. He wrote a philosophical work entitled *On Nature or Being*, in which he systematized, in a sharp and penetrating way, the doctrine of the Eleatic School, which had been poetically presented by Parmenides, and dialectically (but negatively)

defended by Zeno, and which needed a series of precisions and clarifications. The work of Melissus almost certainly preceded that of the Pluralists and is the real and ideal point of departure of the Empedoclean doctrine, the Anaxagorean, as well as that of the Atomists. If Aristotle argues against Melissus and judges him in a negative manner, it depends strictly on doctrinal reasons. Melissus focused his speculations wholly on the concept of the *infinite* understood as that which is absolutely real, whereas Aristotle denied resolutely the reality of an actual infinite. And if modern interpreters have followed Aristotle, they have made the methodological error of conflating the theoretical judgment of the Stagirite with an historical judgment. On these questions see our work entitled *Melisso. Testimonianze e frammenti* 1-268 passim.

2. Cf. 30.B.1 *D-K* 1:268.

3. Cf. G. Reale *Melisso* 34-65.

4. 30.B.1 *D-K* 1:268.; G. Reale *Melisso* 60-98.

5. 30.B.4 *D-K* 1:269; G. Reale *Melisso* 98ff.

6. 30.B.5, B.6 *D-K* 1:269-70; G. Reale *Melisso* 105,123.

7. 30.B.7(7) *D-K* 1:272.

8. 30.B.9 *D-K* 1:275.

9. Cf. the documentation in G. Reale *Melisso* 193-225.

10. 30.B.8(2-6) *D-K* 1:273-275; see the deepening of the questions aroused by this fragment in G. Reale *Melisso* 226-252.

11. Cf. Aristotle *De generatione et corruptione* A8.325a2; 30.A.8 *D-K* 1:266-67; cf. G. Reale *Melisso* 338ff.

(pages 103-8) (1-15)

1. Empedocles was born at Acragas [Agrigentum]. Diogenes Laertius says that he flourished in the eighty-fourth Olympiad, that is, in 444-441 BCE (*DL* 8.74; *LCL* 2.389; 31.A.1 *D-K* 1:276-82). And the same source, on the evidence of Aristotle, tells us that he lived seventy years, which places the dates of his birth and death in 484-81 and 424-421. But since other sources give different chronological indications, it is more prudent to stay with the general indications of the *floruit* given by Diogenes Laertius, without pretending to determine more exactly the dates of his birth and death (cf. G. Reale *Melisso* 12ff.). He was man of very strong personality and of wide-ranging knowledge. In him we find both philosophy and mysticism, medicine and magic. He participated also in political activity, especially in democratic interests (cf. *DL* 8.63-67, 72ff.; *LCL* 2:377, 379, 381, 383 and 387; 31.A.1 *D-K* 1:276-82; Plutarch *Against Colotes* 32.4.1126B; *LCL* 14.303, 305; 31.A.14 *D-K* 1:284). The extant information about his death are from late sources, as that according to which he was taken up to the Gods after a sacrifice or that according to which he threw himself into the volcano, Mount Aetna (cf. *DL* 8.67ff.,

69ff; *LCL* 2:381, 383, 385; 31.A.1 *D-K* 1:276-82). They belong to legend and are the result of fictions aimed at denigrating Empedocles. Empedocles wrote two works, a poem *On Nature* and *Purifications* [*Katharmoi*], of which there are numerous extant fragments. For the romantic transformation of our philosopher see the tragedy of Hölderlin, *Der Tod des Empedokles. Empedokles auf dem Aetna* (1798-1800 posthumous).

2. The translation into English of the fragments are based on Kathleen Freeman's *Ancilla to the Pre-Socratic Philosophers* (Cambridge, Mass. 1977) with some alterations in keeping with the originals or the Italian translation as indicated. The Italian translation of all the fragments of Empedocles used by Reale is Bignone *Empedocle* (Milan, 1916; Rome, 1963²).

3. 31.B.6 *D-K* 1:311-12.

4. The system of the Pythagoreans, in fact, does not, and for a good reason, stand on the same level as the Pluralists's systems, precisely because the Pythagoreans principles, are it is true multiple, but the *multiplicity insofar as it is such* is not taken to the thematic level; only after Zeno and Melissus does the problem of the many and the one emerge on a thematic level.

5. 31.B.17 *D-K* 1:317-18, vv. 27-35.

6. 31.B.28 *D-K* 1:324.

7. 31.B.29 *D-K* 1:324-25.

8. 31.B.110 *D-K* 1:352, v.10. On the Empedoclean doctrine of knowledge see the full testimony of Theophrastus in 31.A.86 *D-K* 1:301-305.

9. 31.B.115 *D-K* 1:356-58.

10. 31.B.117 *D-K* 1:358-59.

11. 31.B.119 *D-K* 1:359.

12. 31.B.146 *D-K* 1:369-70.

13. 31.B.147 *D-K* 1:370.

14. Cf. Zeller-Mondolfo *LFG* 1.5.83ff and the revisions of A. Capizzi in Zeller-Mondolfo *LFG* 1.5.126ff.

15. 31.B.21 *D-K* 1:319, vv. 7-14.

(pages 111-16) (1-17)

1. Anaxagoras was born at Clazomenae probably around 500 BCE, based on the indications which are given to us by Diogenes Laertius 2.7; *LCL* 1:137; 59.A.1 *D-K* 2:5-8 from whom we learn also that the philosopher died around 428 BCE. Anaxagoras was perhaps the first philosopher to bring philosophy to Athens and there he made it take root. He remained at Athens—it seems—for thirty years. Some scholars think that the thirty years ought to be placed between 480 and 450, others between 463 and 433, the year in which Anaxagoras was prosecuted for impiety

at Athens. But our sources do not say that the thirty years must be consecutive necessarily and therefore the two proposed periods are susceptible of being mediated. He was a man of extraordinary learning and love of knowledge. He wrote a work in prose by title *On Nature*, of which there are particularly interesting extant fragments. For a discussion of his chronology consult Zeller-Capizzi *LFG* 351-357. See the bibliography in the fifth volume.

2. The translation into English of the fragments are based on Kathleen Freeman's *Ancilla to the Pre-Socratic Philosophers* (Cambridge, Mass., 1977), with some alterations in keeping with the original or the Italian translation as indicated. The Italian version of the translation of the fragments used by Reale is from D. Lanza, *Anassagora. Testimonianze e frammenti* (Florence, 1966).

3. G. Reale *Melisso* passim; G. Calogero, *Storia della logica antica* 263.

4. Lucretius *De rerum natura* 1.830ff.; *LCL* 61; 59.A.44.*D-K* 2:17.

5. 59.B.4 *D-K* 2:33-35.

6. Cf. 59.B.4, B.6, B.10, B.12 *D-K* 2:33-35, 35, 36-37, 37-39.

7. 59.B.11 *D-K* 2:37.

8. An anonymous scholiast.

9. G. Calogero *Storia della logica antica* 268.

10. 59.B.5 *D-K* 2:35.

11. Zeller-Capizzi *LFG* 378ff.

12. Zeller-Capizzi *LFG* 379.

13. Zeller-Capizzi *LFG* 379, note 55.

14. Zeller-Capizzi *LFG* 379, note 55.

15. C. Carbonara *La filosofia greca, I Presocratici* (Naples, 1962²) 86.

16. Plato *Phaedo* 97Eff.

17. Aristotle *Metaphysics* A4.985a18.

(pages 117-25) (1-27)

1. Concerning Leucippus we possess indications that are so scarce, as is well known, that doubt has been cast on his historical existence (cf. E. Rohde, *Verhandl. d. 34 Philologenvers.*, (1881) 64ff.; also found in E. Rohde, *Kl. Schriften* 1.(1901) 205ff. and 245ff. Apart from, therefore, these supercritical excesses, which were made in their period (previously Diels had given full corrections to the absurd thesis of Rohde in *Verhandl.d.35 Philologenvers.*, (1882) 96ff. in *Rheinisches Museum* (1887) 1ff.; and in *Archiv für Geschichte der Philosophie* (1888) 247ff. there still remains the objective difficulty of a chronological location of our philosopher, even an approximate one. It can be reasonably conjectured that he was a little younger than Empedocles, if, as the testimony states, he was a follower of Zeno and Melissus (cf. 67.A.1, A.4, A.5, A.10 *D-K* 2:70-

71, 72, 72, 74). With respect to his disciple, Democritus was at least twenty years older. And because we know with sufficient certainty that Democritus was born in 460 BCE, it will not be exceptionally improbable to hold that 480-475 BCE are appropriate dates for the birth of Leucippus. Some think with good reason that the journey of Leucippus from his native Miletus was during the period of the revolution of 450-449 BCE. From Miletus he went to Elea and from Elea to Abdera, where he found his School; in 440 he had already taught Democritus atomism, which slowly developed and matured during the collaboration between teacher and student. We certainly know that in 423 the doctrine of Leucippus was widely known, since Diogenes of Apollonia is strongly influenced by the atomistic doctrine, and in that year it was parodied in the play of Aristophanes *The Clouds*. See in this regard the work of V. E. Alfieri *Per la cronologia della Scuola di Abdera* first in *Rivista critica di storia della filosofia* 7 (1952) 488-501 and in *Estudios le historie de la filosifia* (Tucumáman, 1957) 169-1073) [a work in honor of R. Mondolfo], and also in *Atomos Idea. L'origine del concetto dell'atomo nel pensiero greco* (Florence, 1953) 11ff.; Galatina, 1979²). To Leucippus, we can attribute two works *The Great Cosmology* and *On the Intellect*. It seems probable enough, in any case, that the work of Leucippus ended by being absorbed into that of his disciple, who achieved a much greater reputation, ending if not totally obscuring his teacher, at the very least notably overshadowing him. And thus is explained how we possess of Leucippus, in addition to indirect testimonies, only a single direct fragment of his book *On the Intellect*.

2. Democritus was born at Abdera in 460 BCE or generally around that date. This is the conclusion of the reexamination of all the data extant, made by V.E. Alfieri in the above cited work *Per la cronologia della Scuola di Abdera*, which we recommend to the reader who desires to have all the documentation at hand. He was a disciple, in his native Abdera, of Leucippus and then his successor in the government of the school. He took long journeys to the East, visiting Egypt, Asia Minor, and Persia for the sake of knowledge, almost squandering his entire fortune (quite substantial) left to him by his father. He died quite old, some five years after Socrates. They have attributed a great number of works, the list of which can be seen in the testimonies collected in Diels-Kranz under numbers A.31, A.32, and especially A.33 *D-K* 2:90-92; but probably these works constitute, more than the personal productions of Democritus, the *Corpus* of the atomistic School, in which there must have also been subsumed the works of Leucippus and perhaps even those of some other disciple. Democritus was a destroyer of the culture. Zeller writes with appropriate accuracy: "Superior to all preceding and contemporary philosophers by the force of his knowledge, to the greater part of them by the acuteness and rigor of his thinking, Democritus can

be considered through the unusual combination of these two qualities, as the predecessor of Aristotle, who in fact is cited most often, who frequently used his views and speaks of them with evident respect" (Zeller-Capizzi *LFG* 157). Consult the bibliography in the fifth volume.

3. Cf. G. Reale *Melisso* 18, 21, and 278ff.

4. Aristotle *De Generatione et Corruptione* A8.324b35ff.; 67.A.1 *D-K* 2:70-71. The translations into English of the fragments are based on Kathleen Freeman's *Ancilla to the Pre-Socratic Philosophers* (Cambridge, Mass. 1977), with some changes in keeping with the originals or the Italian translation used by Reale of V. E. Alfieri *Atomisti. Frammenti e testimonianze* (Bari, 1936) now included also in the work entitled *I Presocratici* 2 vols. (Bari 1969) 2:643-867).

5. 30.B.8(2) *D-K* 1:273-74.

6. G. Reale *Melisso* 242ff.

7. G. Reale *Melisso* 179ff.

8. V. E. Alfieri *Atomos Idea* 52ff.

9. Zeller-Capizzi *LFG*, 187-208.

10. Apropos this notion V.E. Alfieri *Atomos Idea* 78ff.

11. Cf. V. E. Alfieri *Atomos Idea* 84.

12. Cf. 68.B.118 *D-K* 2:266.

13. Cf. 67.B.2 *D-K* 2:81.

14. *DL* 9.45; *LCL* 2:455; 68.A.1 *D-K* 2:81-84.

15. 68.A.66 *D-K* 2:100-01.

16. Cicero *De natura deorum* 1.43.120; 68.A.74 *D-K* 2:102.

17. The Democratean conception of the divine is however complex enough, see for instance the exhaustive analysis of the problem in V. E. Alfieri *Atomos Idea* 164ff.

18. 68.B.170 *D-K* 2:178.

19. 68.B.171 *D-K* 2:179.

20. 68.B.37 *D-K* 2:155.

21. 68.B.40 *D-K* 2:155; cf. also B.105 *D-K* 2:163.

22. 68.B.214 *D-K* 2:188.

23. 68.B.62 *D-K* 2:158.

24. 68.B.264 *D-K* 2:199.

25. 68.B.41 *D-K* 2:155.

26. 68.B.244 *D-K* 2:194.

27. 68.B.247 *D-K* 2:194.

(pages 127-31) (1-26)

1. Our sources are not in agreement in pointing out the place of origin of

Hippo. According to some he was from Samos (cf. 38.A.1 *D-K* 1:385), according to others Metapontum (cf. 38.A.16 *D-K* 1:387), according to still others Reghium (38.A.16 *D-K* 1:387), finally according to others Croton (38.A.11 *D-K* 1:386). From an indication pointed out by Bergk contained in a scholia to *The Clouds* of Aristophanes (quoted in 38.A.2 *D-K* 1:385) it appears that Hippo would have been active in the Periclean Age.

2. Cf. 38.A.4, A.6, A.8, A.10, A.11 *D-K* 1:385-86.

3. Hippolytus *Ref.* 1.16; Diels, *DG* 566; 38.A.3 *D-K* 1:385.

4. We are not in a condition to identify with absolute certainty who it is. Scholars maintain it is Idaeus of Himera and to him although as a conjecture (cf. 63 *D-K* 2:51) they refer both the affirmations which we reported (cf. also Zeller-Mondolfo *LFG* 1.2.257ff.) Actually, Sextus Empiricus, who expressly names Idaeus of Himera (*Adv. math.* 9.360; *LCL* 3:173; 63 *D-K* 2:51.1-3), places him together with Diogenes of Apollonia and Archelaus, of whom we will speak, among the upholders of the thesis according to which air is a principle. Moreover, in this case, the assertions are of more interest than the name.

5. Aristotle *Metaphysics* A7.988a23ff.; 63 *D-K* 2:51.5ff.

6. Aristotle *De caelo* Γ5.303b10ff.; 63 *D-K* 2:51.9ff.

7. Cf. 63 *D-K* 2:51 lines 11 and 26.

8. Cf. Aristotle *Metaphysics* A3.984a3ff.; 38.A.7 *D-K* 1:385; also *De anima* A2.405b1ff.; 38.A.10 *D-K* 1:386.

9. Cf. above notes 4-6.

10. Diogenes of Apollonia lived in the fifth century BCE. Aristophanes speaks of him in *The Clouds* (which is from 423 BCE) and in that era, Diogenes must have been still living, because, as a rule, the Greek comic writers caricature living persons. If, then, it can also account for the testimony of Theophrastus (Diels, *DG* 477; 64.A.5 *D-K* 2:52-53) which informs us that the thought of Diogenes of Apollonia in addition to being influenced by that of Anaxagoras was also influenced by atomism which is more recent, we can probably conclude that our philosopher was active around 440 and 423 BCE.

11. Cf. 64.B.2 *D-K* 2:52. The Italian translation of this and the rest of the fragments used is from A. Maddalena *Ionici. Testimonianze e frammenti* already cited. For the English translation see the same caution as given above for the translations taken from Kathleen Freeman.

12. Aristotle *De generatione et corruptione* A6.322b12ff.; 64.A.7 *D-K* 2:53.

13. Aetius 1.3.26; 64.A.7 *D-K* 2:53.

14. Simplicius *In Arist. Phys.* 151.28ff.; 64.B.2-5 *D-K* 2:59.15 and 60.11.

15. Cf. 64.B.3 *D-K* 2:60.

16. Cf. 64.B.5 *D-K* 2:61-62.

17. Cf. 64.B.4 *D-K* 2:60-61.
18. Zeller-Mondolfo *LFG* 2.2.282.
19. See also W. Theiler, *Zur Geschichte der teleologischen Naturbetrachtung bis auf Aristoteles* (Zürich,1925); W. Jaeger, *Theology* 155-171. The former of these scholars falls into the opposite excess, because he makes theology and teleology attributed to Socrates date back to Diogenes as well as to Xenophanes. We will see that Socrates is inspired, it is true by Diogenes, but worked a radical reform on both.
20. See especially the section about Socratic theology and teleology, 343-460.
21. All the testimonies still extant of Archelaus are collected by Diels-Kranz under number 60 in the second volume of *Fragmente der Vorsokratiker* 44-49.
22. *DL* 2.16; *LCL* 1:145, 147; 60.A.1 *D-K* 2:44-45.
23. Hippolytus *Ref.* 1.9; Diels *DG* 563; 60.A.4 *D-K* 2:46.
24. Cf. 60.A.11 and A.12 *D-K* 2:47.
25. Cf. 60.A.1, A.2, A.3, A.5, A.7 *D-K* 2:45-47.
26. In *D-K* the verses of Aristophanes *The Clouds* 225ff. and 828ff. are reproduced in the section called "Nachwirkung" related to Diogenes (60.C.1 *D-K* 2:66-69.).

(pages 138) (1)

1. Zeller-Mondolfo *LFG* 1.1.236ff.

(pages 139) (1)

1. For the terminological and conceptual distinctions we owe a great deal to the work of S. Vanni Rovighi *Lezioni di filosofia morale* (Milan, 1954).

(pages 142-45) (1-3)

1. Moral thoughts quite profound and precise moral perspectives are also offered by the tragedians, especially Sophocles and Euripides, which however are contemporary with the Sophists and Socrates and hence their work developed in parallel with the developments of moral philosophy.
2. Plato *Protagoras* 343A; 10.A.2 *D-K* 1:62.
3. Stobaeus *Anthol.* 3.1.172; 10.A.3 *D-K* 1:62-66.

(pages 149-55) (1-17)

1. For the history of the term "Sophist" see M. Untersteiner "Nota sulla parola 'sofista'" in *Sofisti. Testimonianze e frammenti* 1. (Florence: La Nuova Italia, 1961²) 16ff.

2. Plato *Sophist* 231D-E; 79.A.2 *D-K* 2:252-53.
3. Xenophon *Memorabilia* 1.6.13; *LCL*, 73; 79.A.2a *D-K* 2:253.
4. Xenophon *Cynegeticus* 13.8; 79.A.2a *D-K* 2:253.
5. Aristotle *Sophistical Refutations* 1.165a21; 79.A.3 *D-K* 2:253.
6. W.Jaeger *Paideia* 1:291 trans. G. Highet.
7. Cicero *Tusculan Disputations* 5.4.10; *LCL*, 435.
8. Nestle, in Zeller-Nestle *DPG* 1.2.1292.
9. Cf. on this theme, the admirable work of M. Untersteiner "Le origini sociali della sofistica," in *Studi di filosofia greca in onore Rodolfo Mondolfo* ed. V. E. Alfieri and M. Untersteiner (Bari, 1950) 121-180 and also in *I Sofisti* (Milan, 1967²) 2:233-283.
10. Nestle, in Zeller-Nestle *DPG* 1.2.1294.
11. W.Jaeger *Paideia* 1:286-331 trans. G. Highet.
12. Plato *Meno* 91D; 80.A.8 *D-K* 2:257
13. Plato *Protagoras* 328B-C; 80.A.6 *D-K* 2:256.
14. T. Gomperz *Griechische Denker* (Leipzig, 1896).
15. G. Saitta *L'illuminismo della sofistica greca* (Milan, 1938).
16. G. Saitta *L'illuminismo della sofistica greca* (Milan, 1938) 34.
17. L. Robin *La pensée grecque et les origines de l'esprit scientifique* (Paris, 1923).

(pages 157-63) (1-21)

1. Protagoras was born at Abdera, probably in the decade between 491 and 481 BCE. He went to many Greek cities, according to the custom of all the Sophists, and stayed more than once at Athens, where he was quite successful. He was greatly appreciated also for his political activity; Pericles gave him the responsibility for preparing legislation for the new colony of Thuri (444 BCE). Diogenes Laertius states (*DL* 9.52; *LCL* 2:465; 80.A.1 *D-K* 2:253-55) that because of his stated opinions about the Gods (of which we will speak), the Athenians drove Protagoras out of the city, impounded and burned his books in the public square. But the notice is of doubtful authenticity since Plato in the dialogue of the same name (*Protagoras* 317B) concerned with the Sophists has him say that he has suffered no ill effects from being or declaring that he was a Sophist (and, in the dialogue, Protagoras is presented as being experienced and old); and it would be difficult, if what Diogenes says were true, for Plato to have made assertions of that kind. He died toward the end of the century. The greatest work of Protagoras was *On Truth,* which probably, received the subtitle *Destructive Reasoning.* Along side of this work, the work entitled *Controversies* must have occupied a preeminent place in the Protagorean productions. It must have been concerned with the method of discussion of the Sophists. On the life and

work of Protagoras the reader will find ample notices and testimonies in Zeller-Nestle, *DPG* 1.2.1296-1304 and especially in M. Untersteiner, *I Sofisti* 1.13-43. See bibliography in the fifth volume.

2. Sextus Empiricus *Adv. math.* 7.60; *LCL* 2:31-33; Plato *Theaetetus* 151E-152A; 80.B.1 *D-K* 2:262. Cf. also Diogenes Laertius 9.51; *LCL* 2:463, 465; 80.A.1 *D-K* 2:253-55.

3. Cf. especially T. Gomperz *PG* vol. 2.

4. Plato *Theaetetus* 151E-152A; 80.B.1 *D-K* 2:262.

5. Aristotle *Metaphysics* K6.1062b13ff.; 80.A.19 *D-K* 2:259.

6. Sextus Empiricus *Outlines of Pyrrhonism* 1.216; *LCL* 1:131; 80.A.14 *D-K* 2:258.

7. *DL* 9.51; *LCL* 2:463, 465; 80.A.1 *D-K* 2:253-55; 80.B.6(a) *D-K* 2:266; cf. 80.A.20 *D-K* 2:260.

8. Aristotle *Rhetoric* B.24.1402a23; 80.A.21 *D-K* 2:260; 80.B.6(b) *D-K* 2:266.

9. L. Robin, *Storia del pensiero greco* 179. Diogenes Laertius expressly writes, moreover, (*DL* 9.53; *LCL* 2.465, 467; 80.A.1 *D-K* 2:253-55): "the first to point out how to attack and refute any proposition laid down: so Artemidorus the dialectician in his treatise *In Reply to Chrysippus*."

10. *Dissoi Logoi* 1.1-2; 90 *D-K* 2:405.

11. Cf. Plato *Protagoras* 333D, 334A; 80.A.22 *D-K* 2:260.

12. *Dissoi Logoi* 1.17; 90 *D-K* 2:407.

13. Plato *Protagoras* 318E; 80.A.5 *D-K* 2:256; cf. in this regard our commentary on *Protagora* (Brescia, 1969) 49.

14. Plato *Theaetetus* 166D; 80.A.21(a) *D-K* 2:260.

15. Plato *Protagoras* 333D, 334C; 80.A.22 *D-K* 2:260.

16. Cf. note 14 above. It is not improbable that Protagoras maintained "a theory of the ideal State, based on the principle that the primacy must be given to the wise," understood in the sense discussed above (S. Zeppi, *Protagora e la filosofia del suo tempo* (Florence, 1961) 20ff. The testimony discussed by Diogenes Laertius (*DL* 3.37; *LCL* 1:311; 90.B.5 *D-K* 2:412-13) could be explained in such a way (note again S. Zeppi, 22ff.) where he says "Euphorion and Panetius relate that the beginning of the *Republic* was found several times revised and rewritten, and the *Republic* itself Aristoxenus declares to have been nearly all of it included in the *Controversies* of Protagoras." And again (*DL* 3.57; *LCL* 1:469, 471; 90.B.5 *D-K* 2:412-13), "Favorinus, however, in the second book of his *Miscellaneous History* declares that nearly the whole of the *Republic* is to be found in a work of Protagoras entitled *Controversies*." Protagoras, in conclusion, had anticipated the idea that the government of the State must be entrusted to men of wisdom. But we will see that beyond this possibility of contact between the Protagorean state and Plato's there is an abyss.

17. Cf. the passage of the Platonic *Protagoras* read at the beginning of the section.

18. Diogenes Laertius expressly attests to the fact that for Protagoras the soul is nothing other than sensations (*DL* 9.51; *LCL* 2: 463,465; 80.A.1 *D-K* 2:253) with explicit reference also to Plato *Theaetetus* 152ff.

19. Diogenes Laertius 9.51; *LCL* 2: 463,465; 80.B.4 *D-K* 2:265). Eusebius (*Praep. evang.* 14.3.7; 80.B.4 *D-K* 2:265) writes in a wholly comparable way, as follows: "With regard to the Gods, he does not know whether they exist or do not exist, nor of what nature they are."

20. 80.A.23 *D-K* 2:260-61; the judgment which Eusebius arrives at is analogous to that which is reported in 80.B.4 *D-K* 2:265, "Protagoras, being a follower of Democritus, was famous for his atheism etc."

21. The belief in the Gods is clearly presupposed in the attitude of Protagoras in comparison to his followers who argued the issue of the payment of honors, in the Platonic dialogue of the same name (*Protagoras* 328B-C) and to a great extent, in the great myth which we read from 320D in which the Gods are the protagonists.

On Protagoras we can read like antithetical stimuli, the two opposed reconstructions of M. Untersteiner *I Sofisti* 1:13-149 and A. Levi *Storia della sofistica* ed. D. Pesce (Naples, 1966) 79-149 which are particularly useful, since in their antithetical perspectives we come to see the reality of the Sophists as a more complex reality beyond the *cliché*s of the current potted histories of philosophy which are not even suspected. Cf. also S. Zeppi *Protagora e la filosofia del suo tempo* passim. See the bibliography in the fifth volume.

(pages 165-71) (1-30)

1. Gorgias was born at Leontini in Sicily around 485-480 BCE. (cf. 82.A.10 *D-K* 2:274-75) and lived more than a century in complete spiritual and physical health. He was a follower of Empedocles. He journeyed throughout all the cities of Greece and stayed, naturally, at Athens. We know, however, that he came to Athens in 427 BCE coming from his native city as an ambassador (in order to obtain military assistance against Syracuse). He was very successful with his display of rhetorical skill. Philostratus (82.A.1 *D-K* 2:271-72) writes: "He was the teacher of the Sophist's vehement speaking skill, and an audacious innovator of expression, and adapted a sublime and inspired tone for sublime things, a detachment of expression, and he began improvisation, all those things which make discussion more harmonious and solemn." The most philosophically pregnant work must be his *On Nature or On Not Being,* an expression of ancient nihilism. Among the other works of which we have added information the most important must be: *The Encomium of Helen* and *The Apology of Palamedes.* Further information on the life

and works of Gorgias are to be seen in M. Untersteiner *I Sofisti* 1:153-167. See the bibliography in the fifth volume.

2. Cf. G. Reale *Melisso* 22ff. and 24, note 97.

3. There are two redactions of the extant work: one preserved by Sextus Empiricus (*Adv. math.* 7.65ff.; *LCL* 2:35ff.; 82.B.3 *D-K* 2:279-83) and one coming from the anonymous author of the *De Melisso, Xenophane, Gorgia* (it was transmitted among the works of Aristotle, but is certainly spurious), 5-6.979a11-980b21 in the Bekker edition, it is not reported, incorrectly, in Diels-Kranz, but it can be read in the Loeb Classical Library Series *Aristotle: Minor Works* trans. W. S. Hett (Cambridge, Mass.: Harvard University Press, 1955) 496-507 in Greek and English. After the re-evaluation of modern scholars of this anonymous work (on which cf. Zeller-Reale *LPG* 1-54 and G. Reale *Melisso* 27ff. ad 298ff.) the reading of this redaction is indispensible and it is necessary to include it among the fragments of Gorgias (it is as such much more interesting than fragments preserved by Sextus Empiricus).

4. Cf. H. Gomperz *Sophistik und Rhetorik* (Leipzig-Berlin, 1912; reprinted also at Darmstadt, 1965) 1-4.

5. A clear exposition and interpretation of this Gorgean work can be read in A. Levi *Storia della sofistica* 204-236.

6. Sextus Empiricus *Adv. math.* 7.87; *LCL* 45, 47.

7. Ps. Aristotle *De Melisso, Xenophane, Gorgia* 5.979a13ff.; *LCL,* 497ff.

8. For a detailed analysis of this first Gorgian thesis and for a comparison between the two redactions of the versions of Ps. Aristotle and Sextus Empiricus see M. Migliori *La filosofia di Gorgia* (Milan, 1973) 23-62.

9. Sextus Empiricus *Adv. math.* 7.78ff.; *LCL* 2:41; 82.B.3 *D-K* 2:279-83.

10. Sextus Empiricus *Adv. math.* 7.80; *LCL* 2:43; 82.B.3 *D-K* 2:279-83.

11. Sextus Empiricus *Adv. math.* 7.78; *LCL* 2:43; 82.B.3 *D-K* 2:279-83.

12. For a detailed analysis of this section of the Gorgian treatise see M. Migliori *La filosofia di Gorgia* (Milan, 1973) 63ff.and 70ff.

13. Ps. Aristotle *De Melisso, Xenophane, Gorgia* 6.980a20; LCL, 505.

14. Cf. Gorgias *Encomium of Helen* sect. 11; 82.B.11 *D-K* 2:288-94; *The Apology of Palamedes* sect. 24; 82.B.11(a) *D-K* 2:294-303.

15. M. Migliori, *La filosofia di Gorgia* 151ff.

16. M. Migliori, *La filosofia di Gorgia* 134.

17. Cf. Plato *Gorgias* 460Aff.

18. Cf. Plato *Meno* 95C; 82.A.21 *D-K* 2:277.

19. Aristotle *Politics* A.13.1260a27; 82.B.18 *D-K* 2:305.

20. Cf. Plato *Meno* 71E; 82.B.19 *D-K* 2:305.

21. See the preceding section, pp. 237-240.

22. See above, the section on Parmenides, 127ff.

23. See the first part of the Platonic *Gorgias*.
24. W. Jaeger *Paideia* 1.502; [1:290 trans. G. Highet].
25. W. Jaeger *Paideia* 1.502; [1:291 trans. G. Highet].
26. Plato *Gorgias* 452E.
27. Cf. Plato *Gorgias* 459Cff.
28. Plato *Gorgias* 457B.
29. Cf. Gorgias *Encomium of Helen* sect. 9; 82.B.11 *D-K* 2:288-94.
30. Plutarch *De glor. Ath.* 5. 348C; *LCL* 4:509; 82.B.23 *D-K* 2:305-06.

(pages 173-77) (1-19)

1. Prodicus was born at Keos, but we do not know exactly at what date. Scholars conjecture that his date of birth falls between 470 and 460 BCE and that his activity is to be located at the beginning of the Peloponnesian War (since Aristophanes alludes to Prodicus). He was many times at Athens as an ambassador. He gave successful lectures both at Athens and in other Greek cities. His chief work is entitled *Horai* (perhaps derived from the name of the Goddesses of fertility) to whom perhaps belong the famous allegorical tale entitled "The Choice of Heracles" (cf. M. Untersteiner, *I Sofisti* 2:7-11). See bibliography in the fifth volume.

2. Cf. Plato *Protagoras* 341A; *Meno* 96D; *Charmides* 163D; *Cratylus* 384B.

3. Plato *Protagoras* 337A-C; *D-K* 84A13; *Protagoras* 340A; 84.A.14 *D-K* 2:311; *Euthydemus* 277E; 84.A.16 *D-K* 2:311.

4. 84.A.11 *D-K* 2:310 and 84.A.20 *D-K* 2:312.

5. Cf. H. Gomperz, *Sophistik und Rhetorik* 126; cf. also H. Maier, *Sokrates* (Tübingen, 1913).

6. "The Choice of Heracles" is reported by Xenophon (*Memorabilia* 2.1.21-34; *LCL*, 95, 97, 99, 101, 103; 84.B.2 *D-K* 2:313); as we will see the opinion of some interpreters who see Cynic influence here is totally incorrect insofar as the language which is spoken is stamped with hedonism and utilitarianism and has nothing of the Cynic ethic of renunciation and toil.

7. Cf. S. Zeppi "L'etica di Prodico," in *Studi sulla filosofia presocratica* (Florence, 1962) 103-115, first published in *Rivista critica di storia della filosofia*, 1956.

8. Xenophon *Memorabilia* 2.1.23-25; *LCL*, 97; 84.B.2 *D-K* 2:313.

9. Xenophon *Memorabilia* 2.1.27ff.; *LCL*, 97, 99; 84.B.2 *D-K* 2:313.

10. Cf. for example, Plato *Protagoras* 238Bff. and compare this passage with with Xenophon *Memorabilia* 2.1.20, 21; *LCL*, 93, 95 which introduces the story of "The Choice of Heracles."

11. That has been noticed on the contrary by S. Zeppi; cf. note 7 above.

12. Cf. note 15 below.

13. Xenophon *Memorabilia* 2.1.29; *LCL,* 99; 84.B.2 *D-K* 2:313.

14. Xenophon *Memorabilia* 2.1.30-33; *LCL,* 99, 101, 103; 84.B.2 *D-K* 2:313.

15. S. Zeppi "L'etica di Prodico" in *Studi sulla filosofia presocratica* (Florence, 1962) 107ff.

16. The ethics of Protagoras as well as that of Gorgias was in the last analysis utilitarian in tendency. The Sophists of the second generation will tend instead to emphasize hedonism more.

17. Philodemus *De piet.* 9.7.75G; 84.B.5 *D-K* 2:317.

18. Sextus Empiricus *Adv. math.* 9.18; *LCL* 3:11; 84.B.5 *D-K* 2:317.

19. Sextus Empiricus *Adv. math.* 9.52; *LCL* 3:29; 84.B.5 *D-K* 2:317.

(pages 179-82) (1-13)

1. On this point we would call the reader's attention to A. Levi *Storia della sofistica* 30, note 9 and 249ff. A. Levi writes: "As H. Maier observed (*Sokrates* 240, the opposition of φύσις and of νόμος, of nature and convention, is found in Empedocles ... in Philolaus ... in Diogenes of Apollonia ... and in Democritus. Archelaus (introduced such an opposition into the practical life: H. Maier *Sokrates* 241), affirmed that justice and injustice exist by convention and not by nature (*DL* 2.16; *LCL* 1:147). This opposition instead was not made by Protagoras or the Anonymous of Iamblichus (who actually based νόμος on φύσις), nor does it appear in Gorgias or Prodicus."

2. The authors of textbooks have, therefore, attributed to all Sophists a fundamental opposition, which instead solely arises with one of its currents (the "naturalistic" current) which had wholly particular characteristics.

3. Hippias was born at Elis although we do not know exactly when. Toward the end of the fifth century, in any case, he must been a well known and valued teacher. He traveled a great deal, as did all the other Sophists. He lived for a long time and composed—it seems—many works. For further information see M. Untersteiner, *I Sofisti* 2:111-120.

4. The *Hippias Major* (on the beautiful) and the *Hippias Minor* (on lying, a demonstration of the absurdity of the Socratic tenet that no one commits evil voluntarily).

5. Cf. Plato *Protagoras* 315B-C and our commentary in our edition cited above 34, note 45. Cf. *Hippias Minor* 368Bff.; 86.A.12 *D-K* 2:329.

6. Cf. Plato *Hippias Major* 285Bff.; 86.A.11 *D-K* 2:328-29; cf. also *Hippias Minor* 368Bff.; 86.A.12 *D-K* 2:329.

7. Cf. Plato *Protagoras* 318E.

8. Plato *Protagoras* 337C considered in Diels-Kranz and correctly so as a forgery, that is, as a Platonic reconstruction or better a Platonic inven-

tion, made *à la manière de* . . . , as we would say today; cf. the comment on the passage in A. Levi *Storia* 254ff.

9. We possess scarcely any information about Antiphon. His chronological position is extremely difficult to place; his activity seems to be able to be placed with some degree of probability in the last decades of the fifth century BCE. His principal work is entitled *On Truth* and shows the influence of the Eleatic School. The importance of Antiphon for the history of thought only emerged after 1915 and 1922 following the discovery of two papyri at Oxyrhynchus [El Bahnasa], Egypt containing tenets which were audacious and important, as we will see. It is understandable then how the older histories of philosophy and the potted versions did not give much space to him. E. Bignone deserves the major credit for contributing to our knowledge of Antiphon in a series of studies published between 1917 and 1923, then collected into the *Studi sul pensiero antico* (Naples, 1938) 1-226. There is a good deal of discussion as to whether Antiphon the Sophist and Antiphon the Orator are the same person; the question has scarcely any relevance in this context; however we will say that the most recent studies seem to be oriented to reply to this issue in the positive sense; cf. F. Decleva Caizzi *Antiphontis tetralogiae* (Milan-Varese, 1968).

10. 87 fragment A *D-K* 2:346-52.

11. 87 fragment B *D-K* 2:352-55.

12. 87 fragment A *D-K* 2:346-52.

13. 87 fragment B *D-K* 2:352-55.

(pages 183-87) (1-12)

1. Naturally it is not very important to know if Euthydemus and Dionysodorus, protagonists of the Platonic *Euthydemus* are historical persons or not; they are, in any case, "ideal types," if not actual who characterize in a very clear manner the eristic current. Cf. A. Levi *Storia* 52-65 who, although very concerned with preserving the true Sophistic morality, does not give historical space to these people and to the current they represent, which in our judgment, represents one of the almost inevitable outcome of Sophism, even if it is a question of a negative outcome (and a spiritual phenomenon is not understood except by acknowledging it in all its aspects).

2. Ctesippus is considered to be speaking of himself in the third person.

3. Plato *Euthydemus* 285D-286B. The reason can be paraphrased as follows, explicating some implications. If two persons think and speak about the same thing "x," on condition that they speak and think about the same thing, then they agree; if instead one of them has a notion of "x" which is "false," then, actually, he does not speak of "x" since he speaks of another thing "y"; and if it is either one or the other who has

a "false" opinion of "x," then one thought "y" and the other "z" and no one of them thought "x," so that the two in no way contradict each other.

4. Plato *Euthydemus* 286B-E.

5. Critias was a relative of Plato (his mother's cousin). Born probably in the decade between 460-450 BCE. He was part of the Socratic circle, but did not absorb the Socratic spirit. He participated in Athenian political activity without disdaining the most immoral methods. He died in 403. He wrote numerous works in verse and in prose. For further information on his life and works see M. Untersteiner *I Sofisti* 2:179-188.

6. A fragment of the *Sisyphos Satyricos* is reported by Sextus Empiricus *Adv. math.* 9.54; *LCL* 3:31; 88.B.25 *D-K* 2:386-89.

7. Thrasymachus was born at Chalcedon in Bythania, a colony of Megara (Cf. 85.A.1 *D-K* 2:319). His activity is located in the last decades of the fifth century. For detailed information about his life and the works attributed to him see M. Untersteiner *I Sofisti* 2:175-178.

8. Plato *Republic* 338C; 85.A.10 *D-K* 2:320, 85.B.6(a) *D-K* 2:325.

9. Concerning the Callicles that we find portrayed in the Platonic *Gorgias* who is a literary creation and not an historical person, consult also what we said in the Introduction to our translation and commentary to the *Gorgia* 40ff.

10. Plato *Gorgias* 483C-D.

11. Plato *Gorgias* 484A.

12. Plato *Gorgias* 491E-492C.

(page 190) (1)

1. M. Untersteiner *I Sofisti* 1:227ff.

(pages 195-98) (1-12)

1. We know with certainty the date of Socrates's death, which occurred in 399 BCE following his condemnation for "impiety" (Socrates was formally accused of not believing in the Gods of the City and of corrupting the young with his teachings; but behind such an accusation is hidden resentments of various kinds and political manuevering, as Plato so well reveals in the *Apology of Socrates* and in the introduction to the *Euthyphro*). Since Plato himself says that at the moment of the death of Socrates he was seventy years old, we can surmise that he was born in 470-469 BCE. The father of Socrates was named Sophroniscus and it seems he was a sculptor, his mother was named Phenarete and she was a midwife. He married Xanthippe (whose reputation as a difficult woman, at least in great part, is a later invention; the first mention of her being a difficult woman comes from Antisthenes, who described

her as a woman "who was critical of everything present, past, and future" (Xenophon *Symposium* 2.10; but we know how much the Cynics were opposed to the institution of marriage as we will have amply opportunity to see in volume three of this series [*Reale* 3:32-33]). At the time of the death of Socrates he had two young children and an infant child also (cf. *Phaedo* 60A) and hence must have married Xanthippe at an advanced age. A later tradition speaks also of another woman with Socrates, by name Myrto (*DL* 2.26; *LCL* 1:157). If the information is correct it is possible to consider Myrto his first wife and Xanthippe his second. Socrates never left Athens except for his time of military duty (he fought at Potidaea, at Amphipolis and at Delos). It did not want to participate in political activity viewing negatively the way that the public welfare was administered. He was physically quite strong, capable of resisting the fatigue of very hard work and walking barefooted with a light cloak withstanding the rigors of the most intense cold weather. He had moments of such great concentration that were close to ecstatic rapture, as Plato attests, who in the *Symposium* speaks of one of these in which Socrates was prostrate for a day and a night during the campaign of Potidaea (cf. *Symposium* 220C). He was ugly and had a look like the figures of Silenus with bulging eyes but he had an absolutely fascinating charm, like an irresistable force which could both attract and repel others. Plato thus describes him through Alcibiades, "And . . . I say that he is like to the Silenus-figures that sit in the statuaries' shop; those, I mean, which our craftsmen make with pipes or flutes in their hands: when their two halves are pulled open, they are found to contain images of Gods. And I further suggest that he resembles the satyr Marsyas. Now, as to your likeness, Socrates, to these in figure, I do not suppose even you yourself will dispute it; but I have next to tell you that you are like them in every other respect. You are an insolent fellow eh? If you will not confess it, I have witnesses at hand. Are you not a piper? Why, yes, and a far more marvelous one than the satyr. His lips indeed had power to entrance mankind by means of instruments; a thing still possible today for anyone who can pipe his tunes; for the music of Olympus's flute belonged, I may tell you, to Marsyas his teacher. So that if anyone, whether a fine flute-player or paltry flute-girl, can but flute his tunes, they have no equal for exciting a ravishment, and will indicate by the divinity that is in them who are apt recipients of the deities and their sanctifications. You differ from him in one point only—that you produce the same effect with simple prose unaided by instruments" (trans. W.R.M. Lamb *Symposium* 215A; *LCL,* 219). About the "daimon" or the "divine voice" which Socrates is said to hear within himself, we will speak in the course of the exposition although it is appropriate to emphasize the strongly religious character of the man Socrates on the basis of the elements which we have adduced up to this point.

In the life of Socrates it seems again most clear that there are two distinct moments; the first, in which he participated in the philosophical culture of his times and was concerned with the study of the cosmos. As we know already and as we will see further on, Socrates was a disciple of Archelaus (a student of Anaxagoras). Up to what point he followed the teachings of these Physicists it is not possible to say; moreover the doctrines of the Physicists were then in a state of final crisis. A crisis of which Socrates was aware benefiting from the new Sophistic setting of the problems of philosophy, his thought matured slowly, which we know from Plato and Xenophon.

If this is so, it is not so strange that Aristophanes presents us with a Socrates very different from the Platonic and Xenophonean Socrates in 453 (when the *Clouds* by Aristophanes was performed) Socrates was in his forties; while the Platonic and Xenophanean Socrates is the maturer Socrates, it is the Socrates who is between sixty and seventy years of age (Plato was at least forty years younger than Socrates).

Moreover the two moments in the life of Socrates had roots beyond the facts which we have pointed out, in the same historical moment in which he lived. A.E. Taylor writes correctly, "We cannot even begin to understand Socrates historically until we are clear on the point that his youth and early manhood were spent in a society sundered from that in which Plato and Xenophon grew up by the same sort of gulf which divides 'post-war' from 'pre-war' Europe" (*Socrates* 39).

Since the life and philosophy of Socrates are identical further indications concerning his biography and the spiritual history of philosophy will be given in the course of the exposition of his thought. See also the bibliography in the fifth volume.

2. On the relations between Socrates and Aristophanes cf. Leo Strauss *Socrates and Aristophanes* (New York-London, 1966) as well as the relations between Socrates and Xenophon cf. Leo Strauss *Xenophon's Socratic Discourse: An Interpretation of the "Oeconomicus"* (Ithaca-London: Cornell University Press, 1970) and by the same author *Xenophon's Socrates* (Ithaca-London: Cornell University Press, 1972. Also Anton-Hermann Chroust, *Socrates Man and Myth, The Two Socratic Apologies of Xenophon* (London: Routledge & Kegan Paul, 1957).

3. On the problem of Plato as a Socratic source see V. de Magalhães Vilhena *Le problème de Socrate. Le Socrate historique et le Socrate de Platon* (Paris, 1952) with all the indications given there; cf. by the same author, also, *Socrate et la légende platonicienne* (Paris, 1952) as well as a competent but highly compressed analysis by J. Owens, *A History of Ancient Western Philosophy* New York: Prentice-Hall, 1959) 165-169. See also Cornelia de Vogel, "The Present State of the Socratic Problem," *Phronesis* 1 (1955) 26-35.

4. The Anglophone reader will find the Socratic writings of Xenophon translated in the indispensible Loeb Classical Library Series of Harvard University Press and William Heinemann Ltd., London with the Greek text on the facing page. *Memorabilia* and *Oeconomicus* translated by E. C. Marchant in one volume (1965); *Cyropaedia* translated by Walter Miller in two volumes (1900); *Hellenica, Anabasis, Apology,* and *Symposium* translated by E. C. Marchant in three volumes (1900); *Scripta Minora* translated by E. C. Marchant in one volume (1900).

5. All the Aristotelian testimonies concerning Socrates are collected by Th. Deman, *Le témoignage d'Aristote sur Socrate* (Paris, 1942) [Greek text, French translation and full commentary]; cf. also V. de Magalhães Vilhena *Le problème de Socrate* 231-302 and the indications given there.

6. With respect to the minor Socratics see the following section. In addition to the authors we will discuss there, Aeschines of Sphettus is noteworthy about whom consult H. Dittmar *Aischines von Sphettos* (Berlin, 1912).

7. Cf. V. de Magalhães Vilhena *Le problème de Socrate. Le Socrate historique et le Socrate de Platon* (Paris, 1952).

8. See in particular how Aristophanes was used for the reconstruction of the first part of the life and for the first moment of Socratic thought by A. E. Taylor, *Socrates* 39ff. See also F. Adorno *Socrate* (Bari, 1970) 27ff.

9. Cf. H. Maier *Sokrates. Sein Werk und seine geschichtliche Stellung* (Tübingen, 1913).

10. After the work of O. Gigon, *Sokrates. Sein Bild in Dichtung und Geschichte* (Bern, 1947) very few scholars have attempted to write about Socrates. Actually the position of the problem of Socrates which emerges from the work of Gigon (as well as from that of V. de Magalhães Vilhena cf. note 3 above) seems to be without outcome or almost so. The truth is that the historian will never have at his disposal for the reconstruction of the life and thought of Socrates an absolute and unified criterion but must inevitably make use of multiple criteria and then dare to have confidence in his own intuitive powers. On the other hand historiography is not a mathematical science and its methods necessarily are composite.

11. Especially J. Burnet and A. E. Taylor (cf. above note 1 and below note 15).

12. One example will be sufficient to illuminate this assertion of ours; in the famous work of E. Rohde *Psyche* (Tübingen, 1983 and many times revised) Socrates is not cited except incidentally, and he is not acknowledged as an important figure in the development of the Greek notion of *psyche* (and many have simply accepted Rohde's view). On the contrary, as we will show, modern scholars have gone to the point of giving to Socrates even the principal place in the evolution of the concept of *psyche* and have found in Socrates the founder of the typically western conception of the "soul." And with this discovery the sense of the

Socratic philosophy changes radically, as we will see.

(pages 199-223) (1-74)

1. Cf. above pp. 165-168 and Migliori *La filosofia di Gorgia* 29-31.
2. Xenophon *Memorabilia* 1.1.11ff.; *LCL,* 9ff.
3. Xenophon *Memorabilia* 1.1.14; *LCL,* 9.
4. Xenophon *Memorabilia* 4.7.6; *LCL,* 349, 351.
5. Xenophon *Memorabilia* 1.1.12 and 16; *LCL,* 9 and 11.
6. Frag. 11 Blumenthal; *DL* 2.23; *LCL* 1: 153,155.
7. Theophrastus *The Opinions of the Physicists* 4; Diels *DG* 479.
8. Cf. Plato *Phaedo* 97Bff.
9. Xenophon admits that Socrates knows, in the area of the natural sciences, even more than what was strictly necessary and to that which he advised others to limit themselves (*Memorabilia* 4.7; *LCL,* 347, 249, 351, 353); and the mention that he makes of the argument of Socrates against Anaxagoras and his ideas is particularly suggestive (cf. *Memorabilia* 4.7.6; *LCL,* 349, 351). For the later authors see above 346 note 25).
10. Plato *The Apology of Socrates* 19Cff.
11. A.E. Taylor (*Socrates* 56 and following) thinks instead that it was a real spiritual crisis in the life of Socrates, which should be placed in connection with the episode of the oracle of which Plato speaks in the *Apology* 20C. Questioned by Chaeraphon, the oracle responded that Socrates was the wisest man in Greece. (On the interpretation that Socrates gave to this response of the oracle see what we have written further on at page 360). To identify this episode with the spiritual crisis of Socrates is however somewhat hazardous and in any case would be a mere conjecture. As we said above, it would seem logical to think that Socrates had abandoned the speculations of the Physicists through their being obsolete more than through a sudden crisis.
12. Cf. Plato *Phaedo* 96A-102A.
13. Xenophon *Memorabilia* 1.1.16; *LCL,* 11.
14. Plato *The Apology of Socrates* 20D-E.
15. Cf. J. Burnet "The Socratic Doctrine of the Soul" in *Proceedings of the British Academy* 7 (1915-1916) 235ff. republished in *Essays and Addresses* (London, 1929) 126-162; A. E. Taylor *Socrates* 132ff.; W. Jaeger *Paideia* 2:60; [2:40ff. trans. G. Highet].
16. Our student F. Sarri has written a well-documented study to the history of the concept of *psyche* before Socrates and the revolution produced by Socrates entitled *Socrate e la genesi storica dell'idea occidentale di anima* (Rome: Edizioni Abete, 1975) which we recommend for the detailed proof of the thesis. In particular Sarri demonstrates, in the first part,

that the term *psyche* in Homer is even excluded from circulation as a properly psychological term; that in the Orphics *psyche* indicates an individual *daimon* but not the consciousness (man continues to think with the body); in the Naturalists the soul-principle includes (at least in Heraclitus and in Diogenes of Apollonia) intelligence, but in a cosmic and not a personal dimension; in the poets *psyche* circulates as a psychological term, at first indicating the subject of emotions, then, bit by bit, the rational subject, but this occurs in the Socratic period (that is, in the last years of the fifth century BCE). The documentation of Sarri is more complete than that furnished by some of the preceding authors mentioned.

17. A. E. Taylor *Socrates* 137.

18. A. E. Taylor *Socrates* 132.

19. Cf. chiefly the article of J. Burnet cited in note 15 above and A. E. Taylor *Socrates* 132ff.; F. Sarri *Socrates* passim.

20. The extremism of the Scotish School consists in the fact that both Taylor (*Socrates* passim; *Plato, the Man and his Works* 1949[6]) and J. Burnet (cf. the introduction to his *Plato's Phaedo* Oxford, 1911) considered Plato as the faithful historian of Socrates, except in the dialectical dialogues. Plato, as Kant, achieved his most original thought only in his maturity, if not in his old age.

21. Jaeger *Paideia* 2:46-106

22. Jaeger *Paideia* 2:40.

23. Plato *The Apology of Socrates* 29D-30B.

24. Plato *Protagoras* 310B-314C; see also our edition with the related commentary, pp.13-29.

25. Plato *Protagoras* 313D-E.

26. Plato *Laches* 185E.

27. Plato *Charmides* 154D-E.

28. Plato *Alcibiades Major* 128D-130E; that the concept of the body as an "instrument" of the soul expressed splendidly in the passage we have just read is Socratic is confirmed by Xenophon *Memorabilia* 3.12.5ff.; *LCL,* 251, 253.

29. Xenophon *Memorabilia* 4.3.14; *LCL,* 305, 307.

30. Xenophon *Memorabilia* 3.10.1; *LCL,* 231, 233.

31. Xenophon *Memorabilia* 3.10.6ff.; *LCL,* 235ff.

32. For the documentation of this point consult the previously cited work of F. Sarri *Socrate* passim, who gathered all the passages of the Socratics and of the authors influenced by Socrates that allude to the doctrine of the *psyche* and then accurately explained them.

33. Plato *Symposium* 216D-E.

34. Xenophon *Memorabilia* 4.2.34; *LCL,* 293. Obviously, Socrates gave, on

the contrary, an identical evaluation of those things the Greeks maintained as the worst evil; the worst evil for Socrates is ignorance and what is derived from ignorance, just as the highest good is knowledge and what can be derived from it (cf. for example, Plato *Crito* 44D).

35. Plato *Euthydemus* 281D-E.
36. For a detailed interpretation of the *Protagorus* consult our work *Platone: Protagora. Traduzione, introduzione e commento* (Brescia: La Scuola, 1969; 1984⁵) passim.
37. Xenophon *Memorabilia* 3.9.4ff.; *LCL*, 225ff.
38. Aristotle *Nicomachean Ethics* Z.13.1144b28ff.
39. Aristotle *Nicomachean Ethics* H.2.1145b23-27.
40. A. E. Taylor *Socrates* 140-143.
41. Cf. for example how much Aristotle had emphasized it in his *Nicomachean Ethics* Z.13.
42. Cf. Plato *Sophist* 237Aff.
43. Especially in the *Republic* and in the *Phaedo*.
44. Xenophon *Memorabilia* 4.5.8ff.; *LCL*, 329ff.
45. W. Jaeger *Paideia* 2:54 and 2:379 note 126 trans. G. Highet.
46. W. Jaeger *Paideia* 2:54.
47. On the Socratic *enkrateia* the beautiful pages of H. Maier *Sokrates* 2: 32ff. may be read to advantage. Maier, however, does not connect *enkrateia* to the new conception of the *psyche* (about the revolution produced by Socrates with respect to the notion of the soul Maier has not the slightest inkling; but his monograph is fundamental for the understanding of some important aspects of Socrates and Socraticism).
48. Xenophon *Memorabilia* 1.5.4ff.; *LCL*, 65,67.
49. Cf. especially Plato *Gorgias* 491Dff.
50. Xenophon *Memorabilia* 4.5.11ff.; *LCL*, 331,333.
51. Plato *Gorgias* 494B.
52. Xenophon *Memorabilia* 4.5.2ff.; *LCL*, 325, 327.
53. H. Maier *Sokrates* 2:30.
54. Cf. Xenophon *Memorabilia* 1.2.14; *LCL*, 19; 2.6.2; *LCL*, 129.
55. Cf. Plato *Philebus* 67A.
56. Cf. *DL* 6.11; *LCL* 2:13; frag. 70 Decleva Caizzi.
57. In what concerns the teacher of Hippias, by name Egesidamus see Suda under the word *Hippias;* for Hippias consult Plato *Hippias Minor* 368Bff.
58. The thesis of H. Maier (*Sokrates* 2:30, note 1) according to which "the transition from technical *autarcheia* of the Sophists into the moral sense seems to have been accomplished by Antisthenes" is contrary to all the evidence, and contradicts also the affirmation of the scholars

mentioned above. It is true, instead, that Antisthenes was concerned with this concept more than any of the other Socratics.

59. Xenophon *Memorabilia* 1.6.10; *LCL,* 71, 73.
60. W. Jaeger *Paideia* 2:91; [2:56 trans. G. Highet].
61. For the demonstration consult our work cited above in note 36.
62. Xenophon *Memorabilia* 4.5.9ff.; *LCL,* 329, 331.
63. See how H. Maier (*Sokrates* 2:24) in an attempt to leave behind the difficulty of the utilitarian interpretation of Socrates, on the intuitive level grasps the right notion. He writes, "To this tend, according to his [Socrates] conviction, all moral precepts: *to the perfection of the individual soul.* There does not exist any other moral law. Virtue itself is nothing but this perfection." If Maier had gotten to the base of his intuition (many times it was peeping out in his book), he would undoubtedly have anticipated the discovery of J. Burnet and A. E. Taylor.
64. Plato *Gorgias* 470E.
65. Plato *The Apology of Socrates* 30D; and also consult *Crito* 44D.
66. Plato *The Apology of Socrates* 41D.
67. Plato *The Apology of Socrates* 38A.
68. Plato *The Apology of Socrates* 40C.
69. Xenophon *Memorabilia* 2.4-10; *LCL,* 121-165, [every odd numbered page is for the English text JRC.].
70. Plato *The Apology of Socrates* 31Cff.; cf. above 232-235.
71. Plato *Gorgias* 504Dff.
72. Plato *Gorgias* 521D.
73. Plato *Crito* 51B.
74. Xenophon *Memorabilia* 4.4.4; *LCL,* 309.

(pages 225-37) (1-25)

1. Xenophon *Memorabilia* 1.1.1; *LCL,* 3; Plato *The Apology of Socrates* passim; Plato *Euthyphro* 2Cff.
2. Antisthenes frag. 40a, b, c, Decleva Caizzi.
3. Antisthenes frag. 40d, Decleva Caizzi.
4. Plato *Euthyphro* 6A.
5. Cf. above 78ff.
6. H. Maier *Sokrates* 2:152ff.
7. Xenophon *Memorabilia* 1.4 passim; *LCL,* 53-65.
8. Xenophon *Memorabilia* 1.4.8ff.; *LCL,* 57ff.
9. Xenophon *Memorabilia* 1.4.13ff.; *LCL,* 61ff.
10. Xenophon *Memorabilia* 1.4.17ff.; *LCL,* 63ff.
11. Xenophon *Memorabilia* 4.3.1-14ff.; *LCL,* 297-307.

12. Plato in the *Philebus* 28Dff. fully verifies not only the hypothesis that Socrates upheld, that is, the conception of an ordering universal intelligence, but also that he had taken it consciously from the Physicists. Aristotle re-echoed the idea which we find in the passage of the *Memorabilia* read above in his exoteric writings, as, not without surprise H. Maier has pointed out (*Sokrates* 1:98; 2:140). We have confirmed the thesis with respect to the *Treatise on the Cosmos,* which we have shown is probably authentic and belongs among the exoteric works of Aristotle (G. Reale, *Aristotele, Trattato sul cosmo* [Naples: Lofreddo, 1974] and which involves even terminological contacts with Xenophon. It is clear that the original source is not Xenophon, or at least Xenophon is not the author speaking in the first person. Xenophon would not have been able to achieve the reform about which we spoke, that is, to produce the de-cosmologicalization of the discussion of Diogenes Apollonia and to have substituted, at its base, the Socratic understanding. Therefore Plato and Aristotle reconfirm the authenticity of the principal concepts of the discussion on providence-God that Xenophon puts in the mouth of Socrates. (Unsupportable, hence, in our judgment, is the thesis of W. Theiler, *Zur Geschichte der teleologischen Naturbetrachtung,* according to which Xenophon would have taken the material directly from Diogenes).

13. The Sophists, instead, as we have seen, represent the casting of doubt *negatively* on the physicalistic discourse about the Gods.

14. Plato *The Apology of Socrates* 31C-D.

15. Plato *The Apology of Socrates* 27B.

16. Cf. for example Plato *The Apology of Socrates* 40B.

17. This point has not been overlooked by H. Maier *Sokrates* 2:168ff.

18. This point has been nicely brought to light by H. Maier *Sokrates* 2:136-171; cf. especially 143.

19. Plato *The Apology of Socrates* 33C. As can be seen Socrates mentions prophecy (for example the response of the Delphic oracle), dreams and similar things, but rigorously avoids confusing those with his *daimonion* about which we will speak first after this passage.

20. Plato *The Apology of Socrates* 31D.

21. Xenophon *Memorabilia* 1.1.7-9; *LCL,* 5, 7.

22. Zeller, *DGP* 2.1.83ff. is one of the few scholars who have grasped this point.

23. H. Maier *Sokrates* 2:138.

24. Plato *The Apology of Socrates* 41C-D.

25. H. Maier *Sokrates* 2:143ff.

(pages 239-52) (1-27)

1. Cf. Plato *Protagoras* 311B-314C.
2. The protreptic goal of Socratic dialectic is grasped quite well by H. Maier *Sokrates* 2:67ff. who since he does not understand the role that the concept of *psyche* plays in Socrates thought, is unable to achieve clarity about how such a protreptic-dialectic works.
3. Plato *Laches* 187D-188B.
4. Plato *Parmenides* 154D-E.
5. Plato *The Apology of Socrates* 29D-E.
6. Plato *The Apology of Socrates* 39C-D.
7. Plato *Gorgias* 448A.
8. Plato *Protagoras* 318A.
9. Plato *Hippias Minor* 368Bff.
10. Plato *The Apology of Socrates* 21B-22E.
11. Plato *The Apology of Socrates* 23A-B.
12. H. Maier *Sokrates* 2:76ff.
13. Plato *Republic* 337A: "And he [Thasymachus] on hearing this gave a great guffaw and laughed sardonically and said, 'Ye Gods! here we have the well-known irony of Socrates, and I knew it and predicted that when it came to replying you would refuse and dissemble and do anything rather than answer any question that anyone asked you'."
14. Plato *Sophist* 230B-E.
15. Plato *Meno* 80A-B.
16. Plato *Theaetetus* 148E-151D. H. Maier (*Sokrates* 2:68ff.) maintained that the "maieutic" which is described in this passage is an invention of Plato, who (as well as in the *Meno* and in other dialogues) tends to demonstrate the existence of an apriori residue of latent knowledge in the human soul. But the passage which we have read does not connect precisely the maieutic with the Platonic doctrine of innatism which is espoused in the *Meno* and in other dialogues (*Phaedo, Phaedrus*) but even contradicts the doctrine of innatism, in the measure in which he speaks of non-pregnant souls and hence those incapable of benefiting from the company of Socrates and therefore incapable of true parturition. This non-pregnant character of some souls is therefore in clear antithesis with the doctrine of Platonic innatism, *which seems to be true for all souls indiscriminately.* For us therefore "maieutic" (and the page read is the most clear proof) are not in fact identical with the Platonic doctrine of "anamnesis." It is instead the theory that Plato thought up in order to flee from the aporias which the maieutic implied. The maieutic implied that *only some* souls are pregnant with the truth, Platonic anamnesis implies on the contrary that *all* of them are so, indeed in the measure in which they are souls (even those of slaves for example; cf. *Meno* where in order to prove the doctrine of anamnesis a slave is

questioned). Moreover, a ringing confirmation of the thesis of the authenticity of the maieutic doctrine as the *art of delivering pregnant souls* is given by the language which Aristophanes in the *Clouds* puts in Socrates's mouth and which corresponds to that of the *Theaetetus*.

17. F. Schleiermacher, *Ueber den Werth des Sokrates als Philosophen* in *Sämmtliche Werke* 3.2.287-308.

18. E. Zeller *DPG* 2.1.106.

19. Aristotle *Metaphysics* A6.987b1ff.

20. Aristotle *Metaphysics* M4.1078b23-30.

21. Aristotle *Metaphysics* M9.1086b2ff.; cf. M.4.1078b30ff.

22. See our commentary on Book A of the Aristotelian *Metaphysics* passim.

23. W. Jaeger *Paideia* 2:163 trans. G. Highet.

24. Xenophon *Memorabilia* 4.6.1; *LCL,* 333.

25. Xenophon *Memorabilia* 4.5.12; *LCL,* 333.

26. Xenophon *Memorabilia* 4.6.15; *LCL,* 347.

27. A point well clarified by H. Maier but with the cautions made above in note 2.

(pages 253-54) (1-3)

1. Cf. above 359, note 20.

2. A. E. Taylor *Socrates* 139.

3. Xenophon *Memorabilia* 3.8.7; *LCL,* 221.

(pages 259-61)   (1-14)

1. Plato *The Apology of Socrates* 39C-E.

2. *DL* 1.18; *LCL* 1:19.

3. *DL* 2.47; *LCL* 1:177.

4. *DL* 2.48; *LCL* 1:177, 179.

5. *DL* 2.34; *LCL* 1:165; *DL* 2.60; *LCL,* 189, 191.

6. *DL* 6.2; *LCL* 2:3, 5; Giannantoni 5A12.

7. *DL* 6.2; *LCL* 2:3, 5; Giannantoni 5A12.

8. Plutarch *De curios.* 2.516C; *LCL* 6:479 (the passage is quoted on 403).

9. Cf. Gellius *Noctes atticae* 7.10.1-4; *LCL* 2:119; frag. 1 Döring; Giannantoni 2A2; cf. below note 14 and page 371f. note 1.

10. Here is the passage of the *Phaedo* (89A-C; *LCL*:309): "I will tell you. I was sitting at his right hand on a low stool beside his couch, and his seat was a good deal higher than mine. He stroked my head and gathered the hair on the back of my neck into his hand—he had a habit of playing with my hair on occasion—and said, 'Tomorrow [*scil.,* as a sign of mourning for the death of Socrates], perhaps, Phaedo, you will cut this

beautiful hair.'"
"'I suppose so, Socrates,' I said."
"Not if you take my advice."
"What shall I do then?"
"'You will cut it off today, and I will cut mine, if our argument dies and we cannot bring it to life again.' At the beginning of the dialogue Plato had Phaedo say these words: 'I am not busy and I will try to tell you. It is always my greatest pleasure to be reminded of Socrates, whether by speaking of him myself or by listening to someone else'" (Giannantoni *SR* 3A 7).

11. Cf. further on page 373f., note 1.
12. *DL* 3.5; *LCL* 1:281.
13. *DL* 3.5; *LCL* 1:281.
14. An edition of the testimonies and fragments concerning the minor Socratics has been prepared by G. Giannantoni *Socraticorum reliquiae* for the publishing houses Edizioni dell'Ateneo of Rome in co-edition with Bibliopolis of Naples, Volumes I-IV, 1983-1985. The edition of Giannantoni is an outstanding contribution to the scholarship concerning the minor Socratics for which all scholars will be grateful.

(pages 263-69) (1-48)

1. Antisthenes was born at Athens, but he was not of pure Attic descent. His father was Athenian, while his mother came from Thrace. Antisthenes was therefore a semi-barbarian and this, as we will see, is an important element for the understanding of many of his attitudes both practical and theoretical (cf. *DL* 6.1; *LCL* 2:3; *DL* 2.31; *LCL* 1:161,163; Seneca *De const.sap.*18.5; Epiphanius *Adv. haeres.* 3.26). We do not know his year of birth or death; the attempts that have been made to determine his chronology with precision have been wholly unsuccessful; it is possible only to say that Antisthenes lived between the fifth and fourth centuries BCE. (Cf. the chronological indications which are given by Diodorus Siculus 15.76; Eudocia *Violarium* 96.56; Plutarch *Vita Lyc.* 30). He was at first the student of Gorgias (*DL* 6.1; *LCL* 2:3) and he was intimate with other Sophists (Xenophon *Symposium* 4.62ff.); only in advanced old age did he become a disciple of Socrates (hence the cutting remark of Plato [*Sophist* 251B], who called the old man a late learner). Diogenes Laertius (6.15-18; *LCL* 2:15, 17, 19, 21) attributes to him a remarkable number of works, all lost. The most recent collection of the fragments have been edited by F. Decleva Caizzi, *Antisthenes fragmenta* (Milan-Varese, 1966) and by G. Giannantoni in the work cited above page 365, note 14 (the passages cited above on the semi-barbarous origin of Antisthenes are numbered by Decleva Caizzi as fragments 122A, 124, 122C, 122D; the passages concerning the chronology as fragments 140, 141, 171; the other passages which we have cited are listed as fragments

368 / Notes to pp. 263-264

125, 107.1 and are identical with G. Giannantoni's numbering 5A.1, 3, 2, 1; 1.3; 5.35, 10, 11, 13, 41). See bibliography in the fifth volume.

2. *DL* 6.7; *LCL* 2:9; frags. 151 and 152 Decleva Caizzi; Giannantoni *SR* 5A.27. Diogenes writes some anecdotes in which Antisthenes chides Plato for his unbounded pride.

3. Cf. section 2 and the documentation given there.

4. Cf. for example: Stobaeus *Anth.* 2.31.68 and 3.14.17; Epiphanius *Adv. haeres* 3.26; Xenophon *Symp.* 3.8 and 4.2-5 (frags. 64, 84B, 90, 111, 120 Decleva Caizzi; Giannantoni *SR* 5A.163, 131, 107, 81, 83).

5. *DL* 6.11; *LCL* 2:13; *DL* 6.10; *LCL* 2:11, 13; frags. 70 and 23 Decleva Caizzi; Giannantoni *SR* 5A.134.

6. *DL* 6.10; LCL 2:11, 13; frag. 69 Decleva Caizzi; Giannantoni *SR* 5A.134.

7. Cf. above note 5.

8. *DL* 6.12; *LCL* 2:13; frag. 71 Decleva Caizzi; Giannantoni *SR* 5A.134.

9. *DL* 6.13; *LCL* 2:13, 15; frag. 88 Decleva Caizzi; Giannantoni *SR* 5A.134.

10. *DL* 6.13; *LCL* 2:13, 15; frag. 63 Decleva Caizzi; Giannantoni *SR* 5A.134.

11. Stobaeus *Anth.* 2.31.68; frag. 64 Decleva Caizzi; Giannantoni *SR* 5A.163.

12. *DL* 6.11; *LCL* 2:13; frag. 70 Decleva Caizzi; Giannantoni *SR* 5A.134.

13. *DL* 6.11; *LCL* 2:13; frag. 70 Decleva Caizzi; Giannantoni *SR* 5A.134 Giannantoni.

14. It would be an error to understand the logic and epistemology of Antisthenes in separation from Plato, that is, outside this polemical context.

15. Cf. Simplicius *In Arist. Cat.* 208.28ff. and 211.15ff.; Ammonius *In Porphyr. Isag.* 40.6-10 (frags. 50 A-C Decleva Caizzi; Giannantoni *SR* 5A.149).

16. *DL* 6.3; *LCL* 2:5; frag. 45 Decleva Caizzi; Giannantoni *SR* 5A.151. Consult also Alexander Aphrodisias *In Arist. Top.* 42.13ff. (frag. 46 Decleva Caizzi; Giannantoni *SR* 5A.151);

17. That is, as we will immediately see, in an nominalistic and empiricist sense.

18. Aristotle *Metaphysics* H3.1043b4-23ff.; frag. 44A Decleva Caizzi; Consult also Alexander Aphrodisias *In Arist. Met.* 553.31-554.10; frag. 44BDecleva Caizzi; Giannantoni *SR* 5A.150.

19. Aristotle *Metaphysics* H3.1043b4-23ff.; frag. 44A Decleva Caizzi; Consult also Alexander Aphrodisias *In Arist. Met.* 553.31-554.10; frag. 44BDecleva Caizzi; Giannantoni *SR* 5A.150. Consult G. Reale *Aristotele, La Metafisica* vol. 2 the entire commentary to H.3, especially notes 8-19 chiefly the last note (p. 28).

20. Epictetus *Arrian's Discourses of Epictetus* 1.17.10; *LCL* 1:115, 117; frag. 38 Decleva Caizzi; Giannantoni *SR* 5A.160.

21. Cf. Plato *Cratylus* 384B; *Euthydemus* 277Eff.; who writes the thought of Prodicus almost with the same terms; 84.A.11 *D-K* 2:310 and 84.A.16 *D-K* 2:311.

22. Cf. Aristotle *Metaphysics* Δ29.1024b26-34ff.; frag. 47A Decleva Caizzi; Giannantoni *SR* 5A.152; see G. Reale *Aristotele, La Metafisica* 1:483ff. note 5ff. In this passage, as well as in the *Topics* A11.104b19-21 (frag. 47C Decleva Caizzi; Giannantoni *SR* 5A.153), Aristotle records the doctrine of Antisthenes according to which it is impossible that two men contradict each other.

23. Antisthenes was very probably convinced of a kind of *materialism* which maintained that only the bodily existed and it seems that Plato in the *Sophist* 246A-E was aiming at precisely this position of Antisthenes. It is a matter therefore of a naive materialism having an essentially polemic aim (against Plato) and thus like his logical doctrine.

24. Xenophon *Symposium* 4.34ff.; frag. 117 Decleva Caizzi; Giannantoni *SR* 5A.82.

25. Cf. Xenophon *Symposium* 4.45.

26. Epictetus *Arrian's Discourses of Epictetus* 3.24.67-72; *LCL* 2:207; partially reported in Decleva Caizzi frag. 118 and in Giannantoni *SR* 5B.290.

27. An opinion reported by many sources; *DL* 6.3; *LCL* 2:5; Sextus Empiricus *Adv. math.* 9.73-74; *LCL* 3:41, 43; Aulus Gellius *Noctes atticae* 9.5.3; *LCL* 2:177,179; Clement of Alexandria *Stromata* 2.20.121.1; Eusebius *Praep. evang.* 15.13.7; Theodoret *Graec. aff. cur.* 12.47 (frags. 108A-F Decleva Caizzi; Giannantoni *SR* 5A.122).

28. Clement of Alexandria *Stromata* 2.20.107; Theodoret *Graec. aff. cur.* 3.53; frag. 109A-B Decleva Caizzi; Giannantoni *SR* 5A.123.

29. See the preceding note.

30. See especially Plato *Phaedo* passim.

31. Stobaeus *Anthol.* 3.10.41; frag. 94 Decleva Caizzi; Giannantoni *SR* 5A.80.

32. Stobaeus *Anthol.* 3.1.28; frag. 93 Decleva Caizzi; Giannantoni *SR* 5A.125.

33. *DL* 6.8; *LCL* 2:7, 9; frag. 179 Decleva Caizzi; Giannantoni *SR* 5A.114.

34. *DL* 6.8; *LCL* 2:7, 9; frag. 178C Decleva Caizzi; Giannantoni *SR* 5A.89.

35. *DL* 6.11; *LCL* 2:13; frag. 95 Decleva Caizzi; Giannantoni *SR* 5A.134.

36. Clement of Alexandria *Stromata* 2.21.130; Theodoret *Graec. aff. cur.* 11.8; frag. 97A-B Decleva Caizzi; Giannantoni *SR* 5A.111.

37. *DL* 6.11; *LCL* 2:13; frag. 101 Decleva Caizzi; Giannantoni *SR* 5A.134.

38. Consult Philodemus *De pietate* 7.3-8; Cicero *De Natura Deorum* 1.13.32; Minucius Felix *Octav.* 19.7; Lactantius *Div. Instit.* 1.5.18ff.; Lactantius *De ira dei* 11.14; Clement of Alexandria *Stromata* 5.14.108,4; Clement of Alexandria *Protr.* 6.71.1; Eusebius *Praep. evang.* 13.13,35; Theodoret

Graec. aff. cur. 1.75 (frags. 39A-E; 40A-D Decleva Caizzi; Giannantoni *SR* 5A.179-181.

39. *DL* 6.4; *LCL* 2:5, 7; frag. 162 Decleva Caizzi; Giannantoni *SR* 5A.178.

40. *DL* 6.2; *LCL* 2:3; frag. 19 Decleva Caizzi; Giannantoni *SR* 5A.85; "He demonstrated that pain is a good thing by instancing the great Heracles and Cyrus, drawing the one example from the Greek world and the other from the barbarians." Also *DL* 6.11; *LCL* 2:13 (see above, note 35).

41. The testimonies in this regard are very numerous; cf. for example: *DL* 6:13-15; Athenaeus *Deipnosoph.* 5.276B; Clement of Alexandria *Stromata* 1.16.63; Suidas *s.v.*; *DL pooem.* 19; Cicero *De orat.* 3.17 etc.; frags. 128A, 129, 130A, 130B, 134A, 134B, 136A, 136B Decleva Caizzi, and Giannantoni *SR* 5A.22-26.

42. *DL* 6.13; *LCL* 2:13, 15; frag. 136A Decleva Caizzi; cf. frag. 136B; Giannantoni *SR* 5A.22 and 23.

43. *DL* 6.13; *LCL* 2:13, 15; Giannantoni *SR* 5B143.

44. There have been not a few scholars who have denied that Antisthenes should be considered the founder of Cynicism. In addition to the names of famous scholars like E. Schwartz and U. von Wilamowitz Möllendorff (to whom H. Maier *Sokrates* 2:215ff. made a fine rejoinder) we mention D. R. Dudley, *A History of Cynicism* (London, 1937), who did not take into account what Maier had already pointed out in a way difficult to refute, namely that already in Xenophon, a contemporary, "Antisthenes was presented as an authentic Cynic."

45. To some one who faulted him for being the son of a mother who was a barbarian he replied: "The mother of the Gods too is a Phrygian" (*DL* 6.1; *LCL* 2:3; frag. 122A Decleva Caizzi; Giannantoni *SR* 5A.1).

46. *DL* 6.6; *LCL* 2:13, 15; frag. 186 Decleva Caizzi; Giannantoni *SR* 5A.167.

47. Matthew 9:12; Mark 2:17; Luke 5:31.

48. R. Mondolfo *Il pensiero antico* 190. On the developments of Cynicism consult vol. 3:25-54.

(pages 271-79) (1-42)

1. We are not well informed about the dates of his birth or death. His life was lived generally within the parameters of time that moves from the last decades of the fifth century to the first half of the fourth century BCE. He traveled a good deal in Greece and in Sicily. His origin is not Greek, just as the customs of his native city, and perhaps also the tenor of the life he lead within his family must have been etched not a little into his vision of life, so different from that of Socrates. For the life and works of Aristippus see G. Giannantoni *I Cirenaici. Raccolta delle fonti antiche, traduzione e studio introduttivo* (Florence, 1958) 172ff. and 268ff. The numbering of the fragments is given on the basis of the *Socraticorum reliquiae* cited on page 365, note 14 above, the number of which we will

indicate by the abbreviation *SR*. This edition supersedes the previous ones by Giannantoni himself (cited above) and by Mannebach (*Aristippi et Cyrenaicorum fragmenta* Brill: Leiden-Köln, 1961) and claims to be a milestone. The English version is that of the Loeb Classical Library Series. See bibliography in the fifth volume.

2. Plutarch *De curios.* 2.516C; *LCL* 6:479; Giannantoni *SR* 4A.2.

3. To affirm, as some have done, that "it would seem to be correct to maintain that actually the Cyrenaic was not a true follower, but only a friend and admirer of Socrates without any special adherence on a philosophical level" (Giannantoni *I Cirenaici* 28) is impossible. The connection between Aristippus and Socrates was such that Plato in the *Phaedo,* listing the names of the most faithful friends of Socrates who were present the day on which the philosopher drank the hemlock, felt the need to expressly say that Aristippus was not there since he was at Aegina. Also the philosophy of Aristippus and in general Cyrenaicism is explained well only as distortion of Socraticism, while it is not at all explained, if the Socratic matrix is excluded.

4. See further on above in section 3 and the documentation there.

5. *DL* 2.65; *LCL* 1:195; Giannantoni *SR* 4A1.

6. *DL* 2.65; *LCL* 1:195; Giannantoni *SR* 4A1.

7. Xenophon *Memorabilia* 1.2.60; *LCL,* 41, 43; Giannantoni *SR* 4A3.

8. *DL* 2.91; *LCL* 1:221; Giannantoni *SR* 4A.172: "[The Cyrenaics] considered that wealth too is productive of pleasure, though not desirable for its own sake."

9. The exemplary response given by Aristippus to those who remonstrated with him about the relations that he had with the beautiful hetaira Laïs: "I have Laïs, not she me; and it is not abstinence from pleasure that is best, but mastery over them without even being worsted" (*DL* 2.75; *LCL* 1:203, 205; Giannantoni *SR* 4A.96).

10. *DL* 2.66; *LCL* 1:195, 197; Giannantoni *SR* 4A.51.

11. *DL* 2.68; *LCL* 1:197, 199; Giannantoni *SR* 4A.104.

12. *DL* 2.72; *LCL* 1:201; Giannantoni *SR* 4A.160. It is not difficult to understand, already from the little we have read, that Aristippus, more than from his thought, is close to Socrates in many of his traits of character. Here is how Gomperz describes his character: "There was about his [Aristippus] character a gay serenity which preserved him from anxiety and regrets about the events which occurred in the past. There was joined in him, in a marriage, in truth a rarity, the capacity to enjoy and the absence of needs; this aspect of his personality and the calm patience which he maintained in the presence of every provocation produced the greatest impression on his contemporaries" (*PG* 2:667).

13. Here is the list of Cyrenaics and their successors according to Diogenes Laertius, ". . . the disciples of Aristippus were his daughter Arete, Aethi-

ops of Ptolemàs, and Antipater of Cyrene. The pupil of Arete was Aristippus, who went by the name of mother-taught, and his pupil was Theodorus, known as the atheist, subsequently as 'God'. Antipater's pupil was Epitimides of Cyrene, his was Paraebates, and he had as pupils Hegesias, the advocate of suicide, and Anniceris...(*DL* 2.85; *LCL* 1:215, 217; Giannantoni *SR* 4A.160). According to Suda the succession is this: "the daughter Arete was a disciple of Aristippus, from whom came Aristippus the younger, who was called Metrodiddata. Of these Theodorus was a disciple, first called atheist then 'God'; of these Antipater, of these Epitimides the Cyrenaic; of these Parebates; of these Hegesius the death-persuader; of these Anniceris, who rescued Plato" (Giannantoni *SR* 4A.160). Hegesius, Anniceris (or Annicerides) and Theodorus were the heads of the Schools which resulted from the subsequent factionalism and splitting of the School into three branches. Cf. Reale 3: 55-64.

14. *DL* 2.92; *LCL* 1:221; Giannantoni *SR* 4A.172.

15. Ps. Plutarch *Stromata* 9; Giannantoni *SR* 4A.166.

16. Eusebius *Praep. evang.* 15.62.7; Giannantoni *SR* 4A.166. The verse cited in this place just as in the preceding testimony is from Homer *Odyssey* 4.392. Consult also Themistius *Orat.* 34.5.

17. Aristotle *Metaphysics* B2.996a32ff.; Giannantoni SR 4A.170. Cf. also Alexander of Aphrodisias *In Arist. Met.* 182.30-38; Syrianus *In Arist. Met.* 14.31-34; Asclepius *In Arist. Met.* 150.20-26 and 152.35-153, 6; Giannantoni *SR* 4A.170.

18. Cf. for example, Sextus Empiricus *Adv. math.* 7.11; *LCL* 2:7; 1B25 Giannantoni, *SR* 4A.168.

19. *DL* 2.92; *LCL* 1:221; Giannantoni *SR* 4A.172.

20. *DL* 2.92; *LCL* 1:221; Giannantoni *SR* 4A.172.

21. Plutarch *Adv. Colot.* 24.1120D; *LCL* 14:269; Giannantoni *SR* 4A.211.

22. Sextus Empiricus *Adv. math.* 7.191; *LCL* 2:103; Giannantoni *SR* 4A.213.

23. Sextus Empiricus *Adv. math.* 7.194; *LCL* 2:105; Giannantoni *SR* 4A.213.

24. Thus has Th. Gomperz understood them *PG* 2:697ff. The only passage that would seem to suggest this tenet is from Sextus Empiricus: "For the Cyrenaic philosophers assert that only the feelings exist, and nothing else; and hence that sound, not being a feeling but productive of feeling, is not an existent" (*Adv. math.* 6.53; *LCL* 4:397; Giannantoni *SR* 4A.219). But, actually such testimony only repeats what others have said, that is, that *for us* only our feeling exist and that the sound, when it is not a feeling does not exist *for us*.

25. It is precisely this Gorgean element (see above the section on Gorgias, especially, 165-167.

26. Xenophon *Memorabilia* 2.1.9; *LCL,* 87; Giannantoni *SR* 4A.163.

27. See the numerous hints in the various testimonies on his life in Giannantoni *SR* 4A.51ff.
28. Sextus Empiricus *Adv. math.* 7.199; *LCL* 2:107, 109; Giannantoni *SR* 4A.213.
29. *DL* 2.88; *LCL* 1:217, 219; Giannantoni *SR* 4A.172.
30. *DL* 2:89; *LCL* 1:219; Giannantoni *SR* 4A.172.
31. *DL* 2.88; *LCL* 1:217, 219; Giannantoni *SR* 4A.172.
32. *DL* 2.90; *LCL* 1:219, 221; Giannantoni *SR* 4A.172.
33. Elianus *Var. hist.*14.6; Giannantoni *SR* 4A.174.
34. Atheneus 12.544a; Giannantoni *SR* 4A.174.
35. It is appropriate, on this point, that Epicurus will carry on his innovations which transformed Cyrenaic hedonism in an essential way.
36. *DL* 2.87ff.; *LCL* 1:217ff.; Giannantoni *SR* 4A.172.
37. Cf. above subsection 1 and notes 9-12.
38. Cicero *De officiis* 3.33.116; *LCL,* 397; cf. also Lactantius *Div. Instit.* 3.8.6ff.; Giannantoni *SR* 4A.189 and Giannantoni *SR* 4A.193.
39. *DL* 2.91; *LCL* 1:221; Giannantoni *SR* 4A.172.
40. Cicero *Acad. pr.* 2.45.139; Giannantoni *SR* 4A.179.
41. Xenophon *Memorabilia* 2.1.11; *LCL,* 87, 89; Giannantoni *SR* 4A.163.
42. On the development of Cyrenaicism, consult Reale 3:55-64.

(pages 281-85) (1-32)

1. Euclid was born at Megara (Plato *Phaedo* 59B-C; Cicero *Acad. pr.* 2.42.129; Strabo 9.1.8), where he lived and found his School. We do not know the dates of his birth or of his death. As a conjecture some scholars locate the life-span of Euclid between 435 and 365 BCE. He must be older than Plato, if it is true, as has been attested by Diogenes Laertius (*DL* 2.106; *LCL* 1:235), that after the death of Socrates Plato and the other friends of Socrates took refuge at Megara with Euclid for political reasons. Only recently has there been a edition of the fragments of Euclid and his followers: K. Döring, *Die Megariker, Kommentierte Sammlung der Testimonien* (Amsterdam, 1972), and G. Giannantoni *Socraticorum reliquiae* (previously cited in the notes to page 389 note 14). A detailed discussion on the dates, biography as well as chronology may be seen in K. Döring, 73ff. (the passages mentioned above correspond to Döring's order as fragments 3A, 26A, 43A, 4B and in G. Giannantoni as 2A.4, 31, 29 and 5). See bibliography in the fifth volume.
2. And they are scarce and insufficient on the delicate points.
3. The great success of the School occurred with Stilpo of whom Diogenes Laertius records: "And so far did he excel all the rest in inventiveness and sophistry that *nearly the whole of Greece* was attracted to him and

joined the School of Megara" (*DL* 2.113; *LCL*1:241, 243; frag. 163A Döring, Giannantoni *SR* 2O.2).

4. Cf. for example, Kurt von Fritz s.v. *Megariker* in Pauly-Wissowa *Real-enzyclopädie der classischen Altertumswissenschaft,* Supplement 5 (1931) 707-724, the same thesis is taken up and repeated by K. Döring in his recent edition of the fragments (cf. note 1, above), chiefly on 83ff.

5. H. J. Krämer, *Arete bei Platon und Aristoteles* (Heidelberg, 1959; Amsterdam, 1967²) 505f. (K. Döring, *Die Megariker* 88f. attempts in vain to refute this interpretation, which we will see, is imposed by the texts.)

6. *DL* 2.106; *LCL*1:235; frag. 31 Döring, Giannantoni *SR* 2A.30.

7. Cicero *Acad. pr.* 2.42.129; *LCL*635; frag. 26A Döring, 2A31 and 3F17. "A famous school was that of the Megarians, whose founder, as I see it recorded, was Xenophanes whom I just mentioned now; next he was followed by Parmenides and Zeno (and so the school of thought derived from them the name of Eleatic) and afterwards by Euclides, the pupil of Socrates, a Megarian (from whom the same school obtained the title of Megarian); their doctrine was that the sole good is that which is always one and alike and the same. These thinkers also took much from Plato. But from Menedemus, who was an Eretrian, they received the designation of the Eretrian school; they placed their good wholly in the mind and in keenness of mental vision whereby the truth is discerned" (trans. H. Rackham).

8. Aristocles quoted by Eusebius *Praep. evang.* 14.7.1; frag. 27 Döring, Giannantoni *SR* 2O.26.

9. Arguing, that is, against the Platonic doctrine of the Ideas, which broke up the unity of Eleatic being and against the Aristotelian doctrine of potency and act, which broke up the univocity and absolute permanence of Eleatic being provided the means by which becoming was to be admitted within the ambit of being, as we will see in the second volume of the series.

10. Cicero *Acad. pr.* 2.42.129; *LCL* 635 (cf. note 7, above).

11. Cicero *Acad. pr.* 2.42.129; *LCL* 635 (cf. note 7, above).

12. *DL* 2.106; *LCL* 1:235; frag. 24 Döring; Giannantoni *SR* 2A.30).

13. Cf. the passage cited above of Aristocles (cf. note 8).

14. *DL* 2.107; *LCL* 1:235, 237; frag. 30 Döring; Giannantoni *SR* 2A.34.

15. Thus the reasoning is formulated by Th. Gomperz with great effectiveness: "Either the similarity reached is that of complete identity, and in such a case we will do better to obtain our conclusions from things themselves rather than for objects which confront us; or it is a matter of only a partial identity and in that case the comparison introduces an exception (which, we can achieve, perverting our judgment)" *PG* 2:632).

16. *DL* 2.107; *LCL* 1:235, 237; frag. 29 Döring; Giannantoni *SR* 2A.34.

17. See above 91ff.
18. cf. above 225ff.
19. *DL* 2.106; *LCL*1:235; frag. 24 Döring; Giannantoni *SR* 2A.30.
20. There are many interesting observations which are due to von Fritz *Megariker* 876f. which are followed by Döring, *Die Megariker* 85ff.
21. *DL* 7.161; *LCL* 2:265; frag. 25 Döring; Giannantoni *SR* 2A.32; cf. the almost verbal correspondence with Plato *Protagoras* 329D, 349B.
22. Plato *Crito* 48A.
23. A. Levi, "Le dottrine filosofiche della scuola di Megara," *Rendiconti della Reale Accademia Nazionale dei Lincei. Classe di scienze morali, storiche e filologiche* ser. 4, vol. 8, fasc. 5-6, Seduta del 10 giugno 1932, 465-499. It is a work of fundamental importance; unfortunately it has escaped the attention of most of the scholars concerned with Megaricism. The passage we have reported is above on pages 313-314.
24. Cf. above, note 7 toward the end.
25. The exact remark made in this regard by Th. Gomperz (*PG* 2:613): "The attempt by Euclid compared to Platonic speculation is like comparing a living being of a very simple structure to a much more complex organism, which achieves various forms in the different phases of its development. Euclid is content, if we may be permitted this expression, to *ethicize* Eleatic metaphysics and *objectivize* and *existentialize* Socratic ethics.
26. Cf. volume 2, on this topic.
27. *DL* 2.106; *LCL*1:235; frag. 31 Döring; Giannantoni *SR* 2A.22.
28. *DL* 2.107; *LCL* 1:235, 237; frag. 8 Döring; Giannantoni *SR* 2A34.
29. Moreover we have seen that Socrates himself does not remain immune to it.
30. Cf. note 23 above A. Levi "Le dottrine filosofiche della scuola di Megara" 472f.
31. Consult the entire section in which we are concerned with Socratic dialectic above 235ff.
32. On the development of the School consult *Reale* 3:45-54.

(pages 287-88) (1-10)

1. Concerning Phaedo, Diogenes Laertius tells us: "Phaedo was a native of Elis, of noble family, who on the fall of that city was taken captive and forcibly consigned to a house of ill-repute. But he would close the door and so contrive to join Socrates's circle, and in the end Socrates induced Alcibiades or Crito with their friends to ransom him; from that time onwards he studied philosophy as became a free man" (*DL* 2.105; *LCL* 1:233; Giannantoni *SR* 3A.1). He wrote dialogues, among which was *Zopyrus* and *Simon*. Diogenes mentions also other titles, which he says

expressly some did not consider authentic. Cf. also what Gellius *Noctes atticae* 2.18; *LCL* 1:171, 173; and Strabo 9.1.8; Giannantoni *SR* 3A.3 and 1 say about our philosopher.

2. Cf. Timon quoted in Diogenes Laertius 2.107; *LCL* 1:237; Giannantoni *SR* 2A.34 (we quoted the fragment in the preceding chapter on page 284).

3. Cf. Themistius *Orat.* 34.5; Giannantoni *SR* 4A.166.

4. Cicero *Tusc disp.* 4.36.80; *LCL,* 203,205.

5. Cicero *De fato.* 5.10ff. The word *voluntas* is Ciceronian; more exactly, from an historical point of view, the terminology of the preceding passage speaks of *ratio,* that is, of *logos;* actually, the term "voluntas" is unknown to Socratic thought, on the theoretical level.

6. Julian *Epistle* 82.445a Bidez-Cumont; Giannantoni *SR* 3A.2.

7. Seneca *Epistle* 94, 41; *LCL* 3:37, 39; Giannantoni *SR* 3A.12.

8. Cf. above 373, note 1.

9. Cf. *DL* 2.105; *LCL* 1:233, 235. For Menedemus and Asclepiades cf. Giannantoni *SR* 3G.1-25 and 3H.1-5.

10. Cf. *DL* 2.105; *LCL* 1:233, 235; Giannantoni *SR* 3A.1. For Menedemus and Asclepiades cf. Giannantoni *SR* 3F.1-25 and 3G.1-5. See also what we said in Reale 3:55-56.

(pages 289) (1-3)

1. L. Robin *Storia* 204ff.

2. L. Robin *Storia* 217ff.

3. L. Robin *Storia* 218.

(pages 293-304) (1-50)

1. The reader can adequately orient himself with respect to the different ways of addressing and treating the complex problematic of Orphism by reading the following works: E. Rohde, *Psyche, Seelenkult und Unsterblichkeitsglaube der Griechen* 2 vols. (Freiburg im Bresgau, 1890-1894), trans. W. B. Hillis from the eighth edition, *Psyche: the Cult of Souls and Belief in Immortality among the Greeks* (New York and London: Kegan Paul, Trench, Trubner & Co., Ltd. and Harcourt, Brace & Company, Inc., 1925); reprinted by Harper & Row, Publishers [Harper Torch Book] (New York, 1966) in two volumes from which our quotations are taken; V. Macchioro, *Zagreus, Studi intorno all'Orphismo* (Florence, 1930); W. K. C. Guthrie, *Orpheus and Greek Religion* (London, 1935, 1952[2]); K. Ziegler, "Orpheus," in Pauly-Wissowa *Real-enzyclopädie der classischen Altertumswissenschaft* 18 (1939) 1200-1316; the same author and place under *Orphische Dichtung* 18 (1942) 1321-1417; I. M. Linforth, *The Arts of Orpheus* (Berkeley, 1941; New York, 1973[2]); M. P. Nilsson, *Geschichte der*

griechischen Religion vol.1 (Munich, 1941; 1967³); E. R. Dodds, *The Greeks and the Irrational* (Berkeley-Los Angeles, 1951). In these volumes further bibliography may be found.

2. Cf. *Orphica* Rec. G. Hermannus, cum notis H. Stephani, A. Chr. Eschenbachii, J. M. Gesneri, Th. Tyrwhitti (Lipsiae 1805) repro. (Olms: Hildesheim, 1969); *Aglaophamus sive de Theologiae mysticae Graecorum causis libri tres conscripsit* C. A. Lobeck *idemque poetarum Orphicorum dispersas reliquias collegit* (Regimontii Prussorum, 1829); *Orphica* Rec. E. Abel (Lipsiae et Pragae 1885). For the *Hymns* in particular see G. Quandt, *Orphei Hymni* (Berlin, 1955). For the *Argonautica* see also the edition of G. Dottin (Paris, 1930) with French translation.

3. *Orphicorum Fragmenta* Collegit O. Kern (Berlin, 1922; 1963²). A new collection of the fundamental fragments, in a critical edition, with Italian translation and annotations is found in G. Colli, *La sapienza greca* 1. *Dioniso, Apollo, Eleusi, Orfeo, Museo, Iperborei, Enigma* (Milan: Adelphi, 1977) 117-289. Given the soundness and range of this collection, we will use their numbering system (although in addition to that of Kern which is canonic) because it contains new material. Also the translations of the fragments and the testimonies which we report, preserve the contrary indications of Colli himself.

4. Ibycus, frag. 17 Diehl; test. 2 Kern; 4A.1a Colli.

5. Euripides *Alcestis* 962-972 and *Hippolytus* 952-954; tests. 82 and 213 Kern; 4A14 and A16 Kern; Plato *Republic* 364Eff.; frag. 3 Kern; 4A41 Colli.

6. Herodotus 2.81; test. 216 Kern; 4A12 Colli; Aristophanes *The Frogs* 1032ff.; test. 90 Kern; 4A25 Colli.

7. Aristotle *De philosophia* frag. 7 Ross (page 80); test. 188 Kern; 4A56 Colli.

8. Cf. Zeller-Mondolfo *LPG* 1.1.119, note 1.

9. See on the argument W. Jaeger *Theology* 55-72.

10. See the information which we gave in this regard in the volume, G. Reale, *Aristotele, Trattato sul cosmo per Alessandro* (Naples: Lofreddo, 1974) 273ff. We quote the hymn above in the text at 302-303.

11. Pindar frag. 131b Snell; 4A9 Colli.

12. Cf. for example E.R. Dodds *The Greeks and the Irrational* 139ff.

13. Xenophon *Cyropaedia* 8.7.21; *LCL,* 433,435.

14. Aristotle *De philosophia* frag. 12a Ross (page 84).

15. Cf. E. R. Dodds, *The Greeks and the Irrational* 139ff.

16. Plato *Cratylus* 400C; frag. 8 Kern; 4A34 Colli.

17. Frag. 32c Kern; 4A65 Colli.

18. Frag. 32b(I-III) Kern; 4A70a Colli.

19. Euripides *Polydus* frag. 638 Nauck reported by Plato *Gorgias* 492E; *LCL,* 415; 4A23 Colli.

20. Consult *Reale* 3:127.

21. Zeller-Mondolfo *LPG* 1.1.137.

22. U. von Wilamowitz Möllendorff, *Der Glaube der Hellenen* 2 vols. (Darmstadt, 1959³, 1932¹) 2:190ff.

23. Pindar frag. 133 Snell; 4A5 Colli; *LCL* 301, 303 trans. W. R. M. Lamb.

24. Pindar *Olympia* 2.56-72; 4A6 Colli. [Trans. Frank J. Nisetich *Pindar's Victory Songs* (Baltimore: Johns Hopkins University Press, 1980) 90].

25. 44.B.14 *D-K* 1:413-14.

26. Plato *Meno* 81B-C.

27. Aristotle *Protrepticus* frag. 10b Ross (pages 41, 42); 4A55 Colli.

28. Aristotle *De anima* A5.410b27-411a1; 4A60 Colli.

29. *DL* 8.8; *LCL* 2:327, 329; 14.A.19 *D-K* 1:105.

30. Cf. Plato *Phaedo* 80Cff.

31. Plato *Laws* 9.870D-E.

32. Plato *Laws* 9.872D-E.

33. E. R. Dodds, *Greeks and the Irrational* 150-151.

34. Cf. W. K. C. Guthrie *Orpheus and Greek Religion* 167ff.

35. Pindar frag. 129 Snell; 4A7 Colli.

36. Gold plates found at Thuri; frag. 32f Kern; 4A67 Colli.

37. On the theme see: W. K. C. Guthrie *Orpheus and Greek Religion* 83ff.; W. Jaeger *Theology* 55ff.

38. Cf. Eudemus of Rhodes frag. 150 Wehrli; frag. 28 Kern; 4B9 Colli.

39. Damascius *De principiis* 123 bis.1.317.15ff. Ruelle; frag. 54 Kern; 4B72 Colli.

40. E. Rohde *Psyche* 2:339-40.

41. Frag. 21 Kern; 4A71 Colli.

42. W. K. C. Guthrie *Orpheus and Greek Religion* 100.

43. Consult E. Rohde *Psyche* 341ff. and the passages which are referenced there.

44. This point is demonstrated quite well by E. R. Dodds, *The Greeks and the Irrational* 156.

45. Cf. *Reale* 2, on this topic.

46. Cf. W. K. C. Guthrie *Orpheus and Greek Religion* 216ff.

47. On some Orphic ritual formulas cf. W. K. C. Guthrie *Orpheus and Greek Religion)* 231ff.

48. Cf. E. R. Dodds *The Greeks and the Irrational* 154.

49. Cf. above, pages 67ff.

50. Plato *Phaedo* 69C-D.

(pages 307-26) (1-80)

1. Cf. Aristotle *Metaphysics* A1-2.
2. Aristotle *Metaphysics* A3.983b6ff..
3. Plato *Phaedo* 96Aff.; Aristotle *Metaphysics* A8 passim.
4. Aristotle *Metaphysics* A3.983b6ff.
5. Aristotle *Metaphysics* Γ1.1003a21ff.
6. Aristotle *Metaphysics* E1.1025b1ff.
7. Aristotle *Metaphysics* A3.983b20ff.
8. 12.A.15 *D-K* 1:85 and 12.B.3 *D-K* 1:89.
9. 13.B.2 *D-K* 1:95.
10. 22.B.10 *D-K* 1:152-53
11. 22.B.41 *D-K* 1:160.
12. 22.B.50 *D-K* 1:161.
13. 28.B.1 *D-K* 1:230, vv.28-32.
14. Cf. Plato *Republic* 6:485Aff.
15. Cf. Plato *Republic* 6:486Aff.
16. Cf. Plato *Republic* 6:486Aff.
17. Plotinus *Enneads* 6.5.12.
18. Cf. above 157ff.
19. Cf. above 165ff.
20. Cf. above 201ff.
21. Cf. above 199ff.
22. Cf. above 225ff.
23. Cf. *Reale* 3 passim.
24. Plotinus *Enneads* 2.9.9; Marcus Aurelius *Meditations* 2.9.
25. Plato *Republic* 7:537C. Those who are capable of seeing the whole are called *synoptikos;* on this notion cf. W. Jaeger *Paideia* 2:165 and 315ff. and 395, note 22.
26. Cf. Aristotle *Metaphysics* A1 from the beginning.
27. Aristotle *Protrepticus* frag. 41 Düring.
28. Cf. Aristotle *Metaphysics* A1 passim.
29. Aristotle *Protrepticus* frag. 7 Ross (p. 36, 37); 73-77 Düring.
30. Plato *Theatetus* 155D.
31. Aristotle *Metaphysics* A2.982b12ff.
32. Aristotle *Metaphysics* A2.982b18ff.
33. Plato *Theatetus* 173D-174D; *LCL,* 119, 121..
34. Aristotle *Protrepticus* frag. 11 Ross (p. 43-46); 18-19 Düring.
35. Cf. above, note 4.
36. Plato *Republic* 475E.
37. Consult *Reale,* volume 2 on this topic.

38. Aristotle *Protrepticus* frag. 12 Ross (p. 46-47); 42-44 Düring.
39. Cornelia de Vogel *Philosophia* Part I. *Studies in Greek Philosophy* (Assen, 1970) 22ff.
40. Cf. above 328f., note 1; 330, note 1; 337 note 1; 338f., note 1.
41. Cf. above 150ff.
42. Cf. above 221ff.
43. Plato *Gorgias* 521D.
44. Plato *Republic* 6:499B-C
45. Plato *Republic* 7:517C
46. Cf. Plato *Republic* 6:500C-D
47. Cf. Plato *Republic* 7:518C
48. Cf. Plato *Republic* 7:516Aff.
49. Plato *Phaedrus* 248C.
50. Aristotle *Protrepticus* frag. 13 Ross (p. 47-49); 51 Düring.
51. Cf. *Reale* 2, Second Part, Third Section, 6 fin., "Perfect Happiness."
52. Cf. *Reale* 3 passim.
53. *DL* 9.65; *LCL* 2:479; Timon frag. 67 Diels.
54. Sextus Empiricus *Adv. math.* 9.20; *LCL* 3.11; Timon frag. 68 Diels.
55. 22.B.119 *D-K* 1:177.
56. 22.B.4 *D-K* 1:151; cf. above page 54f.
57. 68.B.171 *D-K* 2:179; cf. above page 124.
58. Plato *Gorgias* 470E.
59. Cf. *Reale* 2, Second Part, Third Section, 6 fin., "Perfect Happiness."
60. Cf. *Reale* 2, Second Part, Second Section, 11ff. "The Nature of the Immobile Movent."
61. Epicurus *Epistle to Menoeceus* 122; *DL* 10.122; *LCL* 2:649.
62. 21.B.34 *D-K* 1:137.
63. 22.B.123 *D-K* 1:178.
64. 68.B.117 *D-K* 2:166.
65. Cf. above 199ff; 241ff.
66. Cf. *Reale* 3:309ff.; 4:151ff.
67. Cf. above page 84.
68. Plato *Republic* 5: 476ff.; cf. vol. 2, on this topic.
69. Cf. for example, Aristotle *Metaphysics* Z.3.1029b3ff.
70. Cf. *Reale* 3: 124ff; 221ff.
71. Cf. *Reale,* volume 4 on this topic.
72. See the passages reported in *Reale* 3:3.
73. Cf. above 244ff.
74. Cf. *Reale* 2, on this topic.

75. Cf. *Reale,* volume 4 on this topic.
76. Aristotle *Rhetoric* A1.1355a15-17.
77. Aristotle *Metaphysics* α 1.993b7ff.
78. Cf. *Reale* 2, on this topic.
79. This is not only true of Plato but it seems also of Aristotle himself; cf. *Reale* 2, on this topic.
80. Cf. Aristotle *Metaphysics* Γ3-8.

BIBLIOGRAPHY

The bibliography which is listed here only indicates those works which were expressly cited in the course of the volume. The reader will find all the current bibliography in the fifth volume, arranged according to a new and effective method. For the methodological reasons explained in the Introduction, *the author has given clear pre-eminence to the primary literature, that is, to texts, to the testimonies, and to the ancient sources, with direct citations and with explicit references.*

Adorno, F. *Socrate* (Bari, 1970).

Alfieri, V. E. *Atomisti. Frammenti e testimonianze* (Bari, 1936)

------. "Per la cronologia della Scuola di Abdera," *Rivista critica di storia della filosofia* 7 (1952) 488-501.

------. *Estudios le historie de la filosifia* (Tucumaman, 1957)

------. *I Presocratici* 2 vols. (Bari, 1969).

------. *Atomos Idea. L'origine del concetto dell'atomo nel pensiero greco* (Florence, 1953; Galatina, 1979²).

Bignone, E. *Empedocle* (Milan, 1916; Rome, 1963²).

------. *Studi sul pensiero antico* (Naples, 1938).

Burkert, W. *Weisheit und Wissenschaft: Studien zu Pythagoras, Philolaos und Platon* (Nürnberg, 1962) English translation *Lore and Science in Ancient Pythagoreanism* (Cambridge, Mass.: Harvard University Press, 1972).

Burnet, J. *Plato's Phaedo* (Oxford, 1911).

------. "The Socratic Doctrine of the Soul," in *Proceedings of the British Academy* 7 (1915-1916) republished in *Essays and Addresses* (London, 1929).

------. *Early Greek Philosophy* (London: A. & C. Black, 1930⁴).

Calogero, G. *Storia della logica antica* 1. *L'età arcaica (Bari, 1967).*

------. *Studi sull'eleatismo* (Rome, 1932) [new edition Florence, 1977].

Carbonara, C. *La filosofia greca, I Presocratici* (Naples, 1962²).

Chroust, Anton-Hermann. *Socrates Man and Myth, The Two Socratic Apologies of Xenophon* (London: Routledge & Kegan Paul, 1957).

de Vogel, C. "The Present State of the Socratic Problem," *Phronesis* 1 (1955) 26-35.

Decleva Caizzi, F. *Antisthenes fragmenta* (Milan-Varese, 1966).

------. *Antiphontis tetralogiae* (Milan-Varese, 1968).

Diels, H. "Verhandl.d. 35 Philologenvers.," (1882). *Rheinisches Museum* (1887).

------. *Archiv für Geschichte der Philosophie* (1888).

------. *Die Fragmente der Vorsokratiker* (Berlin: Weidmann, 1903) and Walter

Kranz (Berlin: Weidmann, 1934-37⁵).

Deman, Th. *Le témoignage d'Aristote sur Socrate* (Paris, 1942).

Dittmar, H. *Aischines von Sphettos* (Berlin, 1912).

Dudley, D. R. *A History of Cynicism* (London, 1937).

Frank, E. *Platon und die sogenannten Pythagoreer* (Halle, 1923).

Freeman, K. *Ancilla to the Pre-Socratic Philosophers* (Oxford: B. Blackwell, 1948).

------. *Pre-Socratic Philosophers, A Companion to Diels* (Oxford: B. Blackwells, 1946).

Giannantoni, G. *I Cirenaici. Raccolta delle fonti antiche, traduzione e studio introduttivo* (Florence, 1958).

Gigon, O. *Sokrates. Sein Bild in Dichtung und Geschichte* (Bern, 1947).

Gomperz, T. *Griechische Denker* (Leipzig, 1896).

------. *Sophistik und Rhetorik* (Leipzig-Berlin 1912, Darmstadt 1965).

Gorman, P. *Pythagoras: A Life* (Routledge & Kegan Paul, 1979).

Guthrie, W. K. C. *A History of Greek Philosophy* Vol. 1 (Cambridge, 1962).

Hegel, F. *Vorlesungen über die Geschichte der Philosophie,* K. L. Michelet, ed. 2 vols. 1833-1836.

Highet, G. *Paideia* (Oxford, 1954) [translation of Jaeger's *Paideia*].

Hölderlin, *Der Tod des Empedokles. Empedokles auf dem Aetna* (1798-1800 posthumous).

Jaeger, W. *Paideia. Die Formung des Griechischen Menschen* (Berlin and Leipzig: 1936²).

------. *Die Theologie der frühen griechischen Denker* (Stuttgart, 1953).

Lanza, D. *Anassagora. Testimonianze e frammenti* (Florence, 1966).

Lee, H. D. P. *Zeno of Elea* (Cambridge, 1936, 1967²).

Levi, A. *Storia della sofistica* ed. D. Pesce (Naples, 1966).

Maddalena, A. *Ionici. Testimonianze e frammenti* (Florence, 1963; repr. 1970).

Maier, H. *Sokrates. Sein Werk und seine geschichtliche Stellung* (Tübingen, 1913).

Marchant, E. C. *Memorabilia* and *Oeconomicus* Loeb Classical Library Series, (Harvard University Press, 1965).

------. *Hellenica, Anabasis, Apology,* and *Symposium* (trans.) in three volumes Loeb Classical Library (1900).

------. *Scripta Minora* (trans.) in one volume Loeb Classical Library (1900).

Migliori, M. *La filosofia di Gorgia* (Milan, 1973).

Miller, W. *Cyropaedia* (trans.) Loeb Classical Library Series (1900).

Mondolfo, R. *Il pensiero antico* (Florence, 1950²).

Otto, W. F. *Die Götter Griechenlands* (Frankfurt am Main, 1956⁴).

Owens, J. *A History of Ancient Western Philosophy* (New York: Prentice-Hall, 1959).

------. "The Interpretation of the Heraclitean Fragments" in *An Etienne Gilson Tribute* (Milwaukee: The Marquette University Press, 1959) (ed.) Charles J. O'Neil, 148-68.

Raven, J. E. *Pythagoreans and Eleatics* (Cambridge at the University Press, 1948).

Reale, G. *Protagora. Traduzione, introduzione e commento di G. Reale* (Brescia: La Scuola, 1969, 1984⁵).

------. *Aristotele, Trattato sul cosmo* (Naples: Lofreddo, 1974).

------. *A History of Ancient Philosophy* III. *The Systems of the Hellenistic Age* ed. and trans. J. R. Catan from the third Italian edition (Albany: State University of New York Press, 1985).

------. *Storia della filosofia antica* (Milan: Vita e Pensiero) 5 vols. various dates and editions.

Reinhardt, K. *Parmenides und die Geschichte der griechischen Philosophie* (Bonn, 1916).

Rey, R. *La jeunesse de la science grecque* (Paris, 1933).

Robin, L. *La pensée grecque et les origines de l'esprit scientifique (Paris, 1923). Greek Thought and the Origins of the Scientific Spirit.* Translated by R. M. Dobie. New York: Russell & Russell, 1967.

Robinson, E. S. (trans.), *The Theology of the Early Greek Philosophers* [Gifford Lectures 1936] W. Jaeger (Oxford at the Clarendon Press, 1947; reprinted 1948, 1952, 1960, 1964).

Rohde, E. "Verhandl. d. 34. Philologenvers," (1881).

------. *Psyche* (Tübingen, 1983) and revised many times.

------. *Kl. Schriften* 1. (1901).

Saitta, G. *L'illuminismo della sofistica greca* (Milan, 1938).

Sarri, F. *Socrate e la genesi storica dell'idea occidentale di anima* (Rome: Edizioni Abete, 1975).

Schleiermacher, F. "Ueber den Werth des Sokrates als Philosophen," *Sämmtliche Werke* 3.2.287-308.

Schwabl, H. "Sein und Doxa bei Parmenides" *Weiner Studien* 66 (1953) 50-75.

Snell, B. *Die Entdeckung des Geistes. Studien zur Entstehung des europäischen Denkens bei den Griechen* (Hamburg, 1946).

Strauss, L. *Socrates and Aristophanes* (New York-London, 1966).

------. *Xenophon's Socratic Discourse: An Interpretation of the "Oeconomicus"* (Ithaca-London: Cornell University Press, 1970).

------. *Xenophon's Socrates* (Ithaca-London: Cornell University Press, 1972.

Taylor, A. E. *Plato, the Man and his Works* (New York: Humanities Press,

1949[6]).

------. *Socrates*. (Garden City: Doubleday, 1953).

Timpanaro Cardini, M. La Nuova Italia Editrice (*Pitagorici. Testimonianze e frammenti* 1. (Florence, 1958); 2. (Florence, 1962); 3. (Florence, 1964) "Biblioteca di Studi Superiori."

Theiler, W. *Zur Geschichte der teleologischen Naturbetrachtung bis auf Aristoteles* (Zurich, 1925).

Untersteiner, M. *I Sofisti* (Milan, 1967[2]).

------. "Le origini sociali della sofistica," in *Studi di filosofia greca in onore Rodolfo Mondolfo* ed. V. E. Alfieri and M. Untersteiner (Bari, 1950) 121-80.

------. *Senofane. Testimonianze e frammenti* (Florence, 1956).

------. "La Doxa di Parmenide" *Dianoia* 2 (1956) 203-21.

------. *Parmenide. Testimonianze e frammenti* (Florence, 1958).

------. "Nota sulla parola 'sofista'" in *Sofisti. Testimonianze e frammenti* 1. (Florence: La Nuova Italia, 1961 [2]).

Vilhena, V. de Magalhães. *Le problème de Socrate. Le Socrate historique et le Socrate de Platon* (Paris, 1952).

------. *Socrate et la légende platonicienne* (Paris, 1952).

------. *Pythagoras and Early Pythagoreanism* (Assen: Van Gorcum, 1966).

Wilamowitz-Moellendorff, U. von. *Der Glaube der Hellenen* (Darmstadt, 1959[3]).

Zeller, E. *Die Philosophie der Griechen in ihrer geschichtlichen Entwicklung* (Leipzig: G. R. Reisland, 1892) I.1. (Leipzig, 1919[6]).

Zeller-Mondolfo, *La filosofia dei greci nel suo sviluppo storico* Prima Parte, I Presocratici, vol. 3 [Florence: "La Nuova Italia" Editrice, 1967].

Zeller-Nestle, *Die Philos. der Griechen in ihrer geschichtlichen Entwicklung.* 3 vols. 1844-52. Edited and enlarged by W. Nestle. Leipzig, 1920[6]. Hildesheim: G. Olms, 1963.

Outlines of the History of Greek Philosophy. Translated by L. R. Palmer. London: Kegan Paul, 1931.

Zeppi, S. "L'etica di Prodico," *Rivista critica di storia della filosofia,* 1956. Also in *Studi sulla filosofia presocratica* (Florence, 1962).

------. *Protagora e la filosofia del suo tempo* (Florence, 1961).

INDEX OF NAMES CITED

Wherever possible we have checked the spellings of Greek names in Lempiere's Classical Dictionary (London, Boston; Routledge & Kegan Paul, 1984³), if they were not found there, we have used the spellings in the Loeb Classical Library Series. Where applicable the pages in bold italic face indicate the main treatment of the individual.

INDEX OF GREEK TERMS CITED

ἰδέας 111

κυβερνᾶν 40
Κυνόσαργες 268
κύων 268

νοῦς 113

ὁ βίος θεωρετικός 68
ὁμοῖον 310
ὂν ᾗ ὄν 308
οὐσία 119

πάντα ῥεῖ 50
περιέχειν 40
πόνοι 217
πόνος 176, 268

σημεῖον 232
Σφαῖρος 105, 108, 109
σπέρματα 111
σῆμα 296 v. 16
σημαίνει 296 v. 16
σῴζηται 296 v. 16
σῶμα 296 v. 16

τὰ δαιμόνια 232
τὸ ἄτομον 119
τὸ δαιμόνιον 233
τὸ θεῖον 40
τὸ θειοῦ 232
τὸ μηδενὸς προσδεῖσθαι 264
τῶν ἀνθρωπείων 201

ὑπὸ τοῦ θεοῦ 234

φρόνησις 283
φωνή 232

INDEX OF
CITATIONS OF CLASSICAL SOURCES

The (t) indicates that the text is quoted at this point in the notes.

Aetius

Alexander of Aphrodisias

Ammonius

Antisthenes

Aristophanes

Aristotle

Aristotle *Protrepticus* frag. 13 Ross (p. 47-49); 51 Düring, *378 n. 50.*

Aristotle *Protrepticus* frag. 41 Düring, *377 n. 27.*

Aristotle *De philosophia* frag. 7 Ross (p.80); test. 188 Kern; 4A.56 Colli, *375 n. 7.*

Aristotle *De philosophia* frag. 12a Ross (p.84), *375 n. 14.*

Aristotle *Topics* A 11.104b19-21; frag. 47C Decleva Caizzi; Giannantoni *SR* 5A.153, *367 n. 22.*

Aristotle *Sophistical Refutations* 1.163a21, *347 n. 5.*

Aristotle *Physics* A 4.187a20ff., *330 n. 6.*

Aristotle *Physics* Γ 4.203b6ff., *330 n. 3.*

Aristotle *Physics* Γ 6.213b22ff., *335 n. 10.*

Aristotle *Physics* Z 9.239b14ff., *339 n. 6.*

Aristotle *Physics* Z 9.239b30ff., *339 n. 7.*

Aristotle *De caelo* B 13.295b10ff., *330 n. 11.*

Aristotle *De caelo* Γ 5.303b10ff., *345 n. 6.*

Aristotle *De generatione et corruptione* A 6.322b12ff., *345 n. 12.*

Aristotle *De generatione et corruptione* A 8.324b35ff., *344 n. 4.*

Aristotle *De generatione et corruptione* A 8.325a2, *340 n. 11.*

Aristotle *De anima* A 2.405a19ff., *329 n. 4.*

Aristotle *De anima* A 2.405a19ff., *330 n. 14.*

Aristotle *De anima* A 2.405b1ff., *345 n. 8.*

Aristotle *De anima* A 5.410b27-411a1; 4A.60 Colli, *375 n. 28.*

Aristotle *De anima* A 5.411a7ff., *330 n. 11.*

Aristotle *De anima* A 5.411a7, *329 n. 3.*

Aristotle *Met.* A 1, *377 n. 26.*

Aristotle *Met.* A 1 passim, *377 n. 28.*

Aristotle *Met.* A 1-2, *377 n. 1.*

Aristotle *Met.* A 1.981b23ff., *327 n. 4.*

Aristotle *Met.* A 2.982b11-28, *328 n. 1.*

Aristotle *Met.* A 2.982b12ff., *377 n. 31.*

Aristotle *Met.* A 2.982b18ff., *328 n. 1.*

Aristotle *Met.* A 2.982b18ff., *377 n. 32.*

Aristotle *Met.* A 2.982b29-983a11, *328 n. 2*(t).

Aristotle *Met.* A 3.983b6ff., *329 n. 2.*

Aristotle *Met.* A 3.983b6ff., *377 n. 2.*

Aristotle *Met.* A 3.983b6ff., *377 n. 4.*

Aristotle *Met.* A 3.983b9ff., *329 n. 6.*

Aristotle *Met.* A 3.983b20ff. *377 n. 7.*

Aristotle *Met.* A 3.983b20-27, *329 n. 8.*

Aristotle *Met.* A 3.984a1-3, *330 n. 9.*

Aristotle *Met.* A 3.984a3ff., *345 n. 8.*

Aristotle *Met.* A 4.985a18, *342 n. 17.*

Aristotle *Met.* A 5.985b23-986a3, *334 n. 1.*

Aristotle *Met.* A 5.985b23, *334 n. 5.*

Aristotle *Met.* A 5.986b4ff., *334 n. 3.*

Aristotle *Met.* A 5.986b21ff., *336 n. 14.*

Aristotle *Met.* A 6.987b1ff., *364 n. 19.*

Aristotle *Met.* A 7.988a23ff., *345 n. 5.*

Aristotle *Met.* A 8 passim, *377 n. 3.*

Aristotle *Met.* ā 1.993b7ff., *379 n. 77.*

Aristotle *Met.* B 2.996a32ff.; Giannantoni, *SR* 4A.170, *370 n. 17.*

Aristotle *Met.* Γ 1.1003a21ff., *377 n. 5.*

Aristotle *Met.* Γ 3-8, *379 n. 80.*

Aristotle *Met.* Δ 5.1010a10ff., *332 n. 5.*

Aristotle *Met.* Δ 29.1024b26-34ff.; frag. 47A Decleva Caizzi; Giannantoni *SR* 5A.152, *367 n. 22.*

Aristotle *Met.* E 3.1025b1ff., *377 n. 6.*

Aristotle *Met.* Z 3.1029b3ff., *378 n. 69.*

Aristotle *Met.* H 3.1043b4-23ff.; frag. 44A Decleva Caizzi, *366, n. 18.*

Aristotle *Met.* H 3.1043b4-23ff.; frag. 44A Decleva Caizzi, *366, n. 19.*

Aristotle *Met.* K 6.1062b13ff., *348 n. 5.*

Aristotle *Met.* M 4.1078b23-30, *364 n. 20.*

Aristotle *Met.* M 4.1078b30ff., *364 n. 21.*

Aristotle *Met.* M 9.1086b2ff., *364 n. 21.*

Aristotle *Nicomachean Ethics* H 2.1145b23-27, *360 n. 39.*

Aristotle *Nicomachean Ethics* Z.13 *360 n. 41.*

Aristotle *Nicomachean Ethics* Z 13.1144b28ff., *360 n. 38.*

Aristotle *Politics* A.13.1260a27, *350 n. 19.*

Aristotle *Rhetoric* A.1.1355a15-17, *379 n. 76.*

Aristotle *Rhetoric* B.24.1402a23, *348 n. 8.*

Pseudo-Aristotle

Ps. Aristotle *De Melisso, Xenophane, Gorgia* 5.979a13ff.; *LCL,* 497ff., *350 n. 7.*

Ps. Aristotle *De Melisso, Xenophane, Gorgia* 5-6.979a11-980b21, *350 n. 3*

Ps. Aristotle *De Melisso, Xenophane, Gorgia* 6.980a20; *LCL,* 505, *350 n. 13.*

Asclepius

Asclepius *In Arist. Met.* 150.20-26, *370 n. 17.*

Asclepius *In Arist. Met.* 152.35-153.6; Giannantoni *SR* 4A.170, *370 n. 17.*

Athenaeus

Athenaeus *Deipnosoph.* 5.276B, *368 n. 41.*

Athenaeus *Deipnosoph.*12.544a; Giannantoni *SR* 4A.174, *371 n. 34.*

St. Augustine

Augustine, St. *The City of God* 8.2, *331 n. 9.*

Cicero

Cicero *Acad. pr.* 2.42.129, *371 n. 1.*

Cicero *Acad. pr.* 2.42.129; *LCL,* 635, *372 n. 10.*

Cicero *Acad. pr.* 2.42.129; *LCL,* 635, *372 n. 11.*

Cicero *Acad. pr.* 2.42.129; *LCL,* 635; frag. Döring; Giannantoni *SR* 2A.31 and 3F.17, *372 n. 7*(t).

Cicero *Acad. pr.* 2.45.139; Giannantoni *SR* 4A.179, *371 n. 40.*

Cicero *De fato.* 5.10ff., *374 n. 5.*

Cicero *De natura deorum* 1.10.26, *331 n. 8.*

Cicero *De natura deorum* 1.13.32, *367 n. 38.*

Cicero *De natura deorum* 1.43.120, *344 n. 16.*

Cicero *De officiis.* 3.33.116,*LCL,* 397 *371 n. 38.*

Cicero *De orat.* 3.17, *368 n. 41.*

Cicero *Tusculan Disputations* 4.36.80; *LCL,* 203, 205, *374 n. 4.*

Cicero *Tusculan Disputations* 5.4.10; *LCL,* 435, *347 n. 7.*

Clement of Alexandria

Clem. Alex. *Protr.* 6.71.1, *367 n. 38.*

Clem. Alex. *Stromata* 1.16.63, *368 n. 41.*

Clem. Alex. *Stromata* 1.22 (92, 11 Stählin), *327 n. 2*

Clem. Alex. *Stromata* 2.20.121.1, *367 n. 27.*

Clem. Alex. *Stromata* 2.20.107, *367 n. 28.*

Clem. Alex. *Stromata* 2.21.130, *367 n. 36.*

Clem. Alex. *Stromata* 5.14.108,4, *337 n. 38.*

Clem. Alex. *Stromata* 5.109 (399.16 Stählin), *336 n. 13.*

Damascius

Damascius *De principiis* 132 bis. I.317.15ff. Ruelle; frag. 54 Kern; 4B.72 Colli, *376 n. 39.*

Diels-Kranz

Seven Sages
10.A.2 *D-K* 1:62, *346 n. 2.*
10.A.3 *D-K* 1:62-66, *236 n. 2.*

Thales

11.A.1 *D-K* 1:67, *329 n. 1.*
11.A.1 *D-K* 1:67, *330 n. 13.*
11.A.1 *D-K* 1:67, *330 n. 15.*
11.A.12 *D-K* 1:76-77, *329 n. 2.*
11.A.12 *D-K* 1:76-77, *329 n. 6.*
11.A.12 *D-K* 1:76-77, *329 n. 8.*
11.A.22 *D-K* 1:79, *329 n. 3.*
11.A.22 *D-K* 1:79, *329 n. 4.*
11.A.22 *D-K* 1:79, *330 n. 11.*
11.A.22 *D-K* 1:79, *330 n. 14.*
11.A.23 *D-K* 1:79, *330 n. 12.*
11.B.1 *D-K* 1:80, *330 n. 10.*

Anaximander

12.A.1 *D-K* 1:81, *330 n. 1.*
12.A.2 *D-K* 1:82, *330 n. 1.*
12.A.9 *D-K* 1:83, *330 n. 1.*
12.A.9 *D-K* 1:83, *330 n. 2.*
12.A.9 *D-K* 1:83, *330 n. 6.*
12.A.9 *D-K* 1:83, *330 n. 6.*
12.A.10 *D-K* 1:83, *330 n. 6.*
12.A.10 *D-K* 1:83, *330 n. 9.*
12.A.11 *D-K* 1:83-84, *330 n. 1.*
12.A.11 *D-K* 1:83-34, *330 n. 9.*
12.A.11 *D-K* 1:84, *330 n. 11.*
12.A.12 *D-K* 1:84, *330 n. 1.*
12.A.15 *D-K* 1:85, *330 n. 3.*
12.A.15 *D-K* 1:85, *377 n. 8.*
12.A.17 *D-K* 1:86, *330 n. 5.*

21.B.26 *D-K* 1:135, *336 n. 18.*
21.B.27 *D-K* 1:135, *336 n. 22.*
21.B.29 *D-K* 1:136, *336 n. 23.*
21.B.32 *D-K* 1:136, *336 n. 10.*
21.B.33 *D-K* 1:136, *336 n. 24.*
21.B.34 *D-K* 1:137, *378 n. 62.*

Heraclitus

22.A.1 *D-K* 1:139, *331 n. 1*
22.B.4 *D-K* 1:151, *378 n. 56.*
22.B.10 *D-K* 1:152-53, *332 n. 13.*
22.B.10 *D-K* 1:152-53, *377 n. 10.*
22.B.12 *D-K* 1:154, *332 n. 2.*
22.B.23 *D-K* 1:156, *332 n. 9.*
22.B.30 *D-K* 1:157-58, *332 n. 19.*
22.B.31 *D-K* 1:158, *332 n. 20.*
22.B.41 *D-K* 1:160, *377 n. 11.*
22.B.49a *D-K* 1:161, *332 n. 4.*
22.B.50 *D-K* 1:161, *332 n. 14.*
22.B.50 *D-K* 1:161, *377 n. 12.*
22.B.53 *D-K* 1:162, *332 n. 7.*
22.B.60 *D-K* 1:164, *332 n. 10.*
22.B.66 *D-K* 1:165, *332 n. 22.*
22.B.67 *D-K* 1:165, *332 n. 21.*
22.B.88 *D-K* 1:170, *332 n. 12.*
22.B.90 *D-K* 1:171, *332 n. 18.*
22.B.91 *D-K* 1:171, *332 n. 3.*
22.B.103 *D-K* 1:174, *332 n. 11.*
22.B.111 *D-K* 1:175, *332 n. 8.*
22.B.117 *D-K* 1:177, *333 n. 25.*
22.B.118 *D-K* 1:177, *333 n. 25.*
22.B.119 *D-K* 1:177, *378 n. 55.*
22.B.123 *D-K* 1:178, *378 n. 63.*
22.B.126 *D-K* 1:179, *332 n. 6.*

Parmenides

28.A.1 *D-K* 1:217, *333 n. 1.*
28.A.1 *D-K* 1:217, *337 n. 1.*
28.A.1 *D-K* 1:217, *337 n. 1.*

28.A.12 *D-K* 1:220, *337 n. 1.*
28.A.27 *D-K* 1:222, *339 n. 7.*
28.A.46 *D-K* 1:226, *338 n. 22.*
28.B.1 *D-K* 1:228, vv.1-2, *337 n. 6.*
28.B.1 *D-K* 1:230, vv.28-32, *337 n. 3.*
28.B.1 *D-K* 1:230, vv.28-32, *377 n. 13.*
28.B.2 *D-K* 1:231, *337 n. 4.*
28.B.8 *D-K* 1:235-37 vv.1-21, *337 n. 8.*
28.B.8 *D-K* 1:235 v.6, *337 n. 13.*
28.B.8 *D-K* 1:237 vv.22-25, *337 n. 10.*
28.B.8 *D-K* 1:237 v.24, *337 n. 15.*
28.B.8 *D-K* 1:237-38 vv.26-33, *337 n. 9.*
28.B.8 *D-K* 1:237ff. vv.31ff., *338 n. 17.*
28.B.8 *D-K* 1:238 vv.34ff., *337 n. 7.*
28.B.8 *D-K* 1:238, vv.38-41, *337 n. 14.*
28.B.8 *D-K* 1:238, vv.42-44, *337 n. 12.*
28.B.8 *D-K* 1:239, vv.46-49, *337 n. 11.*
28.B.8 *D-K* 1:239, vv.53ff., *338 n. 20.*
28.B.8 *D-K* 1:240, vv.60ff., *338 n. 18.*

Zeno

29.A.1 *D-K* 1:247, *338 n. 1*(t).
29.A.10 *D-K* 1:250, *339 n. 4.*
29.A.12 *D-K* 1:250, *339 n. 2.*
29.A.13 *D-K* 1:250, *339 n. 3.*
29.A.21 *D-K* 1:252, *339 n. 13.*
29.A.26 *D-K* 1:253, *339 n. 6.*
29.A.27 *D-K* 1:253-54, *339 n. 7.*
29.A.29 *D-K* 1:254-55, *339 n. 18.*
29.B.1 *D-K* 1:255, *339 n. 14.*
29.B.3 *D-K* 1:257-58, *339 n. 16.*

Melissus

30.A.8 *D-K* 1:266-67, *340 n. 11.*
30.B.1 *D-K* 1:268, *340 n. 2.*
30.B.1 *D-K* 1:268, *340 n. 4.*
30.B.4 *D-K* 1:269, *340 n. 5.*
30.B.5, B.6 *D-K* 1:269-70, *340 n. 6.*

Philolaus

44.A.1a *D-K* 1:398, *334 n. 3.*
44.A.2 *D-K* 1:398, *334 n. 3.*
44.A.8 *D-K* 1:400, *334 n.* 3**(t)**.
44.B.2 *D-K* 1:407, *335 n. 6.*
44.B.4 *D-K* 1:408, *335 n. 13.*
44.B.5 *D-K* 1:408, *335 n. 5.*
44.B.11 *D-K* 1:411-12, *335 n. 14.*
44.B.11 *D-K* 1:411-12, *335 n. 2.*
44.B.11 *D-K* 1:411-12, *335 n. 2.*
44.B.14 *D-K* 1:413-14, *376 n. 25.*
44.B.20 *D-K* 1:416, *335 n. 4.*
44.B.20 *D-K* 1:416, *335 n. 4.*

Pythagorean School

58.B.4 *D-K* 1:451, *334 n. 5.*
58.B.4 *D-K* 1:451ff., *334 n. 1.*
58.B.30 *D-K* 1:459-60, *335 n. 10.*

Anaxagoras

59.A.44 *D-K* 2:17, *342 n. 4.*
59.B.4 *D-K* 2:33-35, *342 n. 5.*
59.B.4 *D-K* 2:33-35, *342 n. 6.*
59.B.5 *D-K* 2:35, *342 n. 6.*
59.B.5 *D-K* 2:35, *342 n. 10.*
59.B.10 *D-K* 2:36-37, *342 n. 6.*
59.B.11 *D-K* 2:37, *342 n. 7.*
59.B.12 *D-K* 2:37-39, *342 n. 6.*

Archelaus

60.A.1 *D-K* 2:44-45, *346 n. 22.*
60.A.1 *D-K* 2:45-47, *346 n. 25.*
60.A.2. *D-K* 2:45-47, *346 n. 25.*
60.A 3. *D-K* 2:45-47, *346 n. 25.*
60.A.4 *D-K* 2:46, *346 n. 23.*
60.A.5. *D-K* 2:45-47, *346 n. 25.*
60.A.7. *D-K* 2:45-47, *346 n. 25.*
60.A.11 *D-K* 2:47, *346 n. 24.*

60.A.12 *D-K* 2:47, *346 n. 24.*
60.C.1 *D-K* 2:66-69, *346 n. 26.*

Idaeus of Himera

63 *D-K* 2:51, *345 n. 4.*
63 *D-K* 2:51.1-3, *345 n. 4.*
63 *D-K* 2:51.5ff., *345 n. 5.*
63 *D-K* 2:51.9ff., *345 n. 6.*
63 *D-K* 2:51.11, *345 n. 7.*
63 *D-K* 2:51.26, *345 n. 7.*

Diogenes of Apollonia

64.A.5 *D-K* 2:52-53, *345 n. 10.*
64.A.7 *D-K* 2:53, *345 n. 13.*
64.A.7 *D-K* 2:53, *345 n. 12.*
64.B.2 *D-K* 2:52, *345 n. 11.*
64.B.2-5 *D-K* 2:59.15, *345 n. 14.*
64.B.2-5 *D-K* 2:60.11, *345 n. 13.*
64.B.3 *D-K* 2:60, *345 n. 15.*
64.B.5 *D-K* 2:61-62, *345 n. 16.*
64.B.4 *D-K* 2:60-61, *346 n. 17.*

Leucippus

67.A.1 *D-K* 2:70-71, *342 n. 1.*
67.A.1 *D-K* 2:70-71, *344 n. 4.*
67.A.4 *D-K* 2:72, *342 n. 1.*
67.A.5 *D-K* 2:72, *342 n. 1.*
67.A.10 *D-K* 2:74, *342 n. 1.*
67.B.2 *D-K* 2:81, *344 n. 13.*

Democritus

68.A.1 *D-K* 2:81-84, *344 n. 14.*
68.A.31 *D-K* 2:90, *343 n. 2.*
68.A.32 *D-K* 2:90, *343 n. 2.*
68.A.33 *D-K* 2:90-92, *343 n. 2.*
68.A.66 *D-K* 2:100-1, *344 n. 15.*
68.A.74 *D-K* 2:102, *344 n. 16.*
68.B.37 *D-K* 2:155, *344 n. 20.*
68.B.40 *D-K* 2:155, *344 n. 21.*

68.B.41 *D-K* 2:155, *344 n. 25.*
68.B.62 *D-K* 2:158, *344 n. 23.*
68.B.105 *D-K* 2:163, *344 n. 21.*
68.B.117 *D-K* 2:166, *378 n. 64.*
68.B.118 *D-K* 2:166, *344 n. 12.*
68.B.170 *D-K* 2:178, *344 n. 18.*
68.B.171 *D-K* 2:179, *344 n. 19.*
68.B.171 *D-K* 2:179, *378 n. 57.*
68.B.214 *D-K* 2:188, *344 n. 22.*
68.B.244 *D-K* 2:194, *344 n. 26.*
68.B.247 *D-K* 2:194, *344 n. 27.*
68.B.264 *D-K* 2:199, *344 n. 24.*

Older Sophists

79.A.2 *D-K* 2:252-53, *347 n. 2.*
79.A.2a *D-K* 2:253, *347 n. 3.*
79.A.2a *D-K* 2:253, *347 n. 4.*
79.A.3 *D-K* 2:253, *347 n. 5.*

Protagoras

80.A.1 *D-K* 2:253-55, *347 n. 1.*
80.A.1 *D-K* 2:253-55, *348 n. 2.*
80.A.1 *D-K* 2:253-55, *348 n. 7.*
80.A.1 *D-K* 2:253-55, *348 n. 9.*
80.A.1 *D-K* 2:253-55, *349 n. 18.*
80.A.5 *D-K* 2:256, *348 n. 13.*
80.A.6 *D-K* 2:256, *347 n. 13.*
80.A.8 *D-K* 2:257, *347 n. 12.*
80.A.14 *D-K* 2:258, *348 n. 6.*
80.A.19 *D-K* 2:259, *348 n. 5.*
80.A.20 *D-K* 2:260, *348 n. 7.*
80.A.21 *D-K* 2:260, *348 n. 8.*
80.A.21(a) *D-K* 2:260, *348 n. 14.*
80.A.22 *D-K* 2:260, *348 n. 11.*
80.A.22 *D-K* 2:260, *348 n. 15.*
80.A.23 *D-K* 2:260-61, *349 n. 20.*
80.B.1 *D-K* 2:262, *348 n. 2.*
80.B.1 *D-K* 2:262, *348 n. 4.*
80.B.4 *D-K* 2:265, *349 n. 19.*

80.B.4 *D-K* 2:265, *349 n. 19.*
80.B.4 *D-K* 2:265, *349 n. 20***(t)**.
80.B.6(a) *D-K* 2:266, *348 n. 7.*
80.B.6(b) *D-K* 2:266, *348 n. 8.*

Gorgias

82.A.1 *D-K* 2:271-72, *349 n. 1***(t)**.
82.A.10 *D-K* 2:274-75, *349 n. 1*
82.A.21 *D-K* 2:277, *350 n. 18.*
82.B.3 *D-K* 2:279-83, *350 n. 3.*
82.B.3 *D-K* 2:279-83, *350 n. 9.*
82.B.3 *D-K* 2:279-83, *350 n. 10.*
82.B.3 *D-K* 2:279-83, *350 n. 11.*
82.B.11 *D-K* 2:288-94, *350 n. 14.*
82.B.11 *D-K* 2:288-94, *350 n. 29.*
82.B.11(a) *D-K* 2:294-303, *350 n. 14.*
82.B.18 *D-K* 2:305, *350 n. 19.*
82.B.19 *D-K* 2:305, *350 n. 20.*
82.B.23 *D-K* 2:305-06, *351 n. 30.*

Prodicus

84.A.11 *D-K* 2:310, *367 n. 21.*
84.A.11 *D-K* 2:310, *351 n. 4.*
84.A.13 *D-K* 2:310-11, *351 n. 3.*
84.A.14 *D-K* 2:311, *351 n. 3.*
84.A.16 *D-K* 2:311, *351 n. 3.*
84.A.16 *D-K* 2:311, *367 n. 21.*
84.A.20 *D-K* 2:312, *351 n. 4.*
84.B.2 *D-K* 2:313 *351 n. 6.*
84.B.2 *D-K* 2:313 *351 n. 8.*
84.B.2 *D-K* 2:313 *351 n. 8.*
84.B.2 *D-K* 2:313 *352 n. 13.*
84.B.2 *D-K* 2:313 *352 n. 14.*
84.B.5 *D-K* 2:317 *252 n. 17.*
84.B.5 *D-K* 2:317 *252 n. 18.*
84.B.5 *D-K* 2:317 *252 n. 19.*

Thrasymachus

85.A.1 *D-K* 2:319, *354 n. 7.*

85.A.10 *D-K* 2:320, *354 n. 8.*
85.B6(a) *D-K* 2:325, *354 n. 8.*

Hippias

86.A.11 *D-K* 2:328-29, *352 n. 6.*
86.A.12 *D-K* 2:329 *352 n. 5.*
86.A.12 *D-K* 2:329 *352 n. 6.*

Antiphon the Sophist

87, fragment A. *D-K* 2:346-52, *353 n. 10.*
87, fragment A. *D-K* 2:346-52, *353 n. 12.*
87, fragment B. *D-K* 2:352-55, *353 n. 11.*
87, fragment B. *D-K* 2:352-55, *353 n. 13.*

Critias

88.B.25. *D-K* 2:386-89, *354 n. 6.*

Dissoi Logoi

90 *D-K* 2:405, *348 n. 10.*
90 *D-K* 2:407, *348 n. 12.*
90.B.5 *D-K* 2:412-13, *348 n. 16.*
90.B.5 *D-K* 2:412-13, *348 n. 16.*

Diodorus Siculus

Diodorus Siculus 15.76, *365 n. 1.*

Diogenes Laertius

DL 1.18 *LCL* 1:19, *364 n. 2.*
DL 1.24 *LCL* 1:25, 27, *330 n. 15.*
DL 1.25 *LCL* 1:27, *329 n. 1.*
DL 1.35 *LCL* 1:37, *330 n. 13.*
DL 2.2 *LCL* 1:131, 133, *330 n. 1.*
DL 2.3 *LCL* 1:133, *331 n. 1.*
DL 2.7 *LCL* 1:137, *341 n. 1.*
DL 2.16 *LCL* 1:145, 147, *346 n. 22.*
DL 2.16 *LCL* 1:147, *352 n. 1.*
DL 2.23 *LCL* 1:153, 155; Frag. 11 Blumenthal, *358 n. 6.*
DL 2.26 *LCL* 1:157, *355 n. 1.*
DL 2.31 *LCL* 1:161, 163, *365 n. 1.*

DL 2.34 *LCL* 1:165, *364 n. 5.*

DL 2.47 *LCL* 1:177, *364 n. 3.*

DL 2.48 *LCL* 1:177, 179, *364 n. 4.*

DL 2.60 *LCL,* 189, 191, *364 n. 5.*

DL 2.65 *LCL* 1:195; Giannantoni *SR* 4A.1, *369 n. 5.*

DL 2.65 *LCL* 1:195; Giannantoni *SR* 4A.1, *369 n. 6.*

DL 2.66 *LCL* 1:195, 197; Giannantoni *SR* 4A.51, *369 n. 10.*

DL 2.68 *LCL* 1:197, 199; Giannantoni *SR* 4A.104, *369 n. 11.*

DL 2.72 *LCL* 1:201; Giannantoni *SR* 4A.160, *369 n. 12.*

DL 2.75 *LCL* 1:203, 205; Giannantoni *SR* 4A.96, *369 n. 9.*

DL 2.85 *LCL* 1:215, 217; Giannantoni *SR* 4A.160, *370 n. 13.*

DL 2.87 *LCL* 1:217ff.; Giannantoni *SR* 4A.172, *371 n. 36.*

DL 2.88 *LCL* 1:217, 219; Giannantoni *SR* 4A.172, *371 n. 29.*

DL 2.88 *LCL* 1:217, 219; Giannantoni *SR* 4A.172, *371 n. 31.*

DL 2.89 *LCL* 1:219; Giannantoni *SR* 4A.172 *371 n. 30.*

DL 2.90 *LCL* 1:219, 221; Giannantoni *SR* 4A.172, *371 n. 32.*

DL 2.91 *LCL* 1:221; Giannantoni *SR* 4A.172, *369 n. 8(t).*

DL 2.92 *LCL* 1:221; Giannantoni *SR* 4A.172, *370 n. 14.*

DL 2.92 *LCL* 1:221; Giannantoni *SR* 4A.172, *370 n. 19.*

DL 2.92 *LCL* 1:221; Giannantoni *SR* 4A.172, *370 n. 20.*

DL 2.105 *LCL* 1:233; Giannantoni *SR* 3A.1, *373 n. 1(t).*

DL 2.105 *LCL* 1:233, 325, *374 n. 9.,*

DL 2.105 *LCL* 1:233, 235; Giannantoni *SR* 3A.1 and 3F.,1-25, 3G.1-5, *374 n. 10.*

DL 2.106 *LCL* 1:235, *371 n. 1.*

DL 2.106 *LCL* 1:235; frag. 24 Döring; Giannantoni *SR* 2A.30, *372 n. 12.*

DL 2.106 *LCL* 1:235; frag. 24 Döring; Giannantoni *SR* 2A.30, *373 n. 19.*

DL 2.106 *LCL* 1:235; frag. 31 Döring; Giannantoni *SR* 2A.22, *373 n. 27.*

DL 2.106 *LCL* 1:235; frag. 31 Döring; Giannantoni *SR* 2A.30, *372 n. 6.*

DL 2.107 *LCL* 1:235, 237; frag. 30 Döring; Giannantoni *SR* 2A.30, *372 n. 14.*

DL 2.107 *LCL* 1:235, 237; frag. 8 Döring; Giannantoni *SR* 2A.34, *373 n. 28.*

DL 2.107 *LCL* 1:237; Giannantoni *SR* 2A.34, *374 n. 2.*

DL 2.107 *LCL* 1:235, 237; frag. 29 Döring; Giannantoni *SR* 2A.34, *372 n. 16.*

DL 2.113 *LCL* 1:241, 243; frag. 163A Döring; Giannantoni *SR* 2O.2, *372 n. 3.*

DL 3.5 *LCL* 1:281, *365 n. 12.*

DL 3.5 *LCL* 1:281, *365 n. 13.*

DL 3.9 *LCL* 1:285, *334 n. 3*(t).

DL 3.37 *LCL* 1:311, *348 n. 16*(t).

DL 3.57 *LCL* 1:469, 471, *348 n. 16*(t).

DL 6.1 *LCL* 2:3, *365 n. 1.*

DL 6.1 *LCL* 2:3, *365 n. 1.*

DL 6.1 *LCL* 2:3; frag. 122A Decleva Caizzi; Giannantoni *SR* 5A.1, *368 n. 45.*

DL 6.2 *LCL* 2:3; frag. 19 Decleva Caizzi; Giannantoni *SR* 5A.85, *368 n. 40*(t).

DL 6.2 *LCL* 2:3, 5; Giannantoni *SR* 5A12, *364 n. 6.*

DL 6.2 *LCL* 2:3, 5; Giannantoni *SR* 5A12, *364 n. 7.*

DL 6.3 *LCL* 2:5, *367 n. 27.*

DL 6.3 *LCL* 2:5; frag. 45 Decleva Caizzi; Giannantoni *SR* 5A.151, *366 n. 16.*

DL 6.4 *LCL* 2:5, 7; frag. 162 Decleva Caizzi; Giannantoni *SR* 5A.178, *368 n. 39.*

DL 6.6 *LCL* 2:13, 15; frag. 186 Decleva Caizzi; Giannantoni *SR* 5A.167, *368 n. 46.*

DL 6.7 *LCL* 2:9; frags. 151 and 152 Decleva Caizzi; Giannantoni *SR* 5A.27 *366 n. 2.*

DL 6.8; *LCL* 2:7, 9; frag. 179 Decleva Caizzi; Giannantoni *SR* 5A.114, *367 n. 33.*

DL 6.8; *LCL* 2:7, 9; frag. 178C Decleva Caizzi; Giannantoni *SR* 5A.89, *367 n. 34.*

DL 6.10; *LCL* 2:11, 13; frag. 69 Decleva Caizzi; Giannantoni *SR* 5A.134, *366 n. 6.*

DL 6.11; *LCL* 2:13; frags. 70 and 23 Decleva Caizzi; Giannantoni *SR* 5A.134, *366 n. 5.*

DL 6.11; *LCL* 2:13; frag. 69 Decleva Caizzi; Giannantoni *SR* 5A.134, *366 n. 5.*

DL 6.11; *LCL* 2:13; frag. 95 Decleva Caizzi; Giannantoni *SR* 5A.134, *367 n. 35, 40.*

DL 6.11; *LCL* 2:13; frag. 101 Decleva Caizzi; Giannantoni *SR* 5A.134, *367 n. 37.*

DL 6.11 *LCL* 2:13. frag. 70 Decleva Caizzi; Giannantoni *SR* 5A.134, *366 n. 12.*

DL 6.11 *LCL* 2:13; frag. 70 Decleva Caizzi, *360 n. 56.*

DL 6.11 *LCL* 2:13; frag. 70 Decleva Caizzi; Giannantoni *SR* 5A.134, *366 n. 13.*

DL 6.12 *LCL* 2:13; frag. 71 Decleva Caizzi; Giannantoni *SR* 5A.134, *366 n. 8.*

DL 6.13 *LCL* 2:13, 15; frag. 88 Decleva Caizzi; Giannantoni *SR* 5A.134, *366 n. 9.*

DL 6.13 *LCL* 2:13, 15; frag. 63 Decleva Caizzi; Giannantoni *SR* 5A.134, *366 n. 10.*

DL 6.13 *LCL* 2:13, 15; frag. 136A Decleva Caizzi; cf. frag. 136B; Giannantoni *SR* 5A.22 and 5A.23, *368 n. 42.*

DL 6.13 *LCL* 2:13, 15; Giannantoni *SR* 5B.143, *368 n. 43.*

DL 6.13-15 *LCL* 2:13, 15, *368 n. 41.*

DL 6.15-18 *LCL* 2:15, 17, 19, 21, *365 n. 1.*

DL 7.161; *LCL* 2.265; frag. 25 Döring; Giannantoni *SR* 2A.32, *373 n. 21.*

DL 8.8 *LCL* 2.327, 329, *376 n. 29.*

DL 8.57 *LCL* 2.373, *339 n. 4.*

DL 8.63-67 *LCL* 2:377, 379, 381, 383, *340 n. 1.*

DL 8.67ff. *LCL* 2:381, 383, *341 n. 1.*

DL 8.69ff. *LCL* 2:385, *341 n. 1.*

DL 8.72ff. *LCL* 2:387, *341 n. 1.*

DL 8.74 *LCL* 2.389, *340 n. 1.*

DL 9.1 *LCL* 2:409, *331 n. 1.*

DL 9.3 *LCL* 2:411, *331 n. 1*(t).

DL 9.6 *LCL* 2:413, *332 n. 1*(t).

DL 9.6; *LCL* 2:413, *332 n. 1*(t).

DL 9.21 *LCL* 2:429, *333 n. 1.*

DL 9.23 *LCL* 2:429, *337 n. 1.*

DL 9.23 *LCL* 2:429, *337 n. 1.*

DL 9.25 *LCL* 2:435, *339 n. 4.*

DL 9.25 *LCL* 2:435, 37, *338 n. 1*(t).

DL 9.27 *LCL* 2:437, *338 n. 1.*

DL 9.38 *LCL* 2:447, 449, *334 n. 3.*

DL 9.45 *LCL* 2:455, *344 n. 14.*

DL 9.51 *LCL* 2:463, 465, *348 n. 2.*

DL 9.51 *LCL* 2:463, 465, *348 n. 7.*

DL 9.51 *LCL* 2:463, 465, *349 n. 18.*

DL 9.51 *LCL* 2:463, 465, *349 n. 19.*

DL 9.53 *LCL* 2.465, 467, *348 n. 9*(t).

DL 9.52 *LCL* 2:465, *347 n. 1.*

DL 9.65 *LCL* 2:479, *378 n. 53.*

DL 10.122; *LCL* 2:649, *378 n. 61.*

Elianus

Elianus *Var. Hist.* 3.17; *D-K* 12.A.3 *D-K* 1:82, *330 n. 1*(t).

Elianus *Var. Hist.* 14.6; Giannantoni *SR* 4A.174, *371 n. 33*.

Epictetus

Epictetus *Arrian's Discourses of Epictetus* 1.17.10; *LCL* 1:115, 117; frag. 38
Decleva Caizzi; Giannantoni *SR* 5A.160, *366 n. 20*.

Epictetus *Arrian's Discourses of Epictetus* 3.24.67-72; *LCL* 2:207; (partially
in) Decleva Caizzi frag. 118; and in Giannantoni *SR* 5B.290, *367 n. 26*.

Epicurus

Epicurus *Epistle to Menoeceus* 122; *DL* 10.122; *LCL* 2:649, *378 n. 61*.

Epiphanius

Epiphanius *Adv. haeres.* 3.11, *339 n. 11*.

Epiphanius *Adv. haeres.* 3.26, *365 n. 1*.

Epiphanius *Adv. haeres.* 3.26, *366 n. 4*.

Eudemus of Rhodes

Eudemus of Rhodes frag. 150 Wehrli; frag. 28 Kern; 4B.9 Colli, *376 n. 38*.

Euripides

Euripides *Alcestis* 962-72; test. 82 Kern; 4A.14 Kern, *375 n. 5*.

Euripides *Hippolytus* 952-54; test. 213 Kern; 4A.16 Kern, *375 n. 5*.

Euripides *Polydus*; frag. 638 Nauck; quoted in Plato's *Gorgias* 492E; *LCL*
415; 4A.23 Colli, *375 n. 19*.

Eudocia

Eudocia *Violarium* 96.56, *365 n. 1*.

Eusebius

Eusebius *Praep. evang.* 11.10.14 (28.10ff. Mras), *327 n. 2*.

Eusebius *Praep. evang.* 13.13.35, *367 n. 38*.

Eusebius *Praep. evang.* 14.3.7, *349 n. 19*(t).

Eusebius *Praep. evang.* 14.7.1; frag. 27 Döring; Gainnantoni *SR* 2O.26, *372
n. 8*.

Eusebius *Praep. evang.* 15.13.7, *367 n. 27*.

Eusebius *Praep. evang.* 16.62.7; Giannantoni, *SR* 4A.166, *370 n. 16*.

Favorinus

Favorinus *Miscellaneous History* Bk. 2, *348 n. 16*.

Aulus Gellius

Gellius *Noctes Atticae* 2.18; *LCL* 1:171-73, *374 n. 1*.
Gellius *Noctes Atticae* 7.10.1-4; *LCL* 2:119; frag. 1 Döring; Giannantoni *SR* 2A2, *364 n. 9*.
Gellius *Noctes Atticae* 9.5.3; *LCL* 2:177, 179, *367 n. 27*.

Gorgias

Gorgias *Encomium of Helen* sect. 9, *351 n. 29*.
Gorgias *Encomium of Helen* sect. 11, *350 n. 14*.
Gorgias *The Apology of Palamedes* sect. 24, *350 n. 14*.

Herodotus

Herodotus 2.81; test. 216 Kern; 4A.12 Colli, *375 n. 6*.
Herodotus 2.109, *327 n. 9*.
Herodotus 2.123, *328 n. 6*.

Hippolytus

Hippolytus *Ref.* 1.6.3, *330 n. 11*.
Hippolytus *Ref.* 1.7, *331 n. 2*.
Hippolytus *Ref.* 1.7.2, *331 n. 6*.
Hippolytus *Ref.* 1.9, *346 n. 23*.
Hippolytus *Ref.* 1.16, *345 n. 3*.

Homer

Homer *Odyssey* 4.392, *370 n. 16*.

Iamblichus

Iamblichus *Life of Pythagoras* 199, *334 n. 3*(t).

Ibycus

Ibycus frag. 17 Diehl; test. 2 Kern; 4A.1a Colli, *375 n. 4*.

Julian

Julian *Epistle* 82.445a Bidez-Cumont; Giannantoni *SR* 3A.2, *374 n. 6*.

Lactantius

Lactantius *Div. Instit.* 1.5.18ff., *367 n. 38.*
Lactantius *Div. Instit.* 3.8.6ff.; Giannantoni *SR* 4A.189 and 4A.193, *371 n. 38.*
Lactantius *De ira dei.* 11.14, *367 n. 38.*

Lucretius

Lucretius *De rerum natura* 1.830ff.; *LCL* 61, *342 n. 4.*

Luke

Luke 5:31, *368 n. 47.*

Marcus Aurelius

Marcus Aurelius *Meditations* 2.9, *377 n. 24.*

Mark

Mark 2:17, *368 n. 47.*

Matthew

Matthew 9:12, *368 n. 47.*

Minucius Felix

Minucius Felix *Octav.* 19.7, *367 n. 38.*

Olympiodorus

Olympiodorus *de arte sacra lapidis philosophorum* 25, *331 n. 7.*

Philodemus

Philodemus *De pietate* 7.3-8, *367 n. 38.*
Philodemus *De pietate* 9.7.75G, *352 n. 17.*

Philoponus

Philoponus *In Arist. Phys.* 42,9ff., *339 n. 13.*

Pindar

Pindar *Olympia* 2.56-72; 4A.6 Colli [trans. Frank J. Nisetich, *Pindar's Victory Songs* (Baltimore: Johns Hopkins University Press, 1980) 90], *376 n. 24.*
Pindar frag. 129 Snell; 4A.7 Colli, *376 n. 35.*
Pindar frag. 131b Snell; 4A.9 Colli, *375 n. 11.*

Pindar frag. 133 Snell; 4A.5 Colli; *LCL* 301, 303 trans. W. R. M. Lamb, *376 n. 23.*

Plato

Alcibiades Major 128D-130E, *359 n. 28.*

Apology 19Cff., *258 n. 10.*

Apology 20D-E, *358 n. 14.*

Apology 20C, *358 n. 11.*

Apology 21B-22E, *363 n. 10.*

Apology 23A-B, *363 n. 11.*

Apology 27B, *362 n. 15.*

Apology 29D-E, *363 n. 5.*

Apology 29D-30B, *359 n. 23.*

Apology 30D, *361 n. 65.*

Apology 31Cff., *361 n. 70*

Apology 31C-D, *362 n. 14.*

Apology 31D, *362 n. 20.*

Apology 33C, *362 n. 19.*

Apology 38A, *361 n. 67.*

Apology 39C-D, *363 n. 6.*

Apology 39C-E, *364 n. 1.*

Apology 40B, *362 n. 16.*

Apology 40C, *361 n. 68.*

Apology 41C-D, *362 n. 24.*

Apology 41D, *361 n. 66.*

Charmides 154D-E, *359 n. 27.*

Charmides 163D, *351 n. 2.*

Cratylus 384B, *351 n. 2.*

Cratylus 384B, *367 n. 21.*

Cratylus 400C; frag. 8 Kern; 4A.34 Colli, *375 n. 16.*

Crito 44D, *360 n. 34.*

Crito 44D, *361 n. 65.*

Crito 48A, *373 n. 22.*

Crito 51B, *361 n. 73.*

Euthydemus 277E, *351 n. 3.*

Euthydemus 277Eff., *367 n. 21.*

Euthydemus 281D-E, *360 n. 35.*

Euthydemus 286B-E, *354 n. 4.*

Euthydemus 285D-286B, *353 n. 3.*

Plotinus

Plutarch

Plutarch *De curios.* 2.516C; *LCL* 6:479, *364 n. 8.*

Plutarch *De curios.* 2.516C; *LCL* 6:479; 1A12 Giannantoni *SR* 4A.2, *369 n. 2.*

Plutarch *De prim. frig.* 7.947F, *331 n. 10.*

Plutarch *Adv. Colot.* 24.1120D; *LCL* 14:269; Giannantoni, *SR* 4A.211, *370 n. 21.*

Plutarch *Adv. Colot.* 32.4.1126B; *LCL* 14.303, 305, *340 n. 1.*

Plutarch *Vita Lyc.* 30, *365 n. 1.*

Pseudo-Plutarch

Ps. Plutarch *Stromata* 2, *330 n. 6.*

Ps. Plutarch *Stromata* 9; Giannantoni *SR* 4A.166, *370 n. 15.*

Seneca

Seneca *De const. sap.* 18.5, *365 n. 1.*

Seneca *Epistle* 94.41; *LCL* 3:37, 39; Giannantoni *SR* 3A.12, *374 n. 7.*

Sextus Empiricus

Sextus Empiricus *Outlines of Pyrrhonism* 1.216; *LCL* 1:131, *348 n. 6.*

Sextus Empiricus *Adv. math.* 6.53; *LCL* 4:397; Giannantoni *SR* 4A.219, *370 n. 24***(t)**.

Sextus Empiricus *Adv. math.* 7.60; *LCL* 2:31-33, *348 n. 2.*

Sextus Empiricus *Adv. math.* 7.65ff.; *LCL* 2:35ff., *350 n. 3.*

Sextus Empiricus *Adv. math.* 7.7; *LCL* 2:5, *339 n. 4.*

Sextus Empiricus *Adv. math.* 7.11; *LCL* 2:7; Giannantoni *SR* 4A.168, *370 n. 18.*

Sextus Empiricus *Adv. math.* 7.78ff.; *LCL* 2:41, *350 n. 9.*

Sextus Empiricus *Adv. math.* 7.78; *LCL* 2:43, *350 n. 11.*

Sextus Empiricus *Adv. math.* 7.80; *LCL* 2:43, *350 n. 10.*

Sextus Empiricus *Adv. math.* 7.87; *LCL* 45, 47, *350 n. 6.*

Sextus Empiricus *Adv. math.* 7.191; *LCL* 2:103; Giannantoni *SR* 4A.213, *370 n. 22.*

Sextus Empiricus *Adv. math.* 7.194; *LCL* 2:105; Giannantoni *SR* 4A.213, *370 n. 23.*

Sextus Empiricus *Adv. math.* 7.199; *LCL* 2:107, 109; Giannantoni *SR* 4A.213, *371 n. 28.*

Sextus Empiricus *Adv. math.* 9.18; *LCL* 3:11, *352 n. 18.*

Sextus Empiricus *Adv. math.* 9.20; *LCL* 3:11, *378 n. 54.*

Sextus Empiricus *Adv. math.* 9.52; *LCL* 3:29, *352 n. 19.*

Sextus Empiricus *Adv. math.* 9.54; *LCL* 3:31, *354 n. 6.*

Sextus Empiricus *Adv. math.* 9.73-74; *LCL* 3:41, 43 *367 n. 27.*
Sextus Empiricus *Adv. math.* 9.360; *LCL* 3.173, *345 n. 4.*

Simplicius

Simplicius *In Arist. Cat.* 208.28ff., *366 n.15.*
Simplicius *In Arist. Cat.* 211.15ff., *366 n.15.*
Simplicius *In Arist. Phys.* 23.29, *330 n. 10.*
Simplicius *In Arist. Phys.* 24.13ff., *330 n. 7.*
Simplicius *In Arist. Phys.* 24.13, *330 n. 2.*
Simplicius *In Arist. Phys.* 24, 26, *331 n. 2.*
Simplicius *In Arist. Phys.* 150.24ff., *330 n. 6.*
Simplicius *In Arist. Phys.* 151.28ff., *345 n. 14.*
Simplicius *In Arist. Phys.* 562.1ff., *339 n. 17.*
Simplicius *In Arist. Phys.* 1013.4ff., *339 n. 5.*
Simplicius *In Arist. Phys.* 1015.19ff., *339 n. 8.*
Simplicius *In Arist. Phys.* 1108.181ff., *339 n. 18.*
Simplicius *De caelo* 615.18ff. Heiberg, *331 n. 3.*

Stobaeus

Stobaeus *Anthol.* 1.22.19, *335 n. 8.*
Stobaeus *Anthol.* 2.31.68; frag. 64 Decleva Caizzi; Giannantoni *SR* 5A.163, *366 n. 4, 366 n. 11.*
Stobaeus *Anthol.* 3.1.28. frag. 93 Decleva Caizzi; Giannantoni *SR* 5A.125, *367 n. 32.*
Stobaeus *Anthol.* 3.1.172, *346 n. 3.*
Stobaeus *Anthol.* 3.10.41; frag. 94 Decleva Caizzi; Giannantoni *SR* 5A.80, *367 n. 31.*
Stobaeus *Anthol.* 3.14.17, *366 n. 4.*

Strabo

Strabo 9.1.8, *371 n. 1.*
Strabo 9.1.8; Giannantoni *SR* 3A.3 and 1, *374 n. 1.*

Syrianus

Syrianus *In Arist. Met.* 14.31-34, *370 n. 17.*

Timon

Timon frag. 67 Diels, *378 n. 53.*
Timon frag. 68 Diels, *378 n. 54.*

Themistius

Themistius *Orat.* 34.5, *370 n. 16.*

Themistius *Orat.* 34.5; Giannantoni *SR* 4A.166, *374 n. 3.*

Theodoret

Theodoret *Graec. aff. cur.* 1.75; frags. 39A-E Decleva Caizzi; Giannantoni *SR* 5A.179-81, *368 n. 38.*

Theodoret *Graec. aff. cur.* 3.53; frags. 109A-B Decleva Caizzi; Giannantoni *SR* 5A.123, *367 n. 28.*

Theodoret *Graec. aff. cur.* 11.8; frags. 97A-B Decleva Caizzi; Giannantoni *SR* 5A.122, *367 n. 27.*

Theodoret *Graec. aff. cur.* 11.8; frags. 97A-B Decleva Caizzi; Giannantoni *SR* 5A.111, *367 n. 36.*

Theodoret *Graec. aff. cur.* 12.47; frags. 108A-F Decleva Caizzi; Giannantoni *SR* 5A.122, *367 n. 27.*

Theophrastus

Theophrastus *The Opinions of the Physicists* frag. 2, *330 n. 2.*

Theophrastus *The Opinions of the Physicists* frag. 2, *331 n. 2.*

Theophrastus *The Opinions of the Physicists* frag. 4, *358 n. 7.*

Theophrastus *De sensu* 1ff., *338 n. 22.*

Xenophon

Xenophon *Cynegeticus* 13.8, *347 n. 4.*

Xenophon *Cyropaedia* 8.7.21; *LCL* 433, 435, *375 n. 13.*

Xenophon *Memorabilia* 1.1.1, *LCL* 3, *361 n. 1.*

Xenophon *Memorabilia* 1.1.7-9, *LCL* 5, 7, *362 n. 21.*

Xenophon *Memorabilia* 1.1.11ff., *LCL* 9ff., *358 n. 2.*

Xenophon *Memorabilia* 1.1.12, 16, *LCL* 9 and 11, *358 n. 5.*

Xenophon *Memorabilia* 1.1.14, *LCL* 9, *358 n. 3.*

Xenophon *Memorabilia* 1.1.16, *LCL* 11, *358 n. 13.*

Xenophon *Memorabilia* 1.2.14, *LCL* 19, *360 n. 54.*

Xenophon *Memorabilia* 1.2.60, *LCL* 41, 43; Giannantoni *SR* 4A.3, *369 n. 7.*

Xenophon *Memorabilia* 1.4 passim, *LCL* 53, 55, 57, 59, 61, 63, 65, *361 n. 7.*

Xenophon *Memorabilia* 1.4.8ff., *LCL* 57ff., *361 n. 8.*

Xenophon *Memorabilia* 1.4.13ff., *LCL* 61ff., *361 n. 9.*

Xenophon *Memorabilia* 1.4.17ff., *LCL* 63ff., *361 n. 10.*

Xenophon *Memorabilia* 1.5.4ff., *LCL* 65, 67, *360 n. 48.*

Xenophon *Memorabilia* 1.6.10, *LCL* 71, 73, *361 n. 59.*

Xenophon *Memorabilia* 1.6.13, *LCL* 73, *347 n. 3.*

Xenophon *Memorabilia* 2.1.9, *LCL* 87; Giannantoni *SR* 4A.163, *370 n. 26.*

Xenophon *Memorabilia* 2.1.11, *LCL* 87, 89; Giannantoni *SR* 4A.163, *371 n. 41.*

Xenophon *Memorabilia* 2.1.20, 21, *LCL* 93, 95, *351 n. 10.*

Xenophon *Memorabilia* 2.1.21-34, *LCL* 95, 97, 99, 101, 103, *351 n. 6.*

Xenophon *Memorabilia* 2.1.23-25, *LCL* 97, *351 n. 8.*

Xenophon *Memorabilia* 2.1.27ff., *LCL* 97, 99, *351 n. 9.*

Xenophon *Memorabilia* 2.1.29, *LCL* 99, *352 n. 13.*

Xenophon *Memorabilia* 2.1.30-33, *LCL* 99, 101, 103, *352 n. 14.*

Xenophon *Memorabilia* 2.4-10, *LCL* 121-65, *361 n. 69.*

Xenophon *Memorabilia* 2.6.2, *LCL* 129, *360 n. 54.*

Xenophon *Memorabilia* 3.8.7, *LCL* 221, *364 n. 3.*

Xenophon *Memorabilia* 3.9.4ff., *LCL* 225ff., *360 n. 37.*

Xenophon *Memorabilia* 3.10.1, *LCL* 231, 233, *359 n. 30.*

Xenophon *Memorabilia* 3.10.6ff., *LCL* 235ff., *359 n. 31.*

Xenophon *Memorabilia* 3.12.5ff., *LCL* 251, 253, *359 n. 28.*

Xenophon *Memorabilia* 4.2.34, *LCL* 293, *359 n. 34.*

Xenophon *Memorabilia* 4.3.1-14ff., *LCL* 297, 299, 301, 303, 305, 307, *361 n. 11.*

Xenophon *Memorabilia* 4.3.14, *LCL* 305, 307, *359 n. 29.*

Xenophon *Memorabilia* 4.4.4, *LCL* 309, *361 n. 74.*

Xenophon *Memorabilia* 4.5.2ff., *LCL* 325, 327, *360 n. 52.*

Xenophon *Memorabilia* 4.5.8ff., *LCL* 329ff., *360 n. 44.*

Xenophon *Memorabilia* 4.5.9ff., *LCL* 329, 331, *361 n. 62.*

Xenophon *Memorabilia* 4.5.11ff., *LCL* 331, 333, *360 n. 50.*

Xenophon *Memorabilia* 4.5.12, *LCL* 333, *364 n. 25.*

Xenophon *Memorabilia* 4.6.1, *LCL* 333, *364 n. 24.*

Xenophon *Memorabilia* 4.6.15, *LCL* 347, *364 n. 26.*

Xenophon *Memorabilia* 4.7, *LCL* 347, 349, 351, 353, *358 n. 9.*

Xenophon *Memorabilia* 4.7.6, *LCL* 349, 351, *358 n. 4.*

Xenophon *Memorabilia* 4.7.6, *LCL* 349, 351, *358 n. 9.*

Xenophon *Symposium* 2.10, *355 n. 1.*

Xenophon *Symposium* 3.8; frags. 64, 84B, 90, 111, 120 Decleva Caizzi; Giannantoni *SR* 5A.163, 131, 107, 81, 83, *366 n. 4.*

Xenophon *Symposium* 4.2-5; frags. 64, 84B, 90, 111, 120 Decleva Caizzi; Giannantoni *SR* 5A.163, 131, 107, 81, 83, *366 n. 4.*

Xenophon *Symposium* 4.34ff.; frag. 117 Decleva Caizzi; Giannantoni *SR* 5A.82, *367 n. 24.*

Xenophon *Symposium* 4.45, *367 n. 25.*
Xenophon *Symposium* 4.62ff., *365 n. 1.*